G000109158

THE ROUGH GUIDE TO

London
Restaurants

2004 EDITION

www.roughguides.com

credits

Series editor Mark Ellingham
Text editor Bernice Davison
Production Link Hall
Cartography Maxine Repath
Photography Giles Stokoe, James McConnachie

publishing information

This sixth edition published October 2003 by
Rough Guides Ltd, 80 Strand, London WC2R 0RL.
Penguin Putnam, Inc. 375 Hudson Street, NY 10014, USA.

distributed by the Penguin Group

Penguin Books Ltd, 80 Strand, London WC2R ORL
Penguin Putnam, Inc. 375 Hudson Street, NY 10014, USA
Penguin Books Australia Ltd, 487 Maroondah Highway,
PO Box 257, Ringwood, Victoria 3134, Australia
Penguin Books Canada Ltd, 10 Alcorn Avenue,
Toronto, Ontario, Canada M4V 1E4
Penguin Books (NZ) Ltd,182–190 Wairau Road, Auckland 10, New Zealand

Typeset in Bembo and Helvetica to an original design by Henry Iles.
Printed in Spain by Graphy Cems.

A catalogue record for this book is available from the British Library.
ISBN 1-84353-097-x

Ordnance Survey® This product includes mapping data licensed from Ordnance Survey ® with the
permission of the Controller of Her Majesty's Stationery Office. © Crown copyright.
All rights reserved. Licence No: 100020918.

THE ROUGH GUIDE TO

London
Restaurants

2004 EDITION

written and edited by

Charles Campion

additional research and reviews
Jan Leary, George Theo and Margaret Clancy

ROUGH
GUIDES

About Rough Guides

Rough Guides have always set out to do something different. Our first book, published in 1982, was written by Mark Ellingham. Just out of university, travelling in Greece, he took along the popular guides of the day but found they were all lacking in some way. They were either strong on ruins and museums but went on for pages without mentioning a beach or taverna, or were so conscious of the need to save money that they lost sight of Greece's cultural and historical significance. Also, none of the books told him anything about Greece's contemporary life – its politics, its culture, its people and how they lived.

So, with no job in prospect, Mark decided to write his own guidebook, one which aimed to provide practical information that was second to none, detailing the best beaches and the hottest clubs and restaurants, alongside interesting accounts of sights both famous and obscure, and up-to-the-minute information on contemporary culture. It was a guide that encouraged independent travellers to find the best of Greece, and was an immediate success, getting shortlisted for the Thomas Cook travel guide award, and encouraging Mark and a few friends to expand the series.

The Rough Guide list grew rapidly and the letters flooded in, indicating a much broader readership than anticipated, but one which uniformly appreciated the Rough Guide mix of practical detail and humour, irreverence and enthusiasm. Things haven't changed. The same writers who began the series are still the caretakers of the Rough Guide mission today: to provide the most reliable, up-to-date and entertaining information to independent-minded travellers of all ages, on all budgets.

Rough Guides now publish more than 200 titles, written and researched by a dedicated team based in Britain, Europe, the USA and Australia. We have also created a unique series of phrasebooks, along with an acclaimed series of music guides, and a best-selling pocket guide to the internet. We also publish comprehensive travel information on our Web site: **www.roughguides.com**

About the Author

Charles Campion is an award-winning food writer and restaurant reviewer. He writes a restaurant column for the *London Evening Standard*, which won him the Glenfiddich "Restaurant Writer of the Year" award, and contributes to radio and TV food programmes, as well as a variety of magazines including *Bon Appetit* in the USA. His most recent book publication was *Real Greek Food*, which he wrote with chef Theodore Kyriakou.

Before becoming a food writer, Charles worked in a succession of London ad agencies and had a spell as chef-proprietor of a hotel and restaurant in darkest Derbyshire.

Help Us Update

We've tried to ensure that this sixth edition of *The Rough Guide to London Restaurants* is as up-to-date and accurate as possible. However, London's restaurant scene is in constant flux: chefs change jobs; restaurants are bought and sold; menus change. There will probably be a few references in this guide that are out of date even as this book is printed – and standards, of course, go up and down. If you feel there are places we've underrated or overpraised, or others we've unjustly omitted, please let us know: comments or corrections are much appreciated, and we'll send a copy of the next edition (or any other *Rough Guide* if you prefer) for the best letters. Please address letters to Charles Campion at:

Rough Guides, 80 Strand, London WC2R ORL or
Rough Guides, 4th Floor, 375 Hudson St, New York, NY 10014.
Or send email to: mail@roughguides.co.uk

Contents

Introduction   X

Central London

The City & East London

North London

South London

West London

Indexes

Introduction

Welcome to the sixth edition of the **Rough Guide to London Restaurants**. If you used the earlier books, you will have noticed that the number of restaurants has stabilised around the 350 mark, but it is surprising how many openings and closures there have been within the space of a year. This edition has been extensively revised and as well as reassessing all the previous entries we have added a wide selection of new establishments.

Anyone who has lived or worked in London knows that while it may seem like one big metropolis to the outsider, it is really a series of villages. If you live in Clapham, you know about Clapham and Battersea, and maybe Brixton or Chelsea, while Highgate or Shepherd's Bush are far-off lands. And vice versa. Yet almost every other restaurant guide is divided up by cuisine, which assumes that this is your first criterion when choosing a place to eat. It shouldn't be. If you're meeting friends in Chiswick your best options might be French or Fish; in Wembley or Tooting they might be Indian. But you want to know about that oddball great restaurant, too: whether it's an interesting newcomer like The Real Greek Souvlaki and Bar in Clerkenwell, or a new gastropub like The Barnsbury in Islington. This book divides London into five geographic sections (Central; City & East; North; South; West) and then breaks these down into the neighbourhoods, with restaurants arranged alphabetically in each section. Keep this guide handy and it will tell you where to eat well from Soho to Southall.

Another important thing to note about the restaurants selected and reviewed in this book is that they are **all rec-**

ommended – none has been included simply to make up the numbers. There are some very cheap places and there are some potentially pretty expensive places, but they all represent good value. The only rule we have made for inclusion is that it must be possible to eat a meal for £35 a head or less. In some of the haute cuisine establishments, that will mean keeping to the set lunch, while in some of the bargain eateries £35 might cover a blow-out for four. This guide reviews restaurants for every possible occasion from a quick lunch to a celebration dinner. It also covers many different kinds of food – some 50 cuisines in all. In reality, we cover even more, as for simplicity we have used "Indian" and "Chinese" as catch-all terms.

Prices and credit cards

Every review in this book has at the top of the page a spread of **prices** (e.g. £12 to £40). The first figure relates to what you could get away with – this is the minimum amount per person you are likely to spend on a meal here (assuming you are not a non-tipping, non-drinking skinflint). The second relates to what it would cost if you don't hold back. Wild diners with a taste for fine wines will leave our top estimates far behind, but the figures are there as a guide. For most people, the cost of a meal will lie somewhere within the spread.

For a more detailed picture, each review sets out the prices of various dishes. At some time in the guide's life these specific prices (and indeed the overall price spreads) will become out of date, but they were all accurate when the book left for the printer. And even in the giddy world of restaurants, when prices rise or prices fall, everyone tends to move together. If this book shows one restaurant as being twice as expensive as another, that situation is likely to remain.

Introduction

The reviews also keep faith with original menu spellings of dishes, so you'll find satays, satehs and satés – all of which will probably taste much the same. Opening hours and days are given in every review, as are the credit cards accepted. Where reviews specify that restaurants accept "all major credit cards", that means at least AmEx, Diners, MasterCard and Visa. Acceptance of Visa and MasterCard usually means Switch and Delta, too; we've specified the odd exception, but if you're relying on one card it's always best to check when you book.

Getting off the fence: the best

Every restaurant reviewed in this book is wholeheartedly recommended, but it would be a very strange person who did not have favourites, so here are some "six of the bests".

Best newcomers

Best Chinese or Southeast Asian

Best for a party

Best for serious spending

Best vegetarian dishes

Best classical French

Introduction

Best comfortable French

Best Pakistani or Punjabi

Best post-theatre or cinema

Best real cheapies

Best new wave Indian

Best for fish

Best for a bargain lunch

Best gastropubs

Introduction

Best to impress

Best for eating alfresco

Best British

Best Italian cooking

Best for grazing

Best to clinch a big deal

Best for good, affordable wines

Best "wild cards"

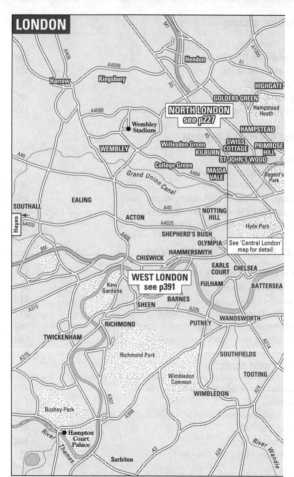

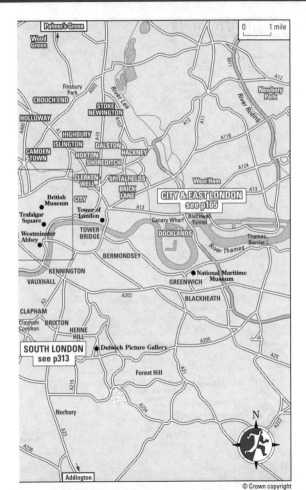

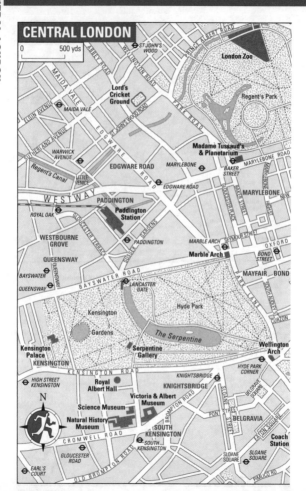

CENTRAL LONDON

0   500 yds

ST JOHN'S WOOD

PRINCE ALBERT ROAD

London Zoo

ABBEY ROAD

WELLINGTON ROAD

MAIDA VALE

Lord's Cricket Ground

Regent's Park

ELGIN AVENUE

MAIDA VALE

ST JOHN'S WOOD ROAD

PARK ROAD

EDGWARE ROAD

Madame Tussaud's & Planetarium

SUTHERLAND AVENUE

WARWICK AVENUE

MARYLEBONE ROAD

BAKER STREET

MARYLEBONE

Regent's Canal

LITTLE VENICE

EDGWARE ROAD

MARYLEBONE

GLOUCESTER PLACE

BAKER STREET

WESTWAY

EDGWARE ROAD

PADDINGTON

ROYAL OAK

GLOUCESTER TERRACE

Paddington Station

SUSSEX GARDENS

OXFORD

WESTBOURNE GROVE

PADDINGTON

MARBLE ARCH

SEYMOUR STREET

BOND STREET

QUEENSWAY

Marble Arch

MAYFAIR   BOND

BAYSWATER

QUEENSWAY

BAYSWATER ROAD

LANCASTER GATE

Hyde Park

PARK LANE

SOUTH AUDLEY STREET

CURZON

QUEENSWAY

Kensington Gardens

The Serpentine

Kensington Palace

KENSINGTON

Serpentine Gallery

Wellington Arch

HIGH STREET KENSINGTON

KENSINGTON ROAD

KNIGHTSBRIDGE

HYDE PARK CORNER

Royal Albert Hall

KNIGHTSBRIDGE

BELGRAVE SQUARE

N

Science Museum

Victoria & Albert Museum

BROMPTON ROAD

PONT STREET

SLOANE STREET

BELGRAVIA

EATON SQUARE

Natural History Museum

SOUTH KENSINGTON

Coach Station

CROMWELL ROAD

SOUTH KENSINGTON

SLOANE SQUARE

EARL'S COURT

GLOUCESTER ROAD

OLD BROMPTON ROAD

PIMLICO RD

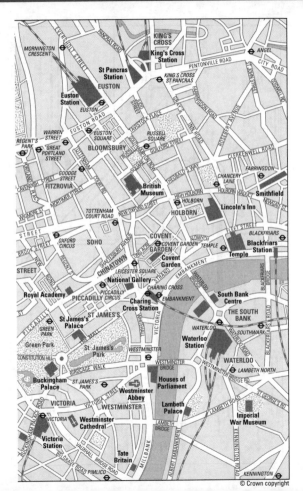

© Crown copyright

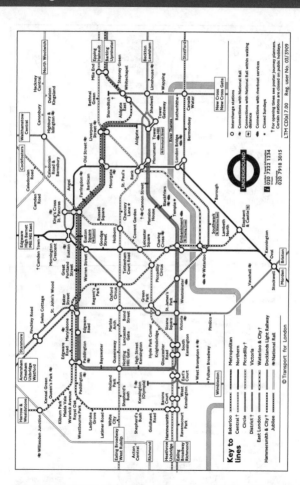

Central

Bloomsbury & Fitzrovia

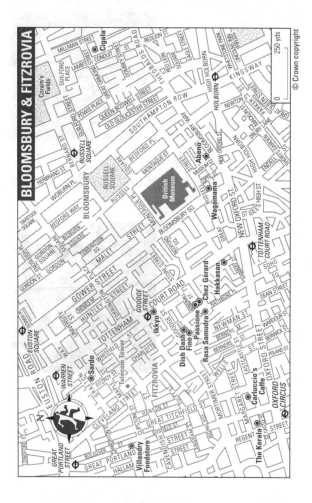

Abeno

JAPANESE

Abeno claims to be Europe's only specialist okonomi-yaki restaurant, and it may well be. London has plenty of teppan-yaki restaurants – where the chef cooks gourmet morsels in front of you on the hotplate – but okonomi-yaki hasn't swept to popularity, perhaps because it is an altogether messier, more grass-roots sort of experience. Even the finest

£9 to £35
Address 47 Museum St, WC1
☏ 020 7405 3211
Station Tottenham Court Road
Open Daily noon–10pm
Accepts All major credit cards except Diners

okonomi-yaki looks a bit like roadkill. Imagine a sloppy pizza crossed with a solid omelette then layered with all manner of odds and ends. Then imagine it being assembled and cooked on the table in front of you. Abeno is saved by the gentle and friendly service, the freshness of the ingredients, the charm of the cooks, and the low, low prices. And it's fun.

You could try yaki-soba (£6.95), a fried noodle dish with chicken, squid or pork. Or soba-rice, a natty combination of rice and noodles which is all the rage in Kansai – try it with pork and kimchi (£9.95). You could even try the upscale teppan-yaki fillet steak (£13.80). But you're here for the okonomi-yaki. The base is cabbage, egg and dough, with spring onions and tempura batter; all this is piled onto the hotplate. You specify whether you want deluxe or super deluxe, trad or wholemeal base, and off they go. Try tofu, corn and extra spring onion (£6.70/8.70); or Osaka mix – pork, kimchi and prawn (£6.95/9.95); or spicy Tsuruhasi – kimchi and an extra egg (£6.70/9.70); or Abeno special – pork, bacon, konn-yaku, asparagus, squid, prawn and salmon, topped with an egg (£14.80); or London mix – pork, bacon, cheese and salmon (£8.80/11.80). These dishes are very tasty, and it's fun to watch the layering at work. And there are nice side dishes that will serve as starters, such as ika itame – squid with garlic and soy (£3.20), and miso soup (£2.20). Set menus take the angst out of ordering.

Don't visit this place in the height of summer, as the red-hot tabletop in front of you chucks out a fierce amount of heat. By the same token, keep your elbows and the menu well away from it – unless the smell of scorching stimulates your taste buds.

ITALIAN

Carluccio's Caffe

When Antonio Carluccio first ambled across our television screens, it was in his role as chef-proprietor of the upscale Neal Street Restaurant, and ultra-passionate mushroom hunter. Now branches of Carluccio's Caffe spring up almost as fast as porcini, and the success is well deserved. Carluccio's Caffe is a much more mainstream concern than Neal Street, and it's also an extremely busy place, which makes for a great

£9 to £26
Address 8 Market Place, W1
☏ 020 7636 2228
Station Oxford Circus
Open Mon–Fri 8am–11pm, Sat & Sun 10am–10pm
Accepts All major credit cards except Diners
⊛ www.carluccios.com
Branches see p.488

atmosphere. The downside is the likelihood of a queue at peak times. The front of the premises is a delicatessen-cum-shop; the mid-section is a bar; the rear is a café-restaurant. Commendable effort has been made to incorporate all that is admirable about Continental coffee shops and so often missing in London. Carluccio's is open throughout the day. Proper meals are available at all hours. The coffee is notably good. Children are welcome.

In the morning the temptations are croissants (from £1.20) and coffee: caffè ristretto (£1.15); cappuccino (£1.70); double espresso (£1.50) – pukka stuff. This segues into the main menu, on which there are always a couple of good soups to be had: zuppa di funghi (£3.95) or pasta ripiena in brodo (£3.75) – note the fair prices. There's a good "bread tin" (£2.85) with sweet stuff at breakfast time and some moody Italian regional breads at meal times. There are sound antipasti, including Sicilian arancini di riso (£3.95), which are crisp, deep-fried rice balls filled with mozzarella or ragu. There are salads. Main courses range from calzone (£4.95) to a trad parmigiano di melanzane (£6.50), and from ravioli (£5.95) to tonno alla griglia con salsa (£10.50). Puds major in ice cream – gelati artigianali (£3.50). For a restaurant serving so many customers, the cooking is very good. Dishes are well seasoned, service is quick and the prices are fair.

Beware the shopping zone, lest you be tempted by the gleaming Piaggio Vespa ET2 50cc. You'll find it listed on the menu under "Trasporti" and described as a "fully automatic scooter, carefully made and imported from Italy". It's priced at £1,650 – up £150 since 2001!

Chez Gérard

When the inner prompting shouts for steak frites, Chez Gérard is a very sound option. Though there are now a host of these popular brasseries spread throughout London, the Charlotte Street branch is the original and, some say, the best. When it opened, over twenty years ago, this type of French restaurant – where the steak is good and the frites are better – was a novelty; today, despite a recent lick of paint, Chez Gérard feels reassuringly old-fashioned. Recently they

£20 to £55

Address 8 Charlotte St, W1
℡ 020 7636 4975
Station Goodge Street
Open Mon–Fri noon–11.30pm, Sat 5.30–11.30pm,
Sun 12.30–10.30pm
Accepts All major credit cards
Branches see p.488
⊛ www.sante-gcg.com

FRENCH

have moved the emphasis gently away from steak, and now there are more fish dishes, as well as chicken and even game. But the approach is always Francophile, so you'll find oeufs poché en meurette, French onion soup, loup de mer, snails and crème brûlée. The bread is crusty, the service Gallic, and the red wine decent. It's not cheap, but the food is generally reliable, and in summer you can eat alfresco at one of the pavement tables.

Start with rock oysters (£4.45 for three, £8.90 for six, £13.35 for nine), pâté de campagne (£4.50), or, for a real belt of nostalgia, a dozen snails in garlic butter (£4.95). The steaks come in all shapes and sizes – Châteaubriand is for two people (£32.50), while côte de boeuf rib-eye is served on the bone (£18.45). There's a 9oz fillet steak (£17.50) and an entrecôte (£13.75). This is also one of the few places in London where you can get onglet (£9.35), a particularly tasty French cut. Everything from the grill comes with pommes frites and sauce Béarnaise. Other dishes are boeuf Bourguignonne (£9.50) and cassoulet Toulousain (£10.50). But don't kid yourself – you're here for the steak frites. Salads, side orders of vegetables, desserts – including tarte Tatin (£4.75) – and a decent selection of regional French cheeses (£4.25) are all nicely in tune with the Gallic ambience. So too are the house wines, which are so good that you can almost disregard the wine list.

There is also a very sound menu prix fixe available every evening and at Sunday lunch – just £13.50 for two courses and £16 for three. Gravadlax; onglet; chocolat pot makes pretty good reading.

Cigala

Cigala has bedded down well in its first few years supported by a hatful of glowing reviews. The chef-proprietor – Jake Hodges, one of the founders of Moro (see p.192) – has settled into a regime of straightforward Iberian dishes, and this is the place to try rabbit, ox tongue, patatas bravas and poached meats, as well as old favourites like the eponymous cigalas na brasa – langoustines with Romesco sauce. Look out for simple dishes. Strong flavours. Fresh ingredients. Real passion.

£18 to £60

Address 54 Lamb's Conduit St, WC1
☎ 020 7405 1717
Station Russell Square
Open Mon–Fri 12.30–2.45pm
& 6–10.45pm Sat 12.30–4pm
& 6–10.45pm, Sun 12.30–
9.30pm
Accepts All major credit cards
🌐 www.cigala.co.uk

The menu changes daily. It is dependent on the markets and what the chef can find that looks good. This makes for seasonal dishes, and that is a huge plus. So a spring menu might start with sopa de picadillo (£5.50) jamon broth with rice, mint and boiled egg. Or revueltos con habas (£5) – scrambled egg with baby broad beans. Or lengua a la Aragonesa (£5.50) – ox tongue with pepper and sherry sauce. Or calamares a la plancha – grilled squid with charrasco sauce (£6.50). All these dishes are simple, well seasoned and have good combinations of flavour. Mains deliver in much the same fashion. Fabadas Asturianas (£13) is a rich, comforting bean stew with good, spicy chorizo, the Spanish blood sausage called morcilla and rashers of fat bacon. Delicious. Paella de conejo (£16.00 per person minimum two people, takes 30 minutes) is the real deal, made with rabbit and chorizo. Or there's tumbet (£13), which is an interesting vegetarian casserole made with aubergine, potatoes and tomatoes. Puddings lie in wait: arroz con leche (£4.50) is a goodly rice pudding. The wine list doffs its cap to a selection of sherries, and features a good range of well-chosen Spanish wines. The cooking here is very adept and Mr Hodges has the sense to stick to simple, unpretentious dishes and simple, unpretentious presentation.

There's a good set lunch here. Two courses cost £15 and three courses cost £18 (Monday to Friday). Tapas are served 3–10.45pm Monday to Friday and all day Saturday, Sunday until 9.30pm and are good value: thirty or so choices mainly between £2 and £4.50 a plate.

CENTRAL

Dish Dash

This modernist Persian restaurant opened as a bar-led, trendy sort of establishment in those heady days of 2000. Since then it has dabbled with takeaways, flirted with different menus and eating styles, and opened another branch in SW12. Things have calmed down somewhat although the bar downstairs – "Sharibar" (open Thursday to Saturday nights 6pm to midnight) – is still a busy and buzzy sort of place attracting a lively crowd.

£12 to £50

Address 57–59 Goode St, W1
℡ 020 7637 7474
Station Goodge Street
Open Mon–Wed noon–3.30pm & 6–10.30pm, Thurs & Fri noon–3.30pm & 6–11pm, Sat 6–11pm
Accepts All major credit cards
ⓦ www.dish-dash.com

PERSIAN

The menu is a multi-sectioned affair, but most of the eccentricities of the ordering system have fallen by the wayside and you should treat the place like any other Middle Eastern establishment ordering a raft of hot and cold "Mazza" (means meze) and then go on to a kebab or other main dishes. You'll find most of the meze stalwarts: hummus (£2.50); panir (£3.50) – a strained cheese served with honey and rose petals; muhummara (£3.50) – roast red peppers; falafel (£3); pan-cooked spinach (£3) ; kookoo (£3) – a Persian classic, a kind of über omelette; or sarpavaran (£3.50), which is deep-fried breadcrumbed squid with black and white sesame seeds. The breads are good – Persian Village bread; Khobez or Barbari nan (£1.50). Under "Kababs" you'll find joojeh (£6) – chicken; mahi (£7) – swordfish; koobideh (£6) – minced lamb with a welcome kick of cumin, coriander and chilli. "Khoresh" is the heading over a selection of stews: joojeh (£6) is a mild chicken curry and bademjan (£5) is a mild dish made with aubergines and chickpeas. Side dishes could be jewelled rice (£1.75), couscous (£1.75) or batatta harra (£2), a Persian take on fried spuds. Puds range from bastani (£4), which are home-made ice creams to various pastries in the classical style. As ever, fresh mint tea (£1) not only complements the food perfectly but is also most refreshing.

There's a short wine list, but the bulk of the drinks is given over to cocktails, which are professionally made and agreeably strong. This means that Dish Dash is popular with a drinking crowd and tends to get loud and boisterous towards the end of the week.

Fino

Why is it that Spanish food seems so out of place in a slick "new-London-restaurant" setting? Say tapas, and the mind makes an involuntary leap towards cool, tiled, old-fashioned places. Fino opened in the spring of 2003 and majors in tapas, but in a setting that is very modernist indeed. It is the brainchild of three urbane young men, two of whom are brothers brought up in the hotel and restaurant trade. Fino is living proof of their admiration for Spain. There's a stylish bar for drinking on the mezzanine and a bar for eating tapas at along the front of the open kitchen downstairs. The food is very sound, and elegantly presented.

£20 to £70

Address 33 Charlotte St, W1, entrance Rathbone St
☎ 020 7813 8010
Station Goodge Street
Open Mon–Fri 10am–3pm & 6–11pm, Sat 6–11pm
Accepts All major credit cards

There are a good range of classic tapas dishes and some items fresh from the plancha (a no-frills grill). Start with some pan tomaquet (£2.20) – a tomatoey, garlicky toast. Add pulpo arroz negro (£6.50), dear little octopi and a very delicious squid ink risotto. Also crisp-fried squid (£4.90), delicious with a squeeze of lemon. The croquetas are good, filled with ham (£4.50); ceps (£4.50); or black with squid ink (£5). From the meat section there are milk-fed lamb cutlets (£7.80) impossibly small, tender and with good gravy; and a good portion of jamon Jabuga (£12.50) – top ham, melting in the mouth. Or a dish of chorizo and white beans (£7.20). The dish of morcilla, octopus, pisto and mash (£8.20) is delicious, a great array of complementary flavours – soft black pudding, chewy octopus. From the vegetable section there is a dish of chickpeas, spinach and bacon (£5.50) to add a welcome savoury note. From the plancha there are scallops (£3 each); squid (£6.50); and a half lobster (£14.20). In keeping with the smartness of the surroundings the wine list is priced on the merciless side.

There are two "set menus" priced at £15.95 per person, and £25 person (both for a minimum of two) and you will get five or seven courses. The constraints of cheffy presentation mean that some dishes come with three items per plate, which can pose the problem of how two people share three prawns without fighting!

Hakkasan

(🍴) As you nod to the doorman and walk down the green slate tunnel that is the staircase, you could easily think that you were entering a superplush theme park ride. Hakkasan opened in 2001 and is as impressive as only the judicious application of more than £3,000,000 can ensure. The double-smart cocktail bar is consistently and fashionably crammed. A large dining area sits inside an elegant and ornate carved wooden cage. Top-name designers from

£30 to £120

Address 8 Hanway Place, W1
☏ 020 7927 7000
Station Tottenham Court Road
Open Mon–Fri noon–2.30pm & 6pm–midnight, Sat & Sun noon–4.30pm & 6pm–midnight (11pm Sun); Thurs–Sat bar open until 1am
Accepts All major credit cards

the worlds of film and fashion have given their all, and this is a smart and elegant place. The food is novel, well-presented, fresh, delicious and, in strangely justifiable fashion, expensive.

The starters are called "small eat" and do not shy away from expensive luxury ingredients. The three-style vegetarian roll (£6) teams a mooli spring roll with a bean curd puff and a yam roll. Live native lobster noodles with ginger and spring onion (£38) cannot be many people's idea of a "small eat". Or there is grilled Shanghai dumpling (£5). The main dishes are innovative and delicious: roast silver cod (£28) comes with champagne and Chinese honey. Try the stir-fry scallop and prawn cake with choi sum (£10.90). Or the jasmine tea smoked chicken (£12.50) Or there is braised aubergine and Morinaga tofu claypot in chilli and black bean (£8.50) – Morinaga tofu is highly prized for its unique texture. There's also sweet and sour organic pork with pomegranate (£9.50), and a very good braised chicken with dried shitake and chestnuts (£11.50). By way of a staple, try the stir-fry glass vermicelli (£7), which enlivens noodles with chicken, crabmeat and fried shallots.

The dim sum (served only at lunchtime) have had a dramatic effect on the critics and for once the acclaim is unanimous. They are not cheap – prawn puff is £3.90, and sesame prawn toast £8.50 – but there are some very interesting dishes. Try asparagus cheung fun with bamboo pith, dried shitake and cloud ear (£3), rock shrimp shumai (£5.50), or a baked venison puff (£3.90). Whisper it … these are better dim sum than you'll find in Chinatown!

Ikkyu

(icon) Busy, basic and full of people eating reliable Japanese food at sensible prices – all in all, Ikkyu is a good match for any popular neighbourhood restaurant in Tokyo. What's more, it's hard to find, which adds to the authenticity. Head down the steps and you'll find that the restaurant has had a much-needed lick of paint. It is still an engaging place, if quite obviously tailored to Japanese customers, but the strangeness comes over as politeness, and you won't feel completely stranded. The first shock is how very busy the place is – you are not the first person to discover some of the best-value Japanese food in London.

£10 to £40
Address 67a Tottenham Court Rd, W1
☎ 020 7636 9280
Station Goodge Street
Open Mon–Fri noon–2.30pm & 6–10.30pm, Sun 6–10.30pm
Accepts All major credit cards

Nigiri sushi is good here and is priced by the piece: tuna (£2); salmon (£1.70); mackerel (£1.40); cuttlefish (£1.70). Or there's sashimi, which runs all the way from mackerel (£4.50) to sea urchin eggs (£13), with an assortment for £13.50. Alternatively, start with soba (£3.60) – delicious, cold, brown noodles. Then allow yourself a selection of yakitori, either a portion of assorted (£5), or mix and match from tongue, heart, liver, gizzard and chicken skin (all £1 a stick). You will need many skewers of the grilled chicken skin, which is implausibly delicious. Moving on to the main dishes, an order of fried leeks with pork (£7.50) brings a bunch of long, onion-flavoured greens strewn with morsels of grilled pork. Whatever the green element is, it is certainly not leeks. Or there's grilled aubergine (£3.40), or rolled five vegetables with shrimp (£8.20), which is like a Swiss roll made with egg and vegetable with a core of prawn.

Ikkyu's menu has a good many delicious secrets, though the Japanese-favoured drink, shouchu and soda (£3.50), is perhaps not among them – shouchu is a clear spirit which tastes like clear spirit and the addition of soda does little to improve it. Asahi and Kirin beers (both £2.70) are a much better choice. Another doubtful order would be fermented soya beans topped with a raw egg (£3.10), which in Japan is considered the perfect start to the day, but is unlikely to woo you away from cornflakes.

The Kerala

(🍴) In 1935, Gough Brothers opened Shirref's wine bar at 15 Great Castle Street at a time when such establishments were something of a novelty. Shirref's stood the test of time and became a favourite watering hole for musicians and actors working around the corner at the BBC in Portland Place. At the end of the 1980s it was taken over by

£8 to £22

Address 15 Great Castle St, W1
☏ 020 7580 2125
Station Oxford Circus
Open Daily noon–3pm &
5.30–11pm
Accepts All major credit cards

David Tharakan and continued to prosper – a good deal of wine was consumed and there was even a short menu of pub food favourites. The big changes came at the end of 1997, when David's wife Millie took over the kitchen and changed the menu. Shirref's started to offer Keralan home cooking, with well-judged, well-spiced dishes at bargain-basement prices. Since then The Kerala restaurant – which is what it has become – has gone from strength to strength.

To start with, you must order a platoon of simple things: cashew nut pakoda (£2.95), potato bonda (£2.75), lamb samosa (£2.75), chicken liver masala (£3.75), mussels ularthu (£3.75). These are honest dishes, simply presented and at a price which encourages experimentation. Thereafter the menu is divided into a number of sections: Syrian Christian specialities from Kerala; coastal seafood dishes; Malabar biryanis; vegetable curries; and special dosas. From the first, try erachi olathiathu (£4.95), a splendid dry curry of lamb with coconut. From the second, try meen and mango vevichathu (£4.95), which is kingfish cooked with the sharpness of green mango. From the biryanis, how about chemmin biryani (£6.45) – prawns cooked with basmati rice? Avial (£3.95) is a mixed vegetable curry with yoghurt and coconut. The breads are fascinating – try the lacy and delicate appams (two for £2.60) made from steamed rice-flour.

The people who run The Kerala are intensely proud of their country and its cuisine, and will be happy to help you discover glorious new dishes. The Kerala would be good value in the suburbs, but being hidden behind Oxford Circus makes it a contender for bargain of the age. Look out for the "lunch buffet" offers – a feast for under £6.95.

Passione

When Passione opened nobody had heard of Gennaro Contaldo, but just about everyone had heard of his protégé, Jamie Oliver, television hero of swathes of Middle England foodies. Gradually, however, Passione has built up a following on its own merits. Sure, the food is in the same idiom as the stuff on the telly, but that's only to be expected, as Oliver spent his formative years in a kitchen run by Contaldo. Passione is a good restaurant. Simplicity, an unpretentious feel to the place, seasonal ingredients and talent in the kitchen – these are sure bets when it comes to eating. Be sure not to miss the splendid breads, including Contaldo's fabled focaccia – the one which the pukka chap is always banging on about.

£22 to £55

Address 10 Charlotte St, W1
℡ 020 7636 2833
Station Goodge Street
Open Mon–Fri 12.30–2.15pm &
7–10.15pm, Sat 7–10.15pm
Accepts All major credit cards
ⓦ www.passione.co.uk

You owe it to yourself to have four courses, and the portions are geared towards being able to manage such a splurge – how nice it is to have four delicious platefuls and not feel overstuffed. If you need any further encouragement, remind yourself that this is a restaurant where some dishes have actually come down in price! The menu changes daily, and there is a constant procession of specials. Among the antipasti, zuppa di funghi (£7.50) is a classic mushroom soup, while petto d'anitra affumicata con pera e rucola (£8.50) combines the richness of smoked duck breast with pear and rocket. Then there is pasta and risotto: taglierini con vongole (£9.50/11.50) has a rich clam sauce, while risotto all'accetosella (£8/10) has the tasty tang of wild sorrel. Mains are rich and satisfying: orata con endiva belga salsina di miele e aceto bianco (£19), seabream with endives and a honey and vinegar sauce; or coniglio con rosmarino e patate saltate (£17.50) – rabbit with rosemary and sauté potatoes. The service is slick here; this is a place where they understand the art of running a comfortable restaurant.

Puddings (all £5) are serious stuff, though it has to be said that the delicious gelato Passione, a swirl of zesty limoncello ice with a splash of wild strawberry folded into it, is for all the world a grown-up's raspberry ripple.

Rasa Samudra

Rasa Samudra represents the "smart fishy" sector in Das Sreedharan's burgeoning portfolio of high-quality South Indian restaurants (see the original Rasa, p.292; and the latest, Rasa Travancore, p.293). The food served is sophisticated fish cookery, the kind of stuff that would be more at home in Bombay than in London, consisting as it does of classy South Indian fish dishes – a million miles from familiar curry-house staples.

> **£18 to £40**
>
> Address 5 Charlotte St, W1
> ☎ 020 7637 0222
> Station Goodge Street
> Open Mon–Sat noon–3pm & 6–11pm, Sun 6–10.30pm
> Accepts All major credit cards
> ⊛ www.rasarestaurants.com

At first glance the menu may seem heart-stoppingly expensive, partly due to a strange and exclusively British prejudice that no curry should ever cost more than a fiver, even if made from the kind of top-quality ingredients that are worth £15 in a French restaurant. Note, however, that all the more expensive choices – which are often based on fish, usually the most pricey of ingredients – come complete with accompaniments. This makes them substantial enough to allow all but the greediest of diners to dispense with starters, except perhaps for the samudra rasam (£5.95) – a stunning shellfish soup – or the array of pappadoms, papparvardi and achappam (£4); or there is banana boli (£4.25) – which are plantain fritters with black sesame seeds. Plus wicked pickles (£3.50). And maybe the meen cutlets (£4.50), which are like fishcakes made with tuna and cassava. For main course, crab varuthathu (£12.50) – a dish of crab stir-fried with ginger – is well offset by pooris (£2.50) and spicy potatoes (£5.25) as side dishes. Other good choices include konju manga curry (£12.95) – prawns cooked dry with turmeric and green mango; fish moily (£11.50) – a curry of kingfish cooked in coconut milk; and varutharacha meen curry (£11.50) – tilapia cooked with shallots, red chillies and tamarind, a dish which is well complemented by beetroot curry (£6.25) and a chapati. The cooking is well judged and the spices well balanced.

If you are still nervous of the bill, don't be – the food is worth it. Serious gastronauts should opt for the Kerala feast (seafood £30; vegetarian £22.50). This takes the worry out of ordering.

Sardo

Sardo has cut out a niche for itself as a self-proclaimed flagship for Sardinian food. The proprietor, Romolo Mudu from Caligari, acts as front of house. Coupled with plain but fairly uninspired decor, this may make elderly diners feel that they have wandered into the Terrazza restaurant circa 1980. Take heart, for the food is more interesting than you would expect and is particularly good when you concentrate on the specials.

£18 to £40

Address 45 Grafton St, W1
☎ 020 7387 2521
Station Warren Street
Open Mon–Fri noon–3pm & 6–11pm, Sat 6–11pm
Accepts All major credit cards
🖰 www.sardo-restaurant.com

Fregola is a Sardinian pasta that comes in small enough pieces to take over the role of rice as a soup thickener; at Sardo such soups crop up on the specials board, so look out for zuppa di fregola ai gamberi e carciofi (£7.90), a thick soup with prawns and artichokes. The alici alla Sardo (£7.90) are also good – marinated anchovies served on rocket and tomatoes, with a few strips of grilled aubergine for good measure. Or there is mosciamo di tonno (£7.90), the prized central fillet of a tuna that is salted and wind-dried and has a very concentrated flavour. Delicious. Move on to something simple, but impressive, like tonno alla griglia (£13.75) – a large chunk of tuna, raw inside, seared outside, spanking fresh and tender as butter. Or maybe salsiccia Sarda (£11.50) appeals? The proprietor will happily discuss his brother's recipe for these home-made sausages, which have a distinctive aniseed tang. For dessert, go trad Sardinian: sebada (£4.50) is a puff pastry filled with orange peel and cheese and topped with honey. Or there is a splendid array of five or six different Pecorino cheeses (£4.50). The wine list includes a page of reasonably priced Sardinian specialities, and there are some distinctive, aromatic whites – note the Vermentinas.

Remember to check out the specials: occasionally this restaurant gets a shipment of the justly famous mountain prosciutto made from mutton, though naturally this is set aside for favoured regulars. Thankfully, other Sardinian delicacies like donkey escalope and vinegared pig's ear have yet to be sighted.

MODERN BRITISH

Villandry Foodstore

As both foodstore and restaurant serving breakfast, elevenses, lunch, tea and dinner, Villandry began in more fashionable but cramped surroundings in Marylebone High Street. Its success brought the need for larger premises and, thus installed in Great Portland Street, a handsome foodstore gives onto a modern and rather stark dining room. Passing displays of some of Europe's most extravagant ingredients may jangle the nerves and alarm the wallet, but if you're serious about your food, and you have time to wait for careful preparation, Villandry won't disappoint.

£22 to £55

Address 170 Great Portland St, W1
℡ 020 7631 3131
Station Great Portland Street
Open Daily 8.30am–10.30pm
Accepts All major credit cards except Diners

The menu changes daily, so you won't necessarily find all – or indeed any – of the dishes mentioned here. But as you'd expect at the back of a foodstore that caters for the well-heeled sector of the foodie faithful, ingredients are scrupulously chosen and prepared with care. At its best, this kind of "informal" menu is surprisingly demanding on the cook – and exact cooking is crucial to ostensibly simple dishes. To start, you may be offered a cream of cauliflower soup with chives (£6); morteau sausage, Puy lentils, caramelized onion and salsa verde (£7.50); poached langoustines with aioli (£10.50); or a plate of charcuterie (£7.25/12.75). Main courses are often hugely impressive: braised lamb shank with champ, red onion and balsamic (£16.50); fillet of halibut with new potatoes, cucumber and Hollandaise (£18.75); roast pork, roast new potatoes, black pudding, apple and sage (£16.50). Desserts include moist chocolate cake with chocolate sauce (£5.50); baked ricotta cheesecake with berry sauce (£5.75); and, unsurprisingly, given the array in the shop, there's an extensive if expensive cheeseboard (£11.50), served with terrific walnut and sourdough breads.

Wine prices, like the food, are distinctly West End, though there are reasonably priced house selections. Overall, standards are high, and the balancing both of flavours and of the menu itself suggests that the kitchen brigade knows what it's doing and isn't afraid to buck the trends. Lunch prices are a tad easier on the purse.

Wagamama

Wagamama has been packed since the day it opened, and its popularity shows no signs of falling off. Which is fair enough, because this is as good a canteen as you'll find, serving simple and generally rather good food at very reasonable prices. What it's not is a place for a relaxed or intimate meal. The basement interior is cavernous and minimalist, and diners are seated side by side on long benches. At regular eating times you'll find yourself in a queue lining the stairway – there are no reservations. When you reach the front, you're seated, your order is punched into a hand-held computer, then the code numbers for your dishes are written on the low-tech placemat in front of you – a legacy of the day when the radio-ordering system failed. There's beer and wine available, as well as free green tea.

£8 to £17

Address 4 Streatham St, WC1
☏ 020 7323 9223
Station Tottenham Court Road
Open Mon–Sat noon–11pm, Sun 12.30–10pm
Accepts All major credit cards
Branches see p.491
⊛ www.wagamama.com

Dishes arrive when they're cooked, so your party will be served at different times. Most people order a main dish – noodles in soup, fried noodles or sauce-based noodles – or a rice dish. Side dishes can also be pressed into service as a starter: yasai yakitori (£4.25) is char-grilled chicken with the ever-popular yakitori sauce, while gyoza (£3.95) are delicious, fried chicken dumplings. The mains include a splendid chilli beef ramen (£8.50) – slivers of sirloin steak in a vat of soup with vegetables. Also good is the yasai katsu curry (£6), which is boiled rice with a light curry sauce and discs of deep-fried vegetables; and yasai chili men (£6.25), a vegetarian "everything-in" dish with courgette, ginger, mushroom, carrot, peas, tomato, tofu and so on, plus ramen noodles. If this all sounds confusing, that's because it is. To enjoy Wagamama you'll need to go with the flow.

It's not often that a restaurant offers a glossary that includes its own name. Wagamama is described as "Willfulness or selfishness: selfishness in terms of looking after oneself, looking after oneself in terms of positive eating and positive living". It seems to work here and at the numerous other branches scattered around town.

Chinatown

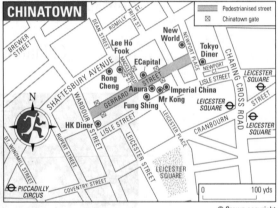

© Crown copyright

Aaura

Aaura is huge, new (summer of 2003) and different. From the lady greeters on the street (who wear short fur-trimmed capes when the weather is foul), to the huge nightclub-style bar (which serves real ale) and the electronic mural of the "lucky couple" (the symbolic dragon and phoenix vital to Chinese

£15 to £60

Address 38 Gerrard Street, W1
℗ 020 7287 8033
Station Piccadilly Circus
Open Daily, 12 noon–11.30pm
Accepts All major credit cards

weddings) – all is slick, if a little over-the-top, and no expense has been spared. There are several floors and mezzanine floors with a warren of dining rooms and private rooms. The chefs have been brought in from Hong Kong, and know their stuff: you will eat well here.

The dim sum are good – a notably delicate shrimp cheung fun (£3.50); Shanghai pork dumplings (£2.50) – a spoonful of soup within the pastry case – eat them whole they explode in your mouth; "deep-fried cuttlefish pasty cake" (£2.80) is a tender, subtle fishcake. The mini glutinous rice in lotus leaf (£3) is good. The barbecued meats are also first-rate – ordering suckling pig (£13.80) brings wafers of über-crackling and tender meat. The main menu has enough old favourites on it to appeal, but ordering crispy aromatic duck (half £13.50) when you could have crispy honey-roast fillet of eel (£15) is unenterprising. Take a look at the section listing "regional" dishes – there are some interesting spicy dishes like double-cooked pork (£7), and Hunan scallops (£9.50); or classics like stir-fried scrambled egg white with seafood Peking style (£10); and steamed sea bass with ginger and spring onion (£13.50). The waiters and managers here are unusually friendly and will happily explain and recommend.

The head chef here was renowned in Hong Kong for his crisp roast pigeon and you may find it on the specials list (£10) – this is a difficult dish to do well: any fool can cook a small bird like a pigeon until crisp, but it is tricky to present it crisp on the outside but still tender on the inside. The pigeon at Aaura is remarkably good and comes with the two dips made famous in Hong Kong – celery salt and Worcestershire Sauce!

Chinatown

ECapital

(🍴) This restaurant, which opened in spring 2002, was a welcome addition to the Chinese scene, as it showcases the somewhat neglected cuisine of Shanghai. The chef is David Tam, who won all manner of awards when at Aroma II. The interior is striking: the ceiling is painted deep fuchsia, the walls are a nondescript cream, the lighting is

£14 to £50
Address 8 Gerrard St, W1
☎ 020 7434 3838
Station Leicester Square
Open Daily noon–midnight
Accepts All major credit cards except Diners

soft – and that's it. For once less really is more. This is a comfortable, unpretentious place to eat and the food is both delicious and fascinating.

For the nervous, the menu offers a safety blanket of familiar favourites, from crispy seaweed to sweet and sour pork; proceed and you'll find a host of good things from Shanghai. Starters include drunken chicken (£8); cold chicken marinated in sweet wine; or paper-thin seasoned beef (£8), a stunning dish of slices of slow-cooked beef in a chilli-spiked, savoury marinade. The warm starters section includes the classic old-fashioned pan-fried dumplings (£5), with good crispy bits, but the out and out star is the thousand-layer pig's ear (£8). It's a slight exaggeration, as there are just 21 layers, but imagine small strips of agreeably chewy streaky bacon, cut thin, and tasting gelatinous and savoury. Pig's ear rarely tastes this good. The grandstand main course is beggar's chicken (£25). The chicken is seasoned with pickled cabbage and shredded pork, then wrapped in lotus leaves and given a casing of flour and water paste; the entire parcel is baked and, when the casing is smashed at table-side, the fragrant chicken is revealed within. You can also try sea bass West Lake style (£16), or Shanghai braised yellow eel (£12). Last, look out for the elite Chinese teas – floral and elegant.

The lunch menu at ECapital showcases all the famous Shanghai cold snacks (priced between £5 and £8 each), and fills in with some more substantial noodle dishes. Look out for a dish called "spring onion deep pan pizza" – it's more refined than the stuffed, flat onion breads you buy at the roadside in Shanghai, but just as tasty.

Fung Shing

Fung Shing was one of the first restaurants in Chinatown to take cooking seriously. Some decades ago, when it was still a dowdy little place with a mural on the back wall, the kitchens were run by the man acknowledged to be Chinatown's number one fish cook, chef Wu. When he died, in 1996, his sous-chef took over. The restaurant itself has changed beyond recognition and now

£22 to £60

Address 15 Lisle St, WC2
☏ 020 7437 1539
Station Leicester Square
Open Daily noon–11.30pm
Accepts All major credit cards
🖳 www.fungshing.com

stretches all the way from Lisle Street to Gerrard Street, ever bigger and ever brassier. Even if there has been a slight decline in overall standards, the menu is littered with interesting dishes, the fish is still very fine and portions are large. Unfortunately, prices are creeping ever upwards, and you need to pick carefully to be sure of a good meal.

By Chinese restaurant standards, the menu is not huge, topping out at around 160 dishes, but the food has that earthy, robust quality which you only encounter when the chef is absolutely confident of his flavours and textures, whatever the cuisine. To start, ignore the crispy duck with pancakes (half for £20), which are good but too predictable, and the lobster with noodles (£19 a pound, with noodles £2 extra), which works out expensive. Turn instead to the steamed scallops with garlic and soya sauce (£2.75 each) – nowhere does them better. Or spare ribs, barbecued or with chilli and garlic (both £8). The prosaically named "mixed meat with lettuce" (£8.50) is also good, a wonderfully savoury dish of mince with lettuce-leaf wraps. You could also happily order mains solely from the chef's specials: stewed belly pork with yam in hot pot (£9.95); crispy spicy eel (£10.95); roast crispy pigeon (£14); or oysters with bean-thread vermicelli in hot pot (£11.50). The other dishes are good too: perfect Singapore noodles (£6), crispy stuffed baby squids with chilli and garlic (£9.50), and steamed aubergine with garlic sauce (£7.50).

The Fung Shing has always been a class act but what is unusual, certainly in Chinatown, is the gracious and patient service. This is a place where you can ask questions and take advice with confidence.

HK Diner

HK Diner is a light, bright, busy, modern sort of place, so if you like your Chinese restaurants seedy and "authentic" you will almost certainly walk past with a shudder. "It looks more like a burger bar, so how can it possibly … " Pre-judging this place would be a major mistake, however, as the food is very good, and there is no iron rule that slickness means rip-off. Prices are not cheap, but they are not over-the-top either, and the prospect of getting decent food very late at night (HK stays open until 5am at the weekend) is a beguiling one. Service is attentive, you don't wait long for food, and the tables turn over at a ferocious pace.

£8 to £35

Address 22 Wardour St, WC2
☏020 7434 9544
Station Piccadilly/Leicester Square
Open Mon–Thurs & Sun noon–4am,
Fri & Sat noon–5am
Accepts All major credit cards
except Diners

The menu offers all the Cantonese favourites, from very good salt and pepper spare ribs (£6.50) to grilled dumplings (four for £3.50) and steamed scallops on the half shell (£2.50 each). For main course, deep-fried squid with salt, pepper and garlic (£8) is as light, crisp and un-rubbery as you could wish, or there's fried mussels in spicy sauce (£8). Fried beef with chilli and black bean sauce (£6) is rich and delicious, as is honey- barbecued pork (£6.50). The Singapore noodles (£4.50) is a model of its kind. From the vegetable dishes, choose the fried snow pea shoots with minced garlic (£7) if you love garlic – this is the one to guarantee that even good friends will keep their distance for the next couple of days. The simple dishes, such as fried noodles with mixed meat (£4.50) or fried noodle with mixed seafood (£6), will hit the spot with diners.

The management has installed a patent Chinese milkshake machine from Hong Kong, and for £3 you can enjoy a tall glass of crushed ice with various flavourings and a secret spoonful of "pearls" – these are chewy, pea-sized balls of agar jelly. You drink your milkshake through a special large-gauge straw and, as you suck up the drink, the pearls shoot into your mouth and rattle around. It's as if you have become a living pinball machine. There are 20 different flavours: coffee is good, passion fruit is OK.

Lee Ho Fook

Encouraged by the glowing reports in the guidebooks, lots of tourists set out to eat at Lee Ho Fook on Macclesfield Street but never actually manage to find it. This is a genuine Chinese barbecue house – small, spartan and cheap, with the food good of its kind. But the restaurant is not so helpful as to have a sign in English. Thus many

£5 to £12
Address 4 Macclesfield St, W1
⊤no phone
Station Leicester Square
Open Daily 11.30am–11pm
Accepts Cash only
Branches see p.489

potential non-Chinese diners find themselves at the larger, grander, more tourist-friendly Lee Ho Fook around the corner in Gerrard Street. These, then, are the directions: Macclesfield Street runs from Shaftesbury Avenue in the north to Gerrard Street in the south; on the west side is a backstreet called Dansey Place and, on the corner, with a red and gold sign in Chinese characters and a host of ducks hanging on a rack, is Lee Ho Fook. Inside there's a chef chopping things at a block in the window and four or five waiters. Sit down and you get tea, chopsticks and a big bottle of chilli sauce placed in front of you. Tables are shared and eating is a brisk business.

The main focus of the short menu is an array of plated meals – a mound of rice with a splash of soy sauce "gravy" and a portion of chopped barbecued meat balanced on top. Choose from lean pork loin, crisp fatty belly pork, soya chicken or duck (all £4.10). You can also mix and match – half pork, half duck, say – or order a "combination" of mixed roast pork, soya chicken and duck with rice (£5). Some choose to eat the meats without rice – perhaps a whole duck (£23) or a portion of soya chicken (£5.50). There's also a thriving takeaway trade.

Because of the specialized nature of this place, the other menu items are all too easily overlooked. Try adding a plate of crisp vegetables in oyster sauce (£3.80) to your order. And, before the main event, perhaps choose a bowl of won ton soup (£2.20), or the even more substantial won ton noodle soup (£2.80). The extension into the shop next door has doubled the number of seats but, aside from that, this establishment continues to do a simple thing very well, which is not as easy a trick to pull off as it sounds.

Chinatown

Mr Kong

You have to wonder whether the eponymous Mr Kong flirted with the idea of calling his restaurant King Kong – despite its marathon opening hours, at all regular mealtimes it's full of satisfied customers who would support such an accolade. Going with a party of six or more is the best plan when dining

£8 to £22

Address 21 Lisle St, WC2
☎ 020 7437 7341
Station Leicester Square
Open Daily noon–3am
Accepts All major credit cards

at Mr Kong, as that way you can order, taste and argue over a raft of dishes. You can share, and if there's something you really don't like, you can exile it to the other end of the table. If there's something wonderful, you can call up a second portion. It's a canny strategy, and means that you can never be caught out.

Sad to say, but several Chinatown stalwarts that have got smarter, busier and richer have lost some of their more obscure menu items along the way. Mr Kong is teetering on the brink. Where once there were three menus, there are now only two. But the Manager's Choice still lists some tempting options – steamed razor clams with glass noodles and garlic (£3.50 each); fried sliced eel and stuffed chilli in black bean sauce (£12); and, most extravagant of all, braised turbot with bitter melon and bean curd stick (£13). The main menu can be rather safety-first, but sliced pork, salted egg and vegetable soup (minimum two people; £2.10 each), something of a house speciality, is worth a try. It's rich and very good, and the salted egg tastes pleasantly cheesy. Then try the braised belly pork with preserved vegetables (£6.80) – a dish much copied by European chefs. Or maybe the special stuffed aubergine with green peppers and bean curd (£7.50); plus the good, spicy take on Singapore noodle (£4.20); Kon Chin king prawn (£7.90) – an interesting prawn dish in a spicy tomatoey sauce; stewed beef flank Cantonese style in a pot (£5.90); and seasonal greens in oyster sauce (£4.60) – dark-green, crunchy and delicious.

Portions are generous and, even when dishes contain exotic ingredients, prices are reasonable. Just ignore the decor, which despite a refurb and new chairs is still resolutely ordinary.

New World

When the 1990s saw the arrival of the mega-restaurants, giant 200- and 300-seater emporiums, the proprietors of this long-established Chinese restaurant were right to feel aggrieved and ask what all the fuss was about. The New World seats between 400 and 600 people, depending on how many functions are going on at any one time. This is probably the largest single restaurant in Europe, but when you arrive you invariably have to wait in a sort of holding pen just inside the door until the intercom screeches with static and you are sent off to your table. The menu, leather-bound and nearly twenty pages long, features everything you have ever heard of and quite a lot you haven't. In any case, you don't need it – go for the dim sum, which are served every day from 11am until 6pm.

£8 to £22

Address 1 Gerrard Place, W1
℗ 020 7734 0396
Station Leicester Square
Open Daily 11am–midnight
Accepts All major credit cards

CHINESE/DIM SUM

The dim sum come round on trolleys. First catch the eye of a waiter or waitress with a bow tie, to order drinks, and then you're at the mercy of the trolley pushers. Broadly speaking, the trolleys are themed: one has a lot of barbecued meat; another is packed with ho fun – broad noodles; another with steamed dumplings; another with soups; another with cheung fun – the long slippery rolls of pastry with different meats inside; and so on. A good mix would be to take siu mai (£2) and har kau (£2) from the "steamers" trolley. Then char sui cheung fun (£3) – a long roll with pork. Then some deep-fried won ton (£2) – little crispy parcels with sweet sauce. Or perhaps try something exotic like woo kwok (£2) – deep-fried taro dumplings stuffed with pork and yam. And something filling like char sui pow (£2) – steamed doughnuts filled with pork; or nor mai gai (£3.50) – a lotus-leaf parcel of glutinous rice and meats.

If you arrive after 6pm, you're on your own: there are literally hundreds of dishes on the main menus. However, Chinese functions apart, New World is really best as an in-and-out dim sum joint. It's about eating and not, as the sticky carpet declares, design and fripperies.

Rong Chen

Rong Chen opened during early summer 2003, and is something of a wild card. It falls into the same category as Lee Ho Fook (page 25) which is just around the corner. But décor-wise, Rong Chen has upped the ante and may well have stolen a march on its rivals – a polished floor, comfortable chairs, solid wood tables. The menu is something of a throwback, there are lots of dishes that are only written up in Chinese and prices are very low indeed. In a strange way it all seems to hark back to several years ago, when these Chinese cafés first became popular. Service is inscrutable, but persevere as the place has an undeniable charm. Cheap charm. Cheap food.

£3 to £15

Address 72 Shaftesbury Avenue, W1
℡ 020 7287 8078
Station Leicester Square
Open Mon–Thurs noon–11.30pm, Fri & Sat noon–midnight
Accepts Mastercard & Visa

CENTRAL

CHINESE

This place specializes in one–plate meals – the main menu offers Fujian fried rice (£4); crispy noodle dishes like chicken vegetable noodles (£3.50); fried ho fun (the broad noodles) with beef (£4.50). Then there is a section devoted to soup noodles – special won ton (£4.50); brisket of beef (£4.80); mixed vegetable (£3) – all of these soups with noodles, rice noodles or ho fun depending on your whim. There's also a range of mainstream dishes such as crispy roast duck (£9 for a half); even lobster at a "seasonal price". But the real business is done off the "platters" menu. These are simple one–plate dishes that come with a free bowl of soup. The soup is interesting, virtually clear and surprisingly strongly flavoured with a few floating lumps of pork. Roast duck rice (£4.50); beef with chilli and black bean sauce rice (£4.30); mixed seafood rice (£4.80); Shanghai spare ribs rice (£4.30). These dishes are all sound enough and cheaper than at most competing establishments, even before you take into account the "free" soup.

There are also a few surprises lurking among the "platters" – five-spices pork rice is what it says on the card. What turns up is a dish of slow-cooked pig's stomach, and before you recoil in horror, if no one had told you, you would never have guessed. Slices of rich, meaty "stuff" arrive in splendid rich gravy – delicious.

Tokyo Diner

Tokyo Diner offers conclusive proof that you needn't take out a second mortgage to enjoy Japanese food in London. Stacked up on three floors of a block that clings to Chinatown's silk skirts, this is a friendly eatery that shuns elaboration in favour of fast food, Tokyo-style. The place was actually set up by a Nipponophile Englishman, but the kitchen staff are all Japanese and its Far Eastern credentials bear scrutiny. The decor, crisp and minimalist, leaves the food to do the talking, which it does fluently – if the number of Japanese who walk through the doors are any indication. If you don't know your teppan-yaki from your kamikaze, or your sushi from your sumo, you'll be glad of the explanatory notes on the menu. When your food arrives, pick a set of chopsticks, snap them apart – the menu recommends that you rub them together to rid them of splinters – and get stuck in. Japanese style, the Tokyo Diner does not accept tips.

£7 to £25
Address 2 Newport Place, WC2 ☎ 020 7287 8777 **Station** Leicester Square **Open** Daily noon–midnight **Accepts** MasterCard, Visa, no cheques

JAPANESE

Top seller is the soba noodle soup (£5.10), thin brown buckwheat noodles in a soya broth. It's pleasant, filling and very popular with the drop-by lunchtime trade. Don't be afraid of slurping it – as the menu explains, slurping is OK. Or try the set lunch in a bento box of rice, noodles, sashimi and your choice of teriyaki, all for around £11.50. Other bento favourites include the ton katsu bento (£11.50), which is a kind of superior breadcrumbed pork escalope. If you don't have appetite enough for a full-on bento box, skip the curries – as the menu admits, they're a bit like school food – and head straight for the sushi and sashimi. They too come in "sets": try the nine-piece nigiri set (£8.90), which is very good value, or the hosi-maki set (£4.90), which comprises six pieces of salmon, three pieces of cucumber and three pieces of pickled radish.

To wash it all down, the Japanese beer Asahi (£1.99) is good, or there's complimentary Japanese tea. For a special treat, try the rich, sweet plum wine (£2.99 for 125ml), which is surprisingly moreish.

Tokyo Diner

Covent Garden & Holborn

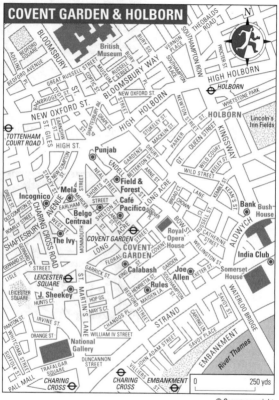

COVENT GARDEN & HOLBORN

© Crown copyright

0   250 yds

Bank

This restaurant may well be the closest London gets to re-creating the all-day buzz and unfussy cuisine of the big Parisian brasseries. Bank opens for breakfast (Continental, Full English, or Caviar); lays on brunch at the weekend; does a good-value pre- and post-theatre (5.30–7pm and 10–11pm) and lunch prix fixe (both are £12.50 for two courses, £15 for three); and has a bustling bar. And then there's the other matter of lunch and dinner for several hundred. Whatever the time of day, the food is impressive, especially considering the large numbers of people fed, and if you like things lively you will have a great time. If you're leaving after 10pm, incidentally, and want a taxi, go for the cabs arranged by the doorman; black cabs are rare as hen's teeth around here after the Drury Lane theatres empty.

> **£16 to £60**
>
> **Address** 1 Kingsway, corner of Aldwych, WC2
> ℡ 020 7379 9797
> **Station** Holborn
> **Open** Mon–Fri 7.30–11.30am, noon–3pm & 5.30–11pm, Sat 11.30am–3.30pm & 5.30–11pm, Sun 11.30am–3.30pm & 5.30–9.30pm
> **Accepts** All major credit cards
> **Branches** see p.487
> 🌐 www.bankrestaurants.com

MODERN BRITISH

The menu changes seasonally, so dishes may come and go. Start with something simple – simple to get wrong, that is – a Caesar salad (£6.95), say, or a smoked haddock and ricotta tart (£6.50); or push the boat out with a well-made foie gras parfait with apple and pear chutney (£7.95). Or go for shellfish. A key role in Bank's history was played by one of London's leading catering fishmongers, so crustacea such as dressed crab with ginger and wasabi dressing (£12.50) should be reliable. The fish dishes are equally good, from an ambitious pan-fried sea bass shrimp sauce, salsify and potato rosti, wild mushrooms (£18.95), to a traditional halibut fish and chips (£18.95), featuring mushy peas and tartare sauce. Meat dishes are well-prepared brasserie fare such as rump of lamb, spiced chickpea casserole, merguez (£17.95); calf's liver, wild mushrooms, creamed polenta, balsamic jus (£16.95); or Cumberland sausage and mash, onion gravy (£11.95). Puds include an assiette au chocolat (£7.50), and panettone bread and butter pudding (£5).

Breakfast specialists may find themselves turning to the "Energiser" cocktail (£6.25). You have to approach a drink that blends passion fruit, melon, banana and pineapple with enthusiasm.

Belgo Centraal

🍴 The Belgians invented mussels, frites and mayonnaise, and Belgo has done all it can to help the Belgian national dish take over London. The Belgo group's flagship restaurant is a massive metal-minimalist cavern accessed by riding down in a scissor-powered lift. Turn left at the bottom and you enter the restaurant (where you can book seats); turn right and you get seated in the beerhall, where diners share

£5 to £30
Address 50 Earlham St, WC2
☏ 020 7813 2233
Station Covent Garden
Open Mon–Wed noon–11pm, Thurs–Sun noon–11.30pm, Accepts All major credit cards
Branches see p.487
🌐 www.belgorestaurants.com

tables. With 95 different beers, some at alcoholic strengths of 8–9 per cent, it's difficult not to be sociable, or perhaps to wile away a few minutes pondering the age-old question … name six famous Belgians.

Belgo has cornered the London mussels market and no mistake. A kilo of classic moules marinières served with frites and mayonnaise (£11.95) has fresh mussels that have clearly been cooked then and there. Other options include classique (£11.95), with cream and garlic; Provençale (£12.50), with tomato, herbs and garlic; or even Thai (£12.50), which comes with a Thai curry sauce. And there are many alternatives for the non-mussel eater. Start with a salade Brabaçonne (£4.95) – a warm salad including bacon, black pudding and duck confit. Or the cheese croquettes (£5.95), made with Orval beer. Move on to carbonade Fla-mande (£9.95) – beef braised in Geuze beer with apples and plums, and served with frites; or loup de mer grillé (£10.95) – sea bass served with baby spinach and Hollandaise sauce; or wild boar sausages made with Chimay beer (£8.95) and served with Belgian mash. Desserts, as you might expect, are strong on Belgian chocolate. They include, among many others, traditional Belgian waffles with dark chocolate and hazelnut ice cream (£4.50). Belgo delights in special offers: there's a £5.95 lunch, and various deals including one called "beat the clock", where the prices shift downwards in relation to how early you eat.

Belgo Centraal is a lively place that delivers value, atmosphere and sound food, but it's the awesome beer list that makes it a must-visit, and also something of a destination restaurant for noisy parties.

Café Pacifico

(🍴) The salsa is hot at Café Pacifico –
both types. As you are seated, a
complimentary bowl of searing salsa dip
with corn chips is put on your table. As
you eat, hot salsa music gets your fingers
tapping. The atmosphere is relaxed and
you're soon in the mood for a cold Tecate
(£3.20) or Negro Modelo (£3.20) beer.
There are nine Mexican beers, a good
selection of wines and dozens of cocktails. Parties can enjoy a pitcher of

£15 to £30

Address 5 Langley St, WC2
☎ 020 7379 7728
Station Covent Garden
Open Mon–Sat noon–midnight, Sun
noon–11pm
Accepts All major credit cards
except Diners
🌐 www.cafepacifico-laperla.co.uk

MEXICAN

Margaritas (£29.95) to serve eight people. But Pacifico's tequila list is the
highlight. There are more than 60 varieties, ranging from £2.90 to £100 a
shot, and including some very old and rare brands.

The menu is a lively mixture of old-style Californian Mexican and
new Mexican, so while favourites like fajitas, flautas and tacos dominate,
there are also some interesting and unusual dishes. Portions are generous
and spicy, and many main courses come with refried beans and rice.
Refried beans at Café Pacifico are smooth and comforting, and just the
thing to balance the spicy heat. Try nachos rancheros (£7.95, £6.95
vegetarian) for starters and enjoy a huge plate of corn chips with beans,
cheese, guacamole, onions, sour cream and olives. Excellent for sharing.
Taquitos (£4.75) – filled fried baby tacos – are very tasty, too, as are
smoked chicken quesadillas (£5.75) – flour tortillas with chicken, red
peppers and avocado salsa. Main courses include degustación del Pacifico
(£9.95), which includes a taste of almost everything. There's the chim-
changa (£9.50) – a deep-fried rolled tortilla like a giant spring roll. The
burrito especial (£9.25) gives you a flour tortilla filled with cheese,
refried beans and a choice of roast beef, chicken or ground beef, covered with ranchero sauce. Roast beef is slow-cooked and falling-apart
tender. Look out for their modern Mexican dishes like char-grilled
Porterhouse steak (£14.95) – these are available from 6pm.

Café Pacifico has been a place to party since 1978 and claims to be
London's oldest Mexican restaurant. And, yes, they do have a bottle of
mescal with a worm in it.

Calabash

The Calabash is a very cool place, in the old-fashioned, laid-back sense of the word. The restaurant, deep within the bowels of the Africa Centre, is at once worthy, comfortable and cheap. The same complex features a splendidly seedy bar, a live music hall, and African arts and crafts for sale. The food is genuine and somewhat unsophisticated, and the menu struggles bravely to give snapshots of the extraordinary diversity of African cuisine. They manage dishes from North, East and West Africa, as well as specialities from Nigeria, Ivory Coast, Senegal and Malawi. So if you're looking for a particular dish you may be out of luck. However, if you want a cheerful atmosphere, a small bill, and wholesome, often spicy and usually unfamiliar food, the Calabash is worth seeking out.

£10 to £25
Address Africa Centre, 38 King St, WC2
☏ 020 7836 1976
Station Covent Garden
Open Mon–Fri noon–2.30pm & 6–10.30pm, Sat 6–10.30pm
Accepts All major credit cards except Diners

Starters include familiar dishes like avocado salad and hummus (both £2.20) along with interesting offerings such as aloco (£2.30), which is fried plantain in a hot tomato sauce, and sambusas (£2.95), a vegetarian cousin of the samosa. Those with an enquiring palate will pick the gizzards (£2.95), a splendid dish of chicken gizzards served in a rich, spiky pepper sauce. Grilled chicken wings (£2.60) are less exotic but very good nonetheless. Main courses are marked according to origin. From Nigeria comes egusi (£6.95), a rich soup/stew with spinach, meat and dried shrimps, thickened with melon seed. Yassa (£6.50) is grilled chicken from Senegal, while doro wot (£6.95) is a pungent chicken stew from Ethiopia, served with injera, the soft and thin sourdough bread. From Malawi there is nyamam yo phika (£7.75), a rich beef stew made with sweet peppers and potatoes. Drink whichever of the African beers is in stock at the time you visit.

One of the best dishes, simply called "chicken" (£6.25), takes the form of superb fried chicken served with a ferocious hot sauce. The chef who handles the frying is a master craftsman who manages to get the outside perfectly crisp and the inside perfectly tender. Order this to get an inkling of what the Colonel has been striving for all these years.

Field and Forest

(🍴) Best to think of Field and Forest as a lively drinking place that serves surprisingly good food. You find your way downstairs into a large space with a vaulted brick roof and a window onto the shops of the Thomas Neil centre. There's an open kitchen, a spacious dining area and, for a basement establishment, everything seems surprisingly light and fresh – helped by pale paintwork and

£12 to £30

Address 22 Shorts Gardens, WC2
☏ 020 7240 5777
Station Covent Garden
Open Mon-Sat noon–3pm & 6pm–midnight.
Accepts All major credit cards
🌐 www.fieldandforest.co.uk

MODERN BRITISH

plenty of lighting. The menu is short and offers good value. Plenty of restaurants bang on about the freshness, the naturalness, and the rarity of their ingredients before making you choose from twelve starters and fifteen mains; a shorter menu gives you so much more confidence. At F and F there are only ten dishes and a few sides.

The food is good and flavour combinations work. Dishes are simply plated and well seasoned. Buffalo mozzarella, tomato, extra virgin olive oil (£5.50) should be renamed "good buffalo mozzarella, good tomato, good extra virgin olive oil" – good value too, and goes well with the salt- crust bread (£2). Other starters include a pissaladière (£3.75), and an aubergine, red pepper and Parmesan pasty (£4). As to mains: grilled black leg chicken, hot French bean vinaigrette (£9.75) shows why the French poulet noir commands a premium price – at last a chicken that tastes of something. Or there's crisp mackerel served with salsa verde (£7.50). The most expensive dish is the grilled Argentinean fillet steak, celeriac slaw (£12.75) – a good steak, precisely cooked and with a nice mustardy celeriac remoulade. As befits somewhere a truckle's roll from the famous Neal's Yard cheese shop, cheeses are good here – Colston Bassett Stilton, Keen's cheddar, quince (£4.50). This equable pricing has also spread to the wine list, where the list tops out in Burgundy, a sound bottle of Givry for around £25.

The set menus are very appealing: three courses and a glass of wine weigh in at £17.50. While at lunch you could have a glass of wine; grilled chicken and merguez sausages, couscous and harissa; followed by fig and almond tart for £11.25 including service.

Incognico

FRENCH

(🍴) The Nico in question is Nico
Ladenis, a respected chef who
sensibly enough has retired to the south
of France leaving his London restaurants
in the capable hands of his daughter.
Fortunately he first took the opportunity
to get the offer here right before abdi-
cating. This is a very French sort of place
and when you are talking about a particular kind of retro French cooking, the

£17 to £70
Address 117 Shaftesbury Ave, WC2
☎ 020 7836 8866
Station Covent Garden/ Tottenham Court Road
Open Mon–Sat noon–3pm & 5.30pm–midnight
Accepts All major credit cards

French have few equals. The dining room is comfortable and done out in
dark-brown tones, the only cavil being that some of the tables are
packed in a bit tightly, so that you could whisper in a loved one's ear and
still share the billing and cooing with your neighbours.

The cooking is very sound here. The menu is a long one and, while
not actually being old-fashioned per se, there are enough old favourites
to please the stickiest stick-in-the-mud. Starters such as fresh salmon and
potatoes (£9.50), brandade of cod (£7.50), and terrine of foie gras
(£14) all strike a chord. As do mains like ossobuco (£15.50), which is
delightfully rich and served with Parmesan risotto. And veal kidneys in
mustard sauce (£12.50). Or monkfish "Roger Verge" (£15.50). Or
entrecôte Béarnaise (£16.50). Or skate with capers and olive oil
(£14.50). Puddings (all £6.50) carry on the theme successfully: pear
tart; crème brûlée; lemon tart. And the cheese selection weighs in at a
rather savage £10.50. Your wallet may also hate the wine list.

The set menu (available at lunch and 5.30–7pm) changes daily and is
an outstandingly good deal. For £12.50 you get three courses and, joy
of joys, there is an equally priced pichet of vin rouge (£7.50 for 50cl).
There are two choices per course and the dishes are appealing. The
choice may be between smoked salmon and horseradish cream, or
ravioli of goat's cheese with red peppers and basil oil; followed by
breast of guineafowl with lentils, or grilled sea bass with basil puree
and red pepper oil; culminating in crème brûlée with soft Italian
cheese and red fruit, or vanilla bavarois with blackcurrant coulis. This is
a very good deal.

India Club

When the India Club opened in 1950, the linoleum flooring was probably quite chic. Situated up two flights of stairs, sandwiched between floors of the grandly named Strand Continental Hotel, the Club is an institution, generally full and mostly with regulars, as you can tell by the stares of appraisal given to newcomers. The regulars are in

£6 to £12

Address 143 Strand, WC2
☎ 020 7836 0650
Station Charing Cross
Open Mon–Sat noon–2.30pm &
6–10.50pm
Accepts Cash or cheque only

INDIAN

love with the strangely old-fashioned combination of runny curry and low, low prices, and don't mind traipsing downstairs to the hotel reception to buy a bottle of Cobra beer. They can be split into two categories: suave Indians from the nearby High Commission, and a miscellany of folk from the BBC World Service down the road in Bush House.

The food at the India Club predates any London consciousness of the different spicing of Bengal, Kerala, Rajasthan or Goa. It is Anglo-Indian, essentially, and well cooked of its kind, although to palates accustomed to more modern Indian dishes it is something of a symphony to runny sauce. Mughlay chicken (£5.20) is a wing and a drumstick in a rich, brown, oniony gravy, garnished with two half hard-boiled eggs; while scampi curry (£6) is runny and brown, with fearless prawns swimming through it. Masala dosai (£3.60) is a well-made crispy pancake with a pleasantly sharp-tasting potato filling. Dhal (£3.30) is yellow and ... runny. Good dishes of bhindi or brinjal (both £3.50). The mango chutney (40p) is a revelation: thick parings of mango, which are chewy and delicious. Breads – paratha (£1.60), puris (two for £1.80) – are good, while the rice is white and comes in clumps (£2).

You should heed the kindly warning of your waiter about the chilli bhajis (£2.60), a dish as simple as it is thought-provoking. Long, thin, extra-hot green chillies are given a thick coating of gram-flour batter and then deep-fried until crisp. These are served with coconut chutney that has a few more chopped chillies sprinkled through it. Eating this actually hurts. Console yourself by remembering that, however bad, chilli burn lasts only ten minutes.

BRITISH

The Ivy

The Ivy is a beautiful, Regency-style restaurant, built in 1928 by Mario Gallati, who later founded Le Caprice. It has been a theatreland and society favourite ever since and never more so than today. The staff, it is said, notice recessions only because they turn fewer people away. That's no joke: The Ivy is booked solid for lunch and dinner right through the week. It behaves like a club even if it is not one, and to get a booking it helps to proffer the name of at least a B-list celebrity. If your heart is set on a visit, try booking at off-peak times a couple of months ahead, or at very short notice, or ask for a table in the bar area. It's also less busy for weekend lunch – three courses for a bargain £17.50 plus £1.50 service charge, with valet parking thrown in.

£28 to £65
Address 1 West St, WC2
☏ 020 7836 4751
Station Leicester Square
Open Daily noon–3pm (Sun 3.30pm) & 5.30pm–midnight
Accepts All major credit cards
✇ www.caprice-holdings.co.uk

And once you're in? Well, first off, whether you're famous or not, the staff are charming and unhurrying. Second, the food is pretty good. The menu is essentially a brasserie list of comfort food – nice dishes that combine simplicity with familiarity. You could spend a lot here without restraint; surprisingly little if you limit yourself to a single course and pudding. You might start with asparagus soup with creamed morels (£6.75), or the risotto primavera (£7.50/11.25), or the eggs Benedict (£6.25/12.50). Then there's deep-fried haddock (£15.25), corned beef hash with double fried egg (£9.25), and well-made versions of classic staples such as the Ivy hamburger with dill pickle (£9.50), shepherd's pie (£12.50) and salmon fishcakes (£11.75). Even the vegetable section is enlivened with homely delights like bubble and squeak (£2.75). For dessert you might turn to chocolate pudding soufflé (£6.50), Eton mess (£9.50), or finish with a savoury – herring roes on toast (£4.75).

The Ivy's present incarnation is the result of a 1990 makeover that meticulously restored the wood paneling and leaded stained glass. It also involved a roll call of British artists. Look around and you may notice works by, among others, Howard Hodgkin, Peter Blake, Tom Phillips and Patrick Caulfield.

J. Sheekey

Sheekey's is one of a handful of restaurants which had shambled along since the war – World War I. Then, in the late 1990s, it was taken over by the team behind The Ivy and Le Caprice (see p.40 and p.98). After a good deal of redesign and refurbishment, it emerged from the builders' clutches as J. Sheekey, with much the same attitudes and style as its senior siblings, but still focused on fish. The restaurant may look new, but it certainly seems old, and its series of interconnecting dining rooms gives it an intimate feel. The cooking is accomplished, the service is first-rate, and the fish is fresh – a good combination!

£18 to £70

Address 28–32 St Martin's Court, WC2
℡ 020 7240 2565
Station Leicester Square
Open Mon–Sat noon–3pm & 5.30pm–midnight, Sun noon–3.30pm & 5.30pm–midnight
Accepts All major credit cards
🖰 www.caprice-holdings.co.uk

FISH

The long menu presents a seductive blend of plain, old-fashioned, classic fish cuisine, such as lemon sole belle meunière (£17.75), with more modern dishes like whole roast gilthead bream with herbs and olive oil (£16.25). There are always handwritten dishes on the menu, "specials" which change on a weekly basis. To start with, there are oysters, crabs and shellfish, plus everything from jellied eels (£5.50) and potted shrimps (£9.75) to seared rare tuna (£9.50) and char-grilled squid with chorizo and red pepper (£9.50). Main courses, like pan-fried wing of skate with capers and brown butter (£13.50), or Cornish fish stew with celery heart and garlic mayonnaise (£19.75), are backed up by classics such as fillet of cod (£17.50) and Sheekey's fish pie (£9.75). Puddings go from spotted dick with butter and golden syrup (£5.25); to raspberry zabaglione (£6.75); or wild strawberry and champagne jelly with Jersey cream (£10.50).

The set menus are good value. At the weekend, lunch costs just £14.25 for two courses, or £18.50 for three (plus a £1.50 cover charge in the main dining room). You could tuck into Italian black figs with Parma ham; then escalope of salmon with mixed courgettes and tomato vinaigrette; and finish with chocolate and Grand Marnier tart. In a further bid to make life at the weekend hassle-free, the restaurant operates a valet parking system on Sunday.

Joe Allen

By some inexplicable alchemy, Joe Allen continues to be the Covent Garden eatery of choice for a wide swathe of the acting profession. It is a dark, resolutely untrendy place that dishes up American comfort food. So saying, you can never have anything better than exactly what you want and, if your heart is set on a Caesar salad, chilli con carne or eggs Benedict, this is a great place to come. Joe Allen also has a splendid attitude to mealtimes: the à la carte runs all day, so you can have lunch when you will. There's a special lunch and pre-theatre menu offering two courses for £14 and three for £16 (noon–4pm), plus a brunch menu on Saturday and Sunday – £17.50 for two courses and £19.50 for three, including a glass of champagne or a bloody Mary.

£16 to £40

Address 13 Exeter St, WC2
☎ 020 7836 0651
Station Covent Garden
Open Mon–Fri noon–12.45am, Sat 11.30am–12.45am, Sun 11.30am–11.30pm
Accepts All major credit cards except Diners
🖳 www.joeallen.co.uk

The food is the kind of stuff that we are all comfortable with. Starters include smoked salmon with cream cheese and herbs (£7.50), deep-fried potato skins with chilli tomato salsa, melted cheese and sour cream (£5.50), and black bean soup (£5). They are followed on the menu by a section described as "salads/eggs/sandwiches" in which you'll find some of Joe Allen's strengths: Caesar salad (£6/8); roast chicken salad with shaved vegetables and Asian dressing (£9); and eggs Joe Allen (£9), a satisfying combination of poached eggs, potato skins, Hollandaise sauce and spinach. Main courses range from grilled tuna with a pepper crust (£14), through barbecue spare ribs with rice, wilted spinach, black-eyed peas and corn muffin (£13), to pan-fried calf's liver with fried caramelized onion polenta and grilled bacon (£14). The side orders, including broccoli with lemon (£3), and grilled courgettes with garlic butter (£3), are most attractive. And the desserts are serious – go for the brownie (£5.50), with hot fudge sauce as an extra (£2).

Joe Allen is also home to its very own urban legend. The hamburger is very highly rated by aficionados everywhere, but you have to be in the know to order one, as it has never been listed on the menu.

Mela

Mela is one of the new breed of Indian restaurants that doesn't follow the time-honoured tradition of Bangladeshi restaurants, with their familiar dishes carefully developed solely for the Brits. At Mela the attitude is more "If it's good enough for Delhi … " The result is a restaurant serving very attractive and remarkably good-value Indian food. Mela may even have cracked the great lunch conundrum – Indian restauraters find it very difficult to persuade Londoners to eat curry for lunch. There's a "Paratha Pavilion" at lunchtime, which may sound a bit kitsch but lists a variety of delicious set lunches, from the insubstantial at £1.95, to the jolly good at £4.95. Stellar value in WC2. In 2003 the decor was tamed slightly: now it is marginally smarter and marginally less garish. Service is slick and friendly.

£5 to £40
Address 152–156 Shaftesbury Ave, WC2
☎ 020 7836 8635
Station Covent Garden
Open Mon–Sat noon–11.30pm, Sun noon–10.30pm
Accepts All major credit cards
🌐 www.melarestaurant.co.uk

At lunch the set meals revolve around bread – parathas, to be precise – much as in Delhi's famous Parathey Wali Gali, a street that is snackers' heaven. The bread may be made from maize, sorghum, millet, wholewheat flour, or chilli- and coriander-flavoured chickpea flour. The latter is particularly good. It may come with the dal or curry of the day for £1.95! Or with a savoury stuffing at £2.95. There may be other breads, too, such as roomalis (large and thin, wholemeal handkerchief bread), puris (fried chapatis), uttapams (rice-flour pancakes) and naans. Dosas come in at £3.95. At these prices you can experiment. The main menu, which is available at lunch but comes into its own in the evening, makes a real attempt to offer genuine regional dishes. Starters range from gosht utthapams (£4.50) – rice pancakes with lamb; to lehsooni whitebait (£3.95). Then tandoor dishes like barrah beer kebab (£10.95) lead on to crab moilee (£14,95); or methi murg (£8.50) – a rich chicken dish. There is also an exemplary gosht rogan josh (£9.25). Good stuff.

As well as bargain lunches, Mela has two further things going for it: the restaurant is located in the West End, and is open all afternoon.

Punjab

In 1951, Gurbachan Singh Maan moved his fledgling Indian restaurant from the City to new premises in Neal Street in Covent Garden, his plan being to take advantage of the trade from the nearby Indian High Commission. It was a strategy that has worked handsomely. Today, his grandson Sital Singh Maan runs what is one of London's oldest curry houses, though one which

£16 to £38

Address 80–82 Neal St, WC2
℡ 020 7836 9787
Station Covent Garden
Open Mon–Thurs noon–3pm &
6–11.30pm, Fri – Sun
noon–11.30pm
Accepts All major credit cards
🖳 www.punjab.co.uk

has always been at the forefront of new developments – in 1962 the Maan family brought over one of the first tandoor ovens to be seen in Britain, and in 2002 they celebrated 40 years in the business with a new extension and a lick of paint. Despite these forays into fashion, the cuisine at the Punjab has always been firmly rooted where it belongs – in the Punjab.

Punjabi cuisine offers some interesting, non-standard Indian dishes, so start by ordering from among the less familiar items on the menu. Kadu and puri (£2.60), for instance, a sweet and sharp mash of curried pumpkin served on a puri; or aloo tikka (£2.60), which are described as potato cutlets but arrive as small deep-fried moons on a sea of tangy sauce; or chicken chat (£2.90), which is diced chicken in rich sauce. To follow, try the acharri gosht (£8.40), or the acharri murgha (£8.30). The first is made with lamb, and the second with chicken, and the Maan family are very proud of the acharri; the meat is "pickled" in traditional Punjabi spices and, as a result, both meat and sauce have an agreeable edge of sharpness. Chicken karahi (£7.95) is good, too – rich and thick. The anari gosht (£8.30) combines lamb with pomegranate, while from the vegetable dishes, channa aloo (£4.70) offsets the nutty crunch of chickpeas with the solace of potatoes. For refreshment, turn to a satisfyingly large bottle of Cobra lager (£3.60), which originated in Bangalore but is now, rather more prosaically, "brewed in Bedford".

On the menu you'll also find benaam macchi tarkari (£8.70), a "nameless fish curry, speciality of chef". This curry may be nameless but it is certainly not flavourless, with solid lumps of boneless white fish in rich and tasty gravy.

Rules

(icon) Rules would be a living cliché but for one essential saving grace – all the fixtures, fittings and studied eccentricities which look as if they have been custom-made in some modern factory are real. Rules is the genuine article, a very English restaurant that has been taking its toll of tourists for 200 years. Dickens, Betjeman, H.G. Wells, Thackeray, Graham Greene and King Edward

£25 to £65

Address 35 Maiden Lane, WC2
(icon) 020 7836 5314
Station Covent Garden
Open Mon–Sat noon–midnight, Sun noon–10.30pm
Accepts All major credit cards
(icon) www.rules.co.uk

VII are just a few of the celebs who have revelled in Rules. In 1984 the restaurant passed into the hands of John Mayhew, and in 1997 he brought in David Chambers as head chef. Rules' proud boast is, "We specialize in classic game cookery". Indeed they do, and the restaurant has become more of a bustling brasserie than the mausoleum it once was, despite a resolute non-smoking policy downstairs that has upset as many people as it has pleased.

First of all you should note that Rules is open from noon till late, which is very handy when circumstances dictate a four o'clock lunch. There is also a competitive pre-theatre offer – £19.95 for two courses. Start with scrambled egg and smoked salmon (£7.95), a Stilton and celeriac soup (£5.95), or an outstanding marbre of foie gras and duck (£11.95). Go on to game in season; whatever the time of year, you'll find something good here. There are also occasional specials: maybe Belted Galloway beef or Tamworth suckling pig, sourced from Rules' own estate in the High Pennines. The steak and kidney pudding with mash (£14.95) is a banker, as are the grilled Dover sole for two (£39.90) and the roast rib of beef for two (£39.90). Also noteworthy is the fillet of venison with a Green Chartreuse sauce, wild mushrooms and herb mash (£19.95). Puddings, such as treacle sponge, or sticky toffee (all £6.50), are merciless. Why not go for the traditional blue Stilton cheese with celery and a glass of port (£9.95)?

And all this in a beautiful Victorian setting. Should you face entertaining out-of-town relations, or foreign visitors in search of something old and English, Rules is a good place to indulge your nostalgia.

Euston & King's Cross

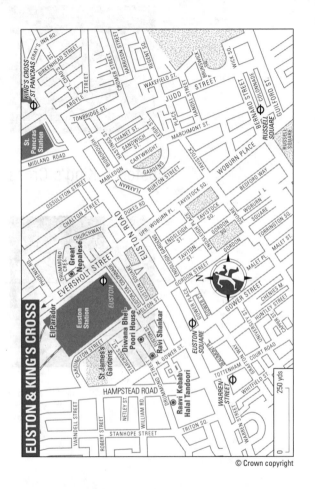

Diwana Bhel-Poori House

All varnished pine and shag-pile carpets, the Diwana Bhel-Poori House puts you in mind of a late 1970s Wimpy bar. Only the Indian woodcarvings dotted around the walls give the game away – that and the heady scent of freshly blended spices. It's a busy place, with tables filling up and emptying at a

£5 to £18

Address 121 Drummond St, NW1
℡ 020 7387 5556
Station Euston
Open Daily noon–11.30pm
Accepts All major credit cards

fair crack, though the atmosphere is convivial and casual rather than rushed. There's no licence, so you can bring your own beer or wine (corkage is free) and a full water jug is supplied on each table. This, the low prices (the costliest dish will set you back just £6), a chatty menu listing "tasty snacks", and fast, friendly service combine to create a deceptively simple stage for some fine Indian vegetarian cooking. There's even a set lunch buffet at £4.95.

Starters are copious, ladled out in no-nonsense stainless steel-bowls. The dahi bhalle chat (£2.30) is a cool, yoghurty blend of chickpeas, crushed pooris and bulghur wheat, sprinkled with "very special spices". The dahi poori (£2.30) is a fragrant concoction of pooris, potatoes, onions, sweet and sour sauces and chilli chutney, again smothered in yoghurt and laced with spices. Stars of the main menu are the dosas, particularly the flamboyant deluxe dosa (£4.80), a giant fan of a pancake with coconut chutney, potatoes and dhal nestling beneath its folds. Also superb is the house speciality, thali Annapurna (£6), a feast of dhal, rice, vegetables, pickles, side dishes, mini bhajees and your choice of pooris or chapatis – divine but unfinishable, especially if you make the mistake of ordering some monstrously proportioned side dishes as well.

Whatever feast you put together, do leave room for dessert, as there's a heavenly kulfi malai (£1.70) to dig into – a creamy pyramid of frozen milk flavoured with kevda, nuts and herbs. Alternatively, try the Kashmiri falooda (£2.20) – cold milk with china grass and rose syrup topped with ice cream and nuts. Though strictly speaking a drink, this is surely pudding enough for anyone.

Great Nepalese

This bit of London behind Euston station is distinctly seedy, and the shops that are neighbours to the Great Nepalese offer strange products for probably quite strange people. Recent years have seen a new shopfront, and a lick of paint, but the giant wall photo showing the Queen and Prince Philip standing with five Gurkha holders of the Victoria Cross has survived all the refurbs. This

£8 to £22

Address 48 Eversholt St, NW1
℡ 020 7388 6737
Station Euston/Euston Square
Open Mon–Sat noon–2.45pm & 6–11.30pm, Sun noon–2.30pm & 6–11.15pm
Accepts All major credit cards

place combines friendly and homely service with authentic Nepalese food and, should your nerve falter, the menu also has a buffer zone littered with standard curry-house favourites – lamb rogan josh is helpfully subtitled "a very popular lamb curry".

But don't order the rogan josh (£5.50) described as "a very popular lamb curry cooked with tomato" unless feeling profoundly unadventurous. It may be a very nice, popular lamb curry but the authentic Great Nepalese dishes are nicer still. Start with masco bhara, a large frisbee-shaped doughnut. It is made from black lentils, but without their black skins, so the result is a nutty-tasting, fluffy white mass with a crisp outside. It comes with a bowl of curry gravy for dipping (£3.50 plain, £3.85 with a hidden core of shredded lamb). Or try haku choyala (£3.75), diced mutton with garlic, lemon juice and ginger. It's spicy and agreeably sharp. For mains, the staff direct you to the dumba curry (£4.95), a traditional Nepalese-style curry, reliant on the same rich gravy as the masco bhara, or the chicken ra piaj (£5.25), with onions and spices. Both are highly recommended. Another very typical Nepalese dish is the butuwa chicken (£5.25). It combines ginger and spices with garlic and green herbs and is delicious. And if you like dhal, you shouldn't miss the kalo dal (£2.95), nutty and dark with black lentils.

A single note of caution. Beware the Coronation rum from Katmandu. This firewater was first distilled in 1975 for the coronation of his majesty, the late King Birendra Bir Bikram Shah Dev, and it comes in a bottle shaped like a glass kukri. You probably have to be a Gurkha to appreciate its finer points.

El Parador

El Parador is a small, no-frills Spanish restaurant and tapas bar, slightly stranded in the quiet little enclave around Mornington Crescent, between King's Cross and Camden. It serves very tasty tapas at very reasonable prices and has a friendly, laid-back atmosphere, even on busy Friday and Saturday nights. It's a good place to spend a summer evening, with a lovely garden out the back, though this is no secret and the sought-after tables here should be booked in advance.

£9 to £22

Address 245 Eversholt St, NW1
℡ 020 7387 2789
Station Mornington Crescent
Open Mon–Thurs noon–3pm & 6–11pm, Fri noon–3pm & 6–11.30pm, Sat 6–11.30pm, Sun 7–10.30pm
Accepts All major credit cards

As ever with tapas, the fun part of eating here is choosing several dishes from the wide selection on offer, and then sharing and swapping with your companions. The plates are small, so allow yourself at least two or three tapas a head – more for a really filling meal – and go for at least one of the fish or seafood dishes, which are treats. Highlights include chipirones salteados (£4.20) – baby squid pan-fried with sea salt and olive oil; gambas al pil-pil (£4.90) – nice fat tiger prawns pan-fried with parsley, paprika and chilli; and salteado de pez espada (£5.20) – fresh swordfish sautéed with garlic and coriander. Carnivores shouldn't miss out on the jamón serrano (£4.80) – delicious Spanish cured ham; or the morcilla de Burgos (£4.60) – sausages that are a cousin of black pudding. Also good is the potaje de lentejas (£4.20) – a classy lentil and vegetable stew. The vegetarian tapas are particularly good here. Try pure de patatas del Parador (£3.80) – mash with pan-fried pepper and Manchego; berenjenas asadas (£4.50) – baked aubergines with cumin; and tortilla Espanola (£3.50), a classic Spanish omelette. Desserts keep up the pace: marquesa de chocolate (£3.30) is a luscious, creamy, home-made chocolate mousse; flan de naranja (£3) is a really good orange crème caramel.

Try a glass of the dry Manzanilla (£3) to start or accompany your meal. It's a perfect foil for tapas. Or delve into El Parador's strong selection of Spanish wines. Enjoyable choices include Muga Crianza '00 (£16.80), a smooth white Rioja, and the Guelbenzu Crianza '00 (£16.80), a rich and fruity red.

Raavi Kebab Halal Tandoori

This small restaurant has been a fixture for more than 25 years, during which time Drummond Street has become one of the main curry centres of London. Competition here is more than just fierce, it is ludicrous, as well-established vegetarian restaurants compete to offer the cheapest "eat-as-much-as-you-can" lunch buffet. It is lucky that vegetables are so cheap. But the Raavi is not just about bargain prices – or vegetables, come to that. It is an unpretentious Pakistani grill house that specializes in halal meat dishes.

£6 to £15

Address 125 Drummond St, NW1
☎ 020 7388 1780
Station Euston/Euston Square
Open Daily 12.30–10.30pm
Accepts All major credit cards

The grills here are good but hot – hot enough for the wildest chilli-head. Seekh kebab (£2.50) – juicy and well-flavoured, straight from the charcoal grill in the doorway – is hot. Chicken tikka (£2.50) is hot. Mutton tikka (£2.50) is hot. The mixed grill (£6.95) brings a bit of everything, and everything is hot! With the kebabs comes a khaki-coloured dipping sauce that is sharp with lemon juice, strongly flavoured with fresh coriander and, as you'd expect, hot with fresh chillies. Lamb quorma (£4.75) is not so fierce; its rich sauce with fresh ginger and garlic is topped with a sprinkle of shaved almonds. Chicken daal (£3.95) brings chunks of chicken on the bone, bobbing on a sea of savoury yellow split-pea dhal, and is thoroughly delicious. Nan breads (90p) are light and crispy. Nihari (£4.95), the traditional Muslim breakfast dish of slow-cooked curried mutton, vies with haleem for the title of bestseller here. Haleem (£4.95) is a dish whose origins are shrouded in mystery. Some say that it was invented in the Middle East, which is certainly where it is most popular today; other devotees track it back to Moghul kitchens. The recipe is arduous. Take some meat and cook it, add four kinds of dhal, a good deal of cracked wheat, and two kinds of rice, plus spices. Cook for up to seven hours, then add some garam masala. The result is a gluey slick of smooth and spicy glop from which any traces of the meat have all but disappeared.

And how does it taste? You'd be hard pushed to be more enthusiastic than "not bad".

Ravi Shankar

As a hotbed of Indian dining, Drummond Street is still a magnet for curryholics and anyone else seeking a good, cheap meal. The Ravi Shankar opened in the 1980s, and its decor is still firmly wedged in an era when plain enough was good enough, even though there was a lick of paint in 2003 and a

£4 to £15

Address 133 Drummond St, NW1
☎ 020 7388 6458
Station Euston
Open Daily noon–10.45pm
Accepts Mastercard & Visa

smart new wood floor. The Ravi Shankar may look plain, and the seating may not be ultra-comfortable, but the vegetarian food is honest and cheap – something that weighs heavily with the loyal clientele.

The daily specials are impressive – maybe a cashew nut pilau rice and cauliflower curry, served with salad and mint yoghurt chutney for the princely sum of £3.95. There are not many sub-£4 meals left anywhere in London, let alone a meal at such a price that is well cooked and satisfying. The cashew nut pilau is rich and nutty, and the cauliflower curry has been made substantial by the addition of chunks of potato. Or there's vegetable biryani with curry (£4.25), Another day will bring aloo palak with chapati (£3.95), and the specials wind onwards to the extravagance of chana bhatura (£4.50) – a delicious fried bread with a chickpea curry. The main menu starters fall into two categories. There are hot snacks from Western India, including samosas (three for £2.30), bhajis (£2.30) and potato bonda (£2.50) – a solid, tasty, deep-fried sphere made from potato and lentils. Then there are cold "snacks and chat", billed as coming from Bombay's famed snack city, Chowpatty beach. At Ravi Shankar there are bhel puri, pani puri and potato puri (all £2.30). Try the pani puri – a plate of tiny spherical shells arrives with a bowl of cooked chickpeas in tamarind and date sauce. You punch a hole in the top of the puri then add a spoonful of chickpeas. Good fun. Breads are good – treat yourself to an ace stuffed paratha (£1.95).

Or try a thali – these complete meals come on stainless-steel trays, and range from rice and dhal (£2.30) to the Shankar thali (£6.95), which comes with dhal soup, four different curries with rice, raita, a pappadom and puris or chapatis, plus a dessert.

Kensington

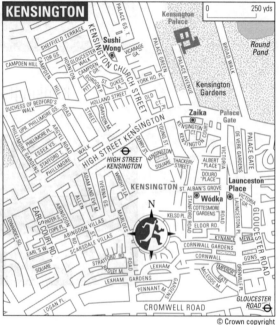

Launceston Place

Launceston Place is one of those small, chic streets where you cannot help feeling a pang of envy for anyone rich enough to live in the slick little houses. As the road curves you'll find a sprinkling of high-ticket shops on one side and the Launceston Place restaurant on the other. The restaurant sprawls its way through a nest of rooms and is pleasantly formal. Or perhaps that should be formal and pleasant. Service is efficient but not in your face and there is a traditional feel to everything. This is a neighbourhood restaurant, but one that is the product of a very swish neighbourhood, which makes some sense of the fact that a couple of years after opening here the team went on to create Kensington Place (see p.446) – another establishment in tune with its surroundings.

£18 to £65

Address 1a Launceston Place, W8
☎020 7937 6912
Station High Street Kensington
Open Mon–Fri 12.30–2.30pm &
7–11.30pm, Sat 7–11.30pm, Sun
12.30–2.30pm & 7–10pm
Accepts All major credit cards

MODERN BRITISH

The menu changes every six weeks or so and dishes match traditional combinations with fashionable ingredients in an unstuffy way. Starters range from a classic dish such as smoked haddock and leek soup with chopped quail egg (£6), to deep-fried oysters with Bloody Mary salsa (£9), or crispy duck spring rolls with spicy lentil and mango salsa (£7.50). Mains range from plain dishes such as deep-fried beer-battered cod with tartare sauce and fat chips (£17), to pan-fried John Dory with Morecambe Bay shrimps and Chardonnay cream (£17), and on to meatier offerings like salt beef and ox tongue with parsley sauce and gherkins (£15); roast chump of lamb with English mustard and herb crust (£17.50); or possibly grilled sirloin steak with Béarnaise sauce (£17.50). The dessert menu ticks all the appropriate boxes: there's Eve's pudding and custard (£6.50) and a double chocolate torte (£6.50). The wine list is strong in traditional areas, so think French.

The set lunch is much beloved by local ladies-who-lunch and is priced reasonably at £15.50 for two courses and £18.50 for three. Caesar salad, seared salmon with dill and cucumber dressing, chocolate mousse cake, coffee, a tsunami of chilled white wine and gossip – just about perfect.

Kensington

Sushi Wong

Sushi Wong is the kind of name you either love or hate but, whichever side you take, it is certainly slick – just like this deceptively sized restaurant. On the ground floor there's a modernist Japanese restaurant-cum-sushi-bar seating about 25 people. Downstairs there's a teppan-yaki table and room for a further sixty diners. Looking in from the street it's hard not to admire the stark blue and bright-yellow colour scheme, and the tables, each topped with ground glass backed by a blue neon tube. In the face of all this brightness and modernity, the service is so low-key that it almost seems timid, but Sushi Wong is a confident and efficient place for all that.

£15 to £40

Address 38c–d Kensington Church St, W8
℡ 020 7937 5007
Station High Street Kensington
Open Mon–Fri noon–2.30pm & 6–10.30pm, Sat noon–10.30pm, Sun 6–10pm
Accepts All major credit cards

Sushi is delicious here. Ordering the sushi matsu set (£18) brings a round lacquer tray with six pieces of salmon or tuna roll flanked by ten pieces of various sushi – the chef's selection. The fish is fresh, the wasabi strong, the gari delicious and the sushi well prepared. A good array at a fair price. The menu emphasizes hosomaki (roll sushi), ranging from edo (£4.20) – crab meat, salmon and cucumber – to "Kensington roll" (£3.80), which is a crispy salmon and asparagus concoction "specially made for Kensington dwellers!" There is also a wide range of à la carte selections: starters like agedashi tofu (£3.50), fried tofu with dashi sauce; tempura soft-shell crab (£7.50); yakitori (£4.50); and gyoza (£4), which are steamed dumplings. Mains include lobster tail with mixed mushroom and asparagus (£11.50); steak teriyaki (£11.50); pork tonkatsu (£9); nabeyaki udon (£7.50) - a soupy dish with chicken, vegetables and prawns – and the Sushi Wong tempura selection (£12.80), which includes king prawns, fish and vegetables.

The set menus do make life simpler. The Makunochi bento (£15.90) seems to bring a bit of everything; and the sashimi tempura dinner (£14.50) combines both delicacies. In 2003 this restaurant took the emphasis away from teppan-yaki and introduced a new menu section featuring a whole range of Thai dishes – which is to somehow miss the point of Japanese food.

Wódka

Wódka is a restaurant that lies in wait for you. It's calm and bare, and the food is better than you might expect – well cooked, and thoughtfully seasoned. The daily lunch menu represents extremely good value at £11.50 for two courses and £14.50 for three, a large proportion of the dishes being refugees from the evening à la carte. Where, you wonder, is the streak of madness that helped the Polish cavalry take on German tank regiments with sabres drawn? On the shelves behind the bar, that's where, in the extensive collection of moody and esoteric vodkas, which are for sale both by the shot and by the carafe.

£15 to £50

Address 12 St Albans Grove, W8
℡ 020 7937 6513
Station High Street Kensington
Open Mon–Fri 12.30–2.30pm &
7–11.15pm, Sat & Sun 7–11.15pm
Accepts All major credit cards
ⓦ www.wodka.co.uk

POLISH

The soup makes a good starter: Ukrainian barszcz (£4.50) is a rich, beetrooty affair. Blinis are also the business: they come with smoked salmon (£7.50/10.90), aubergine mousse (£5.50/8.90) or 40g of Oscietra caviar (£23.50). A lunchtime selection (£6.90/10.50) will get you all except the caviar. Also good is the kaszanka (£5.90) – grilled black pudding with pickled red cabbage and pear puree. For a main course, the fishcakes (£11.90) with leeks and a dill sauce are firm favourites with the regulars. In line with the Polish love of wild game, when partridge is available it is roasted and served with a splendid mash of root vegetables. Or there may be haunch of venison with sour cherries and honey-roasted pears (£14.50). Puddings tend to be of the oversweet, under-imaginative gateaux variety.

Consider the list of vodkas – there is a host of them: Zubrówka (made with bison grass); Okhotnichya (for hunters); Jarzebiak (that's rowan berries); Cytrynówka (lemon); Sliwowica (plum); Sliwówka (plum, but hot and sweet); Czarna Porezecka (blackcurrant); Ananas (pineapple); Krupnik (honey, and served hot); Roza (rose petals); Goldwasser (made with flakes of gold and aniseed); Soplica (dried fruits). They cost from £2.25 to £2.75 a shot, and from £37.90 to £38.90 per 50cl carafe. Try this simple test: pick any three of the above names and say them quickly. If anyone shows signs of understanding, you need another shot.

Zaika

Zaika is an upmarket Indian restaurant that gives the lie to any snobs who still maintain that Indian food can never amount to anything. Not content with netting one of the first Michelin stars to be given to an Indian restaurant, this establishment has hung onto that bauble and grows in confidence. The head chef is Vineet Bhatia and he is an accomplished cook. The spicing is well balanced, the presentation above average and, though your bill will not be a small one, it will not be a West End wallet-breaker either. There are novel dishes to be sampled but they sit alongside classics – you can still enjoy an impeccable rogan josh served on the bone.

£12 to £80

Address 1 Kensington High St, W8
℡ 020 7795 6533
Station High Street Kensington
Open Mon–Fri noon–2.45pm &
6.30–10.45pm, Sat 6.30–
10.45pm, Sun noon–2.45pm &
6.30–9.45pm
Accepts All major credit cards
except Diners
ⓦ www.zaika_restaurant.co.uk

Start with the samundri khazana (£9.95) – this teams the Zaika signature dish (a well-marinated chunk of salmon is cooked in the tandoor) with carom-infused prawns and pan-grilled tuna. Or there is the murghabi milan (£7.95), which is a platter with minced duck rolls, and duck samosa. A good deal of thought goes into the main courses. This is not a seasonal menu in the strictest sense of the term, but in season the grey mullet will switch with sea bass or the cauliflower may be changed for broccoli. The nariyal jhinga (£15,25), made from prawns cooked in a coconut masala tempered with lime leaves, stands out. Or there's murg makhanwala (£13.95), our old friend butter chicken. The koh-e-rogan josh (£15.75) is very good. Or there is parda jungli dhingri biryani (£13.95), a crusted wild mushroom biryani served with yellow lentils. Inspirational stuff. The simpler dishes are also good – try the dubkiwale aloo (£4.95), a straightforward dish of potatoes with cumin. And the breads are splendid. Try the cheese nan (£2.95) with your starters – it's cheesy, sticky, self-indulgent. For dessert you might choose the chocomosa – crisp samosas containing an admirably bitter melted chocolate.

As well as elaborate multi-course set dinners at £33.50 and £50 per person, Zaika offers an express lunch platter for £9.25. This is probably the cheapest way to eat Michelin-starred food in London.

Knightsbridge & Belgravia

Boxwood Café

(Y) If the term "café" conjures up images of fag smoke and fried slice, you're better off thinking of this place as Boxwood. When it opened in mid-May 2003 this addition to Gordon Ramsay's stable of hotel eateries was billed as offering simple seasonal dishes in an informal setting. Sure. This is a café in the same way that the Café Royal on Regent Street, or the Union Square Café in New York, is a café. The dining room is

£18 to £70

Address The Berkeley,
Knightsbridge, SW1
☎ 020 7235 1010
Station Knightsbridge
Open Daily, breakfast 7–10.30am;
lunch noon–3pm; dinner 6–11pm
Accepts All major credit cards
except Diners

MODERN BRITISH

more stylish now than it was when it was home to Vong. The tables are well spaced, the chairs are comfortable, the service swarms over you like a well-disciplined, smartly dressed rash. The standard of cooking is high, very high. Dishes are well presented, and while the prices may not be café prices they are forgiving. This is a very impressive restaurant indeed.

The menu is seasonal and changes to suit what is on the market. In May there may be a nettle and potato soup with poached quail egg (£4.50), service is made much of, your bowl arrives with the egg in it, then the soup is poured over it. The soup is green, rich and well seasoned – tastes of spring. Or there may be a spider crab, squid and borlotti bean salad (£7.50); or a butter-fried duck's egg with green and white asparagus (£6.50). Mains are also good. Roast Dorset blue lobster with garlic butter and chips (£16) comes in a flat iron dish from under the grill, the whole lobster split and sizzling. There may be a warm roast chicken salad with Jerusalem artichokes, shallots and baby spinach (£12.25); or an accurately cooked piece of roast suckling pig with a grain mustard sauce (£13.25). The wine list has some accessibly priced bottles.

The dessert list is a long one (all priced at £5). The seasonal theme is carried through and in spring there may be rhubarb fool or elderflower jelly. The poppy seed Knickerbocker Glory with roasted apricots and panacotta is notable. As are the warm sugared doughnuts that are served with a truly splendid blood orange and yoghurt sorbet. You do get doughnuts in cafés, but not like these!

Knightsbridge & Belgravia

The Capital

The Capital Hotel has quietly gone about its business since 1971. The cooking has always been top-flight, but it took the arrival of a voluble and passionate French chef called Eric Crouillère-Chavot to lift things to the current exalted level. In January 2001 Mr Michelin gave The Capital two stars, putting it firmly in the top half-dozen restaurants in London, and for once he was right. The dining room looks a tad old-fashioned, but pilgrims come for the food not the decor. This is not a cheap restaurant. In the evening starters cost £18, mains £26, and puds £10. The five-course dégustation menu is £65. All of which makes the £28.50 three-course lunch a bargain!

£35 to £150
Address 22–24 Basil St, SW1
ⓣ 020 7589 5171
Station Knightsbridge
Open Mon–Sat noon–2.30pm & 7–11pm, Sun noon–2.15pm & 7–10.30pm
Accepts All major credit cards
ⓦ www.capitalhotel.co.uk

Chavot's menu is an exciting one. Dishes are full-flavoured and elegantly plated. Sometimes presentation strays into the fussy zone beloved of the Michelin inspectors, but expect classically rich and satisfying flavours. Starters may include a king crab risotto and truffle cappuccino. The risotto is a masterpiece, with buckets of flavour and a slight crunch to the rice. Or a millefeuille of veal sweetbreads in an almond and hazelnut crust with potato gnocchi and pork jus. Or seared duck foie gras with lentils and girolles. Main courses carry on in the same vein – pot-roast pigeon, potato and bacon galette with mushrooms; fillet of turbot braised in red wine fumet with creamed baby leeks; or saddle of rabbit "Provençal", white coco beans, deep-fried calamari and a tomato risotto. Puds are elaborate, sculptural and satisfying – Chavot's interpretation of bread and butter pudding is small, rectangular, fussy and tastes of essence of bread and butter pudding. He may also be offering a praline pear crumble, or an iced coffee parfait with a chocolate fondant.

The wine list here is both expansive and expensive – if feeling flush you can seek out the smartest of the classics. A good many memorable meals are ruined by a final cup of dodgy coffee, but not at The Capital. Choose to have your personal cafetière loaded with Colombian Medellin Excelsor, Mount Kenya AA, Ethiopian Mocha Djimmah, or Prime Honduras.

Zuma

A stylish triumvirate including chef-proprietor Rainer Becker enlisted the Japanese über-design team Super Potato to create this huge restaurant, with the unspoken aim of out-Nobu-ing Nobu (pg. 85). Judging by the crowds of both celebs and celeb spotters, the plan has worked. Now the premises that once used to be home to the Chicago Rib Shack are all stone, rough-hewn granite and unfinished wood. This is a seriously trendy place, and the bar buzzes. The approach to eating is modernist – with Japanese dishes, macrobiotic options and pick-and-mix nibbles portions.

£30 to £120
Address 5 Raphael St, SW7
☎ 020 7584 1010
Station Knightsbridge
Open Mon–Sat noon–3pm & 6–11pm, Sun noon–4pm
Accepts All major credit cards

The menu is a long one, and complicated to boot. Start by nibbling some edamame Zuma style (£4). These are soya beans that have been boiled in the pod – you strip the beans out with your teeth and leave the pods. Or there is tosa dofu (£5.50), which is deep-fried tofu with daikon and bonito flakes. Age watarigani (£8.50) is a dish of fried soft shell crab with wasabi mayonnaise. The sashimi and sushi are exquisite and pricey. The skewers from the robata grill are fresh and appealing. Try satsumaimo no goma shoyo gake (£4.50), sweet potato glazed with sesame; or hotate (£6.50), a scallop with Japanese pepper and black bean sauce. Then there are tempura, seafood dishes, meat dishes, – every dish is presented stylishly, and while prices are high the ingredients are commendably fresh. Nobu fans will be interested to compare and contrast the respective black cod (£19.50) dishes; the Zuma version is marinated and then cooked wrapped in a hoba leaf. One dish introduced in the summer of 2003 is the tsubu-miso gake hinadori no oven yaki (£15.50), a baby chicken marinated in distinctive barley miso and oven-roasted on cedar wood.

This is a restaurant with a complicated sake list of 22 varieties – it even has a sake sommelier. Ozeki (£2 per 50ml) is your starting point, and the only one to be served hot, but experts will prefer the Zuma Daiginjo (£5 per 50ml), which is made from rice that has been finely milled. It has been described as having a flowery and even peachy taste.

Marylebone

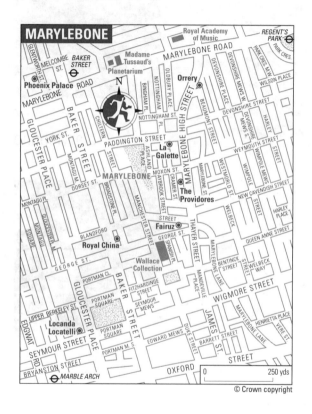

MARYLEBONE

Royal Academy of Music
REGENT'S PARK

Madame Tussaud's Planetarium
Orrery
Phoenix Palace
MARYLEBONE ROAD
BAKER STREET
MELCOMBE ST.
GLENWORTH ST.
PARK CRES M.W.
PARK CRES
MARYLEBONE
ROAD
WILSON PLACE
BINGHAM PL.
NOTTINGHAM PLACE
OLDBURY PLACE
DEVONSHIRE PLACE
DEVONSHIRE MEWS W.
DEVONSHIRE MEWS S.
GLOUCESTER PLACE
YORK ST.
BAKER STREET
CHILTERN STREET
Nottingham St.
DEVONSHIRE STREET
BEAUMONT STREET
HARLEY STREET
PADDINGTON STREET
MARYLEBONE HIGH STREET
La Galette
WEYMOUTH STREET
MONTAGU ST.
ASHLAND PLACE
WIMPOLE STREET
WIMPOLE MEWS
MARYLEBONE
DORSET ST.
MOXON ST.
WESTMORELAND STREET
NEW CAVENDISH STREET
BROADSTONE PL.
CRAMER STREET
The Providores
MONTAGU PL.
GLOUCESTER PL.
MONTAGU SQUARE
MANCHESTER STREET
STREET
WELBECK STREET
HARLEY PLACE
BLANDFORD
Fairuz
GEORGE ST.
THAYER STREET
Royal China
SPANISH PL.
QUEEN ANNE STREET
GEORGE ST.
Wallace Collection
BAKER STREET
MARYLEBONE LANE
BENTINCK STREET
WELBECK WAY
PORTMAN CL.
FITZHARDINGE STREET
MANDEVILLE PLACE
WIGMORE STREET
PORTMAN SQUARE
SEYMOUR MEWS
UPPER BERKELEY ST.
GLOUCESTER PLACE
JAMES STREET
HENRIETTA PLACE
VERE S.
Locanda Locatelli
PORTMAN SQUARE
EDWARD MEWS
DUKE STREET
BARRETT STREET
MARYLEBONE LANE
EDGWAT
SEYMOUR STREET
PORTMAN M. S.
STREET
BRYANSTON STREET
OXFORD
STREET
MARBLE ARCH

0   250 yds

© Crown copyright

Fairuz

Squeezed in between two self-consciously hip and groovy Blandford Street eateries, Fairuz happily carries on doing its own thing, which is Lebanese cooking. As you open the front door, jolly souk music, the smell of Eastern spices and the light of the warm, mud-coloured room assault and beguile the senses. This is one of London's more accessible Middle Eastern restaurants.

£15 to £35

Address 3 Blandford St, W1
℡ 020 7486 8182
Station Bond Street
Open Daily noon–11pm
Accepts All major credit cards
Branches see p.488

The menu is set out in traditional style. There's an epic list of mezze, both hot and cold, to start, followed by a selection of charcoal grills and a couple of oven-baked dishes. You can leave the selection up to the restaurant and order a set mezza (minimum two people, £16.95 per head), or a set menu (minimum two people, £24.95 per head) which combines a mezza with a mixed grill – plus a glass of fiery arak thrown in. The set mezza delivers eight or ten little dishes – plenty for lunch or a light supper. But if you prefer to make your own selection, the menu lists 47 different mezze for you to choose from: cold dishes all cost £3.95; hot dishes £4.95. Particularly recommended are the wonderfully fresh and herby tabbouleh; the warak inab – stuffed vine leaves; the hummous Beiruty; and makanek – spicy lamb sausages. Even that most dangerously indigestible of delicacies, the felafel, is fine here. Main course grills are generous and well prepared. Kafta khashkhash (£10.95) – lamb minced with parsley and grilled on skewers – is unexpectedly delicate and fragrant, but stands up well against its accompanying chilli sauce, while the shish taouk (£10.95) – chicken marinated in garlic and lemon – really is finger-licking good. Round off your meal with excellent pastries (£4.25), and real Lebanese coffee (£2).

Fairuz is a comfortable place, full of sleek and contented Marylebonians. It's not the most authentic, the cheapest or the best Lebanese food that you'll eat, but the ambience at Fairuz is well suited to novice Westerners – staff are friendly and helpful. If you can, get there early to secure one of the nook-and-crannyish, tent-like tables.

La Galette

The proprietors of La Galette have obviously given some thought to the potential of pancakes. La Galette is a bright, modern place with a paint scheme that starts light and gets dark as you travel towards the bare brick wall and the open kitchen at the rear. There's an appealing breakfast served between 8.30am and 4pm, and then there's the main menu, which plunges into the galettes with little more ado.

£8 to £22

Address 56 Paddington St, W1
℡ 020 7935 1554
Station Baker Street
Open Mon–Fri 8.30am–11pm, Sat & Sun 10am–11pm
Accepts All major credit cards except Diners
Ⓦ www.lagalette.com

The hors d'oeuvres are delightful – very simple, and very French. The charcuterie plate (£4.50/7.95) teams some saucisson sec with Bayonne, Jésus and garlic sausage; the vegetarian hors d'oeuvres plate (£4/6.95) majors in those delightful shredded raw vegetable salads – finely grated celeriac with a good mayonnaise, carrot with a light dressing, pickled beetroot and hard-boiled eggs; and there's a good feisty tapenade (£3.50). Or there's soup du jour (£4). The bread is a good chewy-crusted sourdough. When you feel you cannot put off that pancake moment any more, launch into a galette. These large buckwheat pancakes come with a dozen different fillings, and in this instance the use of the word "filling" is not an exaggeration. The "complet" (£6.50), with ham, cheese and a fried egg winking from the centre, is simple and satisfying. Or there's a galette with smoked salmon and crème fraîche (£8.20). Or naked except for rather good Normandy butter (£3.50). Or with chorizo sausage, with piquillo peppers and tomato sauce (£7.80). This is not fancy cooking but the portions are generous and the quality of the ingredients seems agreeably high, while the large pancakes are as crisp as you could wish for. However appealing the galettes, there are still puddies who will proceed directly to the crêpes – "Normandy" comes with caramelized apple and crème Chantilly (£4.95).

There's a Francophile wine list, but much more appealing is the range of Breton ciders served in *pichets* – small jugs – and which must be drunk out of traditional *bollées* – think of a thick, earthenware breakfast cup with the handle knocked off.

Locanda Locatelli

When Giorgio Locatelli opened here in a corner of the Churchill Hotel, it took about a week for the place to get booked out. It opened on Valentine's Day 2002 and by the end of the first week everybody from the Prime Minister to Madonna had been in to sample the startlingly good and honestly priced North Italian food. The room is elegant, the cooking terrific, the prices modest.

£30 to £90

Address 8 Seymour St, W1
℡ 020 7935 9088
Station Marble Arch
Open Mon–Sat noon–3pm &
7–11pm–11pm
Accepts All major credit cards
except Diners
ⓦwww.locandalocatelli.com

ITALIAN

Now there's a phone frenzy at the beginning of each month when everyone struggles to book a table for next month – spontaneous here means five to eight weeks ahead!

There is a large turnover of dishes on the menu but the cooking is always spurred on by the seasons. There may be antipasti like the ox tongue with parsley sauce (£8) – tender and delicate meat with a light, fresh, green dressing. Pan-fried scallops are served with a saffron vinaigrette (£11), and there may be deep-fried calf's head with sweet and sour peppers (£7)? – this is authentic stuff. Pasta dishes delight: tiny fluffy potato gnocchi (£13) come with morels and chives; home-made ravioli (£10) are filled with oxtail, or how about a classic fresh nettle risotto (£11.50)? Every dish looks elegant on the plate, and combines tastes and textures to their best effect. Main courses may include steamed hake in garlic and vinegar (£16.50); roast pigeon with lentils and summer truffle (£22); roast monkfish with a walnut and caper sauce (£24.50); or grilled baby chicken with roast potatoes (£18.50). The service is slick, and the restaurant has an established and comfortable air. The see-and-be-seen crowd discovered this place on day one, yet for such a talked-about restaurant everything is still pretty good value – wine starts at £3 a glass.

Revel in the basket of breads. This is a co-production, the honours being shared by Giorgio Locatelli and master baker Dan Leppard. Seven or eight different breads, all fresh, all majestic, plus metre-long, home-made, cheese-dusted grissini. With a start like this, any meal has a lot to live up to. Locatelli's meets the challenge.

Orrery

There is no doubt that Sir Terence Conran has gone to great lengths to ensure that the public don't see a "formula" in his restaurants. There are large ones, small ones, short ones, tall ones; Italian, French, British; loud music, no music. Even so, Orrery stands out. This is a very good restaurant indeed, driven by a passion for food, and the mainspring is the head chef, Andre Garrett. It may be part of a large group, but they still change the menu daily if need be. Orrery cherishes its own network of small suppliers, going for large, line-caught, sea bass above their smaller, farmed cousins, and selecting the best Bresse pigeon and Scottish beef. The service is slick and friendly, the dining room is beautiful, the cheeseboard has won prizes and the wine list is exhaustive. And the cooking is very good indeed. All of the above is reflected in the bill. For once, you do get what you pay for.

£30 to £120

Address 55 Marylebone High St, W1
℡ 020 7616 8000
Station Baker Street/Regent's Park
Open Mon–Sat noon–2.45pm &
7–10.45pm, Sun noon–2.30pm &
7–10.45pm
Accepts All major credit cards
ⓦ www.orrery.co.uk

What a pleasure to see such a short menu, with simple starters like a tart fine of forme d'Ambert and poire William (£10); or a first-rate terrine of foie gras served with Sauternes jelly and toasted pain Poilâne (£16.50); or seared scallops teamed with pork belly and cauliflower (£16.50). Mains feature well-judged combinations of flavours: roast fillet of venison, violet artichoke barigoule and saffron gnocchi (£22.50); risotto of pumpkin, marjoram and sage (£17); Barbary duck with pain d'épice, red onion and foie gras Tatin, Banyuls jus (£24); Dover sole en papillote, tarta of tuna and langoustine (£26). Presentation is ultra-chic, flavours are intense – this is serious stuff. Puddings span the range from classics such as baked chocolate fondant (£10) to a blueberry soufflé (£10.50).

One way to eat well here is to rely heavily on the set menus: the three-course menu du jour is £23.50; while Sunday dinner, also three courses and including a glass of champagne, costs £30. The Menu Gourmand (which must be ordered by the entire table) brings six courses, coffee and petits fours for £50, rising to £80 when you opt for the specially matched glasses of wine. A stress-free bargain.

Phoenix Palace

To find a large, bright, busy Chinese restaurant just to the north of the Marylebone Road is very unusual. This site was formerly an Indian eatery called the Viceroy of India and, in the transition the rather smart Indian carvings have been left behind. The result is a large room with some tables on a raised dais running around the room, the obligatory feng shui fish tank, and the little wooden idols looking down. This is a very North London sort of place; it may be only just over the river of traffic that flows past Madame Tussaud's, but it has North London attitudes and North London punters.

£12 to £45

Address 3–5 Glentworth St, NW1
℡ 020 7486 3515
Station Baker Street/Marylebone
Open Daily noon–11.30pm
Accepts All major credit cards except Diners

The menu is a huge one, and stretches off into the farthest corners of Chinese chefly imagination. The food is well presented and portions are large – something for which we must thank those North London attitudes? Starters include all the old favourites, but steamed fresh scallops at £3 each are no bargain. Stick to chicken wrapped in lettuce leaf (£5.50), which is well flavoured, if a little short on lettuce leaves. Or order a main-course portion of the deep-fried squid in light batter (£8), which makes a fine opening move. The menu chunters on for over two hundred dishes and is worth a careful read, as there are some interesting discoveries to be made. Salt-baked chicken (£12/21) is a wonderful, savoury roast chicken with juicy meat and crisp skin. The fried minced pork cakes with salted fish (£7.50) are very classy, the salt-fish seasoning the pork mix successfully. The dual seasonal greens with curry (£5.50) is a novelty item – baby sweetcorn and broccoli lurk in a yellow and pretty fierce curry sauce. Very inscrutable. The stewed beef flank (£5.50) is that old favourite, braised brisket – very dark and very rich. The range of noodle dishes is extensive.

The standard of cooking here is good and would not be out of place in the better Chinatown eateries, even if the decor might raise an eyebrow. The Phoenix Palace makes a brave attempt to cheer up a whole tranche of North London.

The Providores

There's only one chef working in London with a 24-carat, bankable reputation for fusion food and that is Peter Gordon, the amiable New Zealander. His showcase is this restaurant which he opened with a consortium of friends. Downstairs, all is informal – you can even have breakfast in the bar before the menu segues gracefully into a host of small dishes for the rest of the day (brunch at the weekend). The resto part occupies an elegant room on the first floor. Chairs are comfortable, table-cloths are white and simplicity rules – which is just as well, as the dishes are amongst the most complicated in town. But what may look like an untidy and arbitrary assemblage on paper becomes wholly satisfying the moment you pop a forkful into your mouth. These dishes all taste fresh, every flavour distinct, and each combination cunningly balanced.

FUSION

£7 to £22

Address 109 Marylebone High St, W1
℡ 020 7935 6175
Station Baker Street/Bond Street
Open Mon–Sat noon–2.45pm & 6–10.45pm, Sun noon–2.45pm & 6–10pm
Accepts All major credit cards except Diners
ⓦ www.theprovidores.co.uk

The menu descriptions read like lists: spicy coconut laksa with grilled tiger prawn, green tea noodles, crab and hijiki dumpling, crispy shallots and coriander (£8.40). Puzzled? The rich, creamy, sweet coconut broth is covered with a scattering of crisp bits of shallot and laced with the contrasting textures of ribbon noodles, and tiger prawns. Or how about a plate of Teruel jamón, prosciutto San Leo, salame Toscano and sweet pickled fig (£10.20)? Mains may include roast sea bass on parsnip and Stornoway black pudding mash, bitter greens with Argan oil and ume-boshi dressing (£18.60), or roast lamb chump on minted barley, saffron, pine nut and broad bean salad with grilled aubergine (£19.20). Or, for a dish to ponder over, roast Trelough duck breast on butter bean, smoked paprika and anchovy stew (£19.20). Desserts are equally elaborate: peanut panacotta with wasabi and kalamansi lime jelly and candied peanuts (£6.90).

This is a place where they understand the majesty of ingredients and give each and every flavour and texture full scope. The Providores will doubtless have its detractors, but this is good and original food – something so rare in London that you shouldn't be surprised if it is not recognized for what it is.

Royal China

Like its more famous sibling, on Queensway, this Royal China is a black-and-gold palace. The effect is a kind of cigarette-packet chic and smacks of the 1970s. But don't let that put you off. The food is not as expensive as the decor would have you believe, the service is efficient and brisk (rather than that special kind of rude and brisk you may encounter in Chinatown) and the

£14 to £27

Address 40 Baker St, W1
℡ 020 7487 4688
Station Baker Street/Bond Street
Open Mon–Thurs noon–11pm, Fri &
Sat noon–11.30pm, Sun 1–10pm
Accepts All major credit cards
except Diners
Branches see p.490

CHINESE/DIM SUN

food is really good. One knowledgeable chef-critic describes the Royal China's sticky rice wrapped in a lotus leaf as the "best ever".

You could eat well from the full menu, which, like everything else in the Royal China, is bound in gold. It goes from "Chef Favourites" – like seafood hotpot (£14) or roast chicken with Monk bean flavour (£12) – through dim sum to lunchtime noodle and rice dishes, but it is the dim sum (served daily until 5pm) that is most enticing here. The roast pork puff (£1.90) is famous, and unusual in that it is made from puff pastry; it is very light and has a sweetish char sui filling. From the "specials", try the lobster dumpling (£3.90) and Thai-style fishcake (£2.50), both of which are tasty. Also worth noting are the prawn and chive dumpling (£2.30), pork and radish dumpling (£1.90), and seafood dumpling (£2.30) – or a selection of three. Also the turnip paste with dried meat (£1.90), and the sesame paper prawn roll (£2.30). The glutinous rice in lotus leaves (£2.80) really is the best ever – it's rich and not too gamey, and two parcels come in each steamer. The Royal China cheung fun (£2.70) is another sampler providing one of each filling – prawn, pork and beef. They take their cheung fun seriously here, with a total of seven variants including mushrooms and dry shrimp (£2.30). The fried rice dishes and the noodles are well priced (£4.50 to £7.50).

This may well be the place finally to take the plunge and try chicken's feet. Spicy chicken feet (£1.90) come thickly coated in a rich, spicy goo and, to be frank, this sauce is so strong that – were it not for the obvious claw shapes – you could be eating almost anything.

Mayfair & Bond Street

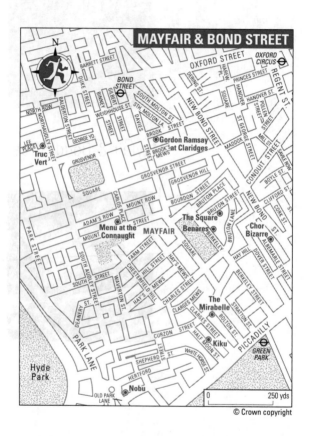

Benares

🍴 Atul Kochar is the man who secured one of the first Michelin stars ever awarded to an Indian restaurant in Britain, and in June 2003 he opened Benares to suitable fanfares. It is certainly a classy place: acres of polished stone floors, large and limpid pools strewn with blossoms and with little candles bobbing about. The dining room is modern and stylish; all is artistic and

£20 to £80

Address 12 Berkeley House,
Berkeley Square, W1
☏ 020 7629 8886
Station Green Park
Open Mon–Fri noon–2.30pm &
5.30–10.30pm, Sat 5.30–10.30pm
Accepts All major credit cards

tranquil. Some of the pricing, and most of the wine list, "goes Mayfair" pretty briskly, but considering the elegance of the setting, the friendliness of the service and the undoubted quality of the cooking, this is a good option as a special occasion Indian restaurant.

When each dish arrives it is beautiful on the plate, lots of influences from smart French chefs but never losing sight of the need to match textures and good assertive tastes – kekdae ki chaat aur tille ka jhinga (£4.50) is a crab salad teamed with a tangy kumquat chutney and topped with a single large prawn deep-fried in a crisp coat. Very fresh, very delicious. Or how about raraha murg masala (£4.50)? This is a spicy fry-up of chicken livers made posh with some chicken meat and button mushrooms, good upfront spicing. The tandoor work is exemplary here – the lamb chops (£12) may work out at £3 each but are exceedingly plump and tender. A classic dish like rogan josh (£12) is as good as you can get – unless you can find it served on the bone. Or there's hare masala ki machchi (£13.50), which is pan-fried John Dory served with a broth of curried mussels. The vegetable side dishes are most interesting: pani singara aur faliyon ki subji (£4) is superb – water chestnuts and French beans with onion seeds and dried mango, an exercise in crunchy textures.

As you would expect in any resto with serious (if unstated) Michelin ambition, there are amuses-gueules before the meal and pretty fabulous petits fours to finish off with. In particular as a final grace note there is a mint leaf dipped into white chocolate that is not only outstandingly refreshing, but the kind of thing we could all do at home!

Chor Bizarre

Chor Bizarre is something of a novelty in London as one of a handful of Indian restaurants that has a "head office" in India. Indeed the London Chor Bizarre is a straight copy of the one in the Broadway Hotel in Delhi. Its name is an elaborate pun (*Chor Bazaar* translates as "thieves' market") and, like the Delhi branch, the London restaurant is

£24 to £45

Address 16 Albemarle St, W1
℡ 020 7629 9802 or 7629 8542
Station Green Park
Open Mon–Sat noon–3pm & 6–11.30pm, Sun 6–10.30pm
Accepts All major credit cards
ⓦ www.chorbizarre.net

furnished with an amazing clutter of Indian antiques and bric-a-brac. Every table, and each set of chairs, is different, and you may find yourself dining within the frame of an antique four-poster bed. The food is very well prepared and encouragingly authentic. Care is taken over the detail, and wine expert Charles Metcalfe has devised a striking wine list. Chor Bizarre does, however, carry the kind of price tag you'd expect of Mayfair.

Start with simple things such as pakoras (£5), which are tasty vegetable fritters, or coconut mussels (£6), which come in a coconut fish broth. Kebabs are taken seriously here, too: try gilouti kebab (£6) – lamb with saffron and served with a white radish salad. Or gazab ka tikka (£12), a bestseller in Delhi, which is a kind of chicken tikka deluxe. Then, for your main course, choose dishes like baghare baingan (£8), a Hyderabadi dish combining aubergine, peanuts and tamarind. Or Kerala prawn curry (£15), marinated king prawns with a kick of black pepper; or goshtaba (£15), the famous Kashmiri lamb curry – very velvety. Breads are also impressive, including an excellent naan (£2.75); pudina paratha (£3) – a mint paratha; and stuffed kulcha (£3) – choose from cheese, potato or mince.

The many imposing set meals are a good way to tour the menu without watching your wallet implode. South Indian Tiffin (£24) features chicken Chettinad, Kerala prawn, poriyal and sambal, served with rice and Malabari parathas on a banana leaf. Kashmiri tarami (£24) is a copper platter with goshtaba, mirchi korma, rajmah, al yakhni, tamatar chaaman and nadru haaq on rice. Or there is the Maharaja Thali (£24, or £22 vegetarian) – a meal on a tray! TV dinners will never be the same again.

Gordon Ramsay at Claridge's

When Gordon Ramsay took over Claridge's the Mayfair fooderati held their breath. But the transition from faded and genteel dining to mega-busy gastro temple seems to have taken place without a hitch. The dining room is still large, the service is still slick, but the food is much better than it used to be and, it could be argued, better value too. The £25 set lunch here is an even better bargain than the £35 set lunch at Ramsay's Chelsea flagship (see p.407). Unfortunately, like its sibling, Claridge's is booked up far in advance. The à la carte offers three courses for £50 and there is a "prestige menu" option that takes you through six courses for £60.

£30 to £120

Address Brook St, W1
℡ 020 7499 0099
Station Green Park
Open Mon–Fri noon–2.45pm & 5.45–11pm, Sat & Sun noon–3.30pm & 5.45–11pm (10.45pm Sun)
Accepts All major credit cards
ⓦ www.gordonramsay.com

FRENCH

While Gordon Ramsay has his name over the door, the head chef here is Mark Sargeant, who won his spurs in the hothouse of Mr Ramsay's three-star establishment. Starters range from velouté of white onion with sautéed cèpes, baby artichokes and grated fresh truffle; to a panaché of sautéed scallops on a bed of cauliflower puree and sherry caramel. Presentation on the plate is elegant and seasoning spot-on. Main courses may include roast cannon of Cornish lamb served with confit shoulder (cooked for eight hours) white bean puree, baby leeks and rosemary jus; pan-fried fillet of dorade with grilled asparagus, marinated artichokes and a light vanilla sauce; loin of Scottish venison with mushroom "à la crème", roast salsify and balsamic-glazed baby beetroots. The desserts are equally considered: Valrhona chocolate fondant with feuillatine and milk ice cream; or how about something iconic like a Bailey's crème brûlée served with caramelized pears and honeycomb ice cream? This is classy cooking in a classy restaurant in a classy location, but at agreeably accessible prices.

If you thought it was hard to get a booking in the restaurant, don't even consider the chef's table. It seats six comfortably in an air-conditioned alcove overlooking the kitchen. You get to watch the blood, sweat and tears from a safe distance while toying with a special multi-course menu, and listening to your wallet whimper.

Mayfair & Bond Street

Kiku

🍴 There's no doubt it sounds like a bit of a porky. Kiku is a Japanese restaurant (translates as pricey), deep in the heart of Mayfair (translates as very pricey) and one that serves top-class sushi with a classical ambience – without charging the earth. Your bill will prove it. In helpful, Oriental fashion it lists the huge number of sushi portions you are alleged

£16 to £55

Address 17 Half Moon St, W1
℡ 020 7499 4208
Station Green Park
Open Mon–Sat noon–2.30pm
& 6.30–10.15pm, Sun 5.30
–9.45pm
Accepts All major credit cards

to have consumed and an average price. For one memorable meal this figure was under £3 per dish. What's more, Kiku is laid out around a traditional sushi bar where you can sit and wonder at the dexterity of the knife man, who effortlessly keeps pace with the appetites in his section. Wander along smack on opening time, snatch a seat at the counter and go for it.

Knowledgeable Japanese folk always start a meal of sushi with tamago (£1.70) – the sweetish, omelettey one which allows the diner to properly assess the quality of the rice before getting serious with the fishy bits. Who knows? The toro (£5), or tuna belly, is good; the suzuki (£2.90), or sea bass, is good; the amaebi (£2.30), or sweet shrimp, is … sweet. Hiramei (£2.70), or turbot, is very delicate. You must have the hotate (£2.70) – slices of raw scallop, translucent and subtle, very good indeed. From the rolled sushi section, pick the umeshiso maki (£3.20), made from rice perked up by pickled plums and fresh green shiso leaves. There are so many good things here that you might feel emboldened to try some of the more challenging sushi, like akagai (£3), or ark shell; or uni, which is sea urchin roe (£4.50). Verging on the "experts" category is tobiko (£2.70), which is flying fish roe and really rather good. A successful strategy might be to try a few sushi and then turn to the main menu: perhaps tempura moriawase (£14.50), which is mixed tempura; or sake teriyaki (£9.80), which is grilled teriyaki salmon. Drink the very refreshing Asahi beer and only venture into the realms of sake if you understand it.

If you feel your nerve breaking, there is a grand assortment of sushi combinations such as tokujyo nigiri (£30) or jyongiri (£22).

Menu at the Connaught

(🍴) After wild success at Claridge's (pg. 81) this was the next Grand Hotel to fall under Gordon Ramsay's spell (he also has outposts at the Berkeley (pg.63) and Savoy). When these venerable institutions succumb there is always a major fuss: on the one hand the leave-well-alone brigade, and on the other the about-time-toos. At the Connaught the management have hedged their bets and if the old guard still want to

£30 to £120

Address Carlos Place, W1
☏ 020 7592 1222
Station Green Park
Open Mon–Fri noon–3pm &
5.45–11pm, Sat noon–3.30pm &
5.45–11pm, Sun noon–3.30pm &
5.45–10.30pm
Accepts All major credit cards

dine there is a special "stuffy" menu served in the Grill Room entitled "Old Favourites". Gordon Ramsay's protégée Angela Hartnett plies her trade in "Menu". The room is comfortably traditional and the service is ball-bearing-smooth. The food is modern and good. The set lunch is a bargain.

The main menu offers three courses for £45 – ten starters and ten mains. Dishes are Italian in spirit and set more store by the quality and freshness of ingredients than by classical Italian names. Starters may include tortelli of oven-roast potato with a rabbit ragout and shaved Pecorino – nice pasta, rich sauce. Or a salad of roast pigeon with confit foie gras, beetroot crisps, sherry vinegar reduction. Or a well-made vialone nano risotto of Barolo wine with sautéed baby squid – imposing flavours and good textures. Mains range from "Classic" bouillabaisse served with braised celery hearts and saffron potatoes; to smoked pork belly with caramelized root vegetables and thyme bouillon – meltingly tender, full of flavour; and pan-fried sweetbread with white turnip puree, potato fondant and truffle jus – it is hard to see how this dish could be improved upon, well-matched flavours and skilfully done. Puds range from lemon panna cotta with thyme syrup and compote of blueberries, to a perfect apple tarte Tatin. The wine list is a book. There are some sensible bottles around the £40 mark!

The set lunch (£25) is a grand way to show off: mosaïque of rabbit with mustard fruits; then confit salmon with lobster and tarragon reduction, herb gnocchi, peas and fèves; followed by a selection of cheeses. Worth every penny.

The Mirabelle

(icon) Anyone hoping to open their own restaurant should have lunch at The Mirabelle. It's not just the touch of Marco Pierre White, London's own culinary Rasputin, the whole operation is superlative. Forgive them the mind-numbingly arrogant and extensive wine list – surprisingly no one has yet ordered the 1847 vintage Chateau d'Yquem at £30,000 – and concentrate on the food, which is quite reasonably priced for this

£25 to £110

Address 56 Curzon St, W1
(T) 020 7499 4636
Station Green Park
Open Mon–Fri noon–2.30pm &
6–11.30pm, Sat noon–3pm &
6–11.30pm, Sun noon–3pm &
6–10.30pm
Accepts All major credit cards
(W) www.whitestarline.org.uk

kind of cooking. The ingredients are carefully chosen. The presentation on the plate is stunning. The surroundings are elegant, and the service attentive. The bar is inviting. Go on, splash out.

Start with a classic: omelette "Arnold Bennett" (£9.50). It's no wonder that Arnold liked these so much – they're rich, buttery and light, made with smoked haddock. Or there's ballottine of salmon with herbs (£8.95). Or fresh asparagus with sauce mousseline (£10.50). Step up a level for some triumphant foie gras "en terrine" dishes: with green peppercorns, gelée de Sauternes and toasted brioche (£16.95); or "parfait en gelée" (£9.95). Believe it or not, these two are actually bargains. For a fishy main course, how about fillet of red mullet au Marocaine, sauce cumin (£14.50)? Or the classical grilled lemon sole served on the bone with sauce tartare (£18.95)? In the meat section, choose from roast venison au poivre, sauce grand veneur (£16.50); or braised pig's trotter with morels, pommes purées, sauce Perigueux (£19.50); or roast duck Montmorency, fumet vin de Banyuls (£18.50). Puddings (all at £7.95) are deftly handled. The star is tarte sablée of bitter chocolate.

Choose the set lunch, don't let the wine list sneak up on you (there's a decent enough Montes Sauvignon Blanc for £15.50) and you could be enjoying a fine meal of ceviche of mackerel with tomato in vinaigrette, followed by confit leg of duck with beetroot salad, and finally Bakewell tart with vanilla ice cream. Monday to Saturday, two lunchtime courses go for £16.50, and three for £19.95; at Sunday lunch, three courses cost £19.50.

Nobu

It's hard to know just what to make of Nobu. On the face of it, a restaurant owned by Robert de Niro, Drew Nieporent and Matsuhisa Nobuyuki sounds like the invention of a deranged Hollywood producer. And then there is the cocoon of hype: the restaurant is amazingly expensive, it has a broom cupboard where Boris Becker qualified for his paternity suit and it's within the

£30 to £100
Address 19 Old Park Lane, W1
☎ 020 7447 4747
Station Hyde Park Corner
Open Mon–Thurs noon–2.15pm & 6–10.30pm, Fri & Sat noon–2.15pm & 6–11pm, Sun 6–9.30pm
Accepts All major credit cards

mega-cool Metropolitan hotel. As is often the case with hype, some of the above is gossip and some is gospel, but which is which? Don't worry, the food is innovative and superb. Ingredients are fresh, flavour combinations are novel and inspired, and presentation is elegant and stylish. See for yourself – the lunchtime bento box, which includes sashimi salad, rock shrimp tempura, black cod and all the trimmings costs just £25.

Chef Matsuhisa worked in Peru, and South American flavours and techniques segue into classical Japanese dishes – some of the dishes here defy classification. There are lists of Nobu "special appetisers" and "special dishes"; the problem is where to begin. Tiradito Nobu-style (£10.50) is a plate of wafer-thin scallop slices, each topped with a dab of chilli, half a coriander leaf and a citrus dressing – delicate and utterly delicious. The sashimi is terrific: salmon (£10) is sliced and just warmed through to "set" it, before being served with sesame seeds – the minimal cooking makes for a superb texture. The black cod with miso (£24) is a grandstand dish – a piece of perfectly cooked, well-marinated fish with an elaborate banana-leaf canopy. Other inspired dishes are the rock shrimp tempura (£8.75) and, for dessert, the chocolate and almond parfait with red berry compote (£7.95).

Nobu is probably the only place in London where none of the customers fully understands the menu. No one on a first visit could hope to make sense of it. For once it is no cop-out to opt for the omakase (chef's choice) menu, which costs £70 in the evenings and £50 at lunch. Don't be intimidated: book your table well in advance and settle back for a stunning gastronomic experience.

The Square

The Square is very French: food is terribly important here. And in the gastro premier league – an arena where almost every commentator bows to the supremacy of French chefs and French cuisine – you cannot help a slight smirk that head chef Philip Howard, an Englishman, has got it all so very, very right. At The Square, the finest ingredients are sought out, and then what is largely a classical technique ensures that each retains its essential character and flavour. Eating here is a palate-expanding experience.

£30 to £130

Address 6–10 Bruton St, W1
☎ 020 7495 7100
Station Green Park
Open Mon–Fri noon–3pm &
6.30–10.45pm, Sat 6.30–10.45pm,
Sun 6.30–9.30pm
Accepts All major credit cards
🌐 www.squarerestaurant.com

This is a very gracious restaurant. Service is suave, silent and effortless. Seasoning is on the button. Presentation is elegant. The wine list seems boundless in scope and soars to the very topmost heights (where mortals dare not even ask the price). Go for lunch and experience real excellence. For £25 you might have a ballottine foie gras, or a velouté of celery and celeriac with a soft-boiled gull's egg and smoked haddock; followed by either fillets of Cornish plaice with creamed potato and a ragout of mussels, pot au feu of duck. Add the extra fiver and go on to crêpe soufflé with rhubarb and orange. In the evening three courses cost £55 (plus a few supplements for serious extravagances). The menu changes on a broadly seasonal basis but you will choose from nine starters – dishes like lasagne of crab with a cappuccino of shellfish and basil; or hot and cold consommé of chicken with celeriac, tarragon and foie gras; or assiette of red mullet with fennel and saffron. Then ten mains, which may include steamed turbot with leeks and champagne foam; or roast loin of veal with wilted greens and Gruyère beignet; or roast pigeon from Bresse with hand-rolled macaroni and truffled consommé. Puddings – such as a fondant of chocolate with coffee and orange – are classics. Howard is an able man and Michelin's two-star measure of his worth is an underestimate.

There's also a eight-course "tasting" menu for £75 plus service (for the entire table only). Book now. This is one treat you will never regret.

Truc Vert

(🍴) Truc Vert is one of those hybrid restaurants. You want it to be a deli, with fine cheeses, artisan chocolate and obscure wild boar salami? Then it's a deli. You want it to be a restaurant, with proper starters, mains and puds? Then it's a restaurant. The Truc is open all day during the week, and it makes a very decent fist of being all things to all customers. The quality, provenance and

£12 to £40
Address 42 North Audley St, W1
(📞) 020 7491 9988
Station Bond Street
Open Mon–Fri 7.30am–9pm, Sat noon–4pm, Sun 1–3pm
Accepts All major credit cards except Diners

freshness of all the ingredients get top priority, and the menu changes daily. It comes in two halves: "From the shop" means quiche, salads, chicken from the rotisserie, pâtés, cakes, pastries and cookies. There is also a novel approach to the magnificent cheese counter: you nominate a few different cheeses, they make up an elegant plateful and then weigh it, and you are charged by weight. The same deal works for charcuterie. With all these instant goodies you would expect the "From the kitchen" section to be a poor relation, but the cooking seems adept and the seasoning spot on.

The menu is rewritten daily, but by way of starter you could be offered a roast Jerusalem artichoke soup (£4.95); Truc Vert crab cakes with baby gem salad and Caesar dressing (£7.95); and bruschetta of buffalo ricotta with asparagus and roast tomato, avocado and chilli salsa (£7.50). Mains run the gamut from grilled swordfish loin steak with salad of French beans, butter beans, Parma ham and tomato salsa (£15.45); to farfalle pasta with smoked salmon, chives, peas and cream (£11.90); and grilled lamb cutlets with sweet potato, spring onion, mangetout salad (£13.95). Puds are accomplished – try pain au chocolat pudding with clotted cream (£4.75), or baked apple with vanilla Anglaise (£4.75) – but they pale beside the prospect of the epic array of fine cheeses. At lunch the Truc Vert quiches (£4.95); the rotisserie chickens (half £9, whole £18); and the selection of pâté with cornichons (£5.95) make the "From the shop" option most appealing,

Wines also get a very sympathetic treatment here. You pay the shop price and they add on £4.50 corkage, a very un-Mayfair approach.

Paddington & Edgware Road

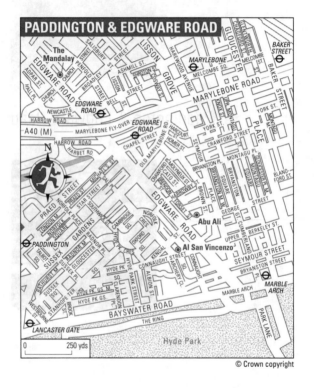

PADDINGTON & EDGWARE ROAD

The Mandalay

Abu Ali

Al San Vincenzo

0   250 yds

© Crown copyright

Abu Ali

(🍴) You can only suppose that, in the Lebanon, going out to eat is man's work. That certainly seems to be the case around the Oxford Street end of the Edgware Road, where you'll find Abu Ali's bustling café. This is an authentic place, the Lebanese equivalent of a northern working man's club, and men gather to

£7 to £25
Address 136–138 George St, W1
☎ 020 7724 6338
Station Marble Arch
Open Daily 9.30am–11pm
Accepts Cash or cheque only

smoke at the pavement tables. It's a bit spartan in appearance, but the food is honest and terrific value. Although you are unlikely to find many Lebanese women here, female diners get a dignified welcome. There's nothing intimidating about the place or its clientele.

You will want a selection of starters. Tabouleh (£2.50) is bright green with lots of fresh parsley, lemon juice, oil and only a little cracked wheat – it even tastes healthy. Hommos (£2.50) is rich and spicy, garnished with a few whole chickpeas and cayenne pepper. Warak inab (£3) are thin and pleasantly sour stuffed vine leaves, served hot or cold. Kabis is a plate of tangy salt and sour pickles – cucumber, chillies and red cabbage – that comes free with every order. For main dishes there's kafta billaban (£5.50) – minced lamb kebabs served hot under a layer of sharp yoghurt and with a sprinkling of pine kernels. Or there's kibbeh bissiniyeh (£5), which is a strange dish: a ball of mince and pine kernels coated with a layer of mince and cracked wheat, then baked until crispy in the oven. The plain grilled meats are also good: try the boned-out poussin – farrouge moussahab (£7). To drink, there is mint tea (£2) – a Lipton's teabag and a bunch of fresh mint in every pot – or soft drinks.

At Abu Ali's, bubble pipes cost £5 a go, and you can choose apple or strawberry. The long strands of black tobacco are mixed into a squelchy mess with chopped fruit and then covered with a piece of foil, on top of which is placed a chunk of blazing charcoal – hubble your way to sweet-smelling smoke. Some of the cognoscenti take this procedure a step further and replace the water in the pipe with ice and Appletise. It certainly makes for a perfumed environment from which to watch the world go by.

The Mandalay

🍴 In the Edgware Road desert – north of the Harrow Road but south of anything else – Gary and Dwight Ally, Scandinavian-educated Burmese brothers, have set up shop in what must be an ex-greasy spoon. The resulting restaurant is rather bizarre, with just 28 seats, the old sandwich counter filled with strange and exotic ingredients, and greetings and decoration in both Burmese and Norwegian. Gary is in the kitchen and smiley, talkative Dwight is front of house. The Ally brothers have perhaps correctly concluded that their native language is unmasterable by the English, so the menu is written in English with a Burmese translation – an enormous help when ordering. But the food itself is pure unexpurgated Burmese, and all freshly cooked.

> ## £6 to £16
>
> **Address** 444 Edgware Rd, W2
> ☎ 020 7258 3696
> **Station** Edgware Road
> **Open** Mon–Sat noon–2.30pm & 6–10.30pm; closed Sun & bank holidays
> **Accepts** All major credit cards
> ⊛ www.bcity.com/mandalay

The cuisine is a melange of different local influences, with a little bit of Thai and Malaysian, and a lot of Indian, and a few things that are distinctly their own. To start there are papadums (two for £1.20) or a great bowlful of prawn crackers (£1.90), which arrive freshly fried and sizzling hot (and served on domestic kitchen paper to soak up the oil). First courses range from spring rolls (from £1.90 for two) and samosas (£1.90 for four), to salads like raw papaya and cucumber (£3.90) or chicken and cabbage (£3.90). There are soups, noodle soups and all manner of fritters as well. Main courses are mainly curries, or rice and noodle dishes, spiced with plenty of ginger, garlic, coriander and coconut, and using fish, chicken and vegetables as the main ingredients. The cooking is good, flavours hit the mark, portions are huge, and only a handful of dishes cost over £6.50. Vegetable dishes are somewhat more successful than the prawn ones, but at this price it's only to be expected.

Even with its eccentric setting, tiny room and rigorous no-smoking policy, The Mandalay has built up a loyal following over the years. The tables are minuscule and the acoustics are good, so be careful what you talk about and keep your ears open – you may be sitting next to an ex-pat Burmese diamond dealer.

Al San Vincenzo

Al San Vincenzo is not a cheap restaurant. But then you'll find it smack bang in the middle of a patch of serious affluence near the bottom end of the Edgware Road, so the local clientele are not over-bothered. This is a very passionate place with a small dining room and a single-minded chef in the kitchen, which perhaps accounts for the mercifully simple dishes and good seasonal food. The front-of-house attitudes are more relaxed, but if there were a motto over the door it would probably read "No compromise". The pricing is straightforward: two courses may be had for £28.50 and three courses cost £34.50; supplements are rare but some of the more expensive ingredients, like fresh fish, can bump the price up a bit.

£35 to £65
Address 30 Connaught St, W2
☎ 020 7262 9623
Station Marble Arch
Open Mon–Fri 12.15–3pm & 7–11pm, Sat 7–11pm
Accepts Major credit cards except AmEx and Diners

The menu changes to reflect the seasons, but there are usually six or seven starters to choose from. Dishes range from the plain but satisfying, such as a risotto of snails; root and green vegetable soup; to interesting combinations like breast of pigeon with black olive pesto served with bruschetta di polenta. Flavours are intense and presentation gloriously unfussy. The perfect example is fresh eels pan-fried with chilli, onions and lemon – the richness of the boneless eel fillets is cut by the lemony tang and a belt of chilli. This tastes as good as it sounds. Main courses are in similar vein: fillet of brill with mussels, saffron and potato puree; rack of venison with red cabbage and green beans; or risotto of cannellini beans, celery and Parmesan cheese. The dessert menu ranges from the expected – vin santo with biscotti – to more surprising puds such as fresh dates stuffed with marzipan, rolled in pistachio and served with a bitter chocolate sauce and vanilla ice cream.

The wine list covers the mid-ground well, with a well-chosen series of Italian wines priced at between £16 and £37. Look out for the light and bright Vernaccia (£20), which is a good option at lunch. Beer lovers will be intrigued by the full-flavoured Ichinusa beer from Sardinia – this is a real treat.

Piccadilly & St James's

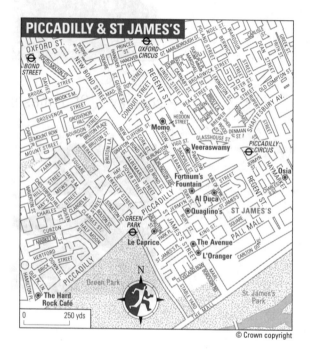

PICCADILLY & ST JAMES'S

The Avenue

The Avenue was one of the first banker-led restaurants in London – a bunch of City chums set up the kind of restaurant where they would choose to eat. Now it's part of a sprawling empire, including Kensington Place (see p.446) and Circus (see p.124), to name just two. This is a stark yet stylish barn of a place, with white walls and pale cherry-wood chairs, and an enormous video wall of moving images around the bar seating area. Entrance is through a glass door, part of a great glass plate fronting the restaurant, and greeting is by designer-clad hosts. Inside it's very noisy, with an upbeat atmosphere. There is not much subtlety about this place – wear your choicest clobber to feel most at home and do not be afraid to gawp.

£25 to £50

Address 7–9 St James's St, SW1
☎ 020 7321 2111
Station Green Park
Open Mon–Thurs noon–3pm &
5.45pm–midnight, Fri & Sat
noon–3pm & 5.45pm–12.30am,
Sun noon–3.30pm & 5.45–10pm
Accepts All major credit cards
ⓦ www.theavenue.co.uk

Cooking is well executed and the menu is a fashionable mix of English and the Med. First courses are generally light and bright: tomato and basil soup with buffalo mozzarella (£5.50); seared smoked salmon with asparagus and chervil butter (£8.50); or tomato, bacon and spinach risotto (£6/11.50). Main courses may include salmon fishcakes with buttered vegetables (£14.50); grilled skate with spinach and Béarnaise sauce (£14.50); crumbed pork cutlet with parsnip puree and apple sauce (£14.50); or calf's liver with champ and bacon (£16). Anyone watching their weight might opt for rare grilled tuna with rocket salsa (£16), while for the opposite persuasion there's braised lamb shank with celeriac mash (£16). Puddings (all £5.75) range from chocolate fudge pudding with clotted cream; to pear and passion fruit zabaglione; or frozen honey nougat with grilled figs. They will appeal to those with a seriously sweet tooth.

The Avenue is huge, so even if you haven't booked it's likely you'll get a table for dinner. Call to check if there have been any cancellations. At lunch both the menu and the pricing are somewhat simpler: you choose and pay £17.95 for two courses, or £19.95 for three. Pre- or post-theatre (5.45–7.30pm & 10.15pm–midnight), you can choose from three starters and three mains, at £14.95 for two courses and £17.95 for three.

Piccadilly & St James's

Le Caprice

Every London socialite worth their salt is a regular at this deeply chic little restaurant, and everyone from royalty downwards uses it for the occasional quiet lunch or dinner. That's not because they'll be hounded by well-wishers or because photographers will be waiting outside. They won't. This restaurant is discreet enough to make an oyster seem a blabbermouth. It's not even particularly plush or comfortable, with a black-and-white-tiled floor, a big black bar and cane seats. What keeps Le Caprice full day in, day out is its personal service, properly prepared food and a bill that holds no surprises.

£25 to £55

Address Arlington House, Arlington St, SW1
☏ 020 7629 2239
Station Green Park
Open Mon–Sat noon–3pm & 5.30pm–midnight, Sun noon–4pm & 5.30pm–midnight
Accepts All major credit cards
🌐 www.caprice-holdings.co.uk

The much-copied menu is enticing from the first moment. Plum tomato and basil galette (£6.75) is simplicity itself, but with decent ingredients that taste of what they should. Crispy duck comes with watercress salad (£9.25), while dressed Dorset crab with celeriac remoulade (£14.25) is so fresh and clean it makes you wonder why other restaurants can't manage this. In season, there are splendid specials – River Spey sea trout with steamed clams and parsley (£18.75). Or perhaps Tamworth pork chop with white asparagus and rosemary butter (£14.50). Or there may be loin of yellow-fin tuna with a spiced lentil salsa (£17.25). If you are still up for pudding, try banana sticky toffee pudding (£6.35) or the baked Alaska with cherries and Kirsch (£7.50) to see just what classic English puds are about. In the winter there is an array of more solid rib-stickers.

Expense aside, the only trouble with Le Caprice is the struggle to get a table. It is so permanently booked up that they only really accept reservations from people they know, or people who book well in advance. If you are able to plan far enough ahead, you should go just for the experience; otherwise you'll have to befriend a regular. But this has its advantages, too. It's too chic and grown-up to attract the fly-by-night fashion people, and you won't find wall-to-wall hip designer wear. All you need to look the part is a Continental tan, a little jewellery, Italian clothes and a few old-fashioned laughter lines.

Al Duca

This restaurant hit the West End scene in 2000, so in the grand scheme of things it now ranks as a grizzled veteran! You get high-quality, sophisticated food, an agreeable setting, slick service, and all at modest prices – what you get here seems to be far more than you pay for. The formula is a simple one: at lunch, two courses cost £17.50, three cost £20.50, and four £23.50. In the evening, the prices go up to £20, £24 and £28. A three-course dinner for £24 within stumbling distance of Piccadilly? More like this, please!

£20 to £40

Address 4-5 Duke of York St, SW1
℡ 020 7839 3090
Station Piccadilly Circus
Open Mon–Fri noon–2.30pm &
6–11pm, Sat 12.30–3pm &
6–11pm
Accepts All major credit cards
except Diners
ⓦ www.alduca-restaurant.co.uk

Anyone who eats out regularly in London might feel cynical about such an offer, doubtful that the cooking and portion sizes could remain uncompromised by the low prices. But do not think London – think Italy. Such regularly changing menus are commonplace there. There are six or more starters at Al Duca: dishes like char-grilled marinated mixed vegetables with balsamic vinegar; or pan-fried wild mushrooms with chicken livers, bacon and crisp polenta. Then there is a raft of dishes under the heading pasta: home-made fettuccine with rabbit ragù and black olives; linguine with clams and Aeolian island pesto (supplement £3); or reginette with peas and bacon. Followed by an array of main courses: pan-fried salmon with poached potatoes in butter and spinach with balsamic; sea bass; chicken; smoked fillet of pork with peach mayonnaise and fennel salad. Finally, six desserts, ranging from a stracchino cheesecake with Acacia honey to a classic almond and pear tart. The standard of cooking is high, with dishes bringing off that difficult trick of being both deceptively simple and satisfyingly rich. The home-made pasta and polenta are fresh and good. The fish is perfectly cooked. Overall there is much to praise here, and the slick service and stylish ambience live up to the efforts in the kitchen.

As seems to be the case with every "all-in" menu, the dreaded supplements do put in an appearance, but they are small and seem fair – an extra £3 for black ravioli with crab, zucchini and cherry tomatoes.

Piccadilly & St James's

Fortnum's Fountain

🍴 The main entrance to Fortnum's Fountain Restaurant is at the back of the store, on the corner of Jermyn Street. This makes it a draw for those working and shopping in the surrounding area. The Fountain reflects their taste and is utterly dependable, delivering just what you expect – well-prepared, very English breakfasts, lunches, teas and early dinners. The ingredients, as you'd expect of London's smartest and most old-fashioned food shop, are top-class. And the Fountain itself is a very pretty room, with classical murals all around.

> **£15 to £30**
>
> **Address** 181 Piccadilly, W1
> ☎ 020 7973 4140
> **Station** Piccadilly Circus /Green Park
> **Open** Mon–Sat breakfast 8.30–11.30am, lunch 11.30am–3pm, tea 3–5.30pm, dinner 5.30–8pm
> **Accepts** All major credit cards
> ⓦ www.fortnumandmason.co.uk

The Fountain is deservedly famous for its selection of Fortnum's teas and coffees accompanied by cream teas and ice-cream sundaes, and on any given afternoon you will see small children being treated by elderly relatives. And beware: the splendid knickerbocker glory (£4.95) has a terrifying ability to turn even grumpy middle-aged men into small children. But the restaurant also serves a very decent breakfast. The full English, called Fortnum's Farmhouse Breakfast (£11.95), is rather better than that found in many hotels, and the grilled kipper with brown toast (£7.95) will gladden the dourest heart. The dishes on the Fountain Menu (which serves for both lunch and dinner) reflect the ingredient-buying power of the food department and, sensibly enough, tend to the straightforward. The excellent London smoked salmon with onion bread (£13.25) is a real treat, as is Fortnum's Welsh rarebit on Cheddar bread with grilled tomato, back bacon or poached egg (£8.75). There are also simple classics such as grilled Dover sole with side salad and new potatoes (£22.95); grilled Aberdeen Angus steak with peppercorn sauce and chips (£15.25); and Highland scramble (£10.25), which teams scrambled eggs with smoked salmon.

The restaurant is always busy and, though they turn tables, you will not be hurried. The downside is that there is no booking. That's great for shoppers, but anyone on a schedule should avoid the lunchtime peak. Give breakfast serious consideration.

The Hard Rock Café

🍴 The Hard Rock Café is a genuine celebration of rock 'n' roll, which makes its location, in Hyde Park's trad hotel strip, all the more strange. Perhaps it was chance, or clever marketing, as the bulk of the café's customers are tourists. Whatever the reason, this is the original Hard Rock Café, here since the 1970s, and it's the original theme restaurant. As such, it's a hard act to follow. The queue to get in is legendary. There is no booking and you will find a queue almost all day long, every day of the year – and it kind of adds to the occasion. Once in, there is a great atmosphere, created by full-on rock music, dim lighting and walls dripping with rock memorabilia. The Hard Rock food is not bad, either, predominantly Tex-Mex and burgers.

> **£15 to £30**
>
> **Address** 150 Old Park Lane, W1
> ☎ 020 7629 0382
> **Station** Hyde Park Corner
> **Open** Mon–Thurs & Sun
> 11.30am–midnight, Fri & Sat
> 11.30am–1am
> **Accepts** All major credit cards
> ⊛ www.hardrock.com

Scanning the menu is a serious business here, dishes get short but complex essays attached to them, so boneless bodacious tenders (£5.75) are explained as "boneless chicken tenders, lightly breaded and coated in our Classic Rock (medium), Heavy Metal (hot) sauce or tangy Bar-B-Que sauce. Served with celery and Bleu cheese dressing" – the job of copywriter is an important one here. The burgers knock spots off those at the high-street chains and cover the spectrum from natural veggie burger (£7.25) to HRC burger (£7.75) and hickory Bar-B-Que bacon cheeseburger (£9.25). There are also Tex-Mex specials like the grilled fajitas (£11.95), which are a pretty good example of the genre (they are billed as "HRC's famous grilled" etc – everything is famous here). Further along, among the Smokehouse Specialities, there's the pig sandwich (£7.35) and Bruce's famous Bar-B-Que ribs (£10.95). Puddings are self-indulgent, and the hot fudge brownie (£4.95) elevates goo to an art form.

Elderly lords and ladies who used to totter up Piccadilly in search of the branch of Coutt's bank that stood on the opposite corner will be deeply puzzled to find that it is now the Hard Rock's museum and memorabilia shop. Perhaps they could try for a T-shirt and cashback?

Momo

🍴 Momo is an attractive and very
trendy Moroccan restaurant tucked
away in a backwater off Regent Street.
For dinner, you usually have to book at
least a week in advance and to opt for an
early or late sitting. If you apply for the
late shift, be prepared for a noisy, nightclub ambience, especially on Fridays and
Saturdays. The design of the place is

£30 to £50
Address 25 Heddon St, W1
☎ 020 7434 4040
Station Piccadilly Circus/Oxford Circus
Open Mon–Sat noon–2.15pm & 7–10.30pm, Sun 7–11.30pm
Accepts All major credit cards

clever, with bold, geometric, kasbah-style architecture, decked out with
plush cushions and lots of candles. Downstairs there's an even more
splendid-looking Moorish bar, annoyingly reserved for members only – a
shame, as Momo is the kind of place where you could happily carry on
the evening, especially if you're booked in for the earlier (7–9pm) of its
two dining slots.

Whenever you arrive, get into the mood with a Momo special (£6), a
blend of vodka, lemon juice and sparkling water, topped with a pile of
chopped mint. While you're downing that, you can check out the
starters. Briouat au cabillaud, mousseline de poivron (£8) are mouth-
watering little parcels of paper-thin pastry filled with cod potatoes and
chermoula and served with a red pepper mousse, while Méchouia
(£6.50) is made with grilled peppers, tomatoes, cumin and coriander.
For main course, choose from four tagines, which are North African-
style stews served in a large clay pot. Try the tagine of chicken with
preserved lemons (£14) or the tagine of lamb with prunes, quinces and
almonds (£15). Alternatively, opt for couscous: brochettes de poulet
(£14.50) combines the staple with marinated spicy chicken and a pot
of vegetables; couscous Méchouia (£32 for two) is based around roasted
spiced lamb. Or treat yourself to the Fès speciality of pastilla (£10), the
super-sweet pigeon pie in millefeuille pastry – a main course that has
been relegated to the starters list. Desserts (all around £5.50) include
pastries, deep-fried filo parcels of fruit, pancakes and meringues.

Finally, even if you don't make it into the seclusion of the members'
bar, don't miss a trip to the toilets downstairs – the men's urinal is an
installation of some beauty.

L'Oranger

(🍴) From the outside, L'Oranger looks like a very expensive French restaurant dedicated to expense-account diners. While it's not cheap, the inclusive menus do bring serious cooking within reach. At lunch you pay £22 for two courses or £26 for three, and dinner is set at £35 for two and £45 for three courses. For your money you can expect

£28 to £90

Address 5 St James's St, SW1
☏020 7839 3774
Station Green Park
Open Mon–Fri noon–2.30pm &
6.30-11pm, Sat 6-11pm
Accepts All major credit cards

modern Provençal cooking of a high standard. The saucing leans towards light olive-oil bases rather than the traditional "loadsa-cream" approach and, for cooking of this quality, it is most competitively priced.

Starters may include split-pea soup and smoked bacon; home-made tortelli of pumpkin and Parmesan; endive and baby gem salad with lemon and olive oil; ballottine of salmon and soft cheese cream; and sautéed scallops with lettuce velouté and Iberico ham (£5 supplement). In the main, these are well-judged combinations of flavours. For main courses, try canette de Challand with baby artichoke. Or there may be roasted filet of John Dory with langoustines; rump of lamb with pommes fondant and olives Niçoises; whole sea bass baked "en croute de sel" (supplement £5). Puddings include lemon and thyme crème caramel with an apple crisp; warm Caraibe chocolate fondant with vanilla and nougatine ice cream; and a hazelnut soufflé with chocolate sauce. It's one of those menus where you can be spoilt for choice, even though some of the more elaborate dishes carry a small supplement. Side dishes of seasonal vegetables are also served. At lunch the menu is shorter, with slightly simpler dishes. The wine list is encyclopedic, starting at £19 for a Chardonnay and going up to £450 for a bottle of La Tâche de la Romanée-Conti. But there's plenty of good choice at the lower prices.

L'Oranger is refined and elegant with attentive service but a relaxed and unstuffy atmosphere. There's also a secret outside courtyard, which is open at dinner only, and a private function room for twenty. The set-prices policy turns what would be an "expensive treat" menu into accessible dining. More restaurants copy, please.

Piccadilly & St James's

Osia

(🍴) OK .... we're pushing it with this one. You could eat here for less than our threshold price of £35 per head but you would have to dodge round the menu in search of low ticket items. Osia is worth squeezing into the guide because it is so refreshingly different. New attitudes, new ingredients, new flavour combinations. Something gen-

£35 to £100

Address 11 Haymarket, SW1
☎020 7976 1313
Station Piccadilly Circus
Open Mon–Sat noon–3pm &
5.30–11pm
Accepts All major credit cards
except Diners

uinely original, and Australian to boot. The restaurant opened in the spring of 2003, and the man in charge of the kitchen is a genial Aussie called Scott Webster. His food is terrific, the service is accomplished and the room comfortable. The bill will probably end up nerve-racking, but overall it is worth flexing your wallet and trying these dishes.

The menu starts with a range of "cocktails and ceviches", small plates or glasses aimed at fulfilling the role of amuses-gueules. Blue swimmer crab cocktail, minted cucumber threads, flying fish roe (£9); or mackerel ceviche with spicy pineapple coriander dressing (£7). Appetisers may include steamed mussels, lemongrass, basil, chilli broth and grilled lemon bread (£8) – sweet mussels, assertive broth, great bread. Or lemon myrtle–cured smoked salmon, potato pancake, lime butter (£10) – awesome. Or skewered prawns in kunafa pastry, wasabi mayonnaise (£12) – large prawns wrapped in shredded filo and fried. Mains look beautiful on the plate and have well-matched, upfront flavours – Dorrigo-herbed spring lamb, wilted pea shoots, and kumera mash (£18) – stunning, exotic, herby lamb. Fresh tasting greens. Or a suckling pig cutlet that comes with quandong glaze (£17) – quandongs are Aussie wild "peaches": small, orange and stunningly citrusy. Perfect with pork. Puds are outrageous – hot chocolate soup with vanilla pepper ice cream (£7) – dive into a pool of molten choccy! Or a Pavlova with wattleseed cream (£7) – barely set meringue – more like oeufs à la neige. The wine list is long on New World, starts at £18 a bottle and accelerates away.

The side dishes are a treat: fried green tomatoes (£3), disc-shaped fritters, crisp outside, sharp within. Every chef in town will copy these.

Quaglino's

In 1929 Giovanni Quaglino opened a restaurant in Bury Street which became an instant success. He was a daring innovator and is reputed to have been the first person to serve hot dishes as hors d'oeuvres. The thing his new restaurant had, above all else, was glamour. When Sir Terence Conran redesigned and reopened Quaglino's, more than 60 years later, his vision was essentially the same. Love it or loathe it, Quaglino's is glamorous, and when it first opened it attracted a sophisticated crowd. Inevitably that early exclusivity is no more. But the ambience is still impressive – the elegant reception, the sweeping staircase into the bar that overlooks the main restaurant, and the second stairway down to restaurant level. If this kind of thing rings your bell you will be happy here.

£20 to £80
Address 16 Bury St, SW1
℗020 7930 6767
Station Green Park
Open Mon–Thurs noon–3pm & 5.30–11.30pm Fri & Sat noon–3pm & 5.30pm–1.30am, Sun noon–3pm & 5.30–11pm
Accepts All major credit cards
⊛www.conran.com

The menu is simple, classy and brasserie-style, with very little to scare off the less experienced diner. Given the size of the restaurant, it is best to go for the simpler dishes that need less finishing and exactitude – with this number of people to feed, the head chef is not going to have a chance to get to every plate. The plateau de fruits de mer (£33 per person, minimum two people) is as good as you would hope, as is the whole lobster mayonnaise (£29). Fish and chips (£13.50) is served with home-made chips and tartare sauce, and is excellent, while an entrecôte steak with Béarnaise sauce (£18.50) is a treat when served, as it is here, properly cooked. Puddings are straightforward and agreeably predictable – passion-fruit Pavlova (£6.50); chocolate St Emilion (£6.50).

Quaglino's staff can be brusque, but then marshalling large numbers of glamour-seekers is a testing enough job, which would make anyone a little tetchy. You can avoid this altogether by staying in the bar, which offers highlights from the menu – including all the seafood. Furthermore, Quaglino's is open late, which makes it perfect for a genuine after-theatre dinner. There's a prix-fixe menu at lunch and pre- or post-theatre: two courses for £16.50, three for £18.50.

INDIAN

Veeraswamy

(icon) Veeraswamy is Britain's oldest-surviving Indian restaurant, founded in 1927 by Edward Palmer following a successful catering operation at the British Empire Exhibition. Its next owner was Sir William Steward, who pulled in the rich and famous throughout the postwar boom – their numbers included the King of Denmark, whose penchant for a glass of Carlsberg with his curry is said to have first established the link between Indian food and beer. The latest owner is

£20 to £50

Address Victory House, 99 Regent St, W1
(phone) 020 7734 1401
Station Piccadilly Circus
Open Mon–Fri noon–2.30pm & 5.30–11.30pm, Sat 12.30–3pm & 5.30pm–11.30pm, Sun 12.30–3pm & 5.30–10.30pm
Accepts All major credit cards
(web) www.realindianfood.com

Namita Panjabi, who also owns Chutney Mary (see p.404) and Masala Zone (see p.127). She has swept Veeraswamy into the modern era: the old and faded colonial decor has gone, along with the old and faded dishes. In their place there's an elegant, fashionable restaurant painted in the vibrant colours of today's India, and an all-new menu of bold, modern, authentically Indian dishes of all kinds.

You'll need to adjust your pattern of ordering. Main dishes come as a plate with rice, and sometimes vegetables too. They're not designed for sharing, and you will definitely need one each. Street food makes great starters: pani puri (£5.25), rich with tamarind; or green pea tikkis (£5.50), which are little patties made from green peas, nuts and raisins (£5.50). Or there's masala crab cake with fresh plum chutney (£7.50) or mussels moilee (£6.50), which is made from fresh mussels with coconut and ginger. The tandoori dishes could be starters or main – venison chops (£15) appeals. Other mains are well spiced and have a good depth of flavour. Saufiyani gosht (£14.75) is a mild lamb curry made with fennel seeds. You could also try the Malabari lobster curry (£21), with fresh turmeric and raw mango; or chicken salaan (£14), a Keralan dish that's hot with black pepper. Vegetarians are not neglected and there's khahjuri kofta (£11) – vegetable dumplings in a curry sauce; or Nilgiri korma (£11) – a green coconutty curry full of fresh vegetables.

Like its sister restaurant, Chutney Mary, Veeraswamy does an excellent Sunday lunch, and there is also a "tasting menu" at £27.50 per person – a starter, thali and dessert.

Queensway & Westbourne Grove

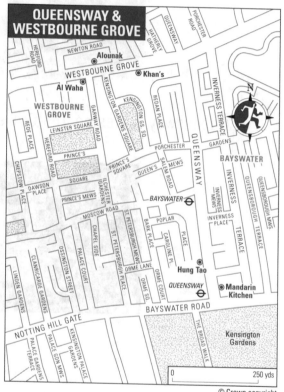

Alounak

Westbourne Grove has always had a raffish cosmopolitan air to it, which makes it the perfect home for this, the second branch of Alounak (actually the third, if you count its early years in a Portakabin opposite Olympia station). Don't be put off by the dated sign outside – this place turns out really good, really cheap Iranian food. The welcoming smell of clay-oven-baked flat bread hits you the moment you walk through the front door, creating a sense of the Middle East that's enhanced further by the gentle gurgling of a fountain, and the strains of Arabic music.

£8 to £20

Address 44 Westbourne Grove, W2
☎ 020 7229 0416
Station Bayswater/Queensway
Open Daily noon–midnight
Accepts All major credit cards
Branches see p.487

The sizable contingent of Middle Eastern locals dining here testifies to the authenticity of the food on offer. As an opening move, you can do no better than order the mixed starter (£8.40), a fine sampler of all the usual dips and hors d'oeuvres, served with splendid, freshly baked flat bread. And then follow the regulars with some grilled meat, which is expertly cooked. Joojeh kebab (£6.90) is melt-in-the-mouth baby chicken, packed with flavour. As you would expect from a Middle Eastern restaurant, lamb dishes feature heavily, and they are simply grilled without fuss or frills. A good way to try two in one is to order the chelo kebab koobideh (£11.10), marinated lamb fillet coupled with minced lamb kebab, which is deliciously rich and oniony. For those with an inquisitive bent there is the innocuous-sounding "kabab tray" (£30 for two), which brings a vast platter best summed up as grilled every-thing. It's worth looking out for the daily specials, too – especially good on a Tuesday, when they offer zereshk polo (£6.20), a stunning chicken dish served on saffron-steamed rice with sweet-and-sour forest berries.

Round things off with a pot of Iranian black tea (£3), sufficient for six and served in ornate glass beakers. Infused with refreshing spices, it does a great job of cleaning the palate, leaving you set for a finale of select Persian sweets. Beware, however, of musty-tasting yoghurt drinks with unpronounceable names.

Queensway & Westbourne Grove

Hung Tao

It is easy to find the Hung Tao: just look out for the much larger New Kam Tong restaurant, and two doors away you'll see this small and spartan establishment. They're actually part of the same group, as is another restaurant over the road (which is where all those singularly appetizing ducks hanging up in the windows of the three establishments are roasted). The reason to choose the Hung Tao above its neighbours is if you fancy a one-plate (or one-bowl) meal. Despite a long and traditional menu, featuring mainly Cantonese and Sichuan dishes, its strengths lie in barbecued meat with rice, noodle dishes and noodle soups. All attract the hungry and are keenly priced.

£8 to £20

Address 51 Queensway, W2
℗ 020 7727 5753
Station Bayswater/ Queensway
Open Daily 11am–11pm
Accepts Cash or cheque only

The very first thing on the menu is delicious – hot and sour soup (£1.90). Uncannily enough, this is both hot, with fresh red chillies in profusion, and sour. There are also a dozen different noodle soups, priced between £4.20 and £5. Then there are twenty dishes that go from duck rice (£4.20) to shrimps and egg with rice (£5.25). Plus about thirty noodle, fried noodle, and ho fun dishes, priced from £3 to £6. The fried ho fun with beef (£4.50) is a superb rich dish – well-flavoured brisket cooked until melting, on top of a mountain of ho fun. And the barbecued meats displayed in the window are very tasty, too: rich, red-painted char sui; soya duckling; and crispy pork or duck.

Towards the front of the menu you'll find a succession of congee dishes. Congee is one of those foods people label "interesting" without meaning it. It is a thick, whitish, runny porridge made with rice, stunningly bland and under-seasoned, but tasting faintly of ginger. Plunge in at the deep end, and try thousand-year egg with sliced pork congee (£4.50). As well as containing pork, there's the "thousand-year" egg itself, the white of which is a translucent chestnut brown and the yolk a fetching green. Inscrutably, it tastes rather like an ordinary hard-boiled egg. Far from being a thousand or even a hundred years old, these eggs acquire their bizarre, slightly cheesy taste after being buried for just one hundred days.

Khan's

If you're after a solid, inexpensive and familiar Indian meal, Khan's is the business. This restaurant, in busy Westbourne Grove, is a long-standing favourite with students and budget-wary locals who know that the curries here may be the staples of a thousand menus across Britain, but they're fresh, well cooked and generously portioned. Just don't expect a restful evening. Tables are turned in a trice, service is perfunctory (this isn't a place to dally over the menu), and it's really noisy. Try to get a table in the vast, echoey ground floor, where blue murals stretch up to the high ceilings – it feels a bit like dining in an enormous swimming pool, but the basement is stuffier and less atmospheric. Wherever you sit, be prepared to be fed briskly and hurried on your way.

> **£8 to £20**
>
> Address 13–15 Westbourne Grove, W2
> ℡ 020 7727 5420
> Station Bayswater
> Open Mon–Thurs noon–3pm & 6–11.45pm, Fri–Sun noon–midnight
> Accepts Cash or cheque only
> ⊕ www.khansrestaurant.com

There are some tasty breads on offer. Try the nan-e-mughziat (£1.60), a coconut-flavoured affair with nuts and sultanas, or the paneer kulcha (£1.45), bulging with cottage cheese and mashed potatoes. You might also kick off with half a tandoori chicken (£2.75), which is moist and well cooked, or a creditable chicken tikka (£3.80). For main dishes, all those curry house favourites are listed here – meat madras or vindalu (£3.20), prawn biryani (£5.25), chicken chilli masala (£3.20), king prawn curry (£6.20) – and they all taste unusually fresh. Especially good is the butter chicken (£4.70), while for lovers of tikka masala dishes, the murgh tikka masala (£3.70) will appeal. There's a typical array of vegetable dishes too: bhindi (£2.70), sag aloo (£2.60) and vegetable curry (£2.60). Desserts include kulfi (£2.15), chocolate bombe (£1.60) and various ice creams – or you could try the lemon or orange delight (£1.70). A pint of lager will set you back £1.90, and there's a small selection of wines: a bottle of Chardonnay costs £8.50, or you can get a glass of house white or red for £1.60.

On an enterprising note (and strangely for a student haunt), this is one of very few curry houses that has a special children's menu. Excellent: start them young.

Mandarin Kitchen

London has its fair share of French fish restaurants, and there are famous English fish restaurants, so why does it seem odd to come across a Chinese fish restaurant? Part of the mystique of the Mandarin Kitchen is the persistent rumour that they sell more lobsters than any other restaurant in Britain. (When questioned about this myth, the management will confirm that they regularly have 100-lobster days!) This is a large restaurant, busy with waiters deftly wheeling four-foot-diameter tabletops around like giant hoops as they set up communal tables for large parties of Chinese who all seem to be eating ... lobster.

£15 to £40

Address 14–16 Queensway, W2
℗ 020 7227 9012
Station Queensway
Open Daily noon–11.30pm
Accepts All major credit cards

Whatever you fancy for the main course, start with as many of the steamed scallops on the shell with garlic soya sauce (£1.80 each) as you can afford. They're magnificent. Then decide between lobster, crab or fish. If you go for the lobster, try ordering it baked with green pepper and onion in black bean sauce (it is priced at about £15 per pound depending on the season), and be sure that you order the optional extra soft noodle (£1.20) to make a meal of it. The crab is tempting, too. Live crabs are shipped up here from the south coast, and a handsome portion of shells, lots of legs and four claws baked with ginger and spring onion is a pretty reasonable £14. Fish dishes require more thought – and an eye to the per-pound prices, which do reflect the gluts and shortages of the fish market. The menu lists "the fish we normally serve" as sea bass, Dover sole, live eels, live carp, monkfish, Chinese pomfret and yellow croaker. Sea bass comes steamed whole at £17–19 per pound, depending on season. The steamed eel with black bean sauce (£10.90) is notably rich. The monkfish (£10.90) is meaty and delicious. The squid in chilli and black bean sauce (£7.90) is good.

After seafood, the never-ending menu wanders off down a road of old favourites, and even features a number of veal dishes such as roasted veal chop with Mandarin sauce (£8.90) – so a seafood allergy is no reason for you to miss out.

Al Waha

Anissa Helou, who has written the definitive book on Lebanese cuisine, nominates Al Waha as London's best Lebanese restaurant. And after cantering through a few courses here you will probably agree with her. Lebanese restaurants are all meze-obsessed, and Al Waha is no exception. What is different, however, is the way in which the chef at Al Waha is obsessive about the main course dishes as well!

£12 to £40

Address 75 Westbourne Grove, W2
☏ 020 7229 0806
Station Bayswater/Queensway
Open Daily noon–midnight
Accepts Mastercard & Visa

When you sit down, a dish of fresh, crisp crudités will be brought to the table. It includes everything from some quartered Cos lettuce through to a whole green pepper. Get the healthy eating part over early. As always with Middle Eastern food, choosing is the problem – there are 21 cold starters and 23 hot ones. Go for a balance and insist on one that you have never had before. Hummus (£3) is good here; tabbouleh (£4.25) is heavy on the parsley; the kabees (£3) are moreish if you like the Lebanese style of heavily salted pickles; and the foul moukala (£4) is good, despite its name – broad beans with garlic, coriander and olive oil. From the hot section, try manakeish bizaatar (£4), which is a mini-bread topped with thyme, like a deluxe pizza, or maybe haliwat (£5), a dish of grilled sweetbreads with lemon juice and herbs. Or there's batata harra (£3.75), potatoes with garlic and peppers. The makanek ghanam (£5) are tiny Lebanese lamb sausages, like a very refined cocktail sausage. For main courses, grills predominate, and they are all spanking-fresh and accurately cooked. Tasty choices include shish taouk (£9), made with chicken, and samakeh harrah (£18), a whole sea bass. Star turn is kafta khashkhash (£9.50), a superb cylinder of minced lamb with parsley, garlic and tomato. Drink the good Lebanese beer or the very good Lebanese wines.

Al Waha's greatest strength is in its superb home-style dishes of the day. Monday means dajaj mahshi – stuffed chicken with rice and pine nuts. Tuesday gets you a good sheikh al mahshi, aubergines stuffed with minced lamb. Friday is kibbeh bil labn – ground lamb, and crushed wheat cooked with yoghurt. They are all priced at £9.50.

Soho

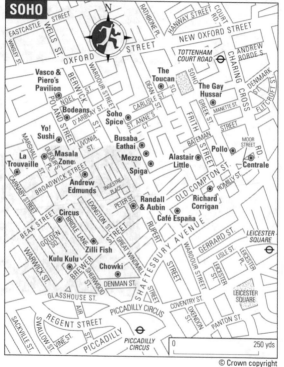

Alastair Little

Alastair Little was the chap who led us out of a world where an Italian restaurant was judged by the size of its peppermills. He was the man who showed us a new style of Mediterranean food: simple, strong flavours; fresh produce; joyful meals, and although it is a very long while since he was a full-time presence in the kitchen, the flame still burns brightly. In 2003 he finally handed over the reins to Juliet Peston, who had been behind the stoves for a variety of stints over the years. The restaurant is still called Alastair Little which in some ways is appropriate because it still serves his kind of food.

£32 to £65
Address 49 Frith St, W1
☎ 020 7734 5183
Station Leicester Square
Open Mon–Fri noon–3pm & 6–11pm, Sat 6–11pm
Accepts All major credit cards

Unlike the decor, which has stayed much the same, the menu changes twice a day. Not radically, although there may be one extra starter or main course to choose from at dinner. Pricing is simple: at lunch £29 buys you three courses; at dinner £35 gets you three courses. The wine list is a largely sub-£30-a-bottle affair, with a sprinkling of more ambitiously priced famous names. The menu runs the gamut – the charcuterie may come from Spain, and there will be French classics mixed in with resolutely Italian dishes – but everything is seasonal. So starters may include chicken broth with parsley pasta; sizzling prawns with chilli, garlic and parsley; a capon salad from Mantua; and, at something of a tangent, six native oysters with shallot vinegar and spicy Thai sausages. Or how about a spring salad with grilled field mushrooms and Parmesan crisps? The main courses are in a similar vein, and may feature dishes like spring lamb with Middle-Eastern style garnishes; or roast chicken with mash, leeks and morels. Fish dishes, such as fillets of brill, braised lettuce, mash and grain mustard sauce, are well handled. And there is always an appealing vegetarian option – perhaps ricotta ravioli with artichokes, pine nuts and rocket.

To end your meal there are splendid puds, like a café Liégeois or rhubarb, Mascarpone and hazelnut trifle – and the satisfying alternative of a plate of British cheeses with oatcakes.

Andrew Edmunds

(🍴) Andrew Edmunds' wine bar, as it is called by Soho locals, has been an institution in the area for over fifteen years – a long time when you consider how speedily so many restaurants come and go. It all started when the lease on the wine bar next door to his print gallery became vacant and he decided that, as he wanted to go on eating there himself, he should take it on. The restaurant now has a loyal band of regulars who like the

£20 to £35

Address 46 Lexington St, W1
☎ 020 7437 5708
Station Oxford Circus
Open Mon–Fri 12.30–3pm &
6–10.45pm, Sat 1–3pm &
6–10.45pm, Sun 1–3pm &
6–10.30pm
Accepts All major credit cards
except Diners

imaginative bistro-style dishes, strong flavours and bold combinations. It's cosy, dark and very crowded, a place where people wave to friends across the room.

The menu changes weekly and combines solid favourites with bright new ideas, so that regular diners can either comfort themselves with the familiar or head off into the unknown. Start with pea and mint soup (£2.95); or dressed crab (£5.50); or black pudding, caramelized apples and sour cream (£4.50). Main courses may include stalwart and straightforward dishes such as best end of lamb, with Dauphinoise, roast aubergine and tzatziki (£13.50); roast cod fillet with panzanella and tapenade (£10.75); or an impressively fresh vegetarian option like penne with peas, broad beans, broccoli, Feta and mint pesto (£7.95); then there may be moodier combinations like Cajun-spiced skate wing, roast sweet potatoes, wild garlic leaves, sweetcorn and avocado salsa (£10.75). This is very like stumbling on a neighbourhood restaurant in some affluent suburb, only you are in the very heart of Soho. Puddings include chocolate mousse cake (£3.50), the ubiquitous tiramisù (£3.50), and plum and almond tart (£4).

Wines are a passion with Andrew Edmunds. The constantly changing, broker-bought list is long and special and, because of his low mark-up policy, there are some genuine bargains. There is an additional list of halves of sweet wines, and daily special wine offers are chalked on a blackboard. Expect to pay a bit more and get much more in return. Booking, especially for the tiny upstairs dining room, is essential.

Bodeans

Bodeans opened in the spring of 2003 with the kind of pizazz you'd expect (it is the latest brainchild of one of the men who set up the first Belgo – page XXX). It's a fair old leap from Belgian mussels to American barbecue but Bodeans seems to have struck a chord and was busy from day one. Upstairs is a kind of diner/deli/sandwich shop. Downstairs is a restaurant. Only somewhere paying serious homage to Americana would have a strident tartan carpet, wall lights made to look like antelope horns and a red-painted ceiling. Even the service is American gushy and there is an authentic "commercial" ring to the place, something that you will either love or hate.

£12 to £42

Address 10 Poland St, W1
☎ 020 7287 7575
Station Piccadilly Circus
Open Mon–Sat noon–3pm &
6–11pm, Sun noon–3pm &
6–10.30pm
Accepts All major credit cards
🌐 www.bodeansbbq.com

The starters are not very impressive – smoke-fired chicken wings (£3.95) come either hot or mild and are the best of the bunch. The fire-kissed jumbo shrimps (£5.95) are neither very jumbo, nor very tender. Cut to the chase and get amongst the smoky barbecued stuff. Baby back ribs (£7.50 for a whole slab, £5.25 for a half) are considered by ribologists to be to tender and a bit of a cop-out. The pork spare ribs (£9.50 for a whole slab, 11-12 ribs; and £6.75 for a half, 5-6 ribs) are terrific. Mains come with average coleslaw and pretty good beans. Fries (£1.95) are good and crisp. The star dish is the beef back ribs (£8.50 for a whole slab, 5 ribs; and £6 for a half-slab), which are dry and chewy. Very good. There are other delicacies like Boston Butt (£6.95) a pulled pork sandwich (Yanks would have it that pulling the pork apart with a fork rather than carving it makes for a particularly satisfying chewy sandwich); and barbecued chicken (half £6.50, a quarter £4.95). But only the ribs will stick to your ribs. Puds tread the ice-cream and pie route, while to drink there is a flotilla of different Bloody Marys (all £5.50), or beer.

One of Bodeans' brave promos on opening was a terrific offer – on Saturdays and Sundays between noon and 6pm, two children could eat for free for every adult eating in the restaurant. This largesse may or may not last but it's worth enquiring.

Busaba Eathai

Busaba occupies a West End site that was once a bank – you remember the days when banks were conveniently positioned all over the place? Former customers stumbling into 106 Wardour St would be more than a little surprised by the dark, designery and implacably trendy Thai eatery that is now bedded in. One of the gents behind this new establishment is the brains behind the original Wagamama (see p.18), and regulars there will find all sorts of echoes

£8 to £22

Address 106–110 Wardour St, W1
📞 020 7255 8686
Station Piccadilly Circus
Open Mon–Thurs noon–11pm,
Fri & Sat noon-11.30pm, Sun
noon–10pm
Accepts All major credit cards
except Diners
Branches see p.488
🌐 www.busaba.com

and resonance at Busaba Eathai. There's the same share-a-table and no-bookings policy, and there's the same half-cod philosophy: "Sanuk is Busaba's living ethos. Based upon traditional Buddhist values ... " You need read no further. The place is saved by serving pretty decent Thai food at low prices, and with consummate lack of pretension. For all the fake Zen, this is a jolly and energetic restaurant and you will probably have a very good time.

Food, grouped into categories, veers towards one-pot dishes, and vegetarians are particularly well served. If you want starters you need to peruse the side dishes. Choose from such things as a good green papaya salad (£5.60); or po-pea jay (£2.90), which are vegetable spring rolls; or fishcakes (£4.20); or Thai calamari (£4.20), which are not unlike everyone else's calamari. There are curries: red ostrich curry (£9.80); green chicken curry (£6.90); green vegetable curry (£6.50); and aromatic butternut pumpkin curry (£5.70). You'll find genuine Thai veg, such as pea aubergines, sweet basil and lime leaves, although dishes do tend to be on the sweet side. Or there's phad Thai (£6.10), and yom yam chicken (£6.40). Stir-fries range from char-grilled duck in tamarind sauce with Chinese broccoli (£7.80); to ginger beef (£6.60); and char-grilled cod with lemongrass and tamarind sauce (£7.80).

The power juice phenomenon has reached Busaba. Nam polamai (£2.90) is organic, and combines carrot, apple and celery with dandelion and nettle extract. Or there's Thai San Sam whiskey (£3.50).

Café España

Situated as it is, at the heart of Soho's pink strip at the Wardour Street end of Old Compton Street, and nestled among the hard-core shops and video stores, Café España is a remarkably balanced restaurant. From the outside it looks rather small and shabby – not very prepossessing at all, in fact, and much like the more tourist-focused trattorias. But once through the door,

£10 to £20

Address 63 Old Compton St, W1
℡ 020 7494 1271
Station Piccadilly Circus
/Leicester Square
Open Mon–Sat noon–midnight, Sun noon–11pm
Accepts Mastercard and Visa

tripping over the dessert trolley, you can sense you're in for something good. You'll be greeted by a friendly maître d' and led up the stairs to join a hubbub of hungry Soho folk with a nose for a bargain.

The menu does give a nod to the trattoria, with a short list of pastas, but it is Spanish, not Italian, cooking that you should be going for here – and if you are anything less than seriously hungry, it's best to stick with the tapas. Mejillones a la marinera (£4.50) delivers enough mussels for a small main course; a portion of tortilla (£4) is the size of a saucer and is likely to be cooked especially for you; ordering the jamón serrano (£6.25) brings a decent portion at a price you'd be hard to match wholesale. For something more substantial, there's plenty of choice, mostly in the form of simple grills. Try chuletas de cordero a la brasa (£9.95) – lamb chops; higado de ternera (£8.95) – calf's liver and bacon; or rodaballo a la plancha (£12.95) – grilled turbot. Or there are the traditional Valenciana and marinera paellas (£22, to feed two), though these are slightly less exciting. Service is swift, if a little harassed. Keeping food prices this low means a rapid turnaround of custom, but the waiters are nonetheless friendly and polite. And given the number of people in the place, you can be sure that whatever you are eating is freshly prepared – the volume of ingredients they get through must be huge.

To enjoy Café España to the maximum, go mob-handed and allow yourself the luxury of running amok with the tapas selections before pouncing on the paella. But be warned – the sangria is a dark and dangerous West End concoction and really quite horrid.

Soho

Centrale

In a grid of streets full of bottom-dollar belly-fillers, Centrale stands out. It has an idiosyncratic charm beloved by its regulars. But don't be misled by its down-at-heel exterior – there's something special about sweeping through the plain glass door and sliding into one of its cracked vinyl banquettes, forced into cosy, chatty

£5 to £15

Address 16 Moor St, W1
℡ 020 7437 5513
Station Leicester Square
/Tottenham Court Rd
Open Mon–Sat noon–9.30pm
Accepts Mastercard and Visa

proximity with strangers across a narrow red Formica table. Maybe it's the small size of the place, maybe it's the crush of students, maybe it's just the cappuccino in smoked-glass cups, but Centrale is not only effortlessly friendly but also strangely glamorous. Odd, really, when this is basically a place to line your stomach with cheap pasta before going on to a pub or club.

Centrale's menu is artless – orange juice (£1) appears as a starter – and the portions are substantial. Appetizers include home-made minestrone (£2.25), salami (£3.75), and pastina in brodo (£2.25) – short pasta snippets in a clear, slightly oily soup. There's a fair spread of diner staples to follow, including pork chop (£4.75) and fried scampi (£4.75), each partnered by an inevitable sprinkling of chips, but the main event here is the pasta. The Bolognese dishes – spaghetti, tagliatelle, rigatoni and ravioli (all £3.75) – are equally dependable, adequately spicy and chewily meaty, as is the lasagne al forno (£4.25). The "specials" include spaghetti vongole (£4.50), and rigatoni Alfredo (£4.25) – a pungent swirl of cream, mushrooms, cheese, tomato and lots and lots of garlic. Rather than a small salad (£1.75), a side order of spinach (£2.25) adds something green to the solid bulk of the pasta.

The menu gives up a bit when it comes to dessert, sticking to just three old favourites: banana split (£1.75), apple pie (£1.75) and ice cream (£1.50), the last being a tripartite scoop of chocolate, strawberry and vanilla. Still, you're not here for puds. You're here for a fix of cheap food – and cheap wine. There's no licence, so you can bring your own bottle for 50p corkage (£1 for a big bottle), from the off-licences just around the corner in Old Compton Street.

Chowki

Chowki is chef Kuldeep Singh's first venture after the runaway success of Mela (see p.43), and it opened in July 2002 to immediate acclaim. This is a large, cheap restaurant serving authentic home-style food in stylish surroundings. The menu changes every month in order

£9 to £25
Address 2–3 Denman St, W1
☎ 020 7439 1330
Station Piccadilly Circus
Open Daily noon–midnight
Accepts All major credit cards

to feature three different regions of India. Thus one month would feature Kashmir, Chettinad and Bengal, then it might be all change to the Gujerat, Goa and Hyderabad for another. During a whole year Chowki showcases 36 different regional styles of food! All the dishes come with accompaniments, they are all authentic, and they are stunning value. Chowki has 120 seats spread across three dining areas, but you'll still probably have to wait for a table at peak times. Cheer up – like Mela, this place is astonishingly good value.

There are three or four starters and three or four mains from each region. When the menu showcased the cuisine of Kashmir, Chettinad and Bengal, starters included epic kabarga lamb chops from Kashmir (£4.25); a dish of spicy lamb liver from Chettinad (£3.25); and "curls" of tiger prawn from Bengal and cooked on the grill (£4.25). This would be a very good standard of cooking at three times the price. Mains follow the lead and come with an appropriate vegetable and the correct rice or bread. From Kashmir comes a classic lamb curry (£8.95). From Chettinad there's a dish of chicken cooked in creamed poppy seeds (£8.50). From Bengal there is a dish made from chunks of tilapia simmered with doodhi vegetables (£8.50). All the dishes have the unmistakable stamp of homely cooking – rich, simple, appetizing flavours. Service is friendly, and this is a comfortable, modern place. Finding anywhere this good – and this cheap – within earshot of Piccadilly Circus is little short of miraculous.

Go for the "regional feast": £10.95 buys you a complete meal, which turns out to be all three main courses plus the side dishes from a particular region. So if you and two companions each ordered a different "feast", your table would get to try the entire menu!

Soho

Circus

When it opened towards the end of the 1990s, Circus was everything a fashionable fin-de-siècle restaurant should be. The decor was cool shades of black and white, there was a de rigueur members' bar downstairs, open till late, and there were spiky "statement" flower arrangements. The service was efficient and good-looking, and the food was very much of the moment. It took little time for Circus to become a destination restaurant for media and design professionals. A few years and several trends later, Circus has proved that it can stand the test of time. It still has the attributes with which it started, it's still pulling the punters in, and it maintains a gloss of confidence that rubs off on its customers.

£16 to £60

Address 1 Upper James St, W1
℡ 020 7534 4000
Station Oxford Circus
Open Mon–Fri noon-3pm &
5.45pm–midnight, Sat
5.45pm–midnight
Accepts All major credit cards
🌐 www.circusbar.co.uk

The menu works hard to offer something for everyone. Tucked in alongside the pan-fried risotto with smoked haddock and soft poached egg (£6.80), and grilled aubergine and red pepper with aged Feta (£6.80), you'll find starters as diverse as spring onion and potato soup (£5.50) – for those spies coming in from the cold – or 30g of Beluga caviar with trimmings (£60). Main courses offer the traditional – roast rump of lamb with bubble and squeak (£16.80), rib-eye steak with mash and chasseur sauce (£18.30) – as well as more modern dishes such as fried squid with tamarind (£13.30). Everything about this place suggests that whatever you choose will be well executed and pleasing to the eye. The kitchen is obviously at ease, cooking good-quality ingredients properly and with predictable results. This being an expense-account eatery ideal for business lunches and dinners, desserts are often skipped. Which is a shame, as the pastry chefs obviously delight in flights of fancy – pear en croûte with spiced ice cream.

Be aware that the sometimes ambitiously priced wine list can further inflate an already not inexpensive dinner bill, but a meal at Circus needn't always be a costly affair. There's a competitively priced set lunch (£12.50 for two courses, £15 for three) available all week, and also as a pre- and post-theatre offer – 5.45pm to 7.15pm and 10.30pm to midnight.

The Gay Hussar

As you walk in off the street, the ground-floor dining room of The Gay Hussar stretches before you: there are banquettes, there are waiters in dinner jackets, there is panelling and the walls are covered with political caricatures. "Aha!" the knowledgeable restaurant-goer murmurs. "How very retro – some fashionable designer has replicated an entire 1950s restaurant dining room." Not so. Granted, it has been spruced up, and the room is clean, neat and comfortable, but The Gay Hussar is the real thing, right down to the faded photo of a naked Christine Keeler.

£16 to £60

Address 2 Greek St, W1
☎020 7437 0973
Station Tottenham Court Rd
Open Mon–Sat 12.30–2.30pm &
5.30–10.45pm
Accepts All major credit cards
ⓦ www.gayhussar.co.uk

Perhaps the politicos like the food, which is solid, dependable, comfortable and tasty. It's also good value: at lunch there is a prix fixe of two courses for £15.50, and three for £18.50. In the evening, dishes get a trifle more complicated. Starters include a fish terrine with beetroot sauce and cucumber salad (£4.90); and hási pástétom (£3.90) – a fine goose and pork pâté; but the most famous (a house speciality that has featured in various novels) is the chilled wild cherry soup (£3.80), which is like a thin, bitterish, sourish yoghurt and is rather good. Main courses are blockbusters. Try the hortobagyi palacsinta (£13.50), a pancake filled with a finely chopped veal goulash and then sealed, deep-fried and served with creamed spinach. Very tasty. Or there are fish dumplings (£11.50), which are served with rice and a creamy dill sauce. Or there's cigány gyors tal (£13.75), billed as a Gypsy fry-up of pork and peppers. The food here is tasty and filling, and best eaten in the chill of winter. Puds are also fierce: poppy-seed strudel comes with vanilla ice cream (£4.50); options like chestnut puree (£4.50) have real substance. The home-made liptoi (£3.50), a savoury amalgam of cream cheese, herbs, paprika and a whiff of onion, is very good.

The wine list is gently priced. Try the good, dry Hungarian whites like the Castle Island Furmint (£14.50). Pudding wine aficionados should sample Tokaji – which, according to Maria Theresa, is both "the king of wines and wine of kings".

Kulu Kulu

Kulu Kulu is a conveyor-belt sushi restaurant that pulls off the unlikely trick of serving good sushi without being impersonal or intimidating. It is light and airy and there are enough coat hooks for a small army of diners. The only thing you might quibble over is the rather low stools, which are so heavy they feel fixed to the floor – anyone over six feet tall will find themselves dining in the tuck position favoured by divers and trampolinists. The atmosphere is Japanese utilitarian. In front of you is a plastic tub of gari (the rather delicious pickled ginger), a bottle of soy and a small box containing disposable wooden chopsticks. After that, as they say at bingo, it's eyes down, look in, and on with the game.

> **£12 to £30**
>
> Address 76 Brewer St, W1
> ☎ 020 7734 7316
> Station Piccadilly Circus
> Open Mon–Fri noon–2.30pm &
> 5–10pm, Sat noon–3.45pm &
> 5–10pm
> Accepts Mastercard, Switch
> and Visa

The plates come round on the kaiten, or conveyor, and are coded by design rather than colour, which could prove deceptive: A plates cost £1.20, B plates are £1.80, C plates are £2.40, and D plates £3. All the usual sushi favourites are here, and the fish is particularly fresh and well presented. Maguri, or tuna, is a B; Amaebi, or sweet shrimp, is a C; Hotategai, or scallops, is a C, and very sweet indeed. Futomaki, a Californian, cone-shaped roll with tuna, is a B. The Ds tend to be ritzier fishes such as belly tuna. The eye-watering wasabi factor, however, is a bit hit-or-miss. Just as you're wishing for a bit more wasabi, you bite into something that makes you long for a bit less. As well as the sushi, the conveyor parades some little bowls of hot dishes. One worth looking out for combines strips of fried fish skin with a savoury vegetable puree. It counts as an A, as does the bowl of miso soup. To drink there is everything from Oolong tea (£1.50) to Kirin beer (£2.60).

Kulu Kulu also offers a range of set options, which represent excellent value and take the strain off keeping your eye fixed on the conveyor belt. They include mixed sashimi (£10) and mixed tempura (£8.60). Look behind the bar and you may see a stack of cardboard cases containing sake supplies. It is strange but true that one of the premium sakes is made in the Rocky Mountains!

Masala Zone

Masala Zone is impossible to pigeonhole. The food is Indian, but modern Indian, with a commendable emphasis on healthy eating – as would be the norm in India, there's a long list of attractive vegetarian options. The dining room is smart and large, but the prices are low. There are fast-food dishes on the menu, but they tend to be the roadside snacks of Bombay. The play-list was put together by one of India's top club DJs. In all, this is an informal, stylish and friendly place, serving food that is simple and delicious.

£6 to £18

Address 9 Marshall St, W1
℡ 020 7287 9966
Station Oxford Circus/
Piccadilly Circus
Open Mon-Fri noon–2.30pm &
5.30–11pm, Sat 12.30–2.30pm &
5.30–11pm, Sun 12.30–2.30pm &
5.30–10.30pm
Accepts Mastercard and Visa
Branches see p.489

INDIAN

The gentle informality extends to the menu, which begins with small plates of street food (most around £2.75). There are sev puris, dahi puris, samosas, a particularly fine aloo tikki chaat, and tokir chaat – an amazing potato basket filled with veg, salad and fruit. Pick several dishes and graze your way along – at these prices it doesn't matter if there's the occasional miss amongst the hits. At lunch there are splendid Indian sandwiches, including a giant masala chicken burger (£4.75) and a Bombay layered-vegetable grilled sandwich (£3.50). There are also half a dozen curries that are well balanced and richly flavoured – served simply, with rice, they cost between £5 and £6.75. But you should move straight on to the thalis, which are the authentic option. At Masala Zone these are steel trays with seven or eight little bowls containing a vegetarian snack (to whet the appetite), a curry, lentils, a root vegetable, a green vegetable, yoghurt, bread, rice and pickles. You just choose the base curry and a complete, balanced meal arrives at table. Choose from chicken thali (£8.75), lamb thali (£9.25), prawn thali (£9.25), or vegetarian thali (£7.75).

The wall decorations are striking. After the surface had been rendered with a close approximation to mud, two tribal artists were flown in to do the painting. The mural depicts their people's history from hunters, to gatherers, to farmers selling to the cities. The artists have also featured their trip to London – look out for the stretch limo, which impressed them quite as much as Buckingham Palace.

Pollo

ITALIAN

You won't find haute cuisine at Pollo, but you do get great value for money. As at its neighbouring rival, Centrale (see p.122), this is comfort food, Latin-style – long on carbohydrate and short on frills. Sophistication is in short supply, too – the interior design begins and ends with the lino floors and tatty

£5 to £16
Address 20 Old Compton St, W1
☎ 020 7734 5917
Station Leicester Square
Open Daily noon–midnight
Accepts Cash or cheque only

pictures. But no matter: devotees return time and again for the cheap platefuls of food and the friendly, prompt service. Diners are shoehorned into booths presided over by a formidable Italian mama who tips you the wink as to what you should order. Downstairs there's more space, but you still might end up sharing a table.

The spotlight of Pollo's lengthy menu falls on cheap, filling pasta in all its permutations. Tagliatelle, rigatoni, ravioli, pappardelle, tortelloni and fusilli are all available. Your choice is basically down to the pasta type, as most of them are offered with the same selection of sauces. The tortelloni salvia (£3.80), which comes with a wonderfully sagey butter sauce, is very good, as is the tagliatelle melanzana (£3.60), whose rich tomato sauce is boosted by melt-in-the-mouth aubergine. Meat courses are less successful: anchovies, for instance, are few and far between in the bistecca alla pizzaiola (£6) – steak in capers and anchovy sauce. But vegetarians are very well catered for here. Meat-free highlights include spaghetti aglio, olio e peperoncino (£3.50), a hot mix of garlic, olive oil and chilli. Meanwhile, a hearty plateful of gnocchi (£3.80) would curb even the most flamboyant appetite. Then there are pizzas – perhaps not the elegant, wood-fired-oven type that are all the rage, but solid and substantial nonetheless, like the Regina (£4.10), which is a hammy, cheesy, mushroomy kind of experience. There is even a selection of risotti (all £3.70) to choose from. A bottle of house wine is a bargain at £7.45; and so are the puddings, at £1.60. After a substantial hit of pasta, the imposing portion of tiramisù is a challenge for even the greediest.

As if Pollo wasn't cheap enough as it is, it offers the same menu as takeaway, on which all the pasta dishes cost just £3.

Randall & Aubin

Formerly a butcher's, Randall & Aubin was recast as a sharp restaurant – as its seafood counter and champagne buckets groaning with flowers suggest – but it's also a rotisserie, sandwich shop and charcuterie to boot. It's the oysters that draw you in, along with the 1900s shop decor. The original white tiles have been cleverly

£12 to £40

Address 18 Brewer St, W1
℡ 020 7287 4447
Station Piccadilly Circus
Open Mon–Sat noon–11pm, Sun 4–10.30pm
Accepts All major credit cards
Branches see p.489

adapted with touches of the French and American diner. But that's part of the plan – Randall's serves good food speedily to folk without a lot of time. In summer, the huge sash windows are opened up, making this a wonderfully airy place to eat, especially if you grab a seat by the window.

There's an extensive menu. An eclectic choice of starters roams the globe, with soupe de poisson (£3.90), Japanese fishcakes (£5.95), and salt and pepper squid with fresh coriander and teriyaki dressing (£7.85). Main courses range from "original" Caesar salad (£6.85), spit-roast herb chicken (£10.50), and sausage with butter-bean mash and onion gravy (£10.50), to organic sirloin steak with pommes frites (£12.85) – sauce Béarnaise £1 extra. There are also some interesting sides, such as gratin Dauphinoise (£2.85), or zucchini frites with basil mayonnaise (£3.95). If you don't mind crowds, drop in at lunchtime for a hot filled baguette (£6.70 to 7.85). How about a lamb souvlaki, tzatziki and salad baguette (£7.85)? Also available in the evening, the baguettes provide an inexpensive yet satisfying meal. The list of fruits de mer offers well-priced seafood, ranging from a whole dressed crab (£11.50), through grilled lobster, garlic butter and pommes frites (half £12.50, whole £20) to "the works" (£26 per head, minimum two people). Puddings all cost £4.50 and range from tarts and brûlées to the more adventurous pear and caramel galette, or chocolate truffle cake. Many dishes are also on the inexpensive takeaway menu, which makes for exciting picnicking.

Hard-core traditionalists with a penchant for chewing gobbets of resilient rubber which taste remarkably like the aroma of pumped-out bilge water will relish the fresh whelks with lemon and vinegar (£8.50).

Richard Corrigan at The Lindsay House

Even among chefs – not usually held to be overly calm and level-headed people – Richard Corrigan is regarded as something of a wild man. He arrived at this deservedly Michelin-starred restaurant in Soho via a spell bringing haute cuisine to a dog track in the East End, but at The Lindsay House he seems to have found his niche. The

£30 to £120

Address 21 Romilly St, W1
℡ 020 7439 0450
Station Leicester Square
Open Main Mon–Fri noon–2.30pm & 6–11pm, Sat 6–11pm
Accepts All major credit cards

restaurant is split into a series of small rooms, the service is attentive, and the food is very good indeed. The menus are uncomplicated and change regularly to keep in step with what is available at the market. Dinner means a choice of seven starters, seven main courses and seven puddings, and costs £48, while at lunch the line-up is smaller, as is the price – a real bargain at £23 for three courses. There is also an epic seven-course tasting menu for £56.

Only a fool would try to predict what dishes Richard Corrigan will have on his menu tomorrow, but you can be sure that they will combine unusual flavours with verve and style. Starters surprise – creamed risotto of cauliflower and pancetta – or are lusciously opulent – tart of foie gras, sautéed foie gras and Muscat grape. Or there are combinations that seem familiar but come with a twist, like globe artichoke, Cornish crab and parsley dressing. Main courses follow the same ground rules (or lack of them!), so you might be offered a poached ballotine of sea bass, pickled cabbage and oysters; or scallops with pork belly and spiced carrots. On a more classical note, roast breast of duck, confit leg, caramelized shallots. The puddings soar towards dessert lover's heaven with such delights as Seville orange tart with chocolate soufflé and buttermilk sorbet; marinated pineapple with coconut sorbet, ginger and lime. The wine list is extensive and expensive.

If there is one thing that marks out the cuisine at the Lindsay House, it is Corrigan's love affair with offal. Sweetbreads, kidneys and tongue all find their way onto the menu, in dishes that perfectly illustrate his deft touch with hearty ingredients.

Soho Spice

Soho Spice is the new face of Indian restaurants. It's large – seating 100 in the restaurant and 40 in the bar – and takes bookings only for parties of six or more. It's busy, with loud music and late opening at the weekends, the decor is based around a riot of colour, and it is very, very successful, which must be mainly down to food that is a large step away from curry house staples. The main menu features contemporary Indian cuisine. What's more, when you order a main course it comes on a thali – with pulao rice, naan, dhal and vegetables of the day – which makes ordering simple and paying less painful.

> **£10 to £28**
>
> Address 124–126 Wardour St, W1
> ☎ 020 7434 0808
> Station Piccadilly Circus
> Open Mon–Thurs
> 11.30am–midnight, Fri & Sat
> 11.30am–12.30am, Sun
> 12.30–10.30pm
> Accepts All major credit cards
> ⓦ www.sohospice.co.uk

On the main menu, starters include seekh kebab (£3.95); achari malai tikka (£3.95) – tikka made with pickling spices; masala jhinga (£4.95), which is a dish of marinated deep-fried prawns; sunhara samosas (£3.50), which are made with chicken or aloo matar tikki (£3.25), which is a sort of super potato cake. Main courses represent good value, given their accompaniments. Good choices are the hara murgh ka tikka (£9.95) – which is made with chicken and green herbs and chillies; and khara masala murgh (£9.95) – chicken, whole spices and tomatoes. Or how about adrakh ke panjai (£12.95) – a dish of spiced lamb chops? Gentler palates will enjoy the tandoori machli (£12.50) – fresh salmon, marinated and cooked in the tandoor. Desserts offer mango or pistachio kulfis (£2.95) – Indian ice creams made with boiled milk – and that sweetest of comfort foods, gulab jamun (£2.95), which is a dumpling soaked in rose syrup.

The special regional menu, called "Seasonal Colour", offers three courses plus tea or coffee for £16.95 and changes every month – so it may be recipes from Rajasthan or dishes from Bengal. For example, when the chosen region was the North West Frontier there were starters like gilafi kebab – lamb dumplings with pearl onions and button mushrooms. Mains included the celebrated murg malai Peshwari – a kebab of chicken breast and cheese; and Kandhari pasanda – lamb with onions, tomatoes, almonds and saffron.

Spiga

(⏺) Spiga has an impeccable pedigree. It comes from the same stable as Aubergine (see p.403), L'Oranger (see p.103) and Zafferano, and has that piece of kit which has long identified any Italian restaurant as serious – a wood-fired oven. But despite its credentials you don't need to pay a king's ransom to eat here, nor do you have to dress up. This is a pleasantly casual affair. The atmosphere is lively – sometimes the music is too lively – and the look is cool. Spiga may have cut the prices but they haven't cut corners – the tableware is the latest in Italian chic.

£14 to £30

Address 84–86 Wardour St, W1
(☎) 020 7734 3444
Station Leicester Square
Open Mon, Tues and Sun noon–3pm
& 6–11pm, Wed–Sat noon–3pm
6pm–midnight
Accepts All major credit cards
Branches see p.490

Menus change monthly, with occasional daily specials, but there's a definite pattern. Starters will get you in the mood. The buffalo Mozzarella (£6.50/£9) is served with fresh tomatoes and basil. Or try something like the carpaccio con indivia e Parmigiano (£7.50/£9.50). But the home-made pasta course is where it's really at. What's good is that, like the starters, most pasta dishes come in large or small portions. Think Italian and enjoy an extra course, such as gnocchi di patate al caprino (£7/£9), or tagliatelle capesante e zucchine (£7.50/£9.50), the pasta served with scallops and courgettes in a saffron cream sauce; or spaghetti pomodoro fresco e basilico (£6/£8) – spaghetti with a fresh tomato sauce. Then consider a pizza – thin crust, crispy and the size of a dustbin lid. Pizza buffala (£9.50) is rich with genuine Mozzarella; pizza pancetta e caprino (£9.50) is topped with goat's cheese and cured ham; pizza montello (£9) comes with Mozzarella and pancetta. Alternatively, main courses offer up char-grilled and pan-fried dishes: filetto d'orata al balsamico di Modena (£14) teams pan-fried sea bream with a dressing of balsamic vinegar; while palliard di pollo con patate e spinaci (£12.50) is a simple but good char-grilled chicken breast. If you aren't already full, the pudding section is well worth a look, too. Highlights include a wickedly indulgent lemon and mascarpone tart (£6) and an excellent tiramisù (£6).

Full marks to the person who can identify the weird loofah-like objects hanging on the walls.

The Toucan

(🍴) When they opened The Toucan the proprietors' first priority was to approach Guinness and ask if they could retail the black stuff. They explained that they wanted to open a small bar aimed single-mindedly at the drinking public, just like the ones they had enjoyed so much in Dublin. Guinness replied that, providing they could shift two barrels a week, they'd be happy to put them on

£8 to £15

Address 19 Carlisle St, W1
℡ 020 7437 4123
Station Leicester Square/
Tottenham Court Road
Open Mon-Sat 11am-11pm
Accepts All major credit cards
Branches see p.491
ⓦ www.thetoucan.co.uk

the list. Neither party imagined that the regular order would end up at more like thirty barrels a week! It's an impressive intake, but then The Toucan is an impressive place, serving home-made, very cheap, very wholesome and very filling food, along with all that Guinness.

Start with six Rossmore Irish oysters (£5), or the vegetable soup with bread (£2). Go on to a large bowl of Irish stew with bread (£5), or Guinness pie and champ (£6) – champ is a kind of supercharged Irish mashed potato with best butter playing a leading role alongside the spring onions. It features in a couple of novelty items – you can have chilli and champ (£5), or garlic mushrooms and champ (£3). And just when you think you have the measure of the place, there's Thai chicken curry and rice (£5.50). The JPs (jacket potatoes, from £3.50) come with various fillings, and there's an array of sandwiches. There's also a great-value smoked salmon salad plate (£6.50). One thing to bear in mind if you've come here hungry is that there are times when The Toucan becomes so packed with people that you can scarcely lift a pint. At those times, all attempts at serving food are abandoned.

Of course, if things have got out of hand, you could spend a happy evening at The Toucan without actually eating. As some Irish sage once remarked, "There's eating and drinking in a pint of Guinness." And if it's a chaser you're after, then be aware that The Toucan also makes a feature of Irish whiskeys, including some exotic and stratospherically expensive Tullamore Dews – 38-, 41- and 42-year-olds. If you have to ask how much it costs, you cannot afford it.

La Trouvaille

VERY FRENCH

Think back to those stalwart English archers who won the famous victories at Agincourt and Crècy. Unfortunately, those away wins were forgotten within a couple of hundred years, and ever since the French have got their own back and given England a bit of a culinary drubbing. Food-wise, French haute cuisine has topped the European Champions League for about a century, and,

£20 to £50
Address 12a Newburgh St, W1
☏ 020 7287 8488
Station Oxford Circus
Open Mon–Fri noon–3pm & 6–10.30pm, Sat 6–10.30pm
Accepts All major credit cards
Branches see p.491

although the English may resent such total dominance, there is a particular kind of French eatery they still adore. At La Trouvaille the proprietors understand the English need for really French Frenchness; they even know that they should provide one or two dishes that are a step too authentic for most Brits. They know that waiters who would be considered too over-the-top for *Allo, Allo* are admired here. They know that their clientele want good food at a price that doesn't break the bank.

The set lunch is £16.95 for two courses and £19.75 for three courses – very good value for this quality of cooking. Starters may include a cardoon and potato soup, or artichoke vinaigrette, which comes with an improbably large artichoke that is all the better for simple presentation. Grilled salsify comes with a herb aioli. Main courses stay in character: boudin blanc with Périgueux sauce; roast pigeon with figs. If you hanker after a "dangerously French" dish, try the andouillette sauce moutarde de Brive - this is a pungent chitterling sausage served with purple mustard. Someone in the kitchen has a truly French respect for the integrity of ingredients. So pick bavette frites, sauce Béarnaise and then revel in excellent Aberdeen Angus beef.

When considering the puds – choccy mousse, crème brûlée, roast pears – divert to the weekly cheese plate, which is outstandingly good. Three cheeses – perhaps a chunk of melting Livarot, a wedge of waxy Brebis, and a richly blued Fourme d'Ambert – plus a little pot of truffled honey. Anyone who hasn't tried that last speciality should do so immediately, it is stunning – a wipe-your-finger-round-the-bowl-unashamedly experience.

Vasco and Piero's Pavilion

🍴 Very much a family-run restaurant, the Pavilion has been a Soho fixture for the past twenty years. But there's nothing old or institutional about the cooking or decor. Vasco himself cooks for his regulars, and the establishment has long been a favourite with diners who appreciate his food, which is fairly simple but made with top-class ingredients.

£16 to £35

Address 15 Poland St, W1
☎ 020 7437 8774
Station Oxford Circus
Open Mon–Fri noon–3pm & 6–11pm, Sat 7–11pm
Accepts All major credit cards
🌐 www.vascosfood.com

Dishes are biased towards Umbrian cuisine. Customers include the great and the good, and the Pavilion's modern yet comfortable atmosphere guarantees them anonymity.

There's only an à la carte menu at lunch (plus a two-course "light menu" which doubles as pre-theatre and costs £14.50), but in the evening the basic deal is that you choose either two courses for £19.50 or three for £23.50. Given the quality, freshness of ingredients and attention to detail, this proves exceptional value. Starters may include roast beetroot, tomato, eggs and anchovies. Or there may be a simple bruschetta with garlic, tomato and basil. Duck salad, mixed leaves and mostarda di Cremona is plate-wipingly good, with the duck shreds crispy yet moist. Pastas, all home-made, are excellent, too, particularly the tagliolini with king prawns and zucchini – perfectly cooked and with a sauce that is prepared from fresh ingredients and tastes like it. Or a risotto with black truffles? Simple is good. For carnivores, however, there is nothing to beat the calf's liver with fresh sage – paper-thin liver that literally melts in the mouth. Piscivores should turn to the scallopine of swordfish with garlic, parsley and cannellini beans; or sautéed monkfish with saffron and lentils.

Puddings continue the theme – they are simple and top-quality. A panna cotta is gelatinously creamy, a praline semi-freddo is rich and soft as well as being crunchy, and a torta della nonna reveals buttery sponge pastry and custard, flavours that remind you of bread and butter pudding and ambrosia. There is a good selection of the less usual Italian wines, as well as some good Italian pudding wines.

Yo!Sushi

(icon) When Yo!Sushi burst upon the scene it was to fanfares and a tidal wave of publicity. This was an event beyond just another kaiten (conveyor-belt) sushi bar. Robotic sushi-makers, robotic drinks trolleys, video screens – and not many restaurants credit "sponsors" like ANA, Sony and Honda. In among all this there is even some food and, while purists may shudder, it's more consistent than the hype would have you suspect.

£8 to £25

Address 52 Poland St, W1
☎ 020 7287 0443
Station Oxford Circus/
Piccadilly Circus
Open Daily noon–midnight
Accepts All major credit cards
Branches see p.491
⊕ www.yosushi.co.uk

Plates are marked in lime (£1.50), blue (£2), purple (£2.50), orange (£3) and pink (£3.50). When satiated you call for a plate count, and your bill is prepared. You sit at the counter with a little waiters' station in front of you – there's gari (pickled ginger), soy and wasabi, plus some little dishes and a forest of wooden chopsticks. Kirin beer costs £3, a small warm sake £3, and unlimited Japanese tea is £1. You're ready to begin. Yo!Sushi claim to serve more than 100 sushi, so be leisurely and watch the belt – and, if in doubt, ask. The sushi range from pickled mushroom and avocado (both £1.50); through salmon, crabstick and avocado (£2); and tuna, grey mullet and salmon skin (£3); and so on up to yellowtail and fatty tuna – which carry the warning that they are "as available" and a pink price tag of £3.50. There are about 20 different maki rolls (with vegetarians well catered for), at all prices. The 10 different sashimi and five different gunkan all command the higher orange and pink prices. As do the isorolls – which are bound with nori and can provide some pretty advanced combinations such as teriyaki chicken and enoki mushroom. It's always worth asking the server what hot dishes are available as they vary from day to day. Dining at Yo!Sushi does call for some restraint and deft mental arithmetic, as the tower of brightly badged empty plates building up in front of you can end up costing more than you expected.

Yo!Sushi is at the forefront of restaurant merchandising and no age group is safe. There are Yo!Sushi T-shirts, books, and even babygros. Even a badged mouse mat has been sighted.

Zilli Fish

Bright, brittle and brash, Zilli Fish is a part of Aldo Zilli's growing empire. You can see into the surprisingly calm kitchen through a large window as you walk along Brewer Street. Inside, in a hectic atmosphere, the restaurant serves a modern Italianate fish menu to London's media workers and the rest of the young Soho crowd. Tables are close

£25 to £60

Address 36-40 Brewer St, W1
℡ 020 7734 8649
Station Piccadilly Circus
Open Mon–Sat noon–11pm
Accepts All major credit cards
Branches see p.492
℗ www.zillialdo.com

ITALIAN/FISH

and everything is conducted at a racy pace. Not ideal for a secret conversation or for plighting your troth, unless you want the whole place to cheer you on.

The starters here are an attractive bunch: pan-fried squid with Thai sauce (£8.90); Dolcelatte, pear and walnut salad with croutons (£7); mussels arrabbiata with bruschetta (£7.50). Then after some pasta dishes the menu goes on to feature a modestly entitled section, "What we are famous for". These are dishes like traditional deep-fried cod, chips and tartare sauce (£15.90); spaghettini with whole fresh lobster (£25); and wild salmon stuffed with crab and spinach, and steamed in ginger and soya (£18.50). Or baked sea bass fillet (£18), wrapped in banana leaf and cooked with cherry tomatoes, ginger, garlic, basil, olive oil and lemon dressing. From the side orders the rocket, Parmesan and roast tomato salad (£4) is a winning combination of flavours. While the list is dominated by fishy favourites, in keeping with the name, there are some modern Italian vegetarian and meat options as well, including a mixed wild mushroom, courgette and Mascarpone risotto (£12.50), and plain grilled chicken breast served with a Caesar salad (£13). Puddings (all £6.50) include a Ricotta and amarena cherry tart with cherry coulis; a home-made tiramisù with Pavesini; and, rather incongruously, a fried banana spring roll with white chocolate ice cream.

Aldo Zilli has built up a reputation in Soho that guarantees that his bar and restaurants are almost always packed. Zilli Fish offers good food, but also good fun. In keeping with so many restaurants nowadays, Signor Zilli is quite happy to give away his secrets, so signed copies of his latest book are always available in the restaurant.

South Kensington

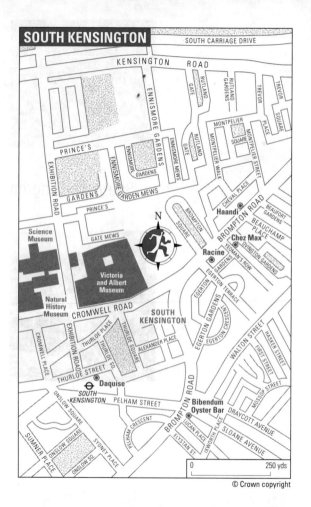

Bibendum Oyster Bar

🍴 Bibendum Oyster Bar is one of the nicest places to eat shellfish in London. The 1911 building, a glorious tiled affair that was a former garage for the French tyre people, is Conranized throughout, but the oyster bar is in what looks like the old ground-floor workshop, and they've done precious little to it. On the forecourt stand two camionettes: one

£12 to £30

Address Michelin House, 81 Fulham Road, SW3
℡ 020 7589 1480
Station South Kensington
Open Mon–Sat noon–10.30pm, Sun noon–10pm
Accepts All major credit cards
🌐 www.bibendum.co.uk

SEAFOOD

a shellfish stall, selling lobsters, oysters and crabs to the Chelsea set; the other a flower stall, with lilies, ginger flowers and roses rather than carnations. Quaint, but very attractive, adding a much-needed initial splash of colour which stays with you in the plain oyster bar, with its cream walls, marble tables and stone floor.

The menu is a shellfish lover's heaven. Here you'll find three different types of rock oyster (£7.50–9.50 per half-dozen) – you can choose your favourite or order a selection to find out the difference. The crab mayonnaise (£9) comes in the shell, giving you the enormous fun of pulling it apart and digging through the claws. Or you can have it done for you in a crab salad (£9.50) – probably just as good, but not nearly so satisfying. If you're really hungry, there's a particularly fine plateau de fruits de mer (£28.50 per head, minimum two people), which has everything: crab, clams, langoustines, oysters, prawns and shrimps, as well as winkles and whelks. There is plenty of choice for those allergic to claw-crushers, though surprisingly there is practically nothing that uses crustacea in hot dishes. Instead there are simple combinations such as lemon chicken with chickpeas (£12.80), and devilled mackerel with spiced cucumber salad (£10). The daily-changing set menu follows suit – smoked haddock and leek tart with green salad (£10); rump of lamb with vegetable chutney and herb oil (£12.50). Desserts are simple and seasonal – raspberries and Jersey cream (£5.50); cheese (£5.50); and the inevitable crème brûlée (£5.50).

Given the nature of the place, there's a sensible wine list, mostly given over to white wine and champagne, with a decent smattering of half-bottles and wines by the glass.

South Kensington

Chez Max

The Max whose name appears over the door of this establishment (latest revamp late 2002) is Max Renzland, who was previously at the helm of a similarly eponymous restaurant in Hampton, Middlesex. On his return to smarter postcodes, Max has thrown in his lot with Marco Pierre White and this is the first of what is planned as a chainlet of Chez Max establishments. The basement room

£15 to £65

Address 3 Yeoman's Row, SW3
℡ 020 7590 9999
Station Knightsbridge/South
Kensington
Open Mon–Sat noon–3pm &
6–11pm, Sun noon–3.30pm &
6–10.30pm
Accepts All major credit cards

looks the part and oozes bourgeois Frenchness from every pore – bistro glass screens between tables, plenty of dark-red paint and old French posters, tiled floor. The menu is more "classic French Brasserie" than you'll find in most Parisian classic French brasseries, and the whole place has a pleasantly old-fashioned feel to it: Chez Max is more Elizabeth David than Alain Ducasse.

The menu opens with what should be seen as Max's signature dish – Cantabrian salted anchovies, shallot, butter, pain Poilaine (Les Entrées are all £6.50). There's also a salad Lyonnaise; snails with garlic butter; boudin blanc fermier, with Puy lentils, wild mushrooms, sauce charcutière; roast crottin de Chavignol. Les plats come in at three price levels: £12.50 gets you a charcoal-grilled Aberdeen Angus rib-eye with beurre maître d'hotel; or feuillette of wild mushrooms; or calf's liver, onions, bacon sauce diable. Spring for £14.50 and you can have a slow-roast lacquered "Bresse" duck with orange sauce – very good, well-judged roast duck with crisp skin and piquant orange sauce. Spend £18.50 and enjoy sole meunière, pommes vapeur. Side dishes are sound – gratin dauphinois (£2). Puds are resolutely old style – rhum baba; crème brûlée; pot au chocolat; good cheese (all at £4.50). Service is Gallic and efficient. The wine list has suitably French strengths.

The "menu Petit Max" is good value – choosing three courses for £16.50: perhaps smoked morteau, warm potato salad, mustard vinaigrette; saucisson à l'ail fermier, Puy lentils, pomme pûrée; and then baba au rhum goes a long way towards restoring your faith in French food.

Daquise

Daquise is more old-fashioned than you could possibly imagine. High ceilings, murky lighting, oilcloth table covers, charming service, elderly customers – the full monty. During the day it serves coffee, tea and rather good cakes to all-comers, breaking off at lunchtime and in the evening to dispense Polish home cooking, Tatra Zwiecka beer, and shot glasses of various vodkas. Several novels have been completed here by penniless writers seeking somewhere warm to scribble – buying a cup of coffee gets you a full ration of patience from the management; all you need supply is a little inspiration. The food is genuine here, and does evolve, albeit at a glacial pace. Regulars were shocked when the magnificent "herrings with potato" became the almost-as-good "herrings with bread". Portions are serious here, but prices are very reasonable, even if you don't take advantage of Daquise's hospitality to wile away the day.

£8 to £25
Address 20 Thurloe St, SW7
☎ 020 7589 6117
Station South Kensington
Open Daily 11.30am–11pm
Accepts Mastercard and Visa

Start with Ukrainian barszcz (£2.50), rich and red, or the new starter, herrings with bread (£3.50) – the herring fillets are amazingly good here. Thick cut, pleasantly salty and with a luxurious smooth texture. Go on to the kasanka (£6), a large buckwheat sausage, cousin to black pudding, made using natural skins. Or, for the fearless, there is giant golonka (£8.80), a marinated pork knuckle which is boiled and served with horseradish sauce. Also welcome back an old friend, Vienna schnitzel (£9.50), with a fried egg on top. And it is hard not to be tempted into ordering an extra dish of potato pancakes (£5.50), which are large, flat and crispy, and come with sour cream or apple sauce. Other side-dishes are an odd kind of sauerkraut (£1.50), served cold and very mild; cucumbers in brine (£1); and kasza (£1.60), the omnipresent buckwheat.

Since the first edition of this guide there have been a succession of rumours that speculators were redeveloping this chunk of Thurloe Street, so inspiring Daquise regulars to band together and defend the place. It is still there.

South Kensington

Haandi

East African Punjabi restaurants are famous for simple dishes, rich, intense sauces and a welcome belt of chilli heat – the kind of food that hitherto has meant a trek to Southall or Tooting. This is a brave initiative. The management decided to expand an empire based on successful establishments in Nairobi and Kampala by adding the long and narrow space, which, in a bygone age, was a Sloaney haven known as the Loose Box. The decor is curry-house- smart, the room is as light and bright as a nearly-basement can be, and you can see into the kitchen through a curved glass wall. The menu and chefs have been flown in from East Africa. The curries are incredibly rich, and got that way by being reduced gradually rather than being thickened with powdered nuts.

£17 to £40

Address 136 Brompton Rd, SW3
☎ 020 7823 7373
Station Knightsbridge/South Kensington
Open Mon–Fri 6–11pm, Sat & Sun noon–3pm & 6–11.30pm
Accepts All major credit cards
🖳 www.haandi-restaurants.com

Start with some kebabs. Machli mahasagar (£8.50) is a dual-purpose dish – it makes a grand, if pricey, starter or a sensible main course; it is a fish kebab, with large chunks of white fish that are marinated and then cooked in the tandoor. The tandoor man knows his job, and every mouthful has a light overshirt of spices and is still moist in the middle. The murg malai tikka (£8.80) is also very good. Another star turn from the tandoor is the Kashmiri kabarga (£8.80), which are implausibly tender lamb chops, richly spiced, with good crispy bits to gnaw. The curries are also very satisfying. Try the lasoni prawns masala (£12.80) – good-sized prawns, which are cooked firm and retain some bite, inhabit a very rich, very strongly flavoured, almost dry masala. Or how about the gosht-ki-haandi (£8.10)? This is a trad lamb curry, chilli-hot. The vegetable dishes are equally good. Dum aloo Kandahari (£6.20) is made with potatoes that have been stuffed with dried fruit before being curried in a rich tomatoey sauce containing apricots – implausible but delicious. The breads are excellent.

Service is smiley. Haandi may be a much more expensive proposition than almost all of London's other East African/Asian restaurants, but the price tags seem less rapacious so close to Harrods, and at Haandi the food is very good.

Racine

Racine opened with suitable fanfares in June 2002, as it brought together what was something of a foodie "dream team" – chef Henry Harris and front-of-house Eric Garnier, – and the signs are that it has fulfilled its early promise. The food is French. Not just any old French, but familiar, delicious, nostalgic dishes from the glory days of French cooking. The dining room at Racine is dark brown and comfortable. The service is friendly and Gallic. The prices are reasonable, and haven't crept up too much during the first year. It's no surprise that this place is busy enough to make booking an imperative.

£18 to £50

Address 239 Brompton Rd, SW3
℡ 020 7584 4477
Station Knightsbridge/South Kensington
Open Mon–Sat noon–3pm & 6–10.30pm, Sat noon–3.30pm & 6–10.30pm, Sun noon–3.30pm & 6–10pm
Accepts All major credit cards

FRENCH

Henry Harris is a very good cook and his menus are invariably skilfully written. Everything tempts, everything is priced reasonably, and he takes a great deal of trouble to source and buy top-quality seasonal ingredients. To start with, expect simple but glorious combinations such as jambon de Bayonne with celeriac rémoulade (£7.25); salade Lyonnaise (£6.50); a cream of onion and thyme soup with melted Raclette (£4.75); and an old-fashioned pâté de foie de volaille et fines herbes (£5.25). Or a truly wonderful warm garlic and saffron mousse with mussels (£7) – light and airy, with a triumphant texture and a delicate taste. Mains continue the "classical" theme: grilled rabbit with mustard sauce and smoked bacon (£10.50); marmite Dieppoise (£12.50); tête de veau with a well-made sauce ravigote (£9.50); plus chicken, chops, steak and fish – but all given the kind of treatment you would expect from the kitchen of a respected restaurant in provincial France. The dessert menu deals in classics: petit pot au chocolat (£6); strawberries in Beaujolais (£5); and Mont Blanc (£5), which is a rich chestnut puree with meringue and chocolate sauce. The wine list is Francocentric but merciful – even the smart bottles seem reasonably priced.

There is a good and bourgeois (in the best possible way) set lunch to tempt Knightsbridge ladies away from a salad of mixed leaves – two courses at £14.50, three courses £16.50.

Racine

Victoria & Westminster

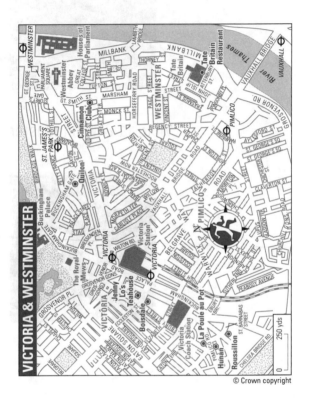

VICTORIA & WESTMINSTER

© Crown copyright

Boisdale

Boisdale is owned by Ranald Mac-donald, who is next in line to be the Chief of Clanranald, and if that information gives you a premonition of what the restaurant is like you are probably thinking along the right lines. This is a very Scottish place, strong on hospitality, and with a befuddlingly large range of rare malt whiskies. Fresh produce – correction, fresh *Scottish* produce – rules wherever possible, and it is no wonder that the clubby atmosphere and reliable cooking makes this a haven of choice for local businessmen, who are also likely to be found in the ultra-Scottish back bar, home to the formidable malt whisky collection.

£16 to £55

Address 15 Ecclestone St, SW1
℡ 020 7730 6922
Station Victoria
Open Mon–Fri noon–1am, Sat 7.30pm–1am
Accepts All major credit cards
Branches see p.487
ⓦ www.boisdale.co.uk

There are three Boisdale menus, one of which is the admirably simple "Flying Scotsman" lunch menu – for £14, diners can enjoy white bean and bacon soup or rocket and Parmesan salad, followed by seared Scottish salmon or breast of chicken with stoved potatoes. Or there's a two-course menu – a choice of five starters and five mains for £17.45 (yes, just like the rebellion!). Starters range from marinated Orkney herring and mini roast Macsween haggis to dill-marinated Scottish salmon. Main courses veer from crofter's pie; to smoked haddock fishcakes to – you've guessed it – roast Macsween haggis. The à la carte includes a good many luxury ingredients. As well as Lochcarnan smoked salmon from South Uist (£9.90), and Rannoch Moor smoked venison with black truffle dressing (£9.90), there's a rabbit, pigeon and foie gras terrine with pear chutney (£8.50). Commendably, the mains feature fresh fish of the day, and fresh offal of the day. There are various Aberdeen Angus beef steaks: fillet with Béarnaise sauce and chips (£21), or rib-eye with black truffle, pommes Dauphinoise, spinach and wild mushrooms (£21.50).

Sensibly enough, you can mix and match all of these menus as you work towards an after-dinner malt, or malts. Perhaps in the Macdonald bar and cigar club, next door, which features jazz every evening from Monday to Saturday (cover charge £3.95)?

The Cinnamon Club

It had to happen. Those brave people who set up smart new restaurants were eventually bound to run out of bank premises to convert. It seems we are entering the next phase, as The Cinnamon Club occupies what was formerly Westminster Library. Banks and libraries have a good deal in common – lofty ceilings, large doors, old wood floors, plenty of panelling – just the stuff to make a cracking formal restaurant. The Cinnamon Club is elegant, substantial and very pukka. Service is polished and attentive, the linen is snowy-white, the cutlery is heavy, the ashtrays stealably elegant, the toilets opulent, and there are huge flower arrangements. The cooking is accomplished, and each dish offers a finely judged combination of flavours, every one distinct. There's an informed wine list. And yes, unlikely as it may sound, this is an Indian restaurant.

From the "Appetisers" section of the menu, chilli-fried squid comes with a squid ink naan (£9); or there is Rajasthani spiced grilled chicken with clove (£7.50); or loin of rabbit stuffed with cottage cheese and dried fruit (£9). Such dishes and prices set the tone. Mains are also well conceived: spice-crusted tandoori monkfish with tomato and lemon sauce (£20); or there is pan-seared Gressingham duck breast with a sesame tamarind sauce (£17); or roast saddle of lamb with green chilli and yoghurt (£20) – not something you'd find on the High Street. There's also a hot, Hyderabadi biryani made with goat (£15.50). Go for the basket of breads (£3) as a side dish, a selection of unusual parathas, naans and rotis. Desserts are elegant: try the warm apple lassi with champagne granita (£6), or the spiced banana tarte Tatin (£6.50), which comes with a deep-purple berry sorbet.

Politicos have already been sighted here prowling amongst the grazing foodies. And to cater for power breakfasters The Cinnamon Club offers the choice of full English (£16) or Bombay scrambled eggs on layered bread (£11). Perhaps this is a sign that refined and elegant Indian food will soon take its place as the lobbyist's weapon of choice.

£25 to £70

Address Old Westminster Library, Great Smith St, SW1
☎ 020 7222 2555
Station St James's Park/ Westminster
Open Mon–Fri 7.30–10am, noon–3pm & 6–11pm, Sat 6–11pm, Sun noon–3.30pm
Accepts All major credit cards
🌐 www.cinnamonclub.com

Hunan

(⊕) The Hunan is the domain of Mr Peng. As you venture into his restaurant you put yourself into his hands, to do with you what he will. It is rather like being trapped in a 1930s B-movie. You order the boiled dumplings … and the griddle-fried lettuce-wrapped dumplings turn up, "because you will like them more". And most likely you will.

£25 to £50

Address 51 Pimlico Rd, SW1
☏ 020 7730 5712
Station Sloane Square
Open Mon–Sat noon–2.30pm & 6–11.30pm
Accepts All major credit cards except Diners

Probably 90 percent of Mr Peng's regular customers have given up the unequal struggle, submitting themselves to the "feast" – a multi-course extravaganza, varied according to the maestro's whims and the vagaries of the market, that might include pigeon soup. Or goose. Or a dish of cold, marinated octopus. This fine food and attentive service is matched by the Hunan's elegant surroundings, but be warned – the prices are Pimlico rather than Chinatown, and they continue to escalate.

If you want to defy Mr Peng and act knowledgeable, you could actually try asking for the griddle-fried lettuce-wrapped dumplings (£6.50), which are exceedingly delicious. Or there are frogs' legs in rich and hot Hunan sauce (£7); or smoked chicken slices (£6.50); or grilled salt and pepper squid (£7). Alternatively, try the camphor-wood-and-tea-smoked duck (£18 for a half, £33 for a whole). Once again, this dish is as interpreted by Mr P, so as well as a southwestern Chinese version of crispy duck (with pancakes etc) there's a sweet-and-sourish sauce. Other standouts include hot and spicy beef (£7), and sizzling prawns (£8), braised scallops in Hunan sauce (£8) and spicy braised eggplant (£6).

However, for all but the strongest wills, resistance is useless and you'll probably end up with what is described on the menu as "Hunan's special leave-it-to-us-feast – minimum two persons, from £29.50 a head. We recommend those not familiar with Hunan cuisine and those who are looking for a wide selection of our favourite and unusual dishes to leave it to the chef Mr Peng to prepare for you his special banquet. Many of the dishes are not on the menu." Even Alexis Gauthier, Michelin-starred head chef from Roussillon (see p.155), has given up and leaves it to Mr P.

Jenny Lo's Teahouse

Jenny Lo's Teahouse in Victoria is the complete opposite of those typically stuffy, over-designed Chinese restaurants. This place is bright, bare and stylishly utilitarian. From the blocks of bright colours and refectory tables to the artifice of framing the emergency exit sign like a picture over the door, this is a somewhat smart, but comfortable, place to eat. And that just about sums up the food too. Service makes you think that you're in the politest cafeteria in the world and the prices don't spoil the illusion. Although portion sizes and seasoning can vary, the food is freshly cooked and generally delicious. All of which meets with unqualified approval from a loyal band of sophisticated regulars.

£7 to £22

Address 14 Eccleston St, SW1
⌖020 7259 0399
Station Victoria
Open Mon–Fri 11.30am–3pm & 6–10pm, Sat noon–3pm & 6–10pm
Accepts Cash or cheque only

The menu is divided into three main sections: soup noodles, wok noodles and rice dishes. Take your pick and then add some side dishes. The chilli beef soup (£7.50) is a good choice: a large bowl full of delicate, clear, chilli-spiked broth which is then bulked out with yards of slippery ho fun – ribbon noodles like thin tagliatelle – plus slivers of beef and fresh coriander. The black bean seafood noodles (£6.95) are an altogether richer and more solid affair, made from egg noodles with prawn, mussels, squid and peppers. Rice dishes range from long-cooked pork and chestnuts (£6.50), to gong bao chicken with pine nuts (£6.95) and the simpler Szechuan aubergine (£5.95). The side dishes are great fun, with good spare ribs (£3.75) and guo tie (£4.50), which are pan-cooked dumplings filled with either vegetables or pork. Spring onion pancakes (£3) are a Beijing street food made from flat, griddled breads laced with spring onions and served with a dipping sauce.

Try the tea here, too. As well as offering Chinese and herbal teas, Jenny Lo has enlisted the help of herbalist Dr Xu, who has blended two special therapeutic teas: long-life tea (£1.85), described as "a warming tonic to boost your energy"; and cleansing tea (£1.85), "a light tea for strengthening the liver and kidneys". It tastes refreshing and faintly gingery, and is doubtless cleansing, too.

La Poule au Pot

You are in trouble at La Poule au Pot if you don't understand at least some French. It is unreservedly a bastion of France in England, and has been for more than three decades. What's more, several of the staff have worked here for most of that time, and the restaurant itself has hardly changed at all, with huge dried-flower baskets and a comfortable rustic atmosphere. The wide windows brighten lunch, but by night, candlelight ensures that La Poule is a favourite for romantic assignations.

£17 to £45

Address 231 Ebury St, SW1
℡020 7730 7763
Station Sloane Square
Open Mon–Sat 12.30–2.30pm & 6.45–11pm, Sun 12.30–3.30pm & 6.45–10pm
Accepts All major credit cards

A small dish of crudités in herb vinaigrette is set down as a bonne bouche. Different fresh breads come in huge chunks. The menu is deceptive, as there are usually more additional fresh daily specials than are listed. The patient waiters struggle to remember them all and answer your questions about the dishes. As a starter, the escargots (£8) deliver classic French authenticity with plenty of garlic and herbs. The soupe de poisson (£8.75) is not the commonly served thick soup, but a refined clear broth with chunks of sole and scallop, plus prawns and mussels. A main course of bifteck frites (£14.50) brings a perfectly cooked, French-cut steak with red-hot chips. The gigot aux flageolets (£14.50) is pink and tender, with beans that are well flavoured and not over-cooked. There's calf's liver (£13.75), and carré d'agneau à l'ail (£17) – rack of lamb with garlic. The pudding menu features standards like crème brûlée (£4.50) – huge, served in a rustic dish, and classically good – and banane à sa façon (£4.50), which is lightly cooked with a caramel rum sauce. There is also a selection of good pudding wines: a glass of Monbazillac (£2.95) makes an excellent companion to the richness of the desserts.

If you are a Francophile, you'll find all your favourites, from French onion soup to boeuf Bourguignon, from quiche to cassoulet. And, such is the atmosphere of the place that, for a few hours at least, you forget that you are in England, particularly if you take advantage of the prix-fixe lunch (£14.50 for two courses, £16 for three).

Quilon

Quilon is about as swish as Indian restaurants get – as you'd expect when you learn that it is owned by the Taj Group, which also runs a dozen of India's most upmarket hotels. Anyone who still unfairly pigeonholes all Indian restaurants as cheap and cheerful should pop along to this elegant 92-seater for a reality check. Quilon has the appearance of a sophisticated restaurant, you get the service you'd expect in a sophisticated restaurant, and you get the quality of cooking you'd expect from a sophisticated restaurant. And, unsurprisingly, you get the size of bill you'd expect from a sophisticated restaurant. The menu, built around "Coastal Food", showcases the splendid cuisine of Kerala – lots of fish, seafood, fresh peppercorns and coconut. The food is very good indeed.

£20 to £60

Address 41 Buckingham Gate, SW1
℡ 020 7821 1899
Station St James's Park
Open Mon–Fri noon–2.30pm & 6–11pm, Sat 6–11pm
Accepts All major credit cards

Start with the Coorg chicken (£5.50) – chunky chicken with rich spicing and a hint of Coorg vinegar. Or pepper shrimps (£6.50) – prawns fried in batter with plenty of chilli and a touch of aniseed. In season there may be partridge masala (£5.50), cooked in really fresh spices. Moving on to the mains, seafood tempters include prawns Byadgi (£18.50) – enormous prawns grilled with the specially imported and pleasantly hot Byadgi chillies. Or try Canara lamb curry (£15.95) – very, very rich with a clean and honest heat; or the guinea fowl salan (£13.75), cooked with coconut milk and yoghurt. These are all fairly spicy choices, but there is also gentler fare, with plenty of chicken options and several duck dishes. All the main courses come with a vegetable of the day. Standouts include masala-stuffed aubergine (£7.50) – whole baby aubergines stuffed with coconut and poppy seeds; and a spinach poriyal (£7.50), made with freshly grated coconut, mustard leaves and split Bengal gram.

In the middle of the dining room there is an outpost kitchen where a busy chef works at an array of burners making fresh appams (£1.95), feathery rice pancakes which are stunning when hot and so-so when cold. The set-lunch menus are good value – £12.95 for two courses and £15.95 for three.

Roussillon

Despite a dining room that has always looked rather stuffy, Roussillon has built up a decent reputation and gathered a shelf-full of awards. The mainspring is a young French chef called Alexis Gauthier, who is obsessed with the quality and freshness of his ingredients. His dishes invariably combine strong flavours, and make good use of fine English foods. To see the advantages of being season- and market-driven, try the terrific-value £18 set lunch. The main menu runs in at three courses for £39, and four for £46. At which point you will probably feel the urge to splash out on one or other of the seven-course showing-off menus – the vegetarian "Garden Menu" (£50) and the "Seasonal Menu" (£60).

£24 to £90

Address 16 St Barnabas St, SW1
℡ 020 7730 5550
Station Sloane Square /Victoria
Open Mon & Tues 6.30–10.45pm, Wed–Fri noon–2.30pm & 6.30–10.45pm, Sat 6.30–10.45pm
Accepts All major credit cards except Diners
🌐 www.roussillon.co.uk

The menu has various sections to it: the classics, the garden, the land, the sea and river – and changes with the seasons. Overlook the coy names and listen to your taste buds. Open with a terrine of duck foie gras with conference pear. Into "the garden": thin cream of broad beans and radish leaves, royale of chicken liver; or autumn vegetables and fruits cooked together in a pot with aged balsamic. Fish dishes may include roast Dublin Bay prawns, salad of purple artichoke and lemon pepper; or grilled halibut, steamed clams, young carrots, garlic leaves. "The land" brings organically raised Aberdeen Angus from Donald Russell, served with braised Swiss chard, bacon and thick French fries (supplement £8); pan-fried lightly battered sweetbreads, sautéed ceps and creamed flat parsley; or Gloucester Old Spot pork in two ways: tenderly braised and pink-roasted, with pommes boulangère. This is gastronomic stuff. Onwards to cheese, fruit and chocolate.

You have to warm to anyone so keen on chocolate puddings. There's white and black chocolate pyramide; chocolate praline finger; and a chocolate soufflé … only eclipsed by the Parthian shot – spicy soufflé of organic goose egg with gingerbread soldiers and maple infusion. During the Chelsea Flower Show, Roussillon offers a special five-course menu for £40 – all those gardening ladies get to eat nettles!

Tate Britain Restaurant

MODERN BRITISH

In these days of a "sandwich at the desk" office culture, you have to think long and hard before recommending a restaurant that is only open for lunch, especially when it has the potential to be a pretty wallet-challenging affair. For the foodie, the Tate Britain Restaurant is worth a visit; for the winey, it is an essential pilgrimage. This restaurant's love affair with wine began in the 1970s, when the food was dodgy and it seemed as if the only customers were wine merchants marvelling at the impossibly low prices. Today there are fewer florid gents enjoying a three-bottle lunch, but the atmosphere is soothing and the wine list is not only fascinating, but offers outstanding value as well.

> **£25 to £100**
>
> Address Tate Britain, Millbank, SW1
> ☎ 020 7887 8877
> Station Pimlico
> Open Mon–Sat noon–3pm, Sun noon–4pm
> Accepts All major credit cards
> ⊕ www.tate.org.uk

The menu changes on a regular basis and offers admirably seasonal dishes. There's also a set lunch, with two courses at £16.75 and three at £19.50. Although there is no indication on the menu, there are dishes to suit the oenophiles, and dishes for civilian diners. Thus wine folk might choose simple starters like salad of smoked chicken (£6.50), or dressed Cornish crab with Melba toast and crab mayonnaise (£9.95), while the others can opt for grilled sardines with pickled vegetables (£8.95). Mains touch most of the bases and dishes are straightforward: escalopes of Loch Duart salmon with asparagus and sauce mousseline (£12.95); roast black leg chicken breast with leeks and truffle sauce (£14.95); or garganelli primavera with broccoli pesto cream (£10.50). The cooking is good. The food is fresh and unpretentious. There are enough tempting puddings to team with dessert wines.

The wine list is wonderful, and constantly changing as bins run out. It takes the form of a vast book, but do not be intimidated, and take your time. The wine waiters are both knowledgeable and helpful. Bottles are served at the right temperature and decanted without fuss when necessary. As a strategy, how about picking a few good half-bottles? For example, a Rully premier cru Les Cloux 2001 from Jean-Marc Boillot (£15.50) and La Petite Eglise 1998 – the second wine of Chateau L'Eglise Clinet, Pomerol – (£19)?

Waterloo & The South Bank

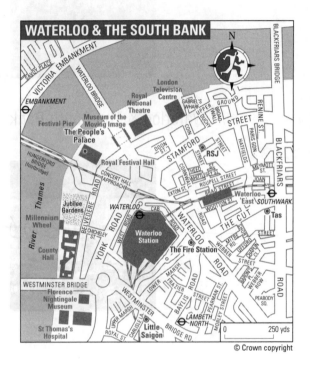

WATERLOO & THE SOUTH BANK

N

Victoria Embankment

Savoy Place

Waterloo Bridge

EMBANKMENT

Festival Pier

Museum of the Moving Image

The People's Palace

Royal National Theatre

London Television Centre

Gabriel's Wharf

Upper Ground

Broad Wall

Doon St

Coin St

Stamford Street

Cornwall Road

Reed St

Whittlesey St

Renne St

Paris Gdn

Hatfields

RSJ

Meymott St

Joan St

Blackfriars Bridge

Blackfriars

Hungerford Bridge (footbridge)

Royal Festival Hall

Concert Hall Approach

Exton St

Roupell Street

Road St

Waterloo East

SOUTHWARK

Wootton St

Thames

Jubilee Gardens

Belvedere Road

York Road

West Road

WATERLOO

CAB

Waterloo Station

The Fire Station

Tas

THE CUT

Mitre Rd

Ufford St

Webber St

Short St

Millennium Wheel

River

County Hall

Chicheley St

Lower Marsh

Frazier Road

Baylis Road

Pearman St

Morley Street

Webber Row

Peabody Sq.

Roberts Pl.

WESTMINSTER BRIDGE

Florence Nightingale Museum

St Thomas's Hospital

WESTMINSTER

Upper Marsh

Royal St

Carlisle La

Little Saigon

Royal Oak

LAMBETH NORTH

BRIDGE RD.

ROAD

0   250 yds

The Fire Station

When you arrive at The Fire Station it's hard to imagine that the food will be of much distinction. This is a big barn of a place with pumping music, and to get to the restaurant at the back you have to fight your way through noisy waves of colourful-drink-swillers. Decoration is scant, consisting mostly of red and cream paint, and blackboards painted with popping champagne corks. At first glance, it looks exactly like a theme hamburger bar. But if you look a little closer you'll see an open-plan kitchen preparing good-looking food, and a lot of happy diners. It's worth persevering.

£18 to £35

Address 150 Waterloo Rd, SE1
℗ 020 7620 2226
Station Waterloo
Open Mon–Fri noon–2.45pm &
5.30–11pm, Sat noon–10.45pm,
Sun noon–9.30pm
Accepts All major credit cards

The menu changes daily but there are some simple things that often feature, including starters such as carrot, orange and coriander soup with croutons (£4.25); Cajun king prawns with mixed leaves and mustard citrus dressing (£6.50); smooth liver terrine (£5.75); and dressed crab on a bed of mixed leaves with lemon dressing (£6.50). Equally appealing are mains such as roast spiced pork belly with sticky rice, pak choi and soy sauce (£10.95); pan-fried salmon fillet with crushed new potatoes and lemon butter sauce (£11.95); and tandoori-seared yellow-fin tuna loin (£12.50). Or how about parsley-crusted calf's liver (£12.50)? Or the Fire Station bouillabaisse (£15.50), a large casserole containing a rather unauthentic mix of prawns, calamari, crab, mussels and salmon? The cooking is sound enough, and the service is friendly. The only problems stem from a tendency towards "sorlin" cooking ("it's-all-in"). Thankfully, puddings are simple, but there are four huge scoops for one helping of caramel ice cream with butterscotch sauce (£3.95). To wash it all down, there's a decent wine list with five reds and whites by the glass, as well as a 50cl carafe (£7.95 for the house white, £9.80 for Rioja).

There's a set menu (available up to 7pm) of two courses for £10.95 and three for £13.50, which makes The Fire Station a sensible place to visit on the way to the Old Vic or the National Theatre. It's a little less frenetic then, as well.

VIETNAMESE

Little Saigon

Little Saigon was the Long family's first restaurant outside Soho. They were driven out by rising rents and set up south of the river. Little Saigon sells good, homely Vietnamese food from a comprehensive menu. You will eat best by sticking to the pukka dishes, and should take this opportunity to get to grips with Vietnamese spring rolls – both the crispy deep-fried kind and the "crystal" variety. The latter are round

£15 to £35

Address 139 Westminster Bridge Rd, SE1
℡020 7207 9747
Station Waterloo/Lambeth North
Open Mon–Fri noon–3pm &
5.30–11.30pm, Sat & Sun
5.30–11.30pm
Accepts All major credit cards

discs of rice pastry like giant, translucent Communion wafers, which you soak in a bowl of hot water until pliable and then roll around a filling made up of fresh salady things, interesting sauces, and slivers of meat grilled on a portable barbecue.

Run amok with the starters. Sugar-cane prawns (two for £3.20) are large prawn "fishcakes" impaled on a strip of sugar cane and grilled. Vietnamese imperial spring rolls (£2.60) are of the crispy fried variety, but they are served cut into chunks and with lettuce leaves to roll them up in. Also good is the strangely resilient Vietnamese grilled squid cake (£3.50). Topping the bill are special spring rolls (four for £2.60) – delicate pancakes, thin enough to read through, filled with prawns and fresh herbs – which in this case have been "pre-rolled" and are quite delicious. It's as if each of the starters comes with its own special dipping sauce, and the table is soon littered with an array of little saucers – look out for the extra-sweet white plum sauce and the extra-hot brown chilli oil. For mains, ha noi grilled chicken with honey (£5.30), special Saigon prawn curry (£6.40), and the house special, fried crispy noodles (£4.80), can be recommended.

Do try and master the "specialities". Make an intermediate course of the crystal pancakes and use them to wrap the crunchy salads and the meats barbecued at the table. You have to soak your own pancakes and it is trickier than it looks. Soak them too long and they stick to the plate; not long enough, and they won't wrap. Grilled slices of barbecued beef (£12) and grilled slices of pork in garlic sauce (£12) both make splendid fillings.

The People's Palace

When this restaurant first opened, there were tales of diners who had finished their dinner late being locked into the Festival Hall, and of others wandering for ages between levels. It is still not the most straightforward venue to find, but it has its own entrance now, opposite Hungerford Bridge. And it's worth seeking out. It's a very large place, run with the high standards you would hope for – considering that it is within the South Bank Centre and many diners are either pre- or post-concert, which makes timing crucial. The food is well presented and accurately cooked. There are occasional flashes of innovation but the menu is mainly composed of well-balanced, satisfying dishes at reasonable prices. Add the fabulous view overlooking the Thames, the sound service, a child-friendly policy (they're nice to kids, and provide high-chairs and children's menus), and it all adds up to an attractive package.

£16 to £45
Address Level Three, Royal Festival Hall, South Bank, SE1
☏ 020 7928 9999
Station Waterloo
Open Daily noon–3pm & 5.30–11pm
Accepts All major credit cards
✆ www.peoplespalace.co.uk

MODERN BRITISH

The bargains at The People's Palace are its fixed-price menus. Daily lunch menus are £12.50 for two courses, while the pre-theatre menu is £16 for two courses, and the all-day Sunday menu is £16.50 for two courses. For this, you choose from a good spread of daily selections. On the à la carte you'll find starters like warm Stilton and red onion tart with frisee and chives (£6.50); smoked eel, treacle-cured bacon, fried egg and horseradish (£9); and venison carpaccio with roast apple (£8.90). Mains may include roast salmon with spiced red lentils (£13.75); coq au vin with parsnip mash (£14.50); duck with a red wine and mushroom risotto (£17); or lemon sole fillet with crevettes and clams (£18). Puddings (£5) ring the sweet-tooth bell: fig and ginger pudding with cinnamon custard; or banana and pecan pudding with clotted cream and toffee sauce.

It's worth figuring the Festival Hall's concert programme into your plans. On a popular night, you'll need to book for pre- or post-concert sittings. When you call to make a reservation, ask the receptionist, who will know just what's on and when it finishes.

RSJ

MODERN EUROPEAN

Rolled Steel Joist may seem a curious name for a restaurant, but it is appropriate – they can point out the RSJ holding up the first floor if you wish! What's more interesting about RSJ is that it's owned by a man with a passion for the wines of the Loire. Nigel Wilkinson has compiled his list mainly from wines produced in this region, and it features

£19 to £55

Address 13a Coin St, SE1
☎ 020 7928 4554
Station Waterloo
Open Mon–Fri noon–2.30pm &
5.30–11pm, Sat 5.30–11pm
Accepts All major credit cards
🌐 www.rsj.uk.com

dozens of lesser-known Loire reds and whites – wines which clearly deserve a wider following. Notes about recent vintages both interest and educate, and each wine is well described.

The menu is based on classical dishes, but with a light touch and some innovative combinations as well. The starters might include purple sprouting broccoli and garlic leaf risotto (£5.25); smoked haddock soup with baby spinach and crème fraîche (£5.25); or terrine of free-range chicken and foie gras (£8.95). Moving on to the main courses, typical choices might include roast cod fillet with a casserole of spicy butter beans (£12.95); fillet of beef, black pepper and chive butter, braised potatoes (£16.95); and breast of guinea fowl, Jersey royal potatoes, spring greens, shallot and carrots (£12.95). The menu also features an above-average number of vegetarian options, some of which are carefully thought out, like fresh sage gnocchi with a blue cheese sauce, new season peas and broad beans (£10.95). The puddings can be the kind of serious stuff that you really should save room for, such as white choco-late and passion fruit mousse (£5.50); or pear and pistachio tart, camomile ice cream (£5.25).

Like The People's Palace (see p.161), RSJ is situated close to the South Bank Centre's cinema, concert halls and theatres, and is clearly enjoyed by patrons. It appears to cater for both the hastier pre-theatre crowd and a late crowd who are not rushed in any way – always a good sign. The set meals at £15.95 for two courses and £16.95 for three represent jolly good value. Use the website to check out the RSJ Wine Company, whose list is a joy to anyone devoted to the fine wines of the Loire.

Tas

Tas is a bright and bustling Turkish restaurant where eating is cheap, the menu and the set menus have proliferated until there is a baffling choice, and there is often live music. All of which explains why the place is heaving with office parties, birthday bashes and hen nights. The management is obviously alert to the possibilities of a modern restaurant serving Turkish dishes – the feel of this place is closer to a busy West End brasserie than to your standard street-corner Turkish grills. Expect colourful crockery and an overdose of noise. If you like lively, then Tas will do just fine.

£9 to £38

Address 33 The Cut, SE1
⊤ 020 7928 1444
Station Southwark
Open Mon–Sat noon–11.30pm, Sun noon–10.30pm
Accepts All major credit cards except Diners
Branches see p.490
www.tasrestaurant.com

TURKISH

The menu is a monster: 4 soups, followed by 12 cold starters, 12 hot starters, 10 salads, 8 rice dishes, 4 side orders, 6 pasta dishes, 10 vegetarian dishes, 14 grills, 10 casseroles (including moussaka, which is stretching things a bit), 14 fish and shellfish dishes, and 9 desserts. Overwhelmed? Everyone else is. Which is probably why Tas also offers four set menus starting at three courses for £7.45 and peaking at a combo of six mezze, a grill, dessert and a coffee at £18.50 (for a minimum of two people). The first thing to say about the food is that it is well presented and tastes wonderfully fresh. From the cold starters, favour the zeytin yagli bakla (£3.40), which is a fine dish of broad beans with yoghurt; or the cacik (£3.25), a simple cucumber and yoghurt dip. The bread is very good. Stars of the hot starter menu are the borek (£3.55), which is filo pastry filled with cheese and deep-fried; and the sucuk izgara (£3.55), a Turkish garlicky sausage. Unless you have particular likes or prejudices to pander to, go on to the good, sound grills: bobrek izgara (£6.95) are lamb's kidneys; and tavuk shish (£7.65) is a chicken kebab. The fish dishes are accurately cooked and come in large portions: grilled halibut (£9.55) comes with tomato sauce, while the calamari (£7.75) brings squid with a walnut sauce.

The menu announces, "Tas is our traditional Anatolian cooking pot, used to prepare casseroles." So try one.

City & East

Brick Lane & Spitalfields

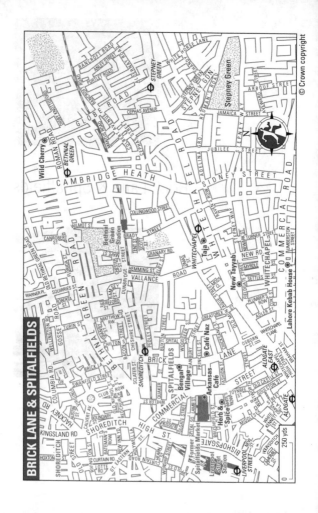

BRICK LANE & SPITALFIELDS

© Crown copyright

0 — 250 yds

Arkansas Café

(🍴) As you approach the Arkansas Café the glow from its steel-pit barbecue invites you in. Bubba Helberg and his wife Sarah claim that they serve the best barbecue this side of the pond, and they may just be right, for they are regularly in demand as the US Embassy's barbecue experts (they will also open here for evening parties of twelve or more). Their food is fresh and simple, and Bubba chooses his own steaks from Smithfield Market to ensure that the meat is marbled through for tenderness. The provenance of his bison and sausages is listed for all to see. He marinates and smokes his own beef brisket and ribs, and his recipe for the latter won him a soul-food award back home. His secret home-made barbecue sauce is on every table, but he won't sell the recipe to anyone.

£10 to £25
Address Unit 12, Old Spitalfields Market, E1
☏ 020 7377 6999
Station Liverpool Street
Open Mon–Fri noon–2.30pm, Sun noon–4pm
Accepts Mastercard, Visa

Decor is spartan – clean-scrubbed tables, canvas chairs and paper plates – but this does not intrude on the quality of the food. There are no starters, and "No fries". Any of the steaks – Irish steak platter (£10.50), bison rib-eye steak platter (£14) – are good bets, char-grilled with Bubba's special sauce and served with seasonal vegetables. Note that the price is genuinely market-sensitive and can rise and fall. Corn-fed French chicken (£7) is tender and full of flavour, and a side order of chilli (50p) provides a spicy sauce-like accompaniment. Most of the other dishes on the menu are platters or sandwiches, the latter including choices like char-grilled Barbary duck breast sandwich (£6); free-range pork sandwich (£6); beef brisket Texas-style sandwich (£7), which comes meltingly tender and smoky; and, of course, hot dog (£4). Puddings (all £2.50) include New York-style lemon cheesecake and New Orleans pecan pie. They are as sweet and as solid as they should be. The wine list is short and to the point, but the beer list is long, with a large selection of serious brews including Budvar and Budweiser (both £3.30), and the American Anchor Steam (£2.50).

Customers at Arkansas often include expat Americans homesick for authentic barbecue, which has to be a good sign. Eat in and take an extra order home.

Bengal Village

No doubt about it, Brick Lane is becoming more sophisticated. Where once all was BYOB restaurants serving rough-and-ready curries at bargain-basement prices to impoverished punters seeking chilli and all things familiar, there's now a growing crop of slick new establishments serving authentic Bangladeshi cooking. The Bengal Village is one such place. There's a blond wood floor and modernist chairs, but it's about more than just design. The menu touches all the bases: trad curryholics can still plough their way through more than a hundred old-style curries – korma, Madras, vindaloo – but now they can also try some more interesting Bangladeshi dishes, too.

£8 to £18

Address 75 Brick Lane, E1
℡ 020 7366 4868
Station Aldgate East/
Liverpool Street
Open Daily noon–midnight
Accepts All major credit cards
🖰 www.bengalvillage.com

Bucking what seems to be becoming the trend, starters are not the best dishes at the Bengal Village. The onion bhajis (£1.95) are, well, onion bhajis, and the chicken tikka (£2.10) is no more than sound. Move straight along to the Bangla specialities. Bowal mas biran (£5.95) is boal fish that has been deep-fried with a rich sauce. There are four shatkora curries – the shatkora being a small green fruit that has a delightful bitter citrus tang and goes very well with rich meats – lamb shatkora (£4.95), for example. Then there are ureebisi dishes, traditionally made with the seeds of a large runner-bean-like plant – in the UK butter beans are often substituted and nobody seems to mind. Try chicken ureebisi (£4.95). There are also some rather splendid vegetarian options: chalkumra (£4.75) – subtitled "ash-ground", and supposed to be made with a pumpkin-like gourd – in practice turns out to be slices of marrow in a korma-ish sauce. The marrow kofta (£4.75) is a curry with large and satisfactorily dense vegetable dumplings floating, or rather sinking, in it. Drink a few a large Cobra beers (£2.95) or follow the great Brick Lane tradition and take your own refreshment with you in a carrier bag.

Perversely the "Chef's Recommendations" seem rather less exotic: chicken makhani (£5.95), coriander lamb (£5.95). Better to try the Bangladeshi dishes than these standard curry house contenders.

Café Naz

Café Naz dominates Brick Lane with its elegant facade complete with an all-glass staircase and spacious upstairs dining room. "Contemporary Bangladeshi Cuisine" is what it says on the menu, and generally speaking that is what you get, though you will find some of the Indian restaurant standards – a list

> **£10 to £24**
>
> **Address** 46–48 Brick Lane, E1
> ℗ 020 7247 0234
> **Station** Aldgate East
> **Open** Daily noon–midnight
> **Accepts** All major credit cards

of baltis and, of course, chicken tikka masala. The decor is certainly contemporary: bright colours, modern furniture and a gleaming open kitchen where you can watch the chefs at work. Prices are reasonable – thirty curry restaurants within a stone's throw makes for serious competition – and service is attentive.

Start with the kebab-e-Naz (£4.95), chicken, cooked in the tandoor and served with a plateful of fresh salad. Or there's chandni lamb tikka (£2.95); or fish cutlet (£2.95), which brings pieces of a Bangladeshi fish called the Ayre, deep-fried-and served with onions. These could be called goujons if they weren't so big and didn't contain a good many large bones. For main courses, the dhansak (£5.95) comes as either mutton or chicken and is very tasty – it's cooked with lentils and turns out at once hot, sweet and sour. Or how about palak lamb (£5.95), a simple dish of lamb and spinach? Then there's a selection of Bukhara dishes – which are essentially biryanis cooked in a sealed pot – chicken or lamb (£6.95), prawn (£7.95). Naan bread (£1.95) is freshly cooked and wiped with butter – delicious. There are a few vegetable dishes – Bombay aloo (£3.95); begun masala (£4.50), which is a dryish aubergine dish; and a vegetable and cashew nut biryani (£5.25). Plus some Banarasi dishes like bhel puri, plus South Indian dishes like dosas, plus all the other familiar favourites. Despite this scatter-gun approach to menu writing, the cooking here is sound enough.

Weekdays, the lunch is a buffet – your chance to go through the card for £7.95, sampling curries, tandoori chicken, rice dishes and a constant flow of hot naans. If you want to do this justice, pick a day when all is serene – a nap after such a lunch is obligatory.

Herb & Spice

🍴 Do not let the tiny, rather cramped and garish dining room put you off this treasure of a curry house on Whites Row, a small road just off Commercial Street and tucked in behind Spitalfields. A loyal clientele from the City means that to secure one of the 22 seats you'll probably have to book! The menu here includes all the curry classics, plus one or two dishes you may not have spotted

£7 to £15
Address 11a Whites Row, E1
☏ 020 7247 4050
Station Aldgate East/
Liverpool Street
Open Mon–Fri 11.30am–2.30pm &
5.30–11.30pm
Accepts All major credit cards

before, but what sets Herb & Spice apart from the pack is that the dishes are freshly cooked and well prepared, and yet the prices are still reasonable. When the food arrives it will surprise you: it's on the hot side, with plenty of chilli and bold, fresh flavours.

It's not often that the popadoms (55p) grab your attention. They do here. Fresh, light and crisp, they are accompanied by equally good home-made chutneys – perky chopped cucumber with coriander leaf, and a hot, yellowy-orange, tamarind-soured yoghurt. The kebabs make excellent starters: murgi tikka (£2.75) – chicken, very well cooked; shami kebab (£2.75) – minced meat with fresh herbs; gosht tikka (£2.75) – tender lamb cubes. For a main course you might try the excellent murgi biryani (£6.95), chicken cooked with saffron rice and served with a good, if rather hot, vegetable curry. Or there's bhuna gosht (£4.95), a model of its type – a rich, well-seasoned lamb curry with whole black peppercorns and shards of cassia bark. Murgi rezala (£6.95) is chicken tikka in sauce; it's much hotter and comes with more vegetables than its cousin, the chicken tikka masala. The breads are good, too: from the decent naan (£1.65) to the shabzi paratha (£1.95), a thin, crisp wholemeal paratha stuffed with vegetables.

For a real tongue-trampler, try the dhal shamber (£2.75), a dish of lentils and mixed vegetables which is often overlooked in favour of that popular garlicky number, tarka dhal. Traditionally served hot, sweet and sour, at Herb & Spice dall shamber comes up very hot, with an almost chemical bite from the large amounts of chilli, and very, very sweet indeed. Not for the faint-hearted.

Lahore Kebab House

For years, the Lahore has been a cherished secret among curry-lovers, a nondescript, indeed dowdy-looking, kebab house serving excellent and very cheap fare. Recent years, however, have seen a few changes, and now the "Original" Lahore Kebab House is bent on world domination, with branches springing up all over London. Thankfully, the food here is still good and spicy, prices are still low, and the service brusque enough to disabuse you of any thoughts that the smart round marquetry tables and posh shopfront are signs of impending mediocrity. What they do here, they do very well indeed.

£4 to £15

Address 2 Umberstone St, E1
☏020 7481 9737
Station Whitechapel/Aldgate East
Open Daily noon–midnight
Accepts Cash or cheque only

Rotis (50p) tend to arrive unordered – the waiter watches how you eat and brings fresh bread as and when he sees fit. For starters, the kebabs are standouts. Seekhe kebab (75p), mutton tikka (£2.50) and chicken tikka (£2.50) are all very fresh, very hot and very good, and served with a yoghurt and mint dipping sauce. The meat or chicken biryanis (£6.50) are also splendid, well spiced and with the rice taking on all the rich flavours. The karahi gosht and karahi chicken (£6) are uncomplicated dishes of tender meat in a rich gravy. And on Friday there is a special dish – lamb chop curry (£6). Also noteworthy is the masala fish (£6). The dal tarka (£5) is made from whole yellow split peas, while sag aloo (£5) brings potatoes in a rich and oily spinach puree. A sad loss from the menu is paya (an awesome dish of long-stewed sheep's feet, thought by some to be the hallmark of any genuine Pakistani restaurant) – apparently it's impossible to get top-quality sheep's feet nowadays. Much more palatable, if you want a very Lahore kind of delicacy, is the home-made kheer (£2), which is a special kind of rice pudding with cardamom.

This Lahore is unlicensed, but happy for customers to bring their own beer or wine – and there's a nearby off-licence ready to oblige. You will certainly need some complement to the generally hot food, though note that alcohol isn't the best cooling agent. For that, order a lassi.

173

Brick Lane & Spitalfields

New Tayyab

(🍴) The Tayyab Empire has come a long way since those first days in 1974. After the initial café came the sweet shop, and then the New Tayyab took over what was once the corner pub. So no.83 was transformed from a scruffy converted pub into a smart new designer restaurant. Now there's art on the walls, smart lighting and the chairs are leather and chrome. Miraculously the food remains straightforward Pakistani fare: good, freshly cooked and served without pretension. And more miraculous still, the prices have stayed lower than you would believe possible. Booking is essential and service is speedy and slick. This is not a place to um and er over the menu.

> **£4 to £15**
>
> **Address** 83 Fieldgate St, E1
> ☎ 020 7247 9543
> **Station** Whitechapel/Aldgate East
> **Open** Daily 5pm–midnight
> **Accepts** Cash or cheque only
> ⊛ www.tayyabs.co.uk

The simpler dishes are terrific, particularly the five pieces of chicken tikka (£2.40), served on an iron sizzle dish alongside a small plate of salady things and a medium-fierce, sharp, chilli dipping sauce. They do the same thing with mutton (£2.40), or there's a plate of four large and splendid lamb chops (£3.80). Sheekh kebabs (70p) and shami kebabs (60p) are bought by the skewer. There are round fluffy naan breads (60p), but try the wholemeal roti (40p), which is deliciously nutty and crisp. The karahi dishes are simple and tasty: karahi chicken (£4 normal portion, £7.80 large) is chicken in a rich sauce; karahi batera (£4/8) are quails; and karahi aloo gosht (£4) is lamb with potatoes in another rich sauce, heavily flavoured with bay leaves. Or there's karahi mixed vegetables (£3). A list of interesting daily specials includes dishes such as the splendidly named meat pillo (£4), which is served every Wednesday, and features chunks of mutton slow-cooked in rice; it's rich, satisfying and seeded with whole peppercorns for bite. Or, for genuine specialists, there's paya (£3.80) – slow-cooked sheep's feet, on Mondays.

The Tayyab is strictly BYOB if you want alcohol. But whether you're going for beer or Coke, make sure you try the Tayyab lassi anyway. A yoghurt drink served in a pint glass, it comes sweet or salted (£1.50), and with mango or banana (£2).

Taja

(‖) Taja's exterior of black and white vertical stripes certainly jolts the eye. Venture in and you find a dining area accommodating 60 covers across two floors. The counter is ultra-modern in stainless steel and the seating has recently been upgraded from stools to comfy chairs. On the ground floor, large windows look out onto the hurly-burly of passing traffic just inches away. The food tastes very fresh, and is markedly cheap.

£5 to £12

Address 199a Whitechapel Rd, E1
☎ 020 7247 3866
Station Whitechapel
Open Mon–Wed & Sun
11am–midnight, Thurs–Sat
11am–12.30am
Accepts All major credit cards
🌐 www.taja.net

So far, so good. By now, those in the know will have recognized that the restaurant in question is a converted toilet in the Whitechapel Road. And, as if that is not novelty enough, Taja is a genuine rarity – a thoroughly modern Bangladeshi restaurant. The menu is both enlightened and lightened, with a host of vegetarian dishes balancing old favourites.

Start with that great test of a tandoor chef, chicken tikka (£1.95). At Taja you get half a dozen sizable chunks of chicken, cooked perfectly – not a hint of dryness – with the obligatory salad garnish (a waste of time) and a yellowish "mint sauce". Or try chotpoti (£1.95), described on the menu as "green peas and potatoes with spices, served with a tamarind chutney – high in protein". Move on to a biryani of mixed vegetables, lamb, chicken or prawn (all £4.95); a good-sized portion comes with a dish of really splendid vegetable curry by way of added lubrication. There are also a host of curryhouse favourites. Chicken bhuna (£4.30) is an outstanding choice, with a really fresh sauce, hot but not too hot, and with lots of fresh herbs. The naan breads – plain (£1.50), peshwari or keema (both £1.75) – are large, thick-rimmed and very fresh, as a naan should be. The Taja got its licence in 1999 but you can still bring your own for a small corkage. Healthier types will enjoy the fresh juices – orange and carrot (£1.95) is especially good.

Taja offers all sorts of set meals and deals. Or you can organize a take-away or delivery by mouse – the website offers a bewildering array.

Wild Cherry

Wild Cherry is a vegetarian restaurant that, as the mission statement by the door proclaims, "exists firstly to provide fresh home-cooked vegetarian meals for the local community". It's part of the London Buddhist Centre around the corner and was once a soup kitchen for workers and devotees.

£6 to £20
Address 241 Globe Rd, E2
☎ 020 8980 6678
Station Bethnal Green
Open Mon 11am–3pm, Tues–Fri 11am–7pm
Accepts All major credit cards except Diners and AmEx

It's a bright, clean, self-service venue with modern wooden tables and Arne Jacobsen chairs. A blackboard lists the daily menu and you choose from selections like layered vegetable, hazelnut and Stilton bake with salad (£4.95); chickpea and spinach curry with coriander and coconut served with basmati rice (£4.95); and hot quiche of the day with two salads (£4.95). There's a choice of three different salads every day, and there's always soup and a quiche and two hot dishes. Baked potatoes include a choice of comforting fillings like humus (£3), grated cheddar (£3.25) and tzatziki (£4.25). Salads (large mixed £4.25, regular mixed £2.95, single scoop £1.50) include choices like arame rice; ruby chard, cherry tomato and fresh chive; mixed leaf; Moroccan chickpea with rocket; and coleslaw with vegan mayonnaise. Puddings include chocolate and beetroot cake (£1.80); prune and honey cake (£1.50); and banoffee pie (£2.25). There's no liquor licence, but you can bring your own for £1 corkage. There are, however, fourteen different teas (80p or 90p), ten of them herbal, plus Free Trade coffee (£1.10 per mug, £1.80 per cafetière), and a choice of soya or cow's milk. Daily choices always include some vegan options and there are usually wheat-free, gluten-free and sugar-free dishes. The portions are huge, it all tastes wholesome and it's amazing value. The resto is relaxed and you can have anything from a full meal to a refreshing cup of camomile tea.

Returning to the mission statement: "We promote vegetarianism by making it both available and, hopefully, irresistible." Read on and discover that Wild Cherry is run by seven Buddhist women whose "working practices are based on the Buddhist principles of non-violence, honesty and generosity". Surely worthwhile aims in any kitchen?

The City

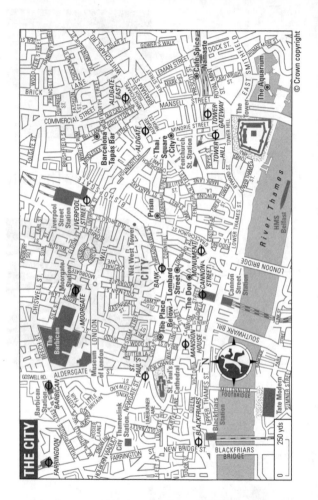

© Crown copyright

1 Lombard Street, The Brasserie

The Brasserie at 1 Lombard Street was formerly a banking hall and the circular bar sits under a suitably imposing glass dome. This is a brasserie in the City, of the City, by the City and for the City. It is connected to Bloomberg – a sort of elitist Teletext-cum-email system which keeps City traders in touch with each other, rather like passing notes at school – and messages flash in and out. The brasserie menu is a model of its kind,

£28 to £75

Address 1 Lombard St, EC3
℡020 7929 6611
Station Bank
Open Mon–Fri Full breakfast
7.30–10am, Continental Breakfast
7.30–11am, 11.30am–3pm &
6–10pm
Accepts All major credit cards
✆ www.1lombardstreet.com

long but straightforward with a spread of dishes that is up to any meal occasion – starters and salads, soups, egg and pasta, caviar, fish, crustacea, meat, puddings. It delivers on pretty much every front, serving satisfying dishes made with good fresh ingredients, and surprisingly it manages to be both stylish and unfussy at the same time. The bar, meanwhile, is like any chic City watering hole – loud, brisk and crowded, with simultaneous conversations in every European language.

The brasserie menu changes every couple of months to satisfy the band of regulars, and there are daily specials in addition. The starters can be ambitious, like a seasonal game pie (£8.75), or simple, like French onion soup (£5.50), while further down the menu there will be some even more comfortable options like a soft-boiled free-range egg (£8.95 or £12.95 main) served with baked potato, smoked haddock, and English mustard sauce. There's enough listed under shellfish and crustacea to fuel even the wildest celebrations, including sautéed scallops with a saffron and chorizo risotto, liquorice velouté (£22.95), and casserole of mussels Marinière (£8.35/£14.50). The Classics section has coq au vin à la Bourguignon (£16.25) and the Meat section lists steak, sausages, liver and chops. During the season you may also find venison stew with glazed root vegetables and suet dumplings (£17.50).

There is a smaller, 40-seater room at the back of the bar set aside for fine dining at fancy prices. It's interesting to note, however, that caviar is a brasserie dish – 50g of Beluga served with blinis, steamed potatoes and sour cream will set you back £120.

The Aquarium

St Katharine's Dock is a strange place, part tourist trap and part haven for millionaire yachties, so the medieval banquet (complete with fighting knights and wenches) rubs shoulders with big boats. The Aquarium is run by Christian and Kerstin Sandefeldt, a Swedish husband-and-wife team and they have put a very personal stamp on the place. This is a fish restaurant and a rather good one. The underlying premise of the place is that the quality and sustainability of ingredients is of paramount importance, so you won't see cod but will see langoustines from the Outer Hebrides and Arctic char. The restaurant is pretty but plain, and has pleasant views across the water. Dishes are well conceived if elaborately presented.

£18 to £60

Address Ivory House, St Katharine's Dock, E1

☎ 020 7480 6116

Station Tower Hill/Tower Gateway

Open Mon noon–3pm, Tues–Fri noon–3pm & 6.30–11pm, Sat brunch (summer) noon–4pm, dinner 6.30–11pm

Accepts All major credit cards

🌐 www.theaquarium.co.uk

There is a very sound lunch menu: two courses for £17.50 and three courses for £20.50. On the à la carte, the starters include a crab and cucumber salad with tomato and ginger dressing (£8.25). Or perhaps carpaccio of tuna and veal with a mint dressing (£9.50) appeals? Main course dishes are full-on – whole roast Swedish perch, curried vegetables and smoked mussel samosa (£15.75). The roast cod with prawn and thyme mash, sauce bois boudrin (£14.75) has been the most popular dish since the Sandefeldts arrived in 2002, but now to save cod it is made with pollock. Stray carnivores get offered a dish or so – such as sweet-and-sour confit of pork belly with chilli udon noodle and pak choi (£14.75). There's a tempting array of desserts, including one dish disarmingly called "lots of chocolate" (£7.50) – the line-up is a choccy crème brûlée, a choccy fondant bun, a choccy milkshake, a choccy orange sorbet, and a three-choccy terrine.

Sandefeldt is a good and passionate fish cook, but if ever a competition were held to determine the world's silliest restaurant plate, the Aquarium would probably have won with one of its 2002 offerings. Picture a punt – those old, smelly, rectangular wooden boats. Then think smaller, about 24 inches long, and imagine it was made of white china.

Barcelona Tapas Bar

(🍴) At the start of the East End, not a hundred yards from the towering buildings of the City, you find yourself among the market stalls of Petticoat Lane and Middlesex Street. On one of the less salubrious corners you'll see a banner bearing the legend "tapas". Note that the arrow points down. As you descend the stairs into a cramped basement, which seats about twenty, try to

£12 to £30

Address 1a Bell Lane, E1
☎ 020 7247 7014
Station Aldgate
Open Mon–Fri 11am–11pm
Accepts All major credit cards
Branches see p.487
🌐 www.barcelona/tapas.com

still the thought that this is an inauspicious start to your lunch or evening. Barcelona is, in fact, one of London's best tapas bars. The range of snacks wouldn't be sniffed at in Barcelona or Madrid, and includes a fair few Catalan specialities – including the classic tomato- and garlic-rubbed bread, a good accompaniment to any tapas session.

You'll find a number of tapas lined up in typical Spanish style along the back half of the bar – these are just a few of the selection on offer. The Barcelona has a vast (in more ways than one) menu, written in Spanish and Catalan with English translations. Many are simple, like Serrano ham (£8.50), or queso Manchego (£4.95), or aceitunas (£1.75-2.95) – olives – and rely on the excellent quality of the raw ingredients. Then there are peasant dishes like fabada Asturiana (£3.50), a stew of white beans with chorizo. More skill is involved in creating the paellas; the paella Valenciana (£11.95 per person) is particularly good. And there is also a chicken brochette (£6.95). Be warned: the Spanish seem blithely unaware of the havoc they wreak with the social lives of unsuspecting diners, and here, as well as being delicious, the gambas al ajillo (£6.95) are pungent enough to give you heartburn and the kind of breath that gets you elbow room in a thronged rush-hour tube.

Unusually for such a small place with such a huge choice, there's no need to worry about freshness. There is a bigger, smarter, newer and less charming Barcelona nearby, and the apparent lull between ordering and receiving your dish may be because the girl is running around the corner to the other kitchen to fetch a portion.

Café Spice Namaste

🍴🍷 During the week this restaurant is packed with movers and shakers, all busily moving and shaking. They come in for lunch at 11.59am and they go out again at 12.59pm. Lunchtimes and even weekday evenings the pace is fast and furious, but come Saturday nights you can settle back and really enjoy Cyrus Todiwala's exceptional cooking. What's more, with the City "closed for the weekend", parking is no

£20 to £50
Address 16 Prescot St, E1
☎ 020 7488 9242
Station Aldgate East/Tower Hill
Open Mon–Fri noon–3pm & 6.15–10.30pm, Sat 6.15–10.30pm
Accepts All major credit cards
Branches see p.488
ⓦ www.cafespice.org

problem. It is well worth turning out, for this is not your average curry house. The menu, which changes throughout the year, sees Parsee delicacies rubbing shoulders with dishes from Goa, North India, Hyderabad and Kashmir, all of them precisely spiced and well presented. The tandoori specialities, in particular, are awesome, fully flavoured by the cunning marinades but in no way dried out by the heat of the oven.

Start with a voyage around the tandoor. The murg kay tikkay (£4.75/9.95) tastes as every chicken tikka should, with yoghurt, ginger, cumin and chillies all playing their part. Or there's venison tikka aflatoon (£5.95/11.50), which originates in Gwalior and is flavoured with star anise and cinnamon. Also notable is the papeta na pattice (£3.95), a potato cake perked up with coconut, green peas and Parsee-style hot tomato gravy. For a main course, fish lovers should consider the tareli machchi nay leeli curry (£12.75) – tilapia fillets marinated and then grilled, and served with a coconut curry. Choose meat and you should try the dhansak (£11.75). This is a truly authentic version of the much-misrepresented Parsee speciality of lamb curried with lentils; it is served with a small kebab and brown-onion rice. Breads are also excellent, and some of the accompaniments and vegetable dishes belie their lowly status at the back of the book-sized menu. Try baingan bharta (£4.50/7.25), an aubergine classic.

It's a good idea at Café Spice Namaste to do as the in-the-know diners do, and choose from the speciality menu that changes every week. Also make a note to try the pickles – they are very good indeed.

The Don

George Sandeman first took over the cellars at 20 St Swithin's Lane in 1798. And very fine cellars they are too, complete with an ornate black iron "Capital Patent Crane" for lowering barrels into the depths. The current incumbent occupying the site is The Don restaurant and bistro, which takes its name from the trademark portrait of Sandeman port's "Don" which has been rehung, with due ceremony, at the gateway to this hidden courtyard. The vaulted brick cellars make a grand backdrop for the bistro, while the lofty room on the ground floor makes a striking restaurant. The restaurant floor is real wood – so real that it squeaks underfoot – and the walls are hung with suitably enigmatic modern art. The whole place reeks of aspiration.

£30 to £75

Address 20 St Swithin's Lane, EC4
℡ 020 7626 2606
Station Bank
Open Mon–Fri noon–3pm & 6–10pm
Accepts All major credit cards

The food in the upstairs restaurant is good – it is setting its cap at great things by aiming directly for the fine-dining market. This is a strategy that seems to be working – the food is accomplished and you couldn't ask for a better-heeled catchment area. Starters range from a Mediterranean fish soup with croutons, rouille and Gruyère cheese (£5.90); a terrine of foie gras, sweetbreads and morel mushrooms with toasted brioche (£9.95); and a warm asparagus salad with a sauce mousseline, summer truffle jus (£6.95); to a salade paysanne of boudin noir with Cox's apples and Calvados dressing (£6.25). Mains may include seared tuna Niçoise (£14.50); loin of young New Zealand venison with roast fig and fondant potato "Oporto" (£16.95); and a well-judged dish of calf's liver with braised chicory and champ potatoes (£15.75). The cooking is good but the presentation is ambitious and tends towards the old-fashioned and elaborate. Puds are comforting: dark chocolate tart with eau de vie Mandarine sorbet (£5.75); hazelnut pistachio parfait (£5.50). And there are savouries, including a delicious French rarebit (£7.75) of grilled Reblochon on toasted potato and garlic bread.

The bistro downstairs offers simpler, cheaper food, and there is a grand private room in the next-door cellar.

The Place Below

Bill Sewell started The Place Below in 1989 and, yes, it is a vegetarian restaurant, and yes it is in the crypt of the St Mary-le-Bow Church. But persevere: it has a splendidly low worthiness rating. If and when you find the restaurant – wander into the wonderfully elegant Wren church and look for the staircase down to the crypt – you'll see that it is split into two halves. The first has an open kitchen at one end and acts as coffee shop and servery. Good pastries and breakfast buns. The restaurant proper is open at lunch (with prices a pound or two cheaper between 11.30am and noon). Choose from the daily changing menu, push a tray along the canteen-style rails, and the chefs will fill a plate for you.

£6 to £15
Address St Mary-le-Bow Church, Cheapside, EC2
☎ 020 7329 0789
Station Bank/St Paul's
Open Mon–Fri 7.30am–3.30pm, lunch 11.30am–2.30pm
Accepts All major credit cards except Diners
⊕ www.theplacebelow.co.uk

The menu is reassuringly short – if everything is freshly cooked, if the menu is seasonal, and if prices are to be kept low, then a short menu is your guarantee. The dining room is lofty, with the large, central communal dining table being the only one with a tablecloth. The menu changes daily. There are a couple of soups, a hot dish, a quichey option, a salad of the day, good trad puds and that's about it. The soups are hearty, such as barley and vegetable broth; or onion potato and Cheddar (both £3.10). Splash out on bread (60p), which is very good indeed – nutty with a good crust. The salad of the day (£7.50) can be triumphant: crisp green beans, a rich savoury dollop of wild rice, shredded carrot with sesame seeds, and plenty of fresh leaves. Or how about a hot dish like the chilli bean casserole (£7)? It's rich and light, with a good spike of chilli, topped with a blob of very decent guacamole and served with bulgur wheat. The field mushroom, fennel and Gruyère quiche (£6.50) is also well made. There are always cakey puddings like carrot cake with passion fruit frosting, or maybe a chocolate and chestnut mousse cake (both £2.80). At The Place Below the cooking is of a high standard, and prices are commendably low.

No alcohol here, so make a beeline for the very good home-made lemonade (£1.50).

Prism

(*) The question we should ask our-selves is: Where have all the banks gone to? And the answer is probably that they have vanished into cyberspace behind hole-in-the-wall machines, leaving free all these tantalizing banking halls with the kind of lofty ceilings and grandiose pillars that make restaurant designers drool. Prism, part of the Harvey Nichols plan for world domination, is an expensive City restaurant. Whether you find it a soul-satisfying experience is probably something that can only be settled by a long interrogation of your wallet (or more probably your expense account). If you work in the City it is undeniably handy. Eating here is rather like being inside a towering, white-painted cube; it's very slick, and very much an old banking hall. The food is a well-judged blend of English favourites and modernist influences. There is the obligatory long bar and the obligatory suave service.

£35 to £110

Address 147 Leadenhall St, EC3
℡ 020 7256 3888
Station Bank
Open Mon–Fri 11.30am–3.30pm &
6–10pm
Accepts All major credit cards
🌐 www.harveynichols.com

Starters are well executed: Jerusalem artichoke soup, wild mushrooms (£6.50); Cornish crab and mango salad, with coriander and mild curry dressing (£9); or bresaola, served with Waldorf salad (£11.50). Risotto of Gorgonzola comes with wild rocket, and a paprika crisp (£8.50). When it comes to main courses, the menu splits half fish and half meat. On the fish side are dishes like poached fillet of Glenarm organic salmon, winter vegetable consommé (£20), as well as more adventurous offerings such as Canadian halibut, citrus crust, braised fennel, broad beans, Pernod butter sauce (£24). The meat side offers Aylesbury duck leg confit with caramelized salsify, Savoy cabbage and girolles (£18.50); Scottish fillet of beef and Colchester oyster stew (£22); and cannon of lamb with sun-dried tomatoes and black olives (£22). Puddings (all £7) include cherry panna cotta pistachio nut waffle; natural yoghurt parfait; blueberry compote; and baked dark chocolate mousse.

Like the pricing, the wine list is for bankers. There are a few bottles to be had for sensible prices but the main thrust is towards whatever the traffic will bear.

Thai Square City

When this restaurant opened in 2001, PR fanfares proclaimed that it was Europe's largest Thai restaurant, and it is plausible enough. In a vast room decorated with temple bells, Buddhas, pots, carved panels, teak, wooden flowers and gold-mosaic rooftop dragons, friendly staff greet customers with a genuine smile. Downstairs there's a 100-seater cocktail bar with a 4–7pm happy hour and a massive bar stocked with brightly coloured drinks. On Thursday and Friday, downstairs at Thai Square turns into a club with a 2am drink and dancing licence.

£12 to £45
Address 136–138 The Minories, EC3
☎ 020 7680 1111
Station Aldgate/Tower Hill
Open Mon–Thurs noon–10pm, Fri noon–11.30pm
Accepts All major credit cards except Diners

The 80-dish menu lists both familiar favourites and more novel ideas. Toong thong (£4) is a dish of minced prawn and chicken in purse-like little sacks, and very moreish. Tod man poo (£5), or Thai crab cakes, will satisfy connoisseurs seeking this favourite, and tom yam kung (£4) will delight lovers of the classic lemongrass soup. Moo ping (£5), or barbecued pork served with a sweet and incredibly hot sauce, is tender and good. The menu suggests that it's especially good with sticky rice (£1.75), and it is. Six Thai curries (all £6.25) offer a choice of red or green and different main ingredients, which boosts the number of menu choices significantly. There are the classic noodle dishes like pad Thai (£6.90). Other treats include Chu-chee lobster (£16.00), which is deep-fried lobster with special curry paste, coconut milk and lime leaves; there's pla neung manau (£16.50) a whole sea bass steamed with lemongrass, fresh lime juice and crushed chillies. There's a twenty-dish vegetarian menu and a wine list that starts at £9.95, threads its way through some decent choices at around the £15–20 mark and rockets to cosset City boys with Krug Grande Cuvée champagne (£140) and a Château Cheval Blanc St Emilion (£245). Puddings include banana with coconut syrup and sesame seeds (£3.50), Thai egg custard (£3.00), and ice creams and sorbets (£3.00).

There's a bargain "Lunch Express" midday menu (noon–4pm), with set meals from as little as £6.50.

Clerkenwell

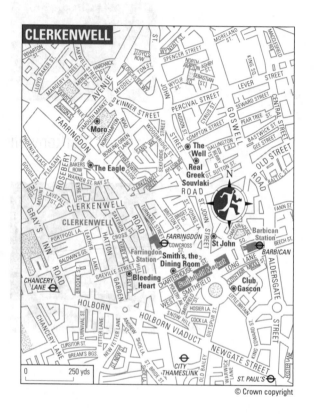

Bleeding Heart

(icon) Just a glance around the deeply traditional basement rooms at Bleeding Heart Yard will tell you instantly what kind of a place this is. The clientele is from the City, the menu is written with City superiority and the wine list is priced for City wallets. And that's not the mufti-wearing, dressing-down, informal sort of City but the pukka, suit-wearing, claret-loving kind. Even during a glorious

£28 to £80

Address Bleeding Heart Yard, off Greville St, EC1
℡ 020 7242 2056
Station Farringdon/Chancery Lane
Open Mon–Fri noon–2.30pm & 6–10.30pm, Sat 6–10.30pm
Accepts All major credit cards

FRENCH

summer these panelled dining rooms will still be packed, and should the forecast veer towards the windy and rainswept this place makes a very agreeable refuge indeed.

The menu changes seasonally and is written in resto-French with Brit subtitles, which may be old-fashioned but obviously suits the customers. Starters may include a little soufflé made with suckling pig, pancetta and a coddled egg (£6.50); home-smoked salmon and sea bass with a quail egg and Caesar salad (£8.45); and a terrine of foie gras with a spiced brioche and a roast fig vinaigrette (£9.50). The mains range from dishes like corn-fed chicken on truffled mash (£15.95); or rack of lamb on crisp potato cake with roast tomato and field mushrooms (£15.95); to tournedos of salmon, basil pomme purée and tapenade (£12.95). The Bleeding Heart empire – restaurant, bistro, tavern, crypt, plus The Don restaurant (see p.183) – also extends to a vineyard in New Zealand, so it's no surprise to see "filet de chevreuil de Nouvelle Zealand avec charlotte des pommes de terre au Reblochon" (£17.45). There's a good, if Franco-centric, cheese trolley, and sound, trad puds (all £5.75). The chef's cooking is precise and unfussy, quality ingredients are left to speak for themselves, and thankfully they speak out loudly. The wine list is an epic tome.

Like everyone else, Bleeding Heart is proud to quote the press, and two hyperbolic comments particularly appeal. According to the *Wine Spectator*, this place has "one of the most outstanding restaurant wine lists in the world", and according to the *New Yorker*, Bleeding Heart Yard is "bleeding hard to find". For once these quotes may even be true.

Clerkenwell

Club Gascon

It's hard to believe it, but Club Gascon opened as long ago as 1998. This place still seems new and still seems fresh, although a vast scrapbook of glowing reviews and a cabinet full of awards testifies to how amazingly successful it has become. If you want a booking, they advise calling two or three weeks ahead, though you may strike lucky with a cancellation. Pascal Aussignac is the chef here, and his cooking is that of the southwest of France, tidied up a little but generally authentic. The menu is set out as six sections, and the portions are larger than some starters but smaller than most mains, the idea being that you indulge in your very own *dégustation*, trying several dishes – which isn't the cheapest way of eating.

£35 to £85

Address 57 West Smithfield, EC1
☎ 020 7796 0600
Station Farringdon
Open Mon–Fri noon–2pm &
7–10pm, Sat 7–10.30pm
Accepts All major credit cards
except Diners

The sections are "La route du sel" – cured meats and charcuterie; "Le potager" – vegetables and cheese; "Les foies gras chauds"; "Les foies gras froids"; "L'océan" – fish and shellfish; "Les pâturages" – mainly duck and cassoulet; "Le marché" – game and offal. There are 40 different dishes. It's important to spread your ordering. Here are some promising combinations: farmhouse jambon du Béarn (£8.50); grilled foie gras of duck with grapes (£10.80); three oysters with truffled chipolata (£6.50); pan-fried beef fillet, winter spirit (£9.50); roast confit of duck, crème forte (£8.50). Or maybe smoked zander roasted on a river stone (£12.50); or home-made French fries with fleur de sel (£4) appeal? The problem with eating like this is that you can hit on a dish that is amazing and therefore too small. You must have the confidence to order a second or even third serving.

If you feel daunted, try the tasting menu, which changes monthly: five courses for £35 (but everyone at the table must order it). One such menu might lead you from a foie gras dish to grilled oysters, carpaccio of duck, to Pyrenean lamb, culminating in a pistachio macaroon with frosted praline. A pretty good way to shed £35. Dig deep and up the ante to £55 and you can have various glasses of specially selected wines as well.

The Eagle

(🍴) The Eagle was for years a run-down pub in an unpromising part of London. Then in 1991 it was taken over by food-minded entrepreneurs who transformed it into a restaurant-pub turning out top-quality dishes. They were pioneers: there should be a blue plaque over the door marking the site as the starting place of the great gastropub revolution. In a decade or so of existence, The Eagle has remained a crowded,

£8 to £20

Address 159 Farringdon Rd, EC1
℡ 020 7837 1353
Station Farringdon
Open Meals served Mon–Fri
12.30–2.30pm & 6.30–10.30pm,
Sat 12.30–3.30pm & 6.30–
10.30pm, Sun 12.30–3.30pm
Accepts Cash or cheque only

MEDITERRANEAN/GASTROPUB

rather shabby sort of place, and the staff still display a refreshing full-on attitude. The kitchen is truly open: the chefs work behind the bar, and the menu is chalked up over their heads. It changes daily, even hourly, as things run out or deliveries come in. The food is broadly Mediterranean in outlook with a Portuguese bias, and you still have to fight your way to the bar to order and pay.

This is a pub with a signature dish. Bife Ana (£8.50) has been on the menu here since the place opened and they have sold tens of thousands of portions. It is a kind of steak sandwich whose marinade has roots in the spicy food of Portugal and Mozambique, and it is delicious. The rest of the menu changes like quicksilver but you may find the likes of the famous caldo verde (£4.50) – the Portuguese chorizo and potato soup which takes its name from the addition of spring greens. There may be a grilled plaice with roast vegetables, and shallots with honey and balsamico (£9.50); or a delicious and simple dish like roast spring chicken with celeriac, celery, cream and bay "al forno" (£9.50); or a shoulder of lamb "en sofrito" with chilli and caraway seeds, and couscous with dried fruit and nuts (£10). To finish, choose between a fine cheese – perhaps a Sardinian Pecorino served with flatbread and marmalade (£6.50), or the siren charms of those splendid, small, Portuguese, cinnamony custard tarts – pasteis de nata – at £1 a piece.

Even with pavement seating providing extra capacity in decent weather, The Eagle is never less than crowded. The music is always loud and the staff are busy and brusque. A great place nonetheless.

Clerkenwell

Moro

(icon) This modern, rather stark restaurant has slipped effortlessly from being new and iconoclastic to occupying a place on the list of London's "must visit" eateries. In feel it's not so very far away from the better pub-restaurants, although the proprietors have given themselves the luxury of a slightly larger kitchen. This has also become a place of pilgrimage for disciples of the wood-fired oven, and as the food here hails mainly from Spain, Portugal and North Africa, it is both Moorish and moreish. There is also a grand list of moody sherries. The only problem lies in Moro's popularity. It's consistently booked up, which places a bit of a strain on both kitchen and waiting staff. A relatively new development is the tapas menu, which is available all day and offers a good range of small dishes priced at £2.50/3.50 rising to £7 for jamon – a good way to test things out.

£18 to £48
Address 34–36 Exmouth Market, EC1
☎ 020 7833 8336
Station Farringdon/Angel
Open Mon–Fri 12.30–2.30pm & 7–10.30pm, Sat 7–10.30pm
Accepts All major credit cards

The a la carte changes every fortnight. There's usually a soup, and its usually amongst the best starters. How does spiced chicken broth with herb and saffron dumplings (£5), sound? Or you may be offered starters such as squid cooked in its own ink with toast (£6); flat bread with minced lamb, pine nuts, cinnamon and pomegranate molasses (£6); or artichoke hearts and leeks poached with dill (£6). Main courses are simple and often traditional combinations of taste and textures. As with the starters, it's the accompaniments that tend to change rather than the core ingredients. Look out for wood-roasted harissa chicken with chips and a rocket salad (£15.50); or charcoal-grilled lamb with a warm chickpea salad and aioli (£16); or perhaps charcoal-grilled sea bass with farika, beetroot, and seasoned yoghurt (£16). There are usually some other fishy options too, along the lines of wood-roasted whole sea bream with pine-nut and raisin pilaf and yoghurt and dill sauce (£16).

Do not miss the splendid Spanish cheeses (£5.50) served with membrillo – traditional quince paste. And there's no excuse to avoid the Malaga raisin ice cream (£4.50), or the serious chocolate coffee and cardamom cake (£5).

Smiths, the Dining Room

Calling Smiths of Smithfield an ambitious project is like saying that pyramid building calls for a large workforce. First take a Grade II listed warehouse overlooking Smithfield Market, then gut it. Rebuild the inside in ultra-modern-meets-*Blade Runner* style and – hey presto – you have two restaurants, two bars, private rooms, kitchens and whatever, spread over four floors. On the ground floor there's a bar and café serving drink and good, sensible food

£18 to £50

Address 67–77 Charterhouse St, EC1
℡ 020 7251 7950
Station Farringdon
Open Café Mon–Fri 7am–11pm, Sat & Sun 10.30am–5pm, restaurants Mon–Fri noon–3pm & 6–11pm, Sat 6–11pm
Accepts All major credit cards
ⓦ www.smithsofsmithfield.com

from breakfast to bedtime. At the top is the "rooftop restaurant", a 70-seater which pays particular attention to quality meat with good provenance. On the second floor is the 130-seater "Dining Room". The culinary mainspring is John Torode, who should be congratulated on his enlightened buying policy – quality, quality, quality.

The Dining Room is a large space around a central hole which looks down onto the smart bar area. Eating here is rather like sitting at the centre of a deactivated factory – a tangle of exposed pipes and girders. The menu is divided into Larder (which means starters), Soups, Mains, Grills, Daily Market Specials, Sides, and Sweet Tooth. The way the prices are expressed, however, is coy and irritating – Larder "all at 4 ¾ Pounds"; "Sides 2 ½ Pounds". Bah humbug. But the starters are simple and good: cured Cumbrian ham, endive and mustard dressing (£4.75); potato gnocchi, creamed Gorgonzola and wild rocket (£4.75); omelette Arnold Bennett (£5.75). Main courses show off the careful buying policy: crisp belly of pork with mashed potato and green sauce (£10.50); Smiths 10oz beef burger with cheese and Old Spot bacon (£11.50); roast hake with creamed tomato and spinach (£10.50). The lunch specials are from the comfort-eating school, and feature such delights as cottage pie (£9.50). Puds are good. Try Bramley apple and cinnamon pie custard (£4).

There's a decent breakfast on offer downstairs, with porridge (£2) or bacon, egg, beans, sausage, mushrooms, black pudding, tomatoes, bubble and toast (£6.50). And it is available all day, so Dr Johnson would have been happy.

Souvlaki & Bar

(🍴) This the latest venture by the team at The Real Greek (see p.217), It opened during spring 2003 and Souvlaki has been busy from day one, partly because the food is cheap and top-quality, and partly because the tone of the place is perfectly in tune with the mood of the times. This is a friendly,

£7 to £28

Address 140–142 St John St, EC1
☎ 020 7253 7234
Station Angel/Farringdon
Open Mon–Sat 10am–11pm
Accepts Mastercard, Switch or Visa

informal, lively bar where you can get simple delicious food. The room is dominated by the bar and open kitchen and there are a series of high, narrow island tables with bar stools. As it says on the menu "Souvlaki and Bar offers Real Greek street food. Regional wines, beers and ouzos complement the flavours" and the good-value Greek wines will convince you. There is also the "Ouzo Mohito" cocktail dreamed up by a superstar mixologist to celebrate the opening, not very trad but surprisingly moreish.

The menu is very short. There are ten mezedes – dolmades (£2.80); taramasalata (£3.80); horta with beetroot (£3.50) – a warm salad – htipiti (£3.20), which is delicious mishmash of cheese, red peppers and roast red onions. The bread is terrific, round, Greek flatbreads, lightly oiled and then crisped on the grill. Then there is the souvlaki. In Greece souvlaki changes with the seasons – so that from November until the end of May it is made from pork and for the rest of the year it is made from lamb. That's the way it is here – £4.75 buys you a flatbread with a splosh of yoghurty tzatziki and some tomato and pepper puree and then a skewer of pork. It is rolled tightly and wrapped in greaseproof paper. For £9.25 you can have a "double" (two of them, unsurprisingly). The same kind of thing made with chicken is (£4.75/9.25). Or there's a smoked sausage from Evritania swaddled in the same bread (£4.75/9.25). Non-souvlakists will find grilled fish (£11.95), grilled pork cutlets (£5.90) and seared scallops (£7.50) to stop them going hungry.

Ultra-traditionalists can have an old-style souvlaki (£3.75/7.50). A piece of toasted sourdough forms the base and the skewer of meat is speared into it; the juices run down onto the bread and not your shirt. Very elegant.

St John

One of the most frequent requests, especially from foreign visitors, is "Where can we get some really English cooking?" Little wonder that the promise of "olde English fare" is the bait in so many London tourist traps. The cooking at St John, however, is genuine. It is sometimes old-fashioned and makes inspired use of all those strange and

£25 to £60

Address 26 St John St, EC1
☎ 020 7251 0848
Station Farringdon
Open Mon–Fri noon–3pm &
6–11pm, Sat 6–11pm
Accepts All major credit cards
🌐 www.stjohnrestaurant.co.uk

unfashionable cuts of meat which were once commonplace in rural Britain. Technically the cooking is of a very high standard, while the restaurant itself is completely without frills or design pretensions. You'll either love it or hate it. But be forewarned: this is an uncompromising and opinionated kitchen, and no place to take a hard-core vegetarian.

The menu changes every session but the tone does not, and there's always a dish or two to support the slogan "nose to tail eating". Charcuterie, as you'd imagine, is good: a simple terrine (£6) will be dense but not dry – well judged. Or, for the committed, what about a starter of roast bone marrow and parsley salad (£6.20)? Anthony Bourdain claimed this as his "Desert Island Dish". Or venison liver and dandelion (£6)? Or potato, bacon and cabbage broth (£5.80)? Be generous to yourself with the bread, which is outstanding (you can purchase a loaf to take home). Main courses may include a pheasant and trotter pie (for two, £26), or braised beef and mash (£14.80). Maybe there will be a dish described simply as "swede cake and watercress" (£12.80); perversely, in this den of offal, the veg dishes are a delight. Puddings are traditional and well executed: rice pudding with plums (£5.40), or a slice of strong Lancashire cheese with an Eccles cake (£6). Joy of joys, sometimes there is even a seriously good Welsh rarebit (£5).

St John has won shedloads of awards, and booking is a must. How encouraging to see a party of Japanese businessmen forsaking tourist pap for roast sirloin, dripping toast and horseradish (£16)! Whatever your feelings about meat and offal cookery, be assured that St John serves food at its most genuine.

Clerkenwell

The Well

Taking its name from the well that served the clerken hereabouts and so inspired the name of the area, The Well is a buzzy bar-cum-gastropub where the diners, staff and owner Tom Martin all appear to be friends having a good time. Scrubbed tables and old church chairs give a fresh, accessible feel to this corner venue, which is open as a bar throughout the day and as a restaurant during kitchen hours. A couple of daily specials on a blackboard complement the modern mixed menu, which appears to be geared to everyone's favourite dishes rather than any particular cuisine. The wine list runs from a respectable Italian house red or white at £11.95 to Dom Perignon 1993 champagne at £95, for the Clerkenwell-heeled.

£30 to £70

Address 180 St John St, EC1
℗ 020 7251 9363
Station Angel/Farringdon
Open Mon–Fri noon–3pm & 6–10.30pm, Sat brunch 10.30am–10.30pm, Sun brunch 10.30am–10pm
Accepts All major credit cards

The menu changes regularly, but starters may include tomato and bread soup (£4.50); "pint o' prawns" with mayonnaise (£6.50); warm salad of squid, chorizo, new potatoes and flat-leaf parsley (£5.95); mussels with rosemary, garlic and white wine (£8); and char-grilled black tiger prawns with lime and chilli dressing (£7.95). Main courses are equally considered. Sausages come with colcannon and gravy (£9.95), but these are Gloucester Old Spot sausages; or there may be home-made cottage pie with green beans (£10.50); or slow-roast rib-eye (£14.95), which comes with Dauphinoise potatoes, roast garlic and crispy bacon. Fish dishes get good representation: whole steamed bream with sticky rice and buttered seaweed (£16.95); or battered coley fillet with fat chips and tartare (£9.50). For veggies there is a Thai green curry with seared tofu and stir-fried vegetables (£11). The desserts (all £3.95) range from the classic – chocolate brownies with vanilla cream, or whisky bread-and-butter pudding with custard – to the more adventurous, like cranberry and cinnamon crème brûlée. British cheeses (£7.50) are from the admirable Neal's Yard Dairy.

The Well attracts an unusually varied crowd from the surrounding dot-com millionaire loft roosts and council estates, but they all seem to enjoy its lively atmosphere and good value.

Docklands

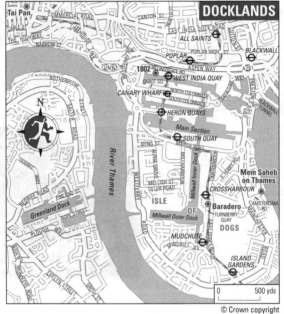

1802

🍴 West India Quay is one of the many stretches of waterfront that have been painstakingly groomed and transformed into a playground for all the people working in the towering glass prisons. A succession of bars and restaurants stretches along the bank, plenty parasols, plenty space heaters, plenty lager, plenty champagne. 1802 is somewhat more stylish. It is the restaurant attached to the Museum of Docklands and was opened by the Searcy's group during June 2003. The operation is driven by a modern bar and there is a selection of simple meals and sandwiches available throughout the day. The main restaurant is more aspirational, and offers a short seasonal menu at lunchtime.

£10 to £50

Address One West India Quay, Hertsmere Rd, E14
☏ 0870 444 3886
Station DLR West India Quay
Open Mon–Sat 11am–10pm, Sun 11am–5pm
Accepts All major credit cards

Dishes are securely based around fresh British ingredients, and all the better for that. Summer starters may include poached asparagus with Hollandaise sauce (£5.85); potted confit duck, apple and gherkin (£6.95) – a well-made dish that is a hair's breadth away from being duck rillettes; if the coarse texture of rillettes has previously left you less than keen, you will enjoy this alternative. Or there may be a Cornish crab and avocado salad (£7.80). Or something very simple like a fresh pea and mint soup (£3.95). Main courses feature a good many fishy options (as befits somewhere a tail's flick from Billingsgate Market). There may be cold poached Scottish salmon, with Jersey Royal potatoes and caviar crème fraîche (£12.50); or lemon herb-crusted cod with slow-roast tomatoes (£12.95); and – as you would expect in the shadow of all that business red in tooth and claw – there is also a rib-eye steak with Béarnaise sauce and hand-cut fat chips (£15.50). Puds are the obvious ones – crème brûlée (£4.50); vanilla panna cotta with summer berries (£5). Service is friendly.

Much is made of the brunch menu here, and it is certainly eclectic – ranging from chicken Caesar salad (£8.95); through Toulouse sausages, champ potato, and red wine jus (£9.95); to trad roast beef (£13.95) – none of which are particularly brunchy dishes, but all of which would make for a pleasant enough weekend lunch.

Baradero

(y) Baradero is modern, light, tiled and airy. And, as far as the view of Millwall dock and proximity to the London Arena will permit, you could almost think yourself in Spain. Essentially a tapas bar, it offers main courses too, and both are of restaurant quality. Take a seat at the bar or at one of the well-spaced tables, order yourself a bottle of Estrella beer or

£8 to £35

Address Turnberry Quay, off Pepper St, E14
℡ 020 7537 1666
Station DLR Crossharbour
Open Mon–Fri noon–11pm, Sat 6–10.45pm
Accepts All major credit cards

a glass of Fino sherry, and set about the tapas. There is even a floor show of sorts in the form of the balletic automatic orange juicer, called a Zumm, which seems to wave the whole oranges about for inspection before squashing them for juice.

Start with an order of pan con aioli (95p) – good bread with a pot of fearsome but seductive garlic mayonnaise. Or pan con tomate (£1.55) – Catalan-style toast drizzled with olive oil and rubbed with garlic and tomato. Add some boquerones (£3.75) – classic white anchovies, sharp with vinegar and garnished with raw garlic slices; and jamón Serrano (£5.75) – a large portion of dark, richly flavoured, dry-cured ham. Then follow up with hot tapas such as croquetas de pollo (£4.25). Whoever would have thought that croquettes could taste so good? Or pulpo a la Gallega (£5.25) – octopus boiled and seasoned in Galician style. Or the particularly delicious fabada Asturiana (£4.95), an Asturian bean stew loaded with chunks of sausage, black pudding and ham hock. Or maybe gambas pil pil (£5.25), prawns with garlic and a belt of chilli heat. If you can restrain your ordering and don't end up crammed full of tapas, move on to the list of main courses, which changes weekly. Try patita de cordero al horno (£16.95), which is a whole roast leg of baby lamb. Or maybe parrillada de pescado y marisco (£17.50) – mixed grilled fish, everything from monkfish to mussels. There is also a simple offer at lunch – pick a couple of tapas, add country bread, aioli and a glass of wine and pay only £7.50.

As well as adding new tapas and main courses each week, to keep regulars from getting bored there is dancing to live music on Friday and Saturday nights.

Mem Saheb on Thames

Mem Saheb on Thames has certainly got an evocative address. "Amsterdam Road" conjures up pictures of old-fashioned docks and wharves, rolling fog banks and cheery East Enders. In practice, this bit of Docklands is a lot like Milton Keynes: Amsterdam Road (along with nearby Rotterdam Drive and Rembrandt Court) are all part of the new

£20 to £40

Address 65–67 Amsterdam Rd, E14
℡ 020 7538 3008
Station DLR Crossharbour
Open Mon–Fri noon–2.30pm &
6–11.30pm, Sat & Sun 6–11.30pm
Accepts All major credit cards

Docklands. Not truly "new" any longer, but new enough for you to notice that some of the paintwork is starting to get chipped. The redeeming factor is the river. As the Thames sweeps round in a majestic arc, the restaurant has a superb view across the water to the Millennium Dome. Mem Saheb is certainly "on-Thames". As a result there's a good deal of squabbling for the middle table in the non-smoking section (pole position as far as the view is concerned). Ultimately, however, the lucky winner must balance the grandstand view of the Millennium folly with the piped-music speaker that hovers directly above the table.

Start by sharing a tandoori khazana (£8.95), which is a platter of mixed kebabs from the tandoor, including good chicken tikka. Or perhaps some salmon samosas (£3.25)? Also tasty is the kabuli salad (£2.95), a winning combination of chickpeas and hard-boiled egg in a sharp tamarind dressing. Of the main courses, macher jhul (£8.95) is tilapia cooked Bengali-style with aubergine and potato. Rajasthani khargosh (£9.95) is an unusual dish pairing rabbit with a mild sauce and served with garlicky spinach. Konju papas (£7.95) is a prawn curry in the South Indian style – tamarind, mustard seeds and coconut. The breads and vegetable dishes are good, particularly the aloo chana (£4.50) – a simple dish of potatoes and chickpeas. The kitchen is to be commended for avoiding artificial additives and colourings.

In pride of place on the menu layout is the "Kitchen Curry" (£7.95) – "Each day our chef cooks a different dish for themselves, also known as Staff Curry. Usually fairly hot, sometimes very hot, meat are always on the bone. Available only from 7pm." Le patron mange ici.

Tai Pan

(🍴) As Sherlock Holmes fans will know, Limehouse was London's first Chinatown, complete with murky opium dens. So, despite the well-intentioned efforts of the Docklands Development Board to promote the area, today's Limehouse seems pretty tame in comparison. It can, however, boast about the Tai Pan. This restaurant is very much a family affair – the ebullient Winnie Wan

£10 to £35

Address 665 Commercial Rd, E14
℗ 020 7791 0118 or 7791 0119
Station DLR Limehouse
Open Mon–Thurs & Sun
noon–11.15pm, Fri noon–
11.45pm, Sat 6–11.45pm
Accepts All major credit cards

is front of house, running the light, bright dining room, while Mr Tsen commands the kitchen. He organizes a constant stream of well-cooked, mainly Cantonese dishes, and slaves over the intricately carved vegetables, which lift their presentation. He's a good cook, and the menu hides one or two surprises as well as all the old favourites. Asking Winnie to recommend something is always a good idea. Sinking your teeth into the carved vegetables is not.

After the complimentary prawn cracker and seriously delicious hot-pickled shredded cabbage, start with deep-fried crispy squid with Szechuan peppercorn salt (£6.90), or fried Peking dumplings with a vinegar dipping sauce (£4.30) – both are excellent. Or try one of the spare-rib dishes (£5.40), or the soft-shell crabs (£4.80 each), or the nicely done, crispy, fragrant aromatic duck with pancakes and the accoutrements (£15.50 for a half). Otherwise, relax and order the Imperial mixed hors d'oeuvres (£8.80 per person, for a minimum of two), which offers a sampler of ribs, spring rolls, seaweed, and prawn and sesame toast, with a carrot sculpture as centrepiece. When ordering main dishes, old favourites like deep-fried shredded beef with chilli (£5.80), and fried chicken in lemon sauce (£5.30), are just as you'd expect. Fried seasonal greens in oyster sauce (£4.30) is made with choi sum, and is delicious, while the fried vermicelli Singapore-style (£5.10) will suit anyone who prefers their Singapore noodle pepped up with curry powder rather than fresh chillies.

For a real bargain pay £13.50 and you can eat as much as you like off the menu (minimum two people); on Sunday between noon and 4pm, the price drops to an awesomely cheap £9.90.

Hackney & Dalston

HACKNEY & DALSTON

© Crown copyright

Armadillo

(🍴) Armadillo is that rare thing – a small neighbourhood restaurant with an unusual menu and staff who care. Chef-owner Rogerio David, from Brazil, has based his dishes on South American home cooking with influences from Spain, North Africa and even Asia. This means adventurous cooking with a modern twist, and if you're looking for unusual combinations of ingredients cooked with a spicy background then be glad to find Armadillo. The dining room is bright, colourful and filled with a lively Broadway Market clientele. The menu uses some unfamiliar South American terms, but after a couple of the excellent Caipirinhas (a mixture of fierce white spirit called Cachaça, with sugar, crushed limes and ice), the friendly explanations from the staff seem to make sense.

£18 to £50

Address 41 Broadway Market, E8
℗ 020 7249 3633
Station Bethnal Green
Open Tues–Sat 6.30–10.30pm, Sun brunch noon–4pm
Accepts All major credit cards
ⓦ www.armadillorestaurant
.co.uk

Coconut sancocho with a peanut and coriander aji sauce (£4) is a rich chunky vegetable soup-stew with a dollop of tasty green chilli and coriander sauce in the middle. Jerusalem artichokes may come sautéed with wild mushrooms and green olives (£4.80). Chicken xim-xim (£10.50) is a dish combining chicken with peppers, nuts, dried shrimp, and coconut stew – served with rice. Roast belly of pork al achiote, with black beans, boniato potatoes and mojo (£12.50), is slow-roasted to melting point with annato spice and South American sweet potatoes. Mojo is the sauce that lubricates – so now you know. Puddings continue in the same vein. Spicy chocolate ice cream and Amaretti (£3.90) is home-made and delivers what it promises; or pionon with manjar (£3.90), which is a kind of Peruvian Swiss roll. Wines are mainly from South America and Spain and are very reasonably priced, from £10.50 to a maximum of £29 for Heidsieck Dry Monopole champagne.

Weather permitting, there's courtyard dining for ten and a balcony with a table for two. Armadillo is deservedly popular on long summer evenings and booking is essential.

FISH & CHIPS

Faulkner's

Faulkner's is a clear highlight among the kebab shops and chippies that line the rather scruffy Kingsland Road – it's a spotless fish-and-chip restaurant, with a takeaway section next door. It is reassuringly old-fashioned with its lace curtains, fish tank, uniformed waitresses and cool yellow walls lined with sepia-tinted piscine scenes, and it holds few surprises – which is probably what makes it such a hit. Usually Faulkner's is full of local families and

£6 to £20
Address 424 Kingsland Rd, E8
☎ 020 7254 6152
Station Liverpool Street
Open Mon–Thurs noon–2pm & 5–10pm, Fri noon–2pm & 4.30–10pm, Sat 11.30am–10pm, Sun noon–9pm
Accepts All major credit cards except AmEx and Diners

large parties, all ploughing through colossal fish dinners while chatting across tables. It also goes out of its way to be child-friendly, with highchairs leaned against the wall, and a children's menu priced at £3.95.

House speciality among the starters is the fishcake (£1.50), a plump ball made with fluffy, herby potato. Or there's smoked salmon (£3.95), which comes in two satisfying wads, or prawn cocktail (£3.75). If you fancy soup, you've got soup of the day (80p) or a more exotic French fish variety (£1.90), which is peppery and dark and comes from Perard in Le Touquet. For main courses, the regular menu features all the British fish favourites, served fried or poached and with chips, while daily specials are chalked up on the blackboard. Cod (from £7.50) and haddock (from £8.75) retain their fresh, firm flesh beneath the dark, crunchy batter, while the subtler, classier Dover sole (from £12.50) is best served delicately poached. The mushy peas (85p) are just right – lurid and lumpy like God intended – but the test of any good chippy is always its chips, and here they are humdingers: fat, firm and golden, with a wicked layer of crispy little salty bits at the bottom. Stuffed in a soft doughy roll they make the perfect chip butty. Most people wet their whistles with a mug of strong tea (70p), but there is wine on offer, including a Beaujolais Villages (£9.90) and a Chablis (£17.25).

Though always lively, Faulkner's is particularly fun at Saturday lunchtime, when traders and shoppers take time out from the local market to catch up, gossip, and joke with the waitresses.

Huong Viet

Huong Viet is the canteen of the Vietnamese Cultural Centre, which occupies a rather four-square and solid-looking building that was once one of Hackney's numerous public bathhouses. It has long had a reputation for really good, really cheap food, and the regulars have stuck with it through a couple of general refurbishments. But, despite acquiring a drinks licence, this place is never going to turn into a trendy bar restaurant, it is too much a focus for the Vietnamese community, so the other customers can breathe a sigh of relief. The food has stayed fresh, unpretentious, delicious and cheap, although prices are creeping upwards. The service is still friendly and informal. And the building still looks a lot like an ex-council bathhouse.

£7 to £25

Address An Viet House, 12–14 Englefield Rd, N1
℡ 020 7249 0877
Station BR Dalston Kingsland
Open Mon–Fri noon–3.30pm & 5.30–11pm, Sat noon–4pm & 5.30–11pm
Accepts Mastercard and Visa

Start with the spring rolls (£3.90) – small, crisp and delicious. Or the fresh rolls (£3.50), which resemble small, carefully rolled-up table napkins. The outside is soft, white and delicate-tasting, while the inside teams cooked vermicelli with prawns and fresh herbs – a great combination of textures. Ordering the prawn and green leaf soup (£3.50/5) brings a bowl of delicate broth with greens and shards of tofu. Pho is perhaps the most famous Vietnamese "soup" dish, but it is really a meal in a bowl. The pho here is formidable, especially the Hanoi noodle soup, filled with beef, chicken or tofu (£3.90/5.50). Hot, rich and full of bits and pieces, it comes with a plate of herbs, crispy beansprouts and aromatics that you must add yourself at the last moment so none of the aroma is lost. The other dishes are excellent too. Look out for mixed seafood with pickled veg and dill (£6.50), which works exceptionally well. You should also try the noodle dishes – choose from the wok-fried rice noodle dishes, or the crispy-fried egg noodles (£3.90 –5.70).

All the food tastes very fresh – it has obviously been freshly cooked and the chef has used spankingly fresh ingredients. There are some good one-plate dishes which are perfect for lunch, such as egg-fried rice with prawns (£5.70).

CITY & EAST

TURKISH

Istanbul Iskembecisi

£8 to £25

Address 9 Stoke Newington Rd, N16
☎ 020 7254 7291
Station BR Dalston Kingsland
Open Daily noon–5am
Accepts All major credit cards

The Istanbul Iskembecisi is just across the road from Mangal II (see p.209), and at heart they are singing off the same sheet. Despite being named after its signature dish – iskembe is a limpid tripe soup – the Istanbul is a grill house. Admittedly it is a grill house with chandeliers, smart tables and upscale service, but it is still a grill house. And because it stays open until late in the morning it is much beloved by clubbers and chefs – they are just about ready to go out and eat when everyone else has had enough and set off home. The grilled meat may be better over at Mangal II, but the atmosphere of raffish elegance at the Istanbul has real charm.

The iskembe (£2.50), or tripe soup, has its following. Large parties of Turks from the snooker hall just behind the restaurant insist on it, and you'll see the odd regular downing two bowlfuls of the stuff. For most people, however, it's bland at best, and even the large array of additives (salt, pepper, chilli – this is a dish that you must season to your personal taste at the table) cannot make it palatable. A much better bet is to start with the mixed meze (£4.95), which brings a good hummus and tarama, a superb dolma, and the rest drawn from the usual suspects. Then on to the grills, which are presented with more panache than usual. Pirzola (£7) brings three lamb chops; shish kebab (£7) is good and fresh; karisik isgara (£8.90) is a formidable mixed grill. For a more interesting option there's arnavaut cigeri-sicak (£6.50) – liver Albanian style. Doubtless somebody somewhere is mourning two casualties of what will probably be seen as the "food scares era" – there is no more kelle sogus (roasted head of lamb) or beyin salata (boiled brain with salad).

Just when you think you're on safe ground with the desserts, the menu is still able to spring one last surprise – kazandibi (£2.50), which is a "Turkish type crème caramel, milk-based sweet with finely dashed chicken breast". When compared with a chicken pudding served as dessert, boiled brain has much to commend it.

Mangal II

The first thing to hit you at Mangal II is the smell. The fragrance of spicy, sizzling char-grilled meat is unmistakably, authentically Turkish. This, combined with the relaxing pastel decor, puts you in holiday mood before you've even sat down. The ambience is laid-back, too. At slack moments, the staff shoot the breeze around the ocakbasi, and service comes with an ear-to-ear grin. All you have to do is sit back, sink an Efes Pilsener (£2.50) and peruse the encyclopedic menu.

£6 to £25
Address 4 Stoke Newington Rd, N16
☎ 020 7254 7888
Station BR Dalston Kingsland
Open Daily noon–1am
Accepts Mastercard and Visa

Prices are low and portions enormous. Baskets of fresh bread are endlessly replenished, so it's just as well to go easy on the appetizers. With a vast range of tempting mezeler (starters), however, resistance is well nigh impossible. The 25 options include simple hummus (£2.50) and dolma (£2.50); imam bayildi (£3) – aubergines stuffed with onion, tomato and green pepper; thin lahmacun (£1.75) – meaty Turkish pizza; and karisik meze (£4) – a large plate of mixed dishes that's rather heavy on the yoghurt. There's a fair spread of salads (£2.50–3) as well, though you get so much greenery with the main dishes that it's a wasted choice here. The main dishes (kebablar) themselves are sumptuous, big on lamb and chicken, but with limited fish and vegetarian alternatives. The patlican kebab (£8) is outstanding – melt-in-the-mouth grilled minced lamb with sliced aubergines, served with a green salad, of which the star turn is an olive-stuffed tomato shaped like a basket. The kebabs are also superb, particularly the house special, ezmeli kebab (£7.50), which comes doused in Mangal's special sauce. Or, if you don't fancy a grill, there's also a choice of three freshly made and hearty "daily stews" (£3.50–5).

After swallowing that lot, dessert might not be feasible, but after a long break – there's no pressure to vacate your table – you might just be tempted by a slab of tooth-achingly sweet baclava (£2). Alternatively, round off the evening with a punch-packing raki (£3). And, for a final blast of Ottoman atmosphere, pay a visit to the bathroom – the no-frills facilities are a real taste of old Istanbul.

Hackney & Dalston

Sông Quê

🍴 A relative newcomer (it opened towards the end of 2002), Sông Quê has made something of an impact among the cluster of Vietnamese eateries strung out along this section of the Kingsland Road. It's a garish place inside, but proximity to other restos means that if you make the journey and can't get a table here (it's best to book), there are several other establishments offering Vietnamese cooking within walking distance including Viet Hoa (see p.220).

£10 to £35

Address 134 Kingsland Rd, EC2
☎ 020 7613 3222
Station Old Street
Open Mon–Sat noon–3pm & 5.30–11pm, Sun noon–11pm
Accepts Mastercard, Visa, Switch or Solo

Sông Quê offers a staggering 170 dishes. 28 starters, 21 noodle dishes, 10 rice dishes, 28 seafood, 13 vegetable dishes and 19 pho or traditional Vietnamese noodle soup dishes – each a meal in itself. The tastes are fresh, hot, sour and heady with basil, coriander and parsley. Try bo nuong la tot (£5.00) and enjoy grilled slices of beef wrapped in betel leaf, or goi cuon (£2.70) – fresh rolls of rice paper with zingy fresh herbs. Larger dishes include diep xao hanh gung (£5.50), scallops with ginger and spring onions, bo chien don sot chua ngot (£4.80), sweet and sour crispy shredded beef and the essential rau muong xao loi (£4.50). Translated as "stir-fried-ong choy with garlic" (but still something of a puzzle), it delivers a dish of the most delicious iron-tasting vegetable, also called water morning glory. Pho, however, is a must. Each comes with rice noodles, shredded onion and coriander simmered in fresh broth with a separate plate of raw beanshoots, a bunch of basil leaves, Vietnamese parsley and sliced red chillies. You dunk the extra raw vegetables in the hot broth, swish around and enjoy, taking great care with the red chillies. Of the 19 varieties (priced between £3.50 and £4.50) each, pho ga is chicken, tai nam is rare sliced steak and well done flank, while hu tiu my tho is mixed pork and prawn. Good simple flavours.

Sông Quê also makes a good job of more mundane Oriental favourites like ruong bien (£3.00) – crispy seaweed – and vit chien don cuon banh trang (£12 for half) – crispy duck with the trimmings!

Hoxton & Shoreditch

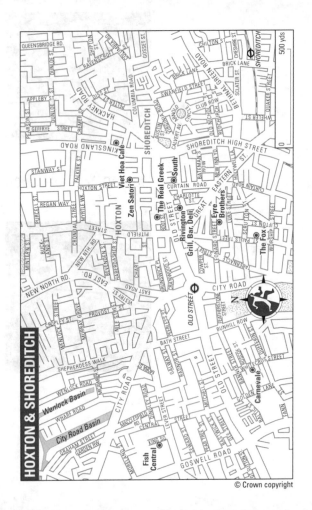

HOXTON & SHOREDITCH

Carnevale

This rather strange little restaurant is tucked into an ordinary shop-like space halfway along a scruffy street which is all street market by day and dingy grubbiness by night. Inside is a clean, light but cramped space, full of blond wood tables and chairs, with carefully selected (if not particularly original) prints on the walls and a faux garden to the rear. The interior has not so much been designed to the hilt, as is the current fashion, but rather put together in

£14 to £25

Address 135 Whitecross St, EC1
℡ 020 7250 3452
Station Old Street
Open Mon–Fri noon–3pm &
5.30–10.30pm,
Sat 5.30–10.30pm
Accepts All major credit cards
except AmEx
ⓦ www.carnevalerestaurant
.co.uk

workable form to meet the needs of the customers. Mercifully, the enduring tendency of vegetarian restaurants to litter the premises with hippy references has been brought under control.

Instead, close attention seems to have been paid to the food, which is cooked with care. Take your time over some very good marinated Greek olives (£2.25) and bread dipped in nutty olive oil while you decide what you'll eat. The menu, which changes every couple of months, is not overlong – ten dishes in all – but is as varied as you could wish for. Starters range from potato, chilli and herb frittata with tomato chilli jam (£4.95); through pennette with cavolo nero, carrots, lemon oil and spiced breadcrumbs (£5.75/8); to a "deli plate" available at lunchtime (£5.50/8). They are good enough to be served in many grander establishments. Main courses are equally eclectic: baby aubergines in pomegranate sauce with potato kibbeh and baby sorrel salad (£10.50); or perhaps celeriac in brioche crust with Puy lentils in red wine sauce and dandelion leaf (£10.50). There is a plentiful list of side orders, though given the size of the portions it is unlikely that you'll need any. If your stamina is up to them, puddings (£4.50) are good, too: try the dairy-free crème caramel with pineapple and blood oranges, or Pavlova with chocolate mousse, pistachio praline and caramelized banana.

Service is relaxed, coffee is good and there are a number of alternative drinks on offer. The set menu deal is available from noon to 3pm and 5.30pm to 7pm; choose between three courses, or two courses and a glass of wine, for £12.50.

Eyre Brothers

(🍴) David Eyre will forever be pigeon-holed as one of the creators of The Eagle (see p.191) and, as such, a founding father of the gastropub revolution. Which makes it all the more surprising to find Eyre and his brother at the helm of a very large, very swish, very elegant 80-seat restaurant. Eyre Brothers is on Leonard Street, deep in the trendy

> ### £25 to £70
>
> **Address** 70 Leonard St, EC2
> ℡ 020 7613 5346
> **Station** Old Street/Liverpool Street
> **Open** Mon–Fri noon–3pm &
> 6.30–11pm, Sat 6.30–11pm
> **Accepts** All major credit cards

part of EC2. There is a long bar with comfortable seats and a sensible footrail so that eating at the bar is a pleasure rather than a contortion. There is a good deal of dark wood and leather and the overall feel is one of comfortable clubbiness. The food is ballsy, with upfront flavours and textures, and scarcely a day goes by without some dishes falling off the menu and being replaced by new ones.

David's cuisine is hard to categorize – there are a few Spanish and Italian dishes, a lot of Portuguese specialities and some favourites from Mozambique. The menu splits into two sections: there is a seasonal menu and a traditional à la carte. Starters range widely, from pulpo a la Gallega (£7), warm octopus and potatoes with smoked paprika; to grilled morcilla with fried turnip greens (£5.50); to scrambled eggs with prawns and wild mushrooms on sourdough (£9). You will also be offered jamón Ibérico "Joselito" gran reserva (£12) – quality is the watchword here. Main courses lead off with grilled Mozambique prawns piri-piri (£25) – these are monsters from the deep waters of the Mozambique channel, scarily large and meaty with a belt of heat from the Portuguese chilli. Or there may be grilled Ibérico pork fillet with paprika and thyme and served with patatas pobres (£17). Or cozido (£13.50), the famous Portuguese stew made with white beans, cabbage and belly pork, and bulked up with chorizo and blood sausage; it's delicious. Puds are classics with a twist, such as basil and Mascarpone ice cream (£4), or chocolate fondant with almond milk sorbet (£5).

This is one place where you can indulge in really good sherry. A rare Manzanilla Passada, a Palo Cortada or an old Oloroso all cost £4 a glass, or £18 for a half-bottle.

Fish Central

The Barbican may appear to be the back of beyond – a black hole in the heart of the City – but perfectly ordinary people do live and work around here. Apart from the theatres and concert hall and the proximity to the financial district, one of the main attractions of the place is Fish Central, which holds its own with the finest fish-and-chip shops in town, and indeed a good many snootier restaurants. People tend to be very snobbish about fish-and-chip shops, but Fish Central is just the place to dispel such delusions.

£8 to £20

Address 151 King's Square, Central St, EC1
℡ 020 7253 4970
Station Barbican
Open Mon–Sat 11am–2.30pm & 4.45–10.30pm
Accepts All major credit cards

FISH & CHIPS

Though at first sight Fish Central appears just like any other chippy – a takeaway service one side and an eat-in restaurant next door – a glance at its menu lets you know that this is something out of the ordinary. All the finny favourites are here, from cod and haddock to rock salmon and plaice (all £5.30), but there's a wholesome choice of alternatives, including grilled Dover sole (£10.90) and roast cod (£8.75) with rosemary and Mediterranean vegetables. These dishes are cooked to order, and a menu note prepares you for a 25-minute wait. You can eat decently even if you are not in the mood for fish. Try the Cumberland sausages (90p each), with onions and gravy, or the chicken breast (£5.95). If you think your appetite is up to starters, try the prawn cocktail (£2.95) – the normal naked pink prawns in pink sauce, but genuinely fresh – or grilled sardines with tomato coulis (£3.45), which puts all of those run-of-the-mill Italian restaurants to shame. Chips (£1.95) come as a side order, so those who prefer can order a jacket potato (£1.60) or creamed potatoes (£1.40). Mushy peas (£1.40) are ... mushy, and wallies (45p) – pickled gherkins to you – come sliced and prettily served in the shape of a flower.

Fish Central certainly pulls in a crowd of devoted regulars. On any given night, half the customers seem to know each other. Unusually for a chippy, it has an alcohol licence, which means there's a palatable dry house white or even champagne – the perfect partner for mushy peas.

The Fox

It may raise a few eyebrows amongst biologists, but this fox is the direct descent of an eagle – The Fox is sibling to the original gastropub, The Eagle (see p.191). Downstairs it is a grand, pubby sort of pub, with decent real ale and the kind of serious pub food that really appeals. Upstairs is the dining room, which has much in common with

£16 to £35

Address 28 Paul St, EC2
℡ 020 7729 5708
Station Old Street
Open Mon–Fri noon–3pm &
6.30–10pm
Accepts All major credit cards
except AmEx

the style of the original Eagle: the tables and chairs are an eclectic mix, the cutlery and china are gleefully mismatched, and the whole has a passing resemblance to Steptoe's lair.

The cooking at The Fox is "school of" The Eagle. Dishes are robust, well seasoned, honest and driven by the seasons. The menu changes every day, and while there isn't a huge amount of choice there should be something to please everyone. Pricing is straightforward: two courses cost £14.95 and three courses £18.75. For starters, a typical choice is between a lentil soup; flatbread, aubergine and feta; brandade and boiled egg; and little foie gras toasts. Note the homeliness of these dishes, their balance and the comfortable combinations of flavour and texture. Main course options include red risotto and fonduta; ham, carrots and parsley sauce; tuna beans and artichoke – which does attract a £1.50 supplement; and a belter of a dish like duck, potato, greens and chorizo. There is always a fish dish and there is always something for vegetarians. Finish off with a couple of puds, such as lemon and almond cake or chocolate tart, as well as a well-chosen cheese. With food like this, and a sensibly priced wine list, The Fox makes for a pleasant, good-value and unpretentious place to eat.

There is an agreeable little suntrap terrace, with a few tables for hardened lovers of the alfresco. The view is largely of the surrounding brick walls, but there are tubs with plants and all is suitably casual for a long, lingering lunch. Competition for the restaurant is close at hand and downstairs in the bar you could lunch on a seriously good salt beef sandwich (£5); terrine and rillettes (£5); or a bespoke dish for two – toad in the hole (£14).

The Real Greek

This particular Real Greek is called Theodore Kyriakou. Traditionally, Greek food has had a pretty rough deal in Britain, as most of the restaurants which call themselves "Greek" are usually run by Greek Cypriots with a menu that concentrates on Cypriot food. Thus, for generations of Brits, Greek food has meant greasy, lukewarm moussaka and lurid-pink cod's roe gloop. Real Greek

£10 to £50

Address 15 Hoxton Market, N1
℡ 020 7739 8212
Station Old Street/Shoreditch
Open Mon–Sat noon–3pm &
5.30–10.30pm
Accepts Mastercard and Visa
ⓦ www.therealgreek.co.uk

GREEK

food is nothing like that, and showing off the authentic dishes of his homeland is the difficult mission Kyriakou has embarked upon. Next door to the restaurant is what was once the Hoxton Mission Hall, but now the lofty room has been converted into a busy mezedopoliou, a bar where you can order a few meze (they cost between £2 and £5 a plateful) and try a dozen stunning Greek wines by the glass or carafaki. It's a relaxed way to sample some seriously good food. In 2003 The Real Greek set up a third establishment – The Real Greek Souvlaki Bar (see p.194).

The original restaurant goes from strength to strength. The menu changes with the seasons. The first section is "Mezedes" and each platter has three or four components. One such might include dolmades; gigandes plaki; cured beef; and pan-fried Kefalotiri cheese (£7.90). Or there may be plate with a scallop; octopus cooked in red wine; potato and caper leaf salad; and beetroots in aged vinegar (£8.60). On to "Fagakia": these small dishes could be either starters or sides. Pot-roast crab claws come with an implausibly rich sauce made from ripe tomatoes and Visanto (£8.50). Main courses are a revelation. Slow-cooked calf's liver and sweetbreads are served with oregano potatoes (£16); lamb cooked with dandelions and cos lettuce (£16.70); pan-fried fresh fish is served simply, with a warm salad of seasonal leaves, yoghurt and garlic (£15). Then there is a whole range of Greek cheeses and desserts – the Manouri ice cream and fig terrine (£5.50) is outstanding.

There is a genuine bargain set lunch and "early doors" dinner (5.30–7pm), which costs just £10 for two courses and £13.50 for three.

BRITISH

Rivington Grill, Bar, Deli

The Rivington Grill, Bar, Deli opened at the very end of 2002. As well as the kind of name that hedges its bets, it has an elegant, high-ceilinged, white-painted dining room, a comfortable bar with high stools for solo diners, and plenty of sofas. The Deli part is to be found in a separate shop just around the corner where you can buy moody artisan packets of pasta and so forth. Before you

£18 to £40

Address 28–30 Rivington St EC2
℡ 020 7729 7053
Station Old Street
Open Mon–Fri noon–3.30pm & 6.30–10.30pm, Sat 6.30–10.30pm.
Accepts All major credit cards
℠ www.fieldandforest.co.uk

dismiss the Rivington as another new restaurant punched from the same mould as all rest, consider the cooking. The menu is seasonal and interesting. This food is not Italian, it is not French, it is not fancy and it is not formal. The dishes don't even answer to Modern British. If there is such a cuisine as Ordinary British, then this is it.

On the face of it everything is simple but someone in the kitchen has given the dishes some thought and the combinations work well together. Ordering chicken and wild mushroom soup (£5.25) brings a small tureen of smooth, thick chicken soup with palpable chunks of chicken, well seasoned. There may be a dish of devilled kidneys on toast (£6.75) – lamb's kidneys cooked perfectly and with a well-made sharp sauce. A watercress salad with goat's cheese and walnuts (£5.50) is triumphant – peppery greens, soothing dressing, good cheese and magnificent toasted walnuts. Main courses also satisfy – hamburger and chips (£7.75); fish fingers and chips with mushy peas (£8.50); grilled whole sea bream (£12.50); hamburger and chips (£7.75). Smoked haddock with a poached egg, colcannon potatoes and mustard sauce (£12.50) is the sort of dish that makes you want to purr. Smoky fish, substance from the spuds, a whiff of mustard from the sauce, egg yolk for contrast. Barnsley chop (£11.75) comes with bubble and squeak – pink lamb, good gravy, nice bubble. Puddings veer from toffee ice cream with fudge sauce (£4.25); to steamed chocolate pudding (£4.75); or lemon meringue pie (£4.25).

The wine list takes a commendable while to get to £30 a bottle, but then skitters on through a handful of pricey bottles to a £120 Vosne-Romanée. Stick with the middleweights for better value.

South

South opened towards the end of 2002, and is a small, pretty, modern restaurant with a mint-green exterior and a great deal of blond wood on show inside. It has an open kitchen, pleasant staff and informal atmosphere – all of which means that it slots right into yoof-trendy Hoxton/Shoreditch. Then you read the menu and your perception changes, because South is a very French restaurant that specializes in "cuisine grand-mère", and you'll find a list of old-fashioned seasonal dishes. This is wonderful food with great belts of flavour, but whether or not it is mainstream enough to succeed with Hoxtonians remains to be seen. While the jury is out, enjoy some really good cooking and some reasonable bills.

£15 to £45

Address 128 Curtain Rd, EC2
℡ 020 7729 4452
Station Old Street
Open Tues–Sat noon–3pm &
6–10.30pm, Sun noon–3pm
Accepts All major credit cards

VERY FRENCH

The menu is uncompromising and it starts with gratinée Lyonnaise (£4.50). Remember French onion soup? Then there is salade de Roquefort, poire et noix (£5.60), and assiette d'hors d'oeuvres (£5.50) – this is so simple and so good. Take a plate and add four mounds: celeriac remoulade good, creamy and mustardy; dressed grated carrot; tangy mushrooms à la Grecque; and the fourth is dressed beetroot. Or there is boudin noir avec pommes (£5.90), or a salade composée (£5.60) – rare beef, good leaves, gherkins, capers. Mains follow through confit de canard; jus de betterave (£11) is the real deal: crisp outside, tender within, stunning mash. When preparing the poulet rôté salade d'ail sauvage (£10.80) the chef started with a really excellent chicken then roasted it to perfection. Job done. Tuna gets the southern treatment – thon grillé et ratatouille (£11.50) comes with tapenade. The puddings are also old friends – croustade des pommes (£4.50); poire vin rouge (£4.50) and a glorious, self-indulgent mousse au chocolat (£5). Meanwhile the wine list keeps faith with this Francophilia and has some interesting bottles from southern France at reasonable prices.

The "prix fixe" lunch weighs in at £12.95 for three courses and transports you to a small town in southern France on market day – pissaladière avec salade anchoiade; saucisse de Toulouse, pommes purée; tarte aux poires.

Viet Hoa Café

The Viet Hoa dining room is large, clean, light and airy, with an impressive golden parquet floor. The café part of the name is borne out by the bottles of red and brown sauce which take pride of place on each table. The brown goop turns out to be hoisin sauce and the red stuff a simple chilli one, but they have both been put into recycled plastic bottles on which the only recognizable words are "Sriracha extra hot chilli sauce – Flying Goose Brand". Apparently this has made all but the regulars strangely wary of hoisin sauce.

> **£8 to £18**
>
> **Address** 72 Kingsland Rd, E2
> ☎ 020 7729 8293
> **Station** Old Street
> **Open** Daily noon–4pm &
> 5.30–11.30pm
> **Accepts** All major credit cards
> except AmEx

As befits a café, there are a good many splendid "meals in a bowl" – soups and noodle dishes with everything from spring rolls to tofu. For diners wanting to go as a group and share, an appetizer called salted prawn in garlic dressing (£4.70) is outstanding – large prawns marinated and fried with chilli and garlic. From the list of fifteen soups, pho (£5.50) is compulsory. This dish is a Vietnamese staple eaten at any and every meal, including breakfast. Ribbon noodles and beef, chicken or tofu are added to a delicate broth. It comes with a plate of mint leaves, Thai basil and chillies, your job being to add the fresh aromatics to the hot soup – resulting in astonishingly vivid flavours. Main courses include shaking beef (£6.70) – cubes of beef with a tangy salad; and drunken fish (£6.70) – fish cooked with wine and cloud-ear mushrooms. Both live up to the promise of their exotic names. There are a good many salad and tofu dishes, including tofu with chilli and black bean (£4.95). Bun tom nuong (£5.75) is a splendid one-pot dish of noodles with char-grilled tiger prawns. Also in one-pot-with-vermicelli territory, you'll find bun nem nuong (£5), which features grilled minced pork, and that old favourite, Singapore noodles (£4.40).

This is a good restaurant in which to make a first foray into Vietnamese food. It is very much a family-run place, with the grandparents sitting at a table rolling spring rolls and the younger generations waiting the tables. They're very helpful to novices.

Zen Satori

Zen Satori is the training restaurant of the Asian and Oriental School of Catering, but do not be deceived into thinking that you might end up with an amateurish meal. Granted, the service may be friendly and charming rather than super-slick, but it is easy to prefer it that way. The room falls into three sections,

£5 to £20

Address 40 Hoxton Street, N1
℡ 020 7613 9590
Station Old Street
Open Mon–Fri 11.30am–3pm &
5–9.30pm, Sat 5–10.30pm
Accepts All major credit cards

there is a well-stocked bar, a series of refectory tables very much in the Wagamama idiom (see p.18), and a small area of pukka tables to the rear. All is glossy and elegant. Running down one side of the room is a gleaming modern, open, kitchen full of bustling cooks – some are students, some are lecturers. Prices are dirt-cheap. The food is fresh, well cooked and well presented. The sooner all these students go out into the world and start spreading this gospel, the better.

Go for lunch. The deals are amazing. There are four different set lunches (all £5.95). Pick Thai and enjoy chicken and mushroom tom yum; chicken and coriander cakes; and then beef with lemongrass and French beans – plus a choice of rice or noodles. Order Chinese and get wonton soup; vegetable spring roll; and lemon chicken – plus either rice or noodles. There is a soup, spring roll and green curried vegetables combo for vegetarians. The Indian option teams mulligatawny soup; samosas; and South Indian chicken curry and rice. The curry is a good one, authentically hot, with well-balanced spices and a complex array of tastes. In the evening these dishes are available à la carte and will be joined by starters like sesame prawn toast (£3.50), chicken tikka (£3.50) – fresh, large chunks, juicy. Then there are further Indian dishes, Chinese dishes, Thai dishes, Vietnamese dishes and Singaporean dishes. The wine list tops out at around £15 and there are several decent beers on offer.

If you are mean enough to think the £5.95 set lunch extravagant, you'll appreciate the range of "special one plate lunch options": Thai chicken with basil broccoli and noodles (£4.75). This school deserves your support: leave a big tip.

Further East

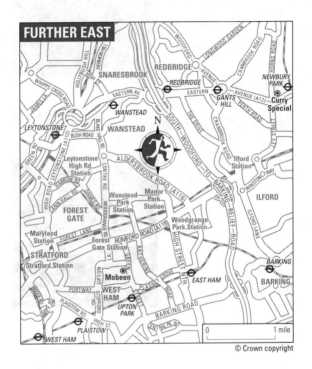
© Crown copyright

Curry Special

Curry Special has been a magnet for curry lovers since 1985. The cuisine is authentic, full-on Punjabi with one or two East African variations. Rich flavours are achieved by long, slow cooking and carefully chosen spices; there are no instant fixes, easy on the cream, yoghurt and handfuls of nuts. During 2002 the restaurant went through a major refurb and emerged triumphant complete with a 25ft waterfall and a lounge bar. Curry Special seats 110 people over two floors.

£10 to £35

Address 2 Greengate Parade, Horns Rd, Newbury Park, Essex
℡ 020 8518 3005
Station Newbury Park
Open Tues–Thurs 12.30–2.30pm & 6–11.30pm, Fri 12.30–2.30pm & 6pm–midnight, Sat 6pm–midnight, Sun 6–11.30pm
Accepts All major credit cards
🖰 www.curryspecial.com

Great pickles. Pause amongst the poppadoms to enjoy the carrot pickle, a genuinely Punjabi-hot super-crunch. Then go on to try the butter chicken (half a chicken £7.50, whole £14), which is suitably, uncannily buttery, and something of a signature dish – as you'd expect, considering the East African influences. There's also jeera (cumin) chicken, at the same price, and chilli chicken (half £8, whole £15) – very tasty. Or perhaps one of the less familiar dishes like pili pili bogo (£4.95), which is a dish of mixed vegetable pieces dusted in spiced flour and deep-fried. For mains the curries are simple and rich: try methi chicken (for one £6.50, half-chicken £17, whole £34), or the delicious palak lamb (£6.50). There is also a section headed chef's special which is always worth a look – and lists starters like murgh haryali (£5.50), a chicken tikka variant green with fresh herbs. From the vegetables section, choose the tinda masala (£4). You will be asked – rather disconcertingly, as how hot is hot? – whether you want your curry mild, medium or hot. Perhaps the spicy Punjabi grub has shocked some previous Essex punters, but whatever the reason, medium here is pretty tame, and you may want to go for hot. Bread-wise, indulge yourself with a hot bhatura (£1.95), which could be subtitled "fried bread meets doughnut".

For all its suburban location opposite B&Q, and its strangely dated name, Curry Special is busy enough to make booking advisable even early in the week. Essex folk seem to know what they like.

Mobeen

If you have never been to West Ham, the whole of Green Street is likely to come as a surprise. It has the feel of Brick Lane and Southall, but everything is much, much cheaper – in the market here you can buy a whole goat for the price of a dozen lamb chops in the West End. Mobeen itself seems to

> **£4 to £16**
>
> **Address** 222–224 Green St, E7
> ☎ 020 8470 2419
> **Station** Upton Park
> **Open** Daily 11am–10pm
> **Accepts** All major credit cards

operate at "factory gate" prices, offering a kind of 1950s Asian works-canteen ethos – with appropriate decor – and it is a strategy that has been so successful that there is now a chain of these strictly halal Pakistani caffs. As you go in, the kitchen lies behind a glazed wooden partition to your left, while to your right are café tables and chairs. The clientele hits this place like a breaking wave – it can be impressively busy at 11.50am.

The dishes and prices are listed above the servery hatches and the food is displayed below. You go up to the hatch, wait your turn and then order up a trayful, which will be reanimated in the microwave. Then it's off to another hatch for fizzy soft drinks and to yet another port of call to pick up cutlery and glasses. This is workmanlike food in large portions at basic prices, and most things are available in two sizes. Chicken tikka (£2.50/3.40) is red and hot, very hot. Sheekh kebabs (70p) are spicy and piping-hot (thanks to the microwave). Meat samosas are just 50p each. Masala fish (£3.30) is rich and good. The biryani (£3/4) is commendably ungreasy and may actually have benefited from being cooked and reheated. There's also spinach and meat curry (£2.70/3.50), a meat curry (£2.70/3.50), and a bhuna meat curry (£2/3). The breads are serviceable, and there is a notable kind of very thick, fried, stuffed paratha (£1) that will tip you over your cholesterol allowance for about a fortnight. This establishment is just up the road from West Ham's home ground. You have to wonder what Alf Garnett would have made of it.

Mobeen is unlicensed and bringing your own is not allowed, but among the soft drinks are some novelty items: for 50p you can try a fizzy mango juice in a lurid can. Just the thing to tempt a jaded palate.

North

Camden Town & Primrose Hill

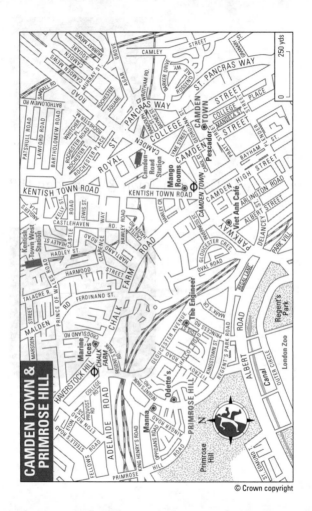

CAMDEN TOWN & PRIMROSE HILL

© Crown copyright

The Engineer

(🍴) The Engineer is now one of London's senior gastropubs – it now has tables in the bar, a more formal restaurant, tables in the garden (for those occasional summer days), and a salle privée on the first floor. Wherever you end up sitting, you'll get offered the same menu (which changes every two weeks) and you'll pay the same price. The cooking is accomplished, with good strong combinations of flavours, and a cheerful, iconoclastic approach to what is fundamentally Mediterranean food. The

£12 to £40

Address 65 Gloucester Ave, NW1
☎ 020 7722 0950
Station Chalk Farm
Open Mon–Fri 9–11.30am, noon–3pm & 7–11pm, Sat 9am–noon, 12.30–3.30pm & 7–11pm, Sun 9am–noon, 12.30–3.30pm & 7–10.30pm
Accepts All major credit cards except AmEx & Diners
🖳 www.the-engineer.com

MEDITERRANEAN/GASTROPUB

latest development is that they open for breakfast seven days a week. When do they sleep?

Your hackles may rise at £2.75 for home-made bread and butter, but the bread is warm from the oven, with a good crust, and the butter is beurre d'Isigny and, as they refill the basket after you've scoffed the lot, you end up feeling happier about paying. Starters are simple and good. There's soup (£3.75) and that price includes the bread mentioned earlier! There may be chicken liver pâté with toasted brioche and sweet onion marmalade (£5.95); or something more exotic like avocado and red pepper maki rolls served with Japanese pickled vegetables (£6.50). Or how about tequila-cured salmon with blinis, horseradish cream and cucumber (£6.25)? At lunchtime the mains will probably be quite light: eggs Benedict (£9), a pan-fried organic beef burger (£10.35). For dinner, expect dishes like char-grilled sea bass fillet with laksa and buckwheat noodles (£14.50); pan-fried soft shell crab with crispy polenta, roast corn salsa (£14); or a free-range duck breast, marinated with blackberries and cinnamon served with spinach, creamed corn pudding and apple fritters (£12.50). A side order of baker fries (£2.25) brings thick wedges of baked potato fried until crispy. There is always a decent pint of beer to be had and the coffee is excellent. All in all, plenty of reasons why it's so busy, and plenty of reasons why you should book.

At the bottom of the menu it says proudly, "Please note that all our fresh meat is free range or organic". Hurrah! They deserve your support.

Mango Rooms

(🍴) Mango Rooms is an engaging place, although it does make you wonder why everyone in this part of London is striving so hard to be laid-back. Hereabouts the coolness seems a little forced, and the casualness somehow elaborate. No matter. This restaurant describes itself as offering "traditional and modern Caribbean cuisine". Despite a recent lick of paint, this

£12 to £38

Address 10 Kentish Town Rd, NW1.
☎ 020 7482 5065
Station Camden Town
Open Tues–Sat noon–3pm &
6pm–midnight, Sun noon–midnight
Accepts Mastercard and Visa
Branches see p.489

is still a homely place, the staff are gentle and the cooking reliable. If there is a fault to be found, it would be that the spicing and seasoning is somewhat tame, as if the act has been cleaned up a little. Perhaps Camden's restaurateurs simply have an unusually good grasp of what their customers like? Mango Room is certainly very full, and everyone seems to be having a great time, in a laid-back, Camden-cool kind of way.

Traditional starters are the most successful, like the salt cod fritters with apple chutney (£4), or crab and potato balls (£4.50) – the exception to the under-spiced rule. Ebony wings, marinated in chilli pepper, garlic and soya with a hot and sweet dipping sauce (£3.80) is a nice dish but not a hot one. For a main course, "Camden's famous curry goat with hot pepper, scallions, garlic, pimento and spices" (£9) is subtitled "A hot, spicy, traditional dish", which it isn't. But it is very tasty: well presented and with plenty of lean meat. For fish-eaters there is Creole snapper with mango and green peppercorn sauce (£10). The side dishes are excellent – plantain (£2.50), rice and peas (£1.90), white and sweet potato mash (£2.50), and a very good, dry and dusty roti (£2.50). The cooking is consistent and the kitchen makes a real effort with the presentation. If you like your Caribbean food on the sweet side and without the fierce burn of lantern chillies or pepper sauce, you will have a great time here.

Puddings are good – the mango and banana brûlée (£4) sports an exemplary hard top – and the Mango Rooms' special rum punch (£4.50) is sweet enough for most people to class it as a dessert. The bar here is lively and seems to be ever-expanding.

Manna

If your new film – the one where a beautiful American business-woman meets a tongue-tied but cute Brit aristo, you know the kind of thing – needed an authentic 1970s veggie restaurant for a crucial hand-holding scene, the decor at Manna would fit the bill perfectly. In this world of chic modern restos and chic modern restaurant designers, it is increasingly hard for anywhere to look old-fashioned and casual without being sneered at. Manna don't care! (Although they did repaint during 2002.) This stubborn gentleness sometimes extends to the service, so don't pitch up here in a hurry, or without a serious appetite – there is no whimsy about the portions here. The cooking is very sound, and if there is such a thing as a peculiarly "veggie" charm, this place has it.

£16 to £45

Address 4 Erskine Rd, NW1
℗ 020 7722 8028
Station Chalk Farm
Open Mon–Fri 6.30–11pm, Sat & Sun 12.30–3pm
Accepts MasterCard, Visa
ⓦ www.manna-veg.com

VEGETARIAN

The menu devolves into five sections: starters, mains, salads, sides and desserts. You can also order a selection of any three salads or starters as the "Manna meze" (£13.95). Soup of the day (£4.95) is a sound option, as it comes with the solid but satisfying home-made bread. The menu changes regularly but may include starters like organic ravioli (£6.50) – Swiss chard, squash, and Gruyère cheese with sage butter sauce and Parmesan. Or how about parsnip cakes with a creamy tarragon filling and watercress pesto (£5.75)? Mains are an eclectic bunch: a white bean, barley and root vegetable cassoulet comes with chestnut dumplings (£11.50); there's a dish made with coriander, chillies and sesame-braised tofu served with stir-fried glass noodles, baby sweetcorn, straw mushrooms and fresh mango and lime salsa (£10.95) – dishes here do read like recipes. Puds are serious: warm chocolate chip, pecan cheesecake brownie (£5.95) and organic fruit crumble (£4.95) are a challenge to all but the stoutest appetites.

The menu here is decidable: (v) stands for vegan dishes; (vo) means vegan option and adds "please ask"; (org) means an organic dish; and (g) means gluten free. All of which is very helpful. Whether committed vegetarians or not, we should all take more interest in just what it is that we are eating.

Marine Ices

ITALIAN/ICE CREAM

Marine Ices is a family restaurant from a bygone era. In 1947, Aldo Mansi rebuilt the family shop along nautical lines, kitting it out with wood and portholes (hence the name). In the half-century since, while the family ice-cream business has grown and grown, the restaurant and gelateria has just pottered along. All for the good. That means old-fashioned service and home-style, old-fashioned Italian food. It also means that Marine Ices is a great hit with children, for in addition to the good Italian food there is a marathon list of stunning sundaes, coupes, ice creams and sorbets.

£9 to £28

Address 8 Haverstock Hill, NW3
℡ 020 7482 9003
Station Chalk Farm
Open Restaurant Mon–Fri noon–3pm & 6–11pm, Sat noon–11pm, Sun noon–10pm; gelateria Mon–Sat 10.30am–11pm, Sun 11am–10pm
Accepts Mastercard, Switch, or Visa

The menu is long: antipasti, salads, pastas and sauces, vitello, fegato, carne, pollo, pesce, specialities and pizzas. Of the starters, you could try selezioni di bruschetta (£4.10), which combines one each of three well-made and fresh bruschette – roast vegetables, sardines and tomatoes. Or go for the chef's salad (£5), a rocket salad with pancetta and splendid croutons made from eggy bread. Pasta dishes are home-made: mix and match various sauces with various pasta – starters £4.75, mains £5.90. There are a few "oven" dishes like cannelloni and lasagne (both £6.25), then the menu lists nearly every old-style Italian dish you have ever heard of; your favourite is here and will cost between £7.50 and £11. Onwards to a host of pizzas - immense, freshly made and very tasty, in whichever of their many guises you choose (£5.20/6.80). And where others may be set on saving Venice, at Marine they support the Roundhouse fund; for every Roundhouse pizza sold – cheese, tomato, ham, mushroom and fresh chilli (£6.50) – they donate 50p.

When you've had your meal, take a breath and ask for the gelateria menu. There are sundaes from Peach Melba (£2.50) to Knickerbocker Glory (£3.80). There are bombe, coppe, cassate and, best of all, affogati (£4.50) – three scoops of ice cream topped with Marsala or, even nicer, espresso coffee. Or create your own combo from fourteen ice creams and eight sorbets. They're £1.35 a scoop.

Odette's

Odette's is a charming, picturesque restaurant, attuned to pretty Primrose Hill and it underwent a major kitchen refurb in the summer of 2003. There's a pleasant conservatory at the back (with a skylight open in warm weather) and candles flicker in the evenings. Add ambitious Modern British food, the odd local celeb, friendly staff, and you have

£20 to £40
Address 130 Regent's Park Rd, NW1
☎ 020 7586 5486
Station Chalk Farm
Open Mon–Sat 12.30–2.30pm & 7–11pm, Sun 12.30–3.30pm
Accepts All major credit cards

all the ingredients for a very successful local restaurant. In summer, try to get one of the tables that spill out onto the villagey street. As with any long-established place the chef (and the menu) changes from time to time and the trend seems to be towards elaboration.

The food makes commendable use of seasonal produce, so do not expect to find all the dishes listed every time you visit. Starters, if you strike lucky, might include poached morels, shitake and asparagus in a Gewürztraminer and truffle broth (£7), or a risotto of Périgueux truffles and Parmesan with a soft poached organic egg and smoked bacon (£8). When in season, six Irish oysters (£8) is a good choice – half deep-fried and half raw with tartare of mackerel and ginger dressing. Mains generally include at least one choice each of fish, meat, game and chicken. Fillet of halibut comes with braised leeks and asparagus (£18). Or there's grilled milk-fed veal chop with Italian lemons (£22); or slow-roast breast of Gressingham duck (£18), while veggies might go for honey-glazed root vegetables with pickled mushrooms and lentil foam (£14). Puddings (all £5) are wonderfully indulgent, and include lemon curd parfait with strawberries, and an outstanding mango and stem ginger sorbet. The set lunch is worth noting: it's available from Monday to Friday and on Sunday, and costs £14.50 for two courses, £17 for three.

Odette's has a very long wine list, with something to suit all tastes and purses. It's also nice to get such a large choice of wines by the glass and half-bottle. Try a glass of Argentine Chenin Blanc (£3.40), or a half-bottle of Jurançon Sec (£11.25).

Pescador

🍴 This part of Camden is the heartland of Greek Cypriot restaurants and all manner of "tavernas" jostle for prime sites. But venture into Pescador and you might as well be in Portugal, which is a good thing ... always presuming that you like fish. The dining room is a plain, cream-painted room that is in the process of being overwhelmed

£15 to £45
Address 33 Pratt Street, NW1
☎ 020 7482 7008
Station Camden Town
Open Mon–Fri 6–11pm, Sat 1–11pm, Sun 1–10pm
Accepts All major credit cards

by a tidal wave of knick-knacks themed around fish and fishermen. The tables are small and close together and, while the lady of the house takes charge of the till behind the bar, a flotilla of waiters bustles about. This is a busy place and you should book.

Starters range from the simple – pasteis de bacalhau (£3.60): small, fluffy, fried rissoles of potato and salt cod, very good indeed – to all manner of luxurious seafood: giant prawns (£4.90 each), langoustines (£5 each), clams (£4.50), mussels (£4.50). One attractive option is to share a main course portion of sapateira (£15) between two: this is billed as "a crab served with toast", and that's what you get. But it is a very large, very fresh crab and when you have picked out all the white meat you always have the toast on which to spread the rich brown meat. As is the way with good fish restaurants, there is always a daily special and this might be a large, fresh sea bream which is priced according to the market and can be served in fillets or left on the bone, depending how confident you are feeling. Plainly grilled, very fresh fish is always delicious, and there is also halibut (£10.50), scabbard fish (£9.50), squid (£10.80), sea bass (£15.80) and skate (£9.50). If you like rich food and plenty of it, opt for the arroz de marisco (£12.50). You get a large casserole full of shellfish chowder thickened with rice but left sloppy like a very loose risotto. As you explore the dish you'll find clams, mussels, fish and larger prawns. Tremendous.

It's worth noting that the Alvarino vinho verde is crisp, dry and the perfect foil for all these fish dishes. It will also help you blend in.

Viet-Anh Cafe

Authentic, it says on the card, and authentic it tastes on the plate. Viet-Anh is a bright, cheerful café with oilcloth-covered tables run by a young Vietnamese couple. They cook and give service that's beyond helpful. In complete contrast to the occasionally intimidating feel of some of the more obscure Chi-

£15 to £40

Address 41 Parkway, NW1
℡ 020 7284 4082
Station Camden Town
Open Daily noon–4pm &
5.30–11pm
Accepts Mastercard and Visa

VIETNAMESE

nese restaurants, this is a friendly and welcoming place. If there is anything puzzling or unfamiliar, they'll tell you what and show you how. It's the sort of place where single diners feel quite at home.

Vietnamese vegetarian spring rolls (£3) and Vietnamese meat pancake (£3) are classic starters. The former are crisp, well seasoned, and flavoured with fresh coriander; the latter are a delight – two large, paper-thin, eggy pancakes stuffed with vegetables and chicken, and served with large lettuce leaves. You hold these in the palm of your hand and manipulate a slice of the pancake onto the leaf, roll it up together, dip in the pungent lemony sauce and eat. Hot and cold, crisp and soft, savoury and lemony – all in one. Ordering prawn sugar-cane stick (£5.50) brings large prawns skewered on a piece of sugar cane. Eat the prawn then chew the cane – it's savoury and sweet in one mouthful. Pho chicken soup, accurately described as the House Special (£4.50), is made with slices of chicken and vegetables plus flat rice-stick noodles in broth. Slurp the noodles and lift the bowl to drink the soup. Lemongrass chicken on boiled rice (£4.50) is a more fiery dish – you can have it medium-hot or very hot. There are over a hundred items on the menu, ranging from £1 to £12, and most are complete one-plate meals. Wines come in at around the £15 mark, or there is sake (300ml for £8) as well as Far East beers. Try the Shui Sen tea (£1.20) – more fragrant than jasmine tea and just as refreshing.

To complete the café feel, huge (1lb 12oz) plastic bottles of sauce with squeezy tops adorn the tables. They are labelled "Sriracha HOT chilli sauce", and the label is as much a warning as an inducement. If you like your food as spicy as the Vietnamese customers do, you're only a squeeze away.

Hampstead & Golders Green

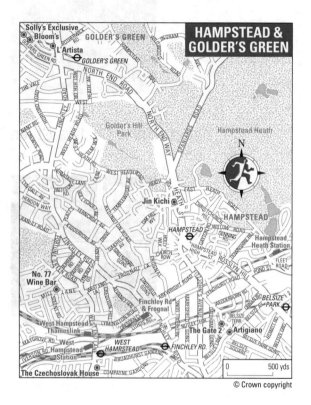

HAMPSTEAD & GOLDER'S GREEN

Solly's Exclusive
Bloom's
L'Artista
GOLDER'S GREEN
GOLDER'S GREEN
GOLDERS GREEN RD
NORTH END ROAD
THE VALE
WEST
NANT RD
DRUKES AVE
HENDON WAY
HARMAN ROAD
Golder's Hill Park
NORTH END WAY
SANDAMS ROAD
Hampstead Heath
WEST HEATH ROAD
FERNCROFT AV
PATTIO RD
FERNDALE LANE
HEATH RD
EAST HEATH ROAD
N
Jin Kichi
FINCHLEY ROAD
FERNCROFT AV
HERMITAGE LANE
KIDDERPORE AV
REDINGTON ROAD
OAK HILL WK
BRANCH HILL
CHURCH ROW
HAMPSTEAD
HAMPSTEAD
WILLOW ROAD
DENNING RD
HAMPSTEAD
Hampstead Heath Station
No. 77 Wine Bar
MILL LANE
WEST END LA
FAWLEY RD
DENNINGTON PK RD
GONDAR GDNS
DASHILL ST
ARKWRIGHT ROAD
FROGNAL
MARESFIELD GDNS
HAMPSTEAD HIGH ST
ROSSLYN HILL
FLEET ROAD
POND ST
FITZJOHN'S AVENUE
LYNDHURST ROAD
WEDDERBURN RD
BELSIZE PARK
Finchley Rd & Frognal
ALVANLEY GDNS
LYMINGTON ROAD
BRIARDALE GDNS
NETHERHALL GDNS
FELLOWS RD
NUTLEY TERR
BELSIZE TERR
The Gate 2
Artigiano
West Hampstead Thameslink
West Hampstead Station
WEST HAMPSTEAD
FINCHLEY RD
BELSIZE PARK GDNS
BELSIZE SQUARE
MAYGROVE RD
IVERSON RD
BROADHURST GARDENS
COMPAYNE GARDENS
The Czechoslovak House

| 0 | 500 yds |

© Crown copyright

ITALIAN

Artigiano

This is one of London's more difficult-to-find restaurants, situated halfway up a dead-end street in the rabbit warren of Belsize Park. Nevertheless, tracking it down is well worth the effort. When you do find it, you will be confronted with a bright, airy restaurant, glass-fronted and with generous skylights. There's more chance of seeing a traffic warden than a passing car and the only disturbance from outside is the

£15 to £28

Address 12 Belsize Terrace, NW3
℡ 020 7794 4288
Station Belsize Park
Open Mon 6.45–11pm, Tues–Sat noon–3pm & 6.45–11pm, Sun noon–3pm & 6.45–10pm
Accepts All major credit cards
ⓦ www.etruscagroup.com

rustle of leaves. For such an out-of-the-way place the restaurant is surprisingly big, with more than 100 covers. It's remarkably busy too, full of 30-something professionals who've sought it out for the same reasons you have – good food and service, convivial atmosphere, and an escape from the rat race.

The menu is longer than you'd expect in such a restaurant, with eight first courses and eight pastas followed by as many main courses, but it seems that the kitchen can cope. There is an admirable tendency to use spanking-fresh ingredients and to let them be themselves. Antipasti might include insalata mista con erbe fresche e pomodori conditti all'aceto balsamico (£5.35) – the Italian for mixed leaves with tomatoes! Or Tuscan prosciutto served with fresh figs and Pecorino (£8.50), or monkfish and tuna (£8.50). Pastas are home-made and sophisticated. Penne comes with grilled vegetables, cherry tomatoes and buffalo Mozzarella (£7.75), or agnolotti ripeni di granchio e cavolo nero (£8.25) – ravioli filled with crab and black cabbage. The "pesce" list also offers a good choice: whole red mullet "en papillotte" (£13.50); or char-grilled tuna steak (£15). Meat-eaters will turn to the ossobuco alla Milanese (£14.50), which is served with a saffron risotto; or the lamb shank, which comes with celeriac and a black olive and Pecorino puree. The chocolate and almond semifreddo (£5.50) is seductive and there are home-made ice creams (£4.75).

Artigiano is settling into a role as a confident neighbourhood eatery. If you are able to make it at lunchtime, go for the set menu – £12 for two courses, £16 for three.

L'Artista

Situated opposite the entrance to Golders Green tube, and occupying an arch under the railway lines, L'Artista is hard to miss. With its pavement terrace, abundant greenery and umbrellas, this is a lively, vibrant restaurant and pizzeria that exercises an almost magnetic appeal to the young and not so young of Golders Green. At the weekend it is literally full to bursting and tables spill onto the terrace – a perfect spot to eat alfresco, providing the traffic isn't too heavy on the Finchley Road. Inside, the plain decor is enhanced by celebrity photographs; the waiters are a bit cagey if asked just how many of them have actually eaten here, but the proximity of the tables ensures that you get to rub shoulders with whoever happens to be around you, famous or otherwise.

£15 to £24
Address 917 Finchley Rd, NW11
☎ 020 8731 7501
Station Golders Green
Open Daily noon–midnight
Accepts Mastercard and Visa
Branches see p.487

The menu offers a range of Italian food with a good selection of main courses such as fegato Veneziana (£7.80), a rich dish of calf's liver with onion and white wine. The trota del pescatore (£7.60) is also good, a simple but effective trout with garlic. But L'Artista's pizzas are its forte. They are superb. As well as traditional thin-crust Capricciosa (£6.50) with anchovies, eggs and ham, or Quattro Formaggi (£6.40), there are more unusual varieties such as Mascarpone e rucola (£6.40), a plain pizza topped with Mascarpone cheese and heaps of crisp rocket, which is actually very good. The calzone (£6.50) – a cushion-sized rolled pizza stuffed with ham, cheese and sausage and topped with Napoli sauce – is wonderful. Pastas are varied and the penne alla vodka (£6.20), made with vodka, prawns and cream, is well worth a try. For something lighter, try the excellent insalata dell'Artista (£5.40), a generous mix of tuna, olives and fennel, with an equally good garlic pizza bread (£2.80).

L'Artista tries hard to bring something of the atmosphere of Naples to Golders Green. By a happy accident this ambience is enhanced by the Vesuvian tremors that occur whenever a Northern Line train rumbles ominously overhead.

Bloom's

Bloom's goes way back to 1920, when Rebecca and Morris Bloom first produced their great discovery – the original veal Vienna. Since then "Bloom's of the East End" has carried the proud tag as "the most famous kosher restaurant in the world". Setting aside the indignant claims of several outraged New York delis for the moment, given its history it's a shame that the East End Bloom's was forced to shut, and that they had to retrench to this, their Golders

£12 to £30

Address 130 Golders Green Rd, NW11
☏ 020 8455 1338
Station Golders Green
Open Mon–Thurs & Sun noon–11pm, Fri 10am–2pm (3pm in summer)
Accepts All major credit cards except Diners
🌐 www.blooms-restaurant.co.uk

JEWISH

Green stronghold, in 1965. Nonetheless, it's a glorious period piece. Rows of sausages hang over the takeaway counter, there are huge mirrors and chrome tables, and you can expect inimitable service from battle-hardened waiters.

So, the waiter looks you in the eye as you ask for a beer. "Heineken schmeineken," he says derisively. At which point you opt for Maccabee, an Israeli beer (£1.90), and regain a little ground. Start with some new green cucumbers (90p) – fresh, crisp, tangy, delicious – and maybe a portion of chopped liver and egg and onions (£4.20), which comes with world-class rye bread. Or go for soup, which comes in bowls so full they slop over the edge: beetroot borscht and potato (£2.90), very sweet and very red; lockshen, the renowned noodle soup (£2.90); or kreplach, full of dumplings (£3.50). Go on to main courses. The salt beef (£14.90) is as good as you might expect, and you can try it in a sandwich on rye bread (£6.90). And there are solid and worthy options like liver and onions (£9.90). Bloom's is now run by Jonathan Tapper – of the fourth generation of the Bloom family – and despite the occasional refurbishment the inimitable ambience remains intact. You can still order extra side dishes like the dreaded, heart-stopping fried potato latke (£1.90), one of the legendarily substantial dishes that underpins the reputation of Jewish food.

Whatever else you try, don't leave without sampling the tzimmas (£2.20), honeyed carrots so cloyingly sweet that they could claim a spot on the dessert menu. This is filling, wholesome, comforting food. Enjoy!

The Czechoslovak House

With its low prices and bafflingly retro decor – the kind of ambience where Harry Lime would feel right at home – The Czechoslovak House is always filled with a happy mix of students and locals. It is situated in the old, established Czechoslovak National House (too good an institution to be sundered – or even to adapt its name), and

£12 to £26

Address 74 West End Lane, NW6
☏ 020 7372 5251
Station West Hampstead
Open Tues–Fri 6–10pm, Sat & Sun
noon–3pm & 6–10pm
Accepts Cash or cheque only

its dining room is a class act. Genuine flock wallpaper gives a unique backdrop for some striking portraits: among them Václav Havel, Winston Churchill and a very young-looking Queen Elizabeth II with her crown and regalia picked out in glitter powder.

Menu-writers across London should be forced to study here – it is hard to improve on the concision of "meat soup" (£3.50). Passing that dish by, try starting with tlacenka (£3), which is home-made brawn with onions. Or Russian egg (£4) – egg mayonnaise with salad, ham and onions. Or the rather good rollmops (£3), again with onions. Main courses deliver serious amounts of home-made, tasty food. Beef goulash (£9) is red with sweet paprika, and cooked long and slow until the meat is meltingly tender. Order smoked boiled pork knuckle (£6.50 small – translates as large; or £7.50 large – translates as enormous), and you get a tasty ham hock, with a small jug of wildly rich pork gravy to go over your dumplings (£1.50). You can have the dumplings with the roast veal (£7.50) but consider the good fried potatoes (£1.50) or the epic sauerkraut (£2.50). For drink, set your sights on beer: Gambrinus on draught is £2.20 a pint, and there are a number of other bottled Czech beers, including one labelled with a motorcycle and sidecar. There is a story behind this design, which the amiable bartender will explain – not that you will be able to remember the tale after drinking the stuff.

There is one pudding that will have any cholesterol-wary diner clutching at their pacemaker. Apricot dumpling (£3.50) is a cricket-ball-sized lump of dough with an apricot inside. It comes under a coat of sour cream, and sits in a sea of melted butter. It is awesome.

The Gate 2

(icon) There are ghetto-like vegetarian restaurants and then there are restaurants in a completely different class that, for one reason or another, happen not to use meat or fish in their cooking. The Gate 2 in Belsize Park, sister to The Gate in Hammersmith (see p.435), is one of the latter, serving excellent and original dishes with intense and satisfying tastes and textures. Even the dedicated carnivore won't miss anything.

> **£25 to £50**
>
> **Address** 72 Belsize Lane, NW3
> ☎ 020 7435 7733
> **Station** Belsize Park
> **Open** Mon–Fri 6–10.30pm, Sat noon–3pm & 6–10.30pm, Sun noon–3pm & 6–9.30pm
> **Accepts** All major credit cards
> ⓦ www.gateveg.co.uk

Starters may include sweet potato and pumpkin tart (£5.75); avocado and baby spinach salad (£4.90); or arancini (£5.50) – those delicious balls of rice filled with cherry tomatoes, Dolcelatte cheese and basil pesto. Or perhaps the mezze platter (£10.50), which provides a sampler of several starters. Main courses are equally adventurous. The Gate lasagna (£10.25) starts with fresh spinach pasta and adds roasted butternut squash, oven-dried tomatoes, courgettes and Gorgonzola with a sauce made from watercress, then plenty of Parmesan as topping. Or celeriac and potato rosti (£11.25), served with roasted root vegetables, braised shallots, and wild mushrooms with a sauce based on ceps. An aubergine schnitzel (£11.25) comes layered with smoked Mozzarella and is served with pan-fried kale, potato Dauphinoise and a horseradish cream sauce. There may also be a root vegetable tagine (£9.50) – it is interesting to see veg like celeriac, sweet potato and fennel given the North African treatment. Breads come in five varieties. For pudding, there may be an Earl Grey tea and honey brûlée (£5); a rice pudding (£5) given an unexpected twist by the addition of tamarillos. Or English cheeses with date and fig compote and oatcakes (£5.50). Wines are well priced, with an organic house white at £10.50 and a Pouilly Fumé les Logères 2001 at £25.

Decor is modern and minimalist, presentation is decorative but not over fussy, and the kitchen downstairs is open to view – always a good sign. If you think vegetarian food is only for the devoted, The Gate 2 might well change your mind.

Jin Kichi

(YI) Unlike so many Japanese restaurants, where the atmosphere can range from austere to intimidating, Jin Kichi is a very comfortable place. It's cramped, rather shabby and has been very busy for over a decade – tables are booked up (even on the quiet nights of the week). It differs from sushi-led establishments in that the bar dominating the ground floor with the stools in front of it is not home to the sushi master, but rather to a short and fierce charcoal grill and an unhurried chef who uses it to cook short skewers of this and that.

£14 to £30

Address 73 Heath St, NW3
℡ 020 7794 6158
Station Hampstead
Open Tues–Fri 6–11pm, Sat
12.30–2pm & 6–11pm, Sun
12.30–2pm & 6–10pm
Accepts All major credit cards

By all means start with sushi. Ordering the nigiri set brings seven pieces of fresh fish for an eminently reasonable £12.70. But then go for the "grilled skewers". Helpfully enough there are two set meals offering various combinations, and each delivers seven skewers (one combo costs £10.80 and the other £8.50). These little, cunningly marinated titbits make for a very splendid kind of eating: each skewer comes hot off the grill. Grilled skewer of fresh asparagus (£1.20) and grilled skewer of quail eggs (£1.20) are steady stuff. Be more adventurous – grilled skewer of fresh asparagus and pork rolls with salt (£1.60) is a big seller. Grilled skewer of chicken wings with salt (£1.30) is simple and very good, but grilled skewer of duck with spring onion (£1.80) is even better. Grilled skewer of ox tongue with salt (£1.80) is tender and delicious, while grilled skewer of chicken gizzard with salt (£1.10) is chewy and delicious. The grilled skewer of chicken skin with salt (£1.50) is crisp and very moreish. To drink there is ice-cold draught Kirin beer served in a frosted glass, as well as a range of sake. The remainder of the menu leads off to fried dishes, tempura, different noodle dishes, soups and so forth, but the undoubted star of the show is the little grill.

The art to eating here lies in second-guessing your appetite. Order too little and you face a wait while more food is grilled; order too much and you feel greedy. Go for greedy: it's an inexpensive place.

No.77 Wine Bar

This rowdy and likable North London wine bar opened its doors in 1982, and by now has survived long enough to match velocities with its clientele. Drawing a veil over a disastrous episode a few years ago when there was an attempt to take the cuisine up market, things now run more smoothly. The food is a kind of refined comfort food and is backed up by a long and informed wine list that offers particularly good value. The "side dishes" make great bar nibbles – chilli almonds, flatbread, marinated fresh anchovies (all £2.50).

£16 to £38
Address 77 Mill Lane, NW6 ℡ 020 7435 7787 **Station** West Hampstead **Open** Mon & Tues noon–11pm, Wed–Sat noon–midnight, Sun noon–10.30pm **Accepts** Mastercard and Visa

Starters range from pan-fried squid with fennel, chilli lemon and wild rocket (£5.95); to bruschetta with marinated peppers, pesto and baked goat's cheese (£4.95); or duck liver pâté with balsamic onions and focaccia toast (£5.25). The soupe de jour has come down to earth as "soup of today" (£3.95), while for main course, also in keeping with the old spirit, there is a pasta dish of the day (£8.25). But what about the wild mushroom stifado (lemon bay and cinnamon) served with braised rice (£8.50)? Or char-grilled rib-eye, roasted garlic mash, French beans and sauce Diane (£14.95)? Or confit duck leg with bubble and squeak (£9.65)? The new polite name for the burger formerly know as the "Fat Bastard" is "No. 77 beefburger topped with smoked Cheddar and served with braised capsicum, onions, potato fries and salad" (£8.75). The pud list is littered with familiar faces such as bitter chocolate and almond torte with rum and raisin and praline ice cream (£4.95) and caramelized clotted-cream rice pudding with brandy oranges (£4.95).

Like the menu, the wine list changes as whim and stocks dictate, but look out for delights such as the Alpha Domus Merlot/Cabernet 1999 from New Zealand (£21.75), or Three Choirs Estate Reserve, lightly oaked 1998 (£13.95). There are a couple of rather good English wines on the list here too. Anyone visiting Mill Lane for the first time should bear in mind that in this part of North London the busiest night of the week is Thursday, which is when the wine bar will be at its liveliest. They certainly know how to party in these parts.

Solly's Exclusive

What makes Solly's Exclusive so exclusive is that it is upstairs. Downstairs is Solly's Restaurant, a small, packed, noisy place specializing in epic falafel. You'll find Solly's Exclusive by coming out of Solly's Restaurant, turning left, and left again around the side of the building, and then proceeding through an unmarked black door. Upstairs, a huge, bustling dining room accommodates 180 customers, while a back room provides another 100 seats, which lie in wait for functions like bar mitzvahs. The decor is interesting – tented fabric on the ceiling, multicoloured glass, brass light fittings – while waitresses, all of them with "Solly's Exclusive" emblazoned across the back of their waistcoats, maintain a brisk approach to the niceties of service.

£16 to £35
Address 146–150 Golders Green Rd, NW11
☎ 020 8455 2121
Station Golders Green
Open Mon–Thurs 6.30–10.30pm, Sat (winter only) an hour after sundown–1am, Sun 12.30–10.30pm
Accepts All major credit cards except Diners

The food is tasty and workmanlike. Start with the dish that pays homage to the chickpea – hoummus with falafel (£4.25), which brings three crispy depth charges and some well-made dip. Even the very best falafel in the world cannot overcome the thunderous indigestibility of chickpeas, but as falafel go these are pretty good. Otherwise, you could try Solly's special aubergine dip (£3.25), or the Moroccan cigars (£5), made from minced lamb wrapped in filo pastry and deep-fried. Solly's pitta (£1.25) – a fluffy, fourteen-inch disc of freshly baked bread – is closer to a perfect naan than Greek-restaurant bread. Pittas to pine for. For mains, the lamb shawarma (£9.75) is very good, nicely seasoned and spiced, and served with excellent chips and good salad. The barbecue roast chicken (£9.50) comes with the same accompaniments, and is also sound. Steer clear of the Israeli salad (£2.75), however, unless you relish the idea of a large bowl of chopped watery tomatoes and chopped watery cucumber.

Solly's Exclusive is kosher, and under the supervision of the London Beth Din, so naturally its opening days and hours don't follow the same rules as non-Jewish establishments. If you're not fully conversant with the Jewish calendar, check before setting out.

Highgate & Crouch End

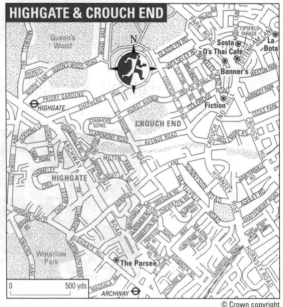

© Crown copyright

Banner's

The 1960s are alive and well at Banner's. This is a characterful restaurant and cocktail bar with a real community feel. Noticeboards proclaim events and accommodation, kids draw using crayons kept in little red wellies, world music plays ... It's a welcoming kind of place if this slant on life matches velocities with your own.

£10 to £30

Address 21 Park Rd, N8
℡ 020 8348 2930
Station Highgate
Open Mon–Thurs 9am–11.30pm,
Fri 9am–midnight, Sat
10am–midnight, Sun 10am–11pm
Accepts Mastercard and Visa

MODERN BRITISH

With all-day breakfasts, small meals, big meals, sandwiches and no-meat sections, Banner's menu pleases all tastes. Small meals include smoked tuna and coriander fish cake with Thai coconut dip (£4.95); tandoori chicken kebabs with mint raita (£4.25); and Greek salad (£4.75). They're all large enough for a light meal. Bigger meals include rib-eye steak, char-grilled with South Carolina barbecue sauce and chips (£10.95); jerk chicken salad with spoon bread and home-made chutney (£9.95); grilled fresh tuna loin with coconut rice and lime butter (£10.65); and Yorkshire sausages and mashed potatoes with Madeira gravy (£8.50) – a generous plateful, tasty and satisfying. Side dishes include cornmeal, sweetcorn and jalapeño spoon bread (£2.95); sweet-potato fries (£2.75); and garlic chips (£2.75) – for the certified lover of the bulb. Desserts include banana cake served warm with ice cream (£4.35); and hot dark chocolate and walnut brownie with ice cream (£4.75). Ices are from Marine (see p.234). But the all-day-breakfast menu is the star, with choices like two Manx kippers with brown or white toast (£5.25); bubble and squeak with two fried eggs (£4.10); and a proper fry-up with everything, including toast (£6.50).

The "world" feel extends to beers from Lapland and Argentina, exotic cocktails by the glass (£4.95) or jug (£20), cigarettes from the US, and postcards from Crouch End. And, to the relief of other diners, parents are warned, for safety reasons, not to let kids rush around on their own. Easy-going and family-oriented by day, Banner's livens up in the evening to become very busy with a lively, cocktail-drinking crowd; booking is advised.

La Bota

This bustling tapas bar and restaurant enjoys a healthy evening trade, and with good reason. It's a Galician (northwest Spanish) place, and that's always a plus sign, particularly for seafood. The best of its tapas fall into two categories: there are the "raw" ones like Serrano ham, which simply need careful buying and good bread as accompaniment, and there are the stews, which have been made in the morning and reheated as necessary – thankfully, most of the rich, unfussy dishes of Galicia

£10 to £25

Address 31 Broadway Parade,
Tottenham Lane, N8
℡ 020 8340 3082
Station Finsbury Park/
Turnpike Lane
Open Mon–Thurs noon–2.30pm &
6–11pm, Fri noon–2.30pm &
6–11.30pm, Sat noon–3pm &
6–11.30pm, Sun noon–11pm
Accepts All major credit cards
except Diners

lend themselves well to this treatment. Your first decision is a crucial one: do you go all out for tapas (there are 30 on the menu, plus 17 vegetarian ones, plus another 18 or so daily specials chalked on a blackboard)? Or do you choose one of the main courses – Spanish omelette, paellas, steaks, chicken, fish and so forth? Perhaps the best option is to play to La Bota's strengths and order a few tapas, then a few more, until you have subdued your appetite and there's no longer a decision to make. In the meantime enjoy the air conditioning – and the house wine at a very reasonable £7.60.

Start with simple things. Boquerones en vinagre (£3) brings a plate of broad white anchovies with a pleasant vinegar tang. Jamón serrano (£4.20) is thinly sliced, ruby-red and strongly flavoured – perfect with the basket of warm French bread that is on every table. Then move on to hot tapas: mejillones pescador (£3.40) is a good-sized plate of mussels in a tomato and garlic sauce; chistorra a la sidra (£3) is a mild sausage cooked in cider; riñones al Jerez (£3) is a portion of kidneys in a sherry sauce, rich and good. Alas de pollo barbacoa (£3) is an Iberian take on chicken wings. Then there's arroz al campo (£3) – rice cooked with saffron and vegetables; rabbit cazuela (£3.25); chicken riojana (£3.25); and patatas bravas (£2), the tasty dish of potatoes in a mildly spicy tomato sauce. Just keep them coming ...

If you like squid, and don't mind looking at a whole one, opt for chipirones a la plancha (£3.85) – four squidlets grilled to perfection.

Fiction

Opposite a hairdresser called Pulp sits the restaurant named Fiction. Fact. But the restaurant was there first, and it was named after the bookshop whose premises it took over – the hairdressers are the film buffs and named their place accordingly. And there's no gore in the tale, as Fiction is strictly vegetarian, although not in the missionary hair-shirt and holier-than-thou style.

£20 to £40

Address 60 Crouch End Hill, N8
℡ 020 8340 3403
Station Finsbury Park/Highgate
Open Wed–Sat 6.30–10.30pm, Sun 6.30–10.30pm
Accepts Mastercard and Visa
Ⓦ www.fiction-restaurant.co.uk

VEGETARIAN

Rather, the idea is to rediscover the use of indigenous herbs, and to cook, with plenty of wine, dishes that were popular in the days when people ate a lot less meat than they do now. All dishes and wines are marked as vegetarian, vegan and organic, where relevant.

Fiction's menu changes with the seasons. Starters will include a soup, and often it is an original one, like spiced roasted pumpkin soup (£3.95). Or try herby onion polenta cake with a cream and sage sauce (£4.95), or chunky cheese, sweetcorn and coriander fritters served with salad garnish and a delicious sweet chilli sauce (£4.45) – a bit like Thai crab cakes without the crab. The signature main courses are wood-roasted butternut squash (£10.95) and "The Good Gamekeeper's Pie" (£10.95); the former is described fulsomely as "a succulent 'steak' of squash filled with lemon-garlic mushrooms"; the latter as "chestnuts, wild mushrooms, 'mock duck', leek, carrot and broccoli, prepared in an old English marinade of red wines, and baked in a puff pastry pie". Both are very nicely flavoured. There's also a "Fictional" take on a North African favourite, styled Marrakesh couscous (£9.25) – roast garlic, tomatoes and olives. Side dishes include roast garlic mash with olive oil (£2.70) and the mini power plate (£3.95), a salad of mixed leaves and organic freshly sprouted legumes and alfalfa. The key pudding is triple chocolate terrine with fresh berry coulis (£3.95) – just one taste will tell you why it stays on the menu.

The large outdoor area with its beautifully planted gardens helps make Fiction a summer favourite, but it is essential to book, whatever the season may be.

O's Thai Café

O's Thai Café is young, happy and fresh – just like O himself. With his economics, advertising and fashion-design background, and a staff who seem to be having fun, O brings a youthful zip to Thai cuisine. His café is fast and noisy, and the music is played at high volume. But that's not to say the food is anything less than excellent, and it's very good value too. Order from the comprehensive and well-explained menu or from the blackboard of specials, which runs down an entire wall.

£12 to £30

Address 10 Topsfield Parade, N8
☎ 020 8348 6898
Station Finsbury Park
Open Mon 6.30–11pm, Tues–Sat noon–3pm & 6.30–11pm, Sun noon–3pm & 6.30–10.30pm
Accepts Mastercard and Visa
🌐 www.oscafesandbars.co.uk

Of the many starters you can do no better than order the special (£8.95 for two), which gives you a taster of almost everything. Satays are tasty, prawn toasts and spring rolls are as crisp as they should be, and paper-wrapped thin dumplings really do melt in the mouth. Tom ka chicken soup (£3.95) is hot and sharp, with lime leaf and lemongrass. Main courses include Thai red and green curries – the gaeng kiew wan, a spicy, soupy green curry of chicken and coconut cream (£5.95), is pungently moreish – as well as an interesting selection of specials such as yamneau, aka weeping tiger (£9.50) – sliced, spiced, grilled steak served on salad with a pungent Thai dressing. If you like noodles, there are a selection of pad dishes all at £6.50. Stir-fries with a host of combinations of vegetables, soy sauce, peanuts, spiciness, chicken, beef, pork, king prawn or bean curd. Puddings may include khow tom mud – banana with sticky rice wrapped in banana leaf (£1.95), Thai ice cream (£2.50), and fruit fritters served with golden syrup and ice cream (£2.50). There is a wide and varied wine list, with Budweiser, Budvar, Gambrinus and Leffe beers on draught. O's does takeaway too.

If you're new to Thai food, O's is a good place to learn, as the staff are happy to explain how it all works and you can specify how hot you like your food. Most main courses are around £6, which makes for very good value, and all of them are served with a delightfully moulded mountain of rice, which is included in the price. They also offer a discount if you eat early and vacate your table by 8.30pm.

The Parsee

London has had an acclaimed Parsee chef for some time now. His name is Cyrus Todiwala and his main restaurant is Café Spice Namaste (see p.182). Since 2001, however, London has also had what may be the world's best Parsee restaurant (there have been murmurings about the other one in Mumbai) and Todiwala is its godfather. Parsees are Zoroastrians who originally came to India from Persia, and in Indian society they seem to have specialized as surgeons and politicians. They are also renowned for their love of food – and for being the most demanding of customers. They start from the admirable standpoint that nothing beats home cooking and complain vehemently if everything is not exactly to their liking. They will be at home in this part of North London, and happy with this Parsee restaurant.

£15 to £40

Address 34 Highgate Hill, N19
☏ 020 7272 9091
Station Archway
Open Mon–Sat 6–10.45pm
Accepts All major credit cards
⊛ www.theparsee.co.uk

The food here is very good. Honest, strong flavours; rich and satisfying. Start with the admirable home-style akoori on toast (£3.50) – splendid, spiced, scrambled egg; or the masala ma murgh ki kalaeji (£4.25) – chicken livers in a typical Parsee masala cooked quickly and served with a roti; or maybe something from the grill such as dhana jeera ni murghi (£4.75/9.75) – a superior chicken "tikka" made with ginger and cumin. Main courses include that most famous of Parsee dishes, the dhaansaak (£10.95), a rich dish of lamb and lentils served with a pulao flavoured with star anise and little crisp meatballs. Then there's the murghi ni curry nay papeto (£9.95) – a distinctive curry made with chicken and potato, cashew nuts, sesame seeds and chickpeas; or the masala nu roast gos (£11.75), which is a Parsee take on roast lamb made with lamb shanks. The breads – rotli (£1.25 for two) – are very good, nutty and moreish. The vegetable dishes are good too: koru nay motta murcha (£4.25) is a simple dish made with cubed pumpkin. Save room for the toffee apricot ice cream (£3.75), rich with concentrated Hunza apricots.

This is a friendly, small, "family" restaurant serving delicious and unfamiliar Indian food. An adventure well worth having.

Sosta

🍴 During the 1970s, Silvano Sacchi was at the helm of two of London's more fashionable eateries – the Barracuda (a smart Italian fish restaurant in Baker Street) and San Martino (an Italian tratt in St Martin's Lane). Having sold out to a plc, Sacchi retired to Italy with his money memories. Just why he would want to return to the maelstrom of the London restaurant scene in the third mil-

£12 to £35

Address 14 Middle Lane, N8
☎ 020 8340 1303
Station Highgate/Finsbury Park
Open Mon–Fri 7–10.30pm, Sat
noon–2.30pm & 7–10.30pm, Sun
noon–3pm & 6.30-10.15pm
Accepts Mastercard and Visa

lennium is a matter for conjecture, but the official party line is that he got bored with doing nothing and, encouraged by his friends' reports of exciting times and record business, decided to return and give it one more go. He opened Sosta and it seems to have been busy from day one, so much so that he has taken on a new partner – chef Daniele Piazza from Milan.

The antipasti range from insalata tricolore (£4.75) – a mozzarella, avocado and tomato salad; to carpaccio di spada (£5.95) – fresh swordfish; or tomato bruschetta (£3.50); or caprese con salsa al Sedano (£5.25) – mozzarella with tomatoes and celery sauce. Onwards to "primi", where you'll find pasta e fagioli alla Veneto (£3.95), a thick pasta and borlotti bean soup, and pasta dishes such as ravioli di zucca (£5.25) – pumpkin ravioli, gnocchi all'aragosta (£8.95), and tagliolini alla rusticana (£4.95). "Secondi" offers five fish and five meat dishes. Orate alla plancha (£9.95) is grilled sea bream. Then there's vitello tonnato antica ricetta (£7.95) – the classic veal and tuna combo; fegato al burro e salvia (£9.95) is calf's liver in butter and sage. Puds are sound: pears poached in Barolo (£2.75); panna cotta (£2.95); and tiramisù al cioccolato (£2.95). The wine list has some trad Italian bottles that appeal greatly, including a bottle of Masi Campofiorin 1997 (£19.95).

At Sosta the service is slick and the tables are close together. The huge pepper mill of the 1970s may have been replaced by a natty modernist Parmesan grater and the offer of a drizzle of home-made chilli oil from a giant bottle, but everyone is attentive in what now seems like an old-fashioned way.

Holloway & Highbury

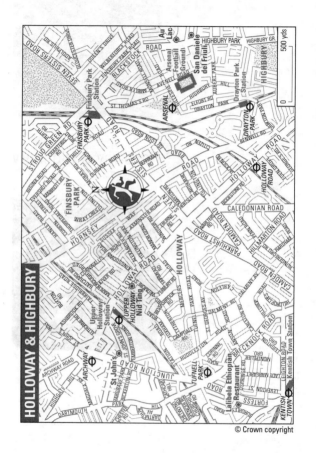

HOLLOWAY & HIGHBURY

© Crown copyright

Au Lac

🍴 Vietnamese restaurants in London tend to divide into two camps. On the one hand there is the spartan canteen – no frills, no nonsense and no concessions to non-Vietnamese speakers. And on the other there is a sprinkling of glossy, West End establishments that charge big bucks and would be puzzled if you wanted authenticity. Au Lac

£8 to £25

Address 82 Highbury Park, N5
☏ 020 7704 9187
Station Arsenal
Open Mon–Fri noon–2.30pm &
5.30–11pm, Sat & Sun 5.30–11pm
Accepts Mastercard and Visa

VIETNAMESE

doesn't fall into either of these categories. For a start, it is hidden away in Highbury and, what is more, it is a genuinely family-run restaurant – the dining room is comfortable in an informal, shabby sort of way, there are knick-knacks on the walls, and the family cover all the bases from the kitchen to the front of house.

Start with goi cuon (two for £2.20). These are soft rice-flour pancakes wrapped around crunchy veg and large grilled prawns, and they're fresh and light. Then there's goi tom (£6) – you get large steamed prawns, a small pot of hot and spicy sauce, and several large iceberg lettuce leaves. Take a leaf, add sauce and prawn, wrap, eat, enjoy. The deep-fried monk-fish with garlic and chilli (£6) is very good. There are good soups, too. The noodle soups – pho, bun bo and tom hue – come in large portions. They are cheap and tasty, good for eating when alone. For a more sociable, sharing meal, try the chicken with lemongrass and chilli (£5). The noodles are also very good – pho xao do bien (£5.50) is a grand dish of stir-fried rice noodles with fresh herbs and seafood, providing a good combination of flavours and textures. Another very impressive dish is the "minced pork with aubergine in hot pot" (£6.50). Ordering this brings a small casserole whose contents appear almost black. Very dark, very rich, very tasty.

Lurking in the drinks section is "Vietnamese sake". This potion was the one thing from his homeland that the head of the household (now banished to the kitchen) pined for. So the family made it for him. This clear hooch is served warm, and tastes like dry-cleaning fluid. To enjoy it you would have to be very homesick indeed.

Lalibela Ethiopian Restaurant

The real Lalibela is a twelfth-century Ethiopian church carved in the shape of a cross from a huge outcrop of solid rock. Its namesake in Tufnell Park is remarkable for serving uncompromisingly authentic Ethiopian food and for its genuine understanding of hospitality. It has a slightly harassed but still laid-back feel that is a great comfort to the diner. And, however ignorant of Ethiopian cuisine and customs you may be, pure ungilded hospitality shines through. The unwary can end up seated on low, carved, wooden seats around traditional low tables (so that you can eat with your hands). If your knee joints won't take that kind of punishment, plead for an ordinary table and resign yourself to dripping sauce down your front.

£12 to £34

Address 137 Fortess Rd, NW5
℡ 020 7284 0600
Station Tufnell Park
Open Daily 6pm–12.30am
Accepts All major credit cards except Diners

Starters are few, but they banish any inkling you may have about being in an odd kind of curry house. The lamb samosas (£3.75) have very dry, papery pastry and a savoury, spicy filling – delicious. The Lalibela salad (£4) is potatoes and beetroot fried together with a spicy sauce and served hot. Main courses are served traditionally, that is to say as pools of sauce set out on a two-foot-diameter injera bread. Injera is cold, made from fermented sourdough, and thin. You tear off a piece and use it to pick up something tasty. Portions are small, which makes prices seem high. But the flavours are intense. If you prefer, you can have the dishes with rice or mashed potato. What goes on the injera? Wot, that's what. Doro wot (£6.50) is a piece of chicken and a hard-boiled egg in a rich sauce, while begh wot (£6.50) is lamb with a bit more chilli. Lalibela ketfo (£8) is savoury mince with amazing, highly spiced cottage cheese – delicious. King prawn special (£7) is prawns in a tomato, onion and chilli sauce.

Do try the Ethiopian traditional coffee (£5.50), which is not only delicious, but also something of a feast for the eyes. After parading a small wok full of smoking coffee beans through the restaurant, a waiter will bring it to you in a round-bottomed coffeepot on a plaited quoit.

Nid Ting

What are restaurants for? Some pundits would have you believe that restaurants are for posing in, some that their mission is to entertain. Nid Ting is a place that feeds people. Lots of them. And it feeds people well, serving good, unfussy Thai food. The dishes here have not been tamed to suit effete Western palates, and you'll get plenty of

£8 to £20
Address 533 Holloway Rd, N19
☎ 020 7263 0506
Station Archway
Open Mon–Sat 6–11.15pm, Sun 6–10.15pm
Accepts All major credit cards

chilli heat and pungent fish sauce. You'll also get good value and brisk service – both of which obviously appeal, as the place is usually packed. This is a genuine neighbourhood restaurant at ease with its surroundings.

The starters are neat platefuls of mainly fried food: chicken satay (£3.95) is sound, although the sauce is a bland one; a much better bet is the "pork on toasted" (£3.95) – this is a smear of rich, meaty paste on a disc of fried bread. The prawns tempura (£4.95) are large and crisp, and the peek ka yas sai (£3.95) is very successful – stuffed chicken wings, battered and deep-fried. The menu then darts off into numerous sections: there are hot and sour soups, clear soups, salads, curries, stir-fries, seafood, rice, noodle dishes and a long, long list of vegetarian dishes – all before you get to the chef's specials. From those specials, try the lamb Mussaman curry (£8.75), which is rich and good, made with green chillies and coconut milk. From the noodles, try pad see ew (£5.50), a rich dish made with thick ribbon noodles and your choice of chicken, beef or pork. As a side order, try the som tum (£4.50), which is a pleasingly astringent green papaya salad. Also worth noting is the pla muk kaprow (£6.95), a dish of squid with chilli, garlic and Thai basil; and the koong kra prow (£6.95), which is a dish of prawns that have been given the same treatment.

One of the commonest criticisms of Thai food is that it can be insubstantial, and that dishes can start out looking cheap but end up as pretty bad value when portion size is taken into account. This is not the case at Nid Ting. Here, the cooking is accomplished, and dishes arrive both immaculately presented and in man-size helpings.

St John's

Archway's unprepossessing Junction Road is an unlikely setting for this fine gastropub, where the emphasis is firmly on the gastro rather than on the pub. The food is broadly Mediterranean, with a passion for all things rich, earthy and flavoursome, and there's a real joie de vivre in the combinations of tastes, textures and colours. Not only that but the dining room, which lies beyond the pub itself, looks fabulous – all louche, junk-store glamour with its high, gold-painted ceiling, low chandeliers and plush banquettes. There's an open kitchen at one end of the room, while at the other a giant blackboard displays the long menu. The proprietors also own The Ealing Park Tavern (see p.411).

£14 to £40

Address 91 Junction Rd, N19
☎ 020 7272 1587
Station Archway
Open Tues–Fri noon–3.30pm & 6.30–11pm, Sat noon–4pm & 6.30–11pm, Sun noon–4pm & 6.30–10.30pm
Accepts All major credit cards

As an opening move, the friendly staff bring fresh bread and bottles of virgin olive oil and balsamic vinegar. The menu changes day by day but there will probably be a soup – perhaps spiced parsnip soup (£4.50), or a ham and white bean broth (£4.50). Other starters might be salmon and cod fishcakes with herb crème fraîche (£5.25) or Taleggio, spinach and artichoke tart (£5.25). The food is robust and mercifully unpretentious. Main courses range from the traditional – braised lamb shank, garlic, tomato, rosemary, spinach, chickpea and chorizo stew (£12.50) – to the more adventurous, shellfish stew (£11.50), which comes with bruschetta and rouille. The fish is invariably good: whether a char-grilled sea bass with all the trimmings (£12), or the roast cod (£11.50), which is teamed with mash spinach, Puy lentils and salsa verde. You'll need to take a breather before venturing into pud territory (all £4.25). The rhubarb and raspberry crumble with ginger ice cream is good, but the star turn must be the blissful strawberry and clotted-cream fool with shortbread. The intelligent wine list includes a dozen by the glass, with a Cava at £4.25.

St John's gets more crowded and more convivial as the night goes on, but it is possible to have a dîner à deux; just make sure you're ready to be romantic by 7.30pm, when you've a chance of getting a table. You should book, whatever time you come.

MEDITERRANEAN/GASTROPUB

San Daniele del Friuli

🍴 Highbury Park is a strange place to find a football club. Lots of grand, renovated houses, wide streets, trees and, just a stroll around the corner, there's the Arsenal. Perhaps that is why they are moving? Until then, don't attempt to go to San Daniele on match days, when it will be packed out with happy, very respectable, middle-class

£16 to £42

Address 72 Highbury Park, N5
☎ 020 7226 1609
Station Arsenal
Open Mon–Sat noon–2.30pm & 6.30–10.45pm
Accepts Mastercard and Visa

footie fans loading up on Italian grub. San Daniele opened in the summer of 1996, with a chef from Friuli – that bit of Italy in the extreme northeast around Trieste. The dining room is large and airy, and the service is family-restaurant style, both attentive and gracious. The dishes lean that way as well, being substantial and unfussy. The menu is a long one. So, unless nostalgia gets the upper hand and you are swept away on a wave of desire for whitebait or insalata tricolore, pay special attention to the "altri Friuliani" (regional delicacies) and to the chef's specials.

The cooking here scales no modern gastronomic heights, and it is not cheap, but portions are large and the hospitality wholehearted. Simple things are well presented, like the vegetali grigliati (£4.50) – grilled vegetables with olive oil; the insalata di mare misto (£6.50) – a seafood salad; or the excellent prosciutto di San Daniele (£7.50), served plain or with melon. Or there may be pasticcio alla Friulana (£7.50), a lasagne made with speck and Asiago cheese. There are also risotto and pasta dishes from an imaginative specials board. For a main course you can choose between a dozen different Neapolitan pizzas (£5.50/7), fresh fish dishes and lots of old favourites. A huge portion of calf's liver (£11) comes in a classic butter and sage sauce and is accurately cooked to order. Scallopine di vitello (£9) is trad veal escalope and there are several options by way of sauce, including the classic Marsala and black pepper.

For pudding there is an old-fashioned tiramisù (£4), rich with alcohol and Mascarpone – delightfully different from the fluffy, faffy fakes that are all the rage in the smarter postcodes.

San Daniele del Friuli

Islington

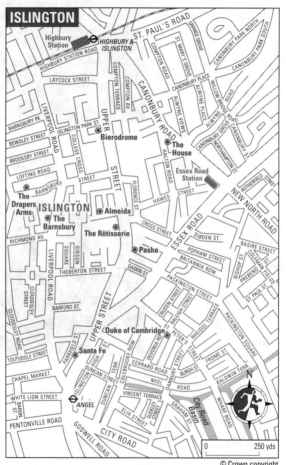

Almeida

(11) It may be located in oh-so-trendy Islington, opposite the home base of the Almeida Theatre, and it may be yet another outpost of Sir Terence Conran's sprawling London empire, but spiritually Almeida is stuck in some faintly remembered rural France. The man behind the stoves here is head chef Ian Wood (who served time at the Orrery with Chris

£18 to £80

Address 30 Almeida St, N1
℡ 020 7354 4777
Station Highbury & Islington
Open Mon–Sat noon–3pm &
6–11pm, Sun noon–3pm &
6–10.30pm
Accepts All major credit cards

FRENCH

Galvin: he's now moved on to a more exalted overseer's role with the Conran Group). The menu at Almeida manages to be a distillation of all that is good about an old-fashioned, gently familiar kind of French cooking and eating. On top of which, the large dining room is comfortable and the service is slick without being oppressive. There is a comprehensive wine list, with a good selection available by the glass.

This is a place to overdose on nostalgia. Soupe à l'oignon (£5) – the genuine article; six or twelve escargots à la Bourguignon (£5/9) – garlic heaven; tarte aux poireaux (£5.50); cuisses de grenouilles persillés (£8); moules gratinées (£5); omelette forestière (£5.50); and best of all, the trolley of charcuterie and rillettes (£10.50). This chariot is wheeled round to your table and you can pig out on well-made pâtés and rillettes to your heart's content. Mains carry the theme forward triumphantly: coq au vin (£14.50); steak au poivre (£19.50); confit de canard, lentils de Puy (£11); rognon de veau grillé (£12). Pukka pommes frites (£2). For pud there's the tantalizingly named "trolley of tarts" (£5.50), plus petit pot au chocolat (£4.50) or pain perdu (£5). With such a single-minded menu, Almeida could have ended up as something of a French resto theme park, but the kitchen is passionate about the classic dishes, and the mood ends up affectionate rather than reverential. No wonder it is busy enough to make booking for dinner a prudent idea.

Lunchtime features the twin attractions of a much less crowded restaurant and a grand deal – £17.50 for three courses. There is also a pre-theatre deal: £14.50 for two courses, and £17.50 for three.

The Barnsbury

🍴 The establishment now know as the Barnsbury took on its new role as a rather good gastropub just before Christmas 2002; prior to that it had been a rather insalubrious drinking den called Hourican's. The new team includes Jeremy Gough, who, after a career working front of house in various smart establishments, changed tack and now he runs the kitchen. He makes a great job of it. This is a pleasant, informal, pubby type pub with good food. And wonder of wonders it serves pub food rather than restaurant food. The management have got the menu right, the prices right, the service right and the ambience right. The Barnsbury deserves to succeed.

£10 to £30

Address 209–211 Liverpool Rd, N1
☎ 020 7607 5519
Station Highbury & Islington
Open Mon–Fri noon–3pm & 6.30–10pm, Sat noon–4pm & 6.30–10pm, Sun 12.30–5pm
Accepts All major credit cards except AmEx
⊕ www.thebarnsbury.co.uk

The menu changes day to day and offers seven starters, seven mains and half a dozen puds, the proprietors must be congratulated for not succumbing to the lure of fancy dishes, In the colder months starters will probably include a couple of soups – French onion soup (£3.95) or carrot and coriander soup (£3.50). Other starters may be a well-made salt and pepper squid salad with sweet chilli dressing (£5.50) – well seasoned, good leaves. Or Parma ham with caramelized beetroot and red onions (£5.50) – lots of (admittedly ordinary rather than great) ham and an interesting mound of warm beetroot, good complimentary flavours. Mains are "in-your-face-ordinary" and none the worse for that. Chicken and ham pie (£9.50); char-grilled sirloin steak (£9.50); fresh tuna steak pan-fried (£11); smoked haddock fishcake, rarebit sauce and spinach (£8.50). The pie is tipped out of its dish onto your plate and the flaky pastry crust added. An enormous portion, well-seasoned, tender meat. The fishcake comes with a splendid cheesy sauce and fresh spinach. Puddings are also satisfying: chocolate cake; apple pie; plum crumble (all £4). The blackboard wine list steers a sensible course between good value at the bottom of the price range and interesting bottles at the top.

The portions here are seriously large. You can confirm this by watching couples sharing a single side order of chips (£2.20) and failing to finish the giant bowlful.

Bierodrome

🍴 Bierodrome is part of the Belgo empire (see p.34), and shares its emphasis on modernist and iconoclastic architecture. The long, low bar is a temple to beer, and with that beer you can eat if you wish. The menu introduces a change of pace from the other branches – yes, there is life after mussels! Here there are sausages with stoemp, along with steaks, lobsters, croquettes and frites. Unsurprisingly the beeriness spreads through the menu – wild boar sausages with beer; roast chickens basted with beer.

£7 to £55

Address 173–174 Upper St, N1
☎ 020 7226 5835
Station Highbury & Islington
Open Daily noon–midnight
Accepts All major credit cards
Branches see p.490
🌐 www.belgo.restaurants
.co.uk

BELGIAN

It is no surprise that when the Bierodrome first opened they found that the customers were walking off with the beer and wine list. It makes stunning reading, with more than seventy beers to pore over and ultimately pour out. At random, consider: a banana beer – 25cl (£2.55); a very strong beer – Kasteel tripel 11% 35cl (£3.95); and a pretty delicious beer – Gulden Draak 75cl 10.5% (£4.75). As you work your way through your sumptuous malty glassful, what you will need is some food. Croquettes make good starters: try the Trappist cheese with piccalilli (£4.50). Or there is onion soup glazed with Gruyère croutons (£3.50). Wild boar sausages (£7.95) are made with dark Chimay beer and are served with stoemp, a superior kind of mashed potato indigenous to Belgium. Then there are the famous Belgo mussel pots: a kilo pot costs £9.95 and can be had marinière, Provençale, Dijon or even Congo – the latter cooked with creamed coconut and lemongrass. Or there's half a spit-roast chicken with frites (£7.95). Steaks include a 6oz sirloin with frites, salad, tomatoes and garlic butter (£10.95). There is a burger with smoked bacon and Swiss cheese (£7.95). There is an "express" lunch bargain, with a main course for £5.

The atmosphere in this place is much as you'd expect with such a raft of strong beers on offer. And how about the huge Nebuchadnezzars, which contain fifteen litres of La Veille Bon Secours at a thought-provoking £635 a pop? They do not sell those quite so quickly as the others, but you may still need to order ahead!

The Drapers Arms

(🍴) In October 2001, Paul McElhinny and Mark Emberton took over The Drapers Arms in Barnsbury. The Drapers started life as an old-fashioned double-fronted Georgian pub and that is pretty much how it has remained, despite the refurb. There's a bar downstairs and a dining room upstairs, and out the back is a large walled yard which has been paved over and kitted out with tables and

£12 to £45

Address 44 Barnsbury St, N1
☎ 020 7619 0348
Station Highbury & Islington
Open Mon–Fri noon–3pm &
7–10.30pm, Sat noon–3pm &
7–10.30pm, Sun noon–4pm
Accepts All major credit cards
except AmEx & Diners

chairs, and a pair of huge awnings in case of rain. This "extra dining room" seats another 45 hungry customers, and when the weather is sunny it is a thoroughly charming place. The food at The Drapers is better than standard gastropub fare, and this is reflected in the restaurant-ish pricing levels; it was also one of the factors that won The Drapers the title London *Evening Standard* Pub of the Year in 2003.

The menu changes twice daily and reflects the seasons, but starters may include a truffled cauliflower soup (£3.80); roast scallop and parsley salad with capers, olives and anchovy (£7); or a chicken liver and foie gras parfait with sourdough and red onion marmalade (£8) – this is a skilfully made dish, the parfait light, fluffy and ungreasy. Or how about a pear, walnut, white Stilton and watercress salad (£5.50); or an aggressive mix of flavours like tuna tempura with lime pickle, cucumber and Nam Pla (£6.50)? Mains range from spaghetti with peppers, artichoke, olives and capers (£9.80), and a monster salmon and cod fishcake with spinach and tartare sauce (£9), to rabbit Dijonnaise with char-grilled polenta (£12.50); or fish pie with smoked tomatoes and mash (£13). The chips (£2.50) are stellar, and side dishes may include welcome stalwarts like cauliflower cheese (£3.50). Puds are sound, and sensibly the kitchen sticks to favourites like sticky toffee pudding and custard; double chocolate brownie, hot chocolate sauce and crème fraîche; or a vanilla cheesecake with berry compote (all at £4.50).

The sandwiches and bar snacks also punch their weight – grilled steak and Dijon mayonnaise (£6.20); or toasted chicken BLT (£5.50).

Duke of Cambridge

£15 to £35

Address 30 St Peter's St, N1
☎ 020 7359 3066
Station Angel
Open Mon–Fri 12.30–3pm &
6.30–10.30pm, Sat 12.30–
3.30pm & 6.30–10.30pm, Sun
12.30–3.30pm & 6.30–10pm
Accepts All major credit cards
🖥 www.singhboulton.co.uk

In the canon of organic, things don't get much holier than this, the first gastropub to be certified by the Soil Association. Game and fish are either wild or caught from sustainable resources, and the 40-strong wine list is 95 percent organic. As "organic" becomes every supermarket's favourite adjective it is hard to remember that it was tough going in the beginning, and the Duke was there at the start. There's a small, bookable restaurant at the back, but most diners prefer to share the tables in the noisy front bar – the Duke is for the gregarious as well as the organic battalions.

The blackboard menu changes twice daily and is commendably short; you order from the bar. Robust bread with good olive oil and grey sea salt is served while you wait. Starters may include asparagus and white bean minestrone (£4.50), or smoked mackerel rillettes, rye bread and pickled cucumber (£5.50). Main courses are an eclectic bunch: a pan-fried red mullet may be partnered with linguine, lemon and chilli sauce (£12), while bacon-wrapped scallops come with tartare potato cake and basil creme (£10.50). Home-smoked lamb fillet is served with potato aubergine and Feta gratin (£13). Portions are serious, a million miles away from the mean-spirited bar snacks of many old-style pubs. There are vegetarian choices too, such as a roast vegetable parmigiana with Parmesan and hazelnut crust (£9). Puddings include plum and apple crumble – with custard, of course (£5) – and a chocolate, prune and praline cake with crème fraîche (£5). The wines are well chosen and varied, with a Greek Domaine Spiropoulos Porfyros (£16), and a New Zealand Te Aria Malbec (£21).

There are also many unusual bottled beers and non-alcoholic drinks, all organic. Connoisseurs will seek out the deliciously light and refreshing Eco Warrior ale, or the Freedom Brewery's organic Pilsener. But the zenith of the beer list must be Singhboulton ale. The Pitfield Brewery brews this rich, organic beer exclusively for the Duke of Cambridge, and it is named after the owners, Geetie Singh and Esther Boulton.

The House

As befits a location in one of Islington's smarter enclaves, The House seems more gastro than pub. But what is most unusual about this N1 newcomer is that for once aspirations on the menu seem matched by real talent in the kitchen. The House emerged from a lengthy (and doubtless expensive) transformation from dodgy local to chic eating house in mid-October 2002 but, despite a dining room that has been busy from day one, service is friendly and unstuffy.

£15 to £50

Address 63–69 Canonbury Rd, N1
☎ 020 7704 7410
Station Highbury & Islington
Open Mon 6–10.30pm, Tues–Fri noon–3.30pm & 6–10.30pm, Sat 6–10.30pm, Sun 6–9.30pm (brunch Sat & Sun noon–5pm)
Accepts All major credit cards except AmEx
🕸 www.inthehouse.biz

The kitchen is an open one and before you even get to your food the signs are good – the chefs work quickly, quietly and neatly. On the top of the grill there is an imposing piece of meat warming through: the char-grilled rib of Buccleugh beef, shallot crust, gratin dauphinois, green beans, jus gras (£37.50 for two) – whoever gets to share this particular rib will be thankful that someone didn't just whip it out of the refrigerator and slap it onto the grill. The food comes promptly and doesn't disappoint. Traditional jambon persillé, with warm potato salad, gherkins and Dijon mustard (£5), is well seasoned, well made and the texture is top-drawer. The Stilton, red onion and rocket salad with peppered beef fillet (£5.50) is another good starter: good salad, and melting slices of rare beef. Mains also hit the spot – braised beef in red wine with ceps, bacon and mashed potato (£15) is a Desperate Dan-sized portion, bags of flavour. There's a grilled lemon sole with sauce tartare, broccoli and new potatoes (£16.50). There is also the house shepherd's pie. When talking shepherd's pie a price tag of £10.50 takes a lot of living up to, but this pie just about makes it. Large, "recognizable" chunks of lamb, good gravy, unctuous mash, crisp top. Puds are also accomplished; you'd have to be really picky to say that the crème brûlée (£4.50) was a tad on the firm side.

Brunch is big here: there's a DJ on Sunday, and an array of brunchtime favourites – oyster shooter (£1); smoked haddock rarebit (£6.50); steak and eggs (£11.50); plus a Sunday roast (£11) for purists.

Pasha

If you picture Turkish food as heavy and oil-slicked, think again. Pasha is dedicated to producing fresh, light, authentic Turkish food that's suited to modern tastes. Dishes are made with virgin olive oil, fresh herbs, strained yoghurts and fresh ingredients prepared daily. Pasha doesn't look like a traditional Turkish restaurant either, being open and airy with only the odd brass pot for deco-

£15 to £30

Address 301 Upper St, N1
℡ 020 7226 1454
Station Angel
Open Mon–Thurs noon–3pm & 6–11.30pm, Fri & Sat noon–3pm & 6pm–midnight, Sun noon–11pm
Accepts All major credit cards except Switch

ration. The management describes it as "Modern Ottoman". It has clearly adapted well to its Upper Street location – so well, in fact, that the wine list offers a spritzer for £2.95.

For anyone new to Turkish cooking, the menu is a delight. Dishes are clearly described so that you can try them on a no-risk basis. Staff are helpful and will encourage you to eat in Turkish style with lots of small "meze" dishes. Set menus are popular (minimum two people): £11.95 for twelve meze and £17.95 for the Pasha Feast, ten meze plus main courses, dessert and coffee. Meze may include hummus, tarama, cacik, kisir (a splendid bulgur wheat concoction), falafel, courgette fritters, meatballs and a host of others. Other noteworthy starters include Albanian liver (£3.95), which is lamb's liver served with finely chopped onions and sumac. Main courses are more familiar but the choice is better than usual. Try kilic baligi (£11.95) – fillet of swordfish marinated in lime, bay leaf and herbs, and served with rice; Pasha kofte (£7.95) – the standard minced lamb kebab, but well seasoned and well presented; or istim kebab (£8.95) – roasted aubergine filled with cubes of lamb, green peppers and tomatoes with rice; or yogurtlu iskender (£8.95) – a trio of shish, kofte and chicken on pitta bread soaked in fresh tomato sauce with fresh herbs and topped with yoghurt. Though meat undeniably dominates the menu, there are five vegetarian and three fish selections. Puddings include the usual Turkish stickies but light and freshly made.

Wines are priced fairly, and there is Efes beer from Turkey (£2.50), or that powerful spirit raki (£2.95), for a tongue-numbing blast of the real Near East.

The Rôtisserie

The Rôtisserie is buzzing, brightly painted and unpretentious, with a commitment to quality underlying both food and service. Its South African owner makes regular trips to Scotland to lean on the farm gate and make small talk about Aberdeen Angus steers (which, if they did but know it, will soon be visiting his grill), and his menu's claim, "Famous for our steaks", seems well earned. The kitchen also frets about the quality of their chips, which is no bad thing, as the classic combination of a well-grilled steak with decent French fries and Béarnaise sauce is one of life's little luxuries.

£15 to £30

Address 134 Upper St, N1
℡ 020 7226 0122
Station Highbury & Islington /Angel
Open Mon & Tues 6–10.45pm, Wed–Fri noon–3pm & 6–11pm, Sat noon–11pm, Sun noon–10pm
Accepts All major credit cards
Branches see p.490
ⓦ www.rotisserie.co.uk

Rôtisserie starters are sensibly simple: a good Caesar salad (£3.95); tiger prawns peri peri (£4.95); grilled mushrooms with garlic and Parmesan (£3.95); char-grilled spare ribs (£4.25). Having brushed aside these preliminaries, on to the steaks, all of which are Scottish Aberdeen Angus: 225g rump (£12.95); 300g sirloin (£14.95); 200g fillet (£14.95); 400g T-bone (£16.95). All are carefully chosen, carefully hung, and carefully cooked. All of them (and all other main courses) come with a good-sized bowl of rather good French fries. If you don't want steak, try one of the other rotisserie items, such as the French corn-fed chicken leg and thigh (£5.95); or the wonderful spit-roasted Barbary duck (£12.95) – half a duck with fruit chutney. Or perhaps "simply sausages: with creamed mash and onion gravy" (£8.95). The rest of the menu covers the bases for non-meat-eaters. There's a grilled fish of the day (£12.95), or grilled Mediterranean vegetable skewers with spiced rice (£8.95). Puddings (all £3.95) are sound, and range from pecan pie to the ubiquitous tiramisù, banoffi pie and home-made ice cream.

The South African influence is a constant lurking presence behind these chunks of grilled meat. Occasional specials feature all manner of exotic meats, and sometimes you can opt for "monkey gland" sauce, which is rich and dark, and made to a secret recipe rumoured to include both Coca-Cola and Mrs Ball's Chutney.

Santa Fe

Two words are banned at Santa Fe. They are Tex and Mex. The chef (one Rocky Durham – a name which sounds so appropriate that it must be his own) would like the cuisine at Santa Fe to be described as "American Mexican", presumably to distance his creations from the T and M words, and from the strange southwestern dishes that feature on some London menus. The restaurant is quiet at

£20 to £45

Address 75 Upper St, N1
℡ 020 7288 2288
Station Angel
Open Mon–Fri noon–10.30pm, Sat noon–11pm, Sun noon–10pm
Accepts All major credit cards except Diners

lunchtimes but gets very busy in the evenings and at weekends. Symbols are used to classify dishes as hot, healthy low fat, and vegetarian.

Lovers of the margarita (£4.15–20) will be able to indulge, as there are eleven different versions on offer, together with nineteen classic cocktails (£4.15–6.25) and beers like Negra Modelo (£2.95). You are encouraged to plan your meal over drinks and tortilla chips with salsa (£2.95). Start with a smoked chicken and pesto quesadilla – a grilled tortilla – filled with smoked chicken, Jack cheese and a mild Jalapeño pesto (£4.95); or South Western fishcakes (£4.95) – salmon, cod and smoked haddock given a tortilla crumb crust. Or try five different starters in a Santa Fe sampler (£9.95). Tastes are fresh and clean, but dishes are hot unless you specify otherwise. For mains, try South Western steak and fries (£12.95), or mint-blackened lamb (£12.95). The steak is spice-rubbed and served with fresh salsa and chilli-dusted chips. The use of different chillies brings out the flavours well and makes dishes very moreish. It is possible to escape the chilli, but this isn't the place for anyone who likes bland food. There's also a new Mexican "chop" salad (£6.95): chopped apple, roast corn, poblanos, cherry tomatoes, red onion, toasted pinon with a cumin lemon vinaigrette. Puddings include Santa Fe cheesecake (£3.50), which comes with cinnamon-spiced whipped cream, and a very rich brownie with canella ice cream (£3.65). There are separate lunch and dinner menus, lunch featuring some lighter and more wrap-based dishes.

Santa Fe is a great venue for groups who prefer cocktails and beer to wine, and who like their food chilli-spicy. Quiet and mild it isn't.

Maida Vale & Kilburn

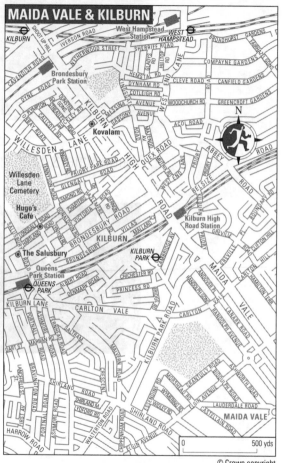

© Crown copyright

Hugo's Café

(🍴) For many years this place was known as the Organic Café before changing hands and being renamed Hugo's Café. But it would take a very perceptive person to pinpoint any differences other than the name. The "mission statement" ticks all the right boxes: organic; seasonal; local produce; non-endangered fish; traditional methods; eco-friendly practices. This place is still a genuine neighbourhood gem in a quiet, semi-private road. When it is too cold to enjoy one of the pavement tables, enter instead the largish yellow-painted dining room, decorated with twisted fig branches and reclaimed chicken-wire light fittings, and relax.

£17 to £35

Address 21–25 Lonsdale Rd, NW6
☎ 020 7372 1232
Station Queens Park
Open Daily 9.30am–11pm
Accepts Mastercard and Visa
Branches see p.489
🌐 www.organiccafe.co.uk

The menu changes sporadically and is divided traditionally into starters, mains and puds, with the addition of one-course dishes consisting of salads and pastas. But you can mix and match as you wish. Vegetarian choices are exceptionally good, but there is plenty for meat eaters as well. The cooking is reasonably classical and well grounded, with little that is unnecessarily fancy. Expect a soup, butternut squash and coconut (£4.50) perhaps, or a mixed crostini platter (£5.80). Or baked goat's cheese with marinated peppers (£6.20), or maybe a gammon hock terrine with home-made piccalilli (£6.50). Thereafter there are three main sections: veggie mains, fish mains and meat mains. Artichoke risotto comes with smoked Mozzarella (£10.50) and vies for attention with steamed halibut with lemon and caper mash and parsley sauce (£14.50). Roast rump of lamb Niçoise-style (£13.95) competes with a stunning steak – organic char-grilled 8oz rib-eye steak, served with hand-cut chips and glazed shallots (£14.50). Puddings (£4.80) are on the heavy side: caramelized apple bread and butter pudding; flourless chocolate pecan and Jack Daniel's cake. The drinks list is short, but there is a range of wines, beers, spirits and juices.

Most of the customers (many of whom are families) are regulars. There is no music to disturb animated conversations (except for occasional jazz nights) and service is informal but efficient. Lunchtime is brunchtime.

Kovalam

In the 1960s and 1970s, Willesden Lane was something of a magnet for curry lovers, as it boasted a couple of London's first authentic South Indian vegetarian establishments. These places shocked diners, who at that time were "curry and chips at closing time" sort of folk, by serving cheap and honest veggie food. Now Willesden Lane is no longer the cutting edge of curry, but that did not

£10 to £25

Address 12 Willesden Lane, NW6
℡ 020 7625 4761
Station BR West Hampstead/ Brondesbury Park
Open Mon–Thurs & Sun noon–2.30pm & 6–11.15pm, Fri & Sat noon–2.30pm & 6–11.45pm
Accepts Mastercard and Visa

dissuade some South Indian entrepreneurs from taking over the curry house at no.12 at the beginning of 2001, and relaunching it as "Kovalam – South Indian cuisine".

Kovalam is a brightly lit if traditionally decorated restaurant where the best dishes are the specials rather than the curry house staples that creep onto the list. So think authentic and order accordingly. Start with the ghee-roast masala dosa (£4.95), which is large, crisp and buttery, and has a suitably chilli-hot potato heart. Ordering the cashew nut pakoda (£2.95) brings a good, big helping of the deep-fried nuts. The paripu vada with chutney (£2.20) are very good – crisp lentil cakes with good, coconutty chutney. For your main courses, look closely at the vegetable dishes and the specials: aviyal (£2.75) is creamy with coconut; kaya thoran (£2.75) is green bananas with grated coconut, shallots and mustard. The koonthal masala (£5.50) is a "worth trying" – it's squid in a very rich sauce that has been sharpened with tamarind. Also try the aaterechi fry (£4.95) – dry-fried cubes of lamb with onion, curry leaves and black pepper; it's very tender and very tasty. Or perhaps the kadachachka kootan (£3.90), which is a dish of curried breadfruit, heavy with coconut? The breads are good, as are the scented plain rices – lemon (£1.95) and coconut (£1.95).

Do not be fooled by the terminology of the menu. Aaterechi Madras sounds authentic, but *aaterechi* is just a South Indian word for lamb, and this is our old friend, meat Madras, in disguise. In fact, the menu includes a good many curry house dishes masquerading under new, "authentic" names.

The Salusbury

(🍴) In a relatively short time The Salusbury has built up a reputation as one of London's better gastropubs; indeed in 2003 the management took on a small group including the Salt House (see p.287) so they are now responsible for a chainlet. Broadly speaking the Salusbury is a U-shaped space. You go in one door through the bar and continue

£16 to £35

Address 50–52 Salusbury Rd, NW6
℡ 020 7328 3286
Station Queens Park
Open Mon 7–10.15pm, Tues–Sat
12.30–3.30pm & 7–10.15pm, Sun
12.30– 3.30pm & 7–10pm
Accepts Mastercard and Visa

ITALIAN/GASTROPUB

round the bar to come out in the dining room – a quieter room filled with the kind of tables your mum had in her living room, stripped and scrubbed, with a display of eclectic art lining the walls.

The excellent and varied menu follows a mainly modern Italian theme rather than the more predictable Modern British bias of so many gastropubs. Starters (and a wave of dishes that could either be starters or mains) may include sautéed prawns with chilli and garlic (£7/11); Tuscan winter minestrone (£4); caponet – stuffed Savoy cabbage (£5.50); papardelle with artichoke and walnut sauce (£7/9.50); or chicken and Parmesan risotto (£6.50/9). There's a practical emphasis on pasta and risotto. Main courses may include sea bass cartoccio with radicchio (£13.50); braised venison with celeriac, olive oil and rosemary mash (£11); and lobster brodetto with shellfish and squid (£15). Moving on to pud territory, Amaretto, Ricotta and almond pudding (£3.95) vies with sgroppina (£3.95) – a soft lemon sorbet doused in grappa – and pure chocolate tart (£3.95). The wine list is not large, but it is well chosen, and runs from a Bandol (£11.60) to Mersault, Michel Bouzereau 2000 (£38.50). Bread and olive oil are served while you wait.

The Salusbury serves a highly critical crowd with excellent food in stimulating surroundings. If there's one niggle, it's that portion sizes can be daunting. In Yorkshire they call it being "over-faced", but if sound, Italian-accented cooking coupled with excellent value is what rings your bell, you'll like The Salusbury a lot.

St John's Wood & Swiss Cottage

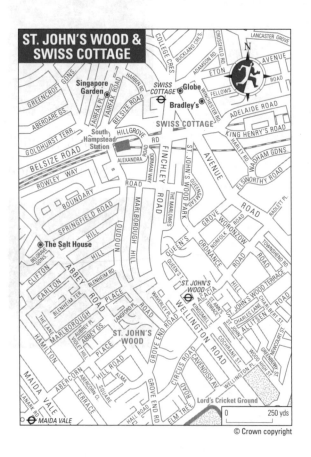

ST. JOHN'S WOOD & SWISS COTTAGE

© Crown copyright

0   250 yds

Bradley's

(ii) Bradley's is tucked away in a side street behind Swiss Cottage and hard to find – you get the impression that the regular clientele would prefer to keep the secret to themselves. The food here is pretty impressive, but that's not all. The atmosphere is warm and inviting, the menu covers and (metal) plates are probably the heaviest in London, and the loos are definitely a must-visit. All of which forms a good backdrop for chef-proprietor Simon Bradley's cooking and presentation. Dishes revolve around a combination of fresh ingredients and are served with a view to making the most of the visual appeal. They can look terrific.

£15 to £40

Address 25 Winchester Rd, NW3
☏ 020 7722 3457
Station Swiss Cottage
Open Mon–Fri & Sun noon–3pm & 6–11pm, Sat 6–11pm
Accepts All major credit cards

MODERN BRITISH

The menu works on a prix-fixe basis. There's a set lunch, £10 for two courses, £14 for three courses, rising to £16/20 on Sunday, when you also get a free apéritif. Dinner costs £24/29, all with mercifully few supplements. Starters range from Cornish crab and vegetable salad with crab Bavarois; to roast stuffed quail with foie gras and grapes; or Ricotta and lemon ravioli with tomatoes and oyster mushrooms. Mains are along straightforward lines: tuna au poivre with French beans and potato galette; pan-fried calf's liver with butternut squash gratin and roasted onions; stuffed globe artichoke heart, aubergine cannelloni and asparagus parcel; venison loin, mushroom torte, celeriac puree and sauce grand veneur; roasted monkfish with braised split yellow peas and crispy pancetta; confit leg and pan-fried loin of rabbit with prunes and potato dumplings. These are enlightened dishes that mix tried and tested combinations of ingredients with flair. Puddings continue the theme: there's a fine apple tart with baked apple ice cream; a blood orange and Campari sorbet with chocolate tuille; and sticky date and ginger pudding with vanilla ice cream.

Bradley's extensive wine list includes some unusual and higher-priced New World wines that can be hard to find. A lively but full-flavoured and biscuity Veuve Delaroy champagne is good value at £29.95, making Bradley's a fine venue for a celebration dinner.

St John's Wood & Swiss Cottage

Globe

MODERN BRITISH

Globe is a successful local restaurant. The proof of this assertion lies in Globe's survival in what has become a more competitive marketplace. The food here used to be "Pacific Fusion" or thereabouts, but over the last couple of years things have got slightly less spooky and slightly more comfortable. The dining room was given a lick of paint in 2002 and the private dining room was trans-

£18 to £35

Address 100 Avenue Rd, NW3
☎ 020 7722 7200
Station Swiss Cottage
Open Mon–Fri noon–2.30pm &
6–11pm, Sat 6-11pm, Sun 7–10pm
Accepts All major credit cards
except Diners
🌐 www.globerestaurant.co.uk

formed into the Globe bar. This restaurant owes its continued success to keeping an ear to the ground so the pricing is very much on a par with that of the competition. For all of the above reasons Globe has a strong local following.

Among the starters you may find duck salad with hoisin dressing on watercress and parsnip chips and watermelon (£5.95); or smoked salmon with avocado salad, caper berries and lemon oil (£6.50). There may be something simple such as a creamed smoked chicken and asparagus soup (£4.50), or something a bit more adventurous like honey-glazed chicken livers with pumpkin, rosemary and truffle oil on rocket (£4.95). Main courses may include an 8oz sirloin steak, tomato, field mushrooms and "big chips" (£13.95); oven-roasted salmon on crushed new potatoes and salsa verde (£11.95); char-grilled calf's liver and bacon, celeriac mash and red wine jus (£13.95). Vegetarians are pretty well treated here: perhaps a mushroom risotto cake with Mediterranean vegetables, Feta and aubergine relish (£11.50)? Puddings include the ubiquitous crème brûlée, here with plums (£4.50), and a mango sorbet with black pepper tuille (£4.50). But the star of the show must be the dark chocolate brownie with chocolate sauce and vanilla ice cream (£4.50).

Globe is built like a conservatory, with a glass roof and sliding doors that pull open, and an open-front courtyard for alfresco dining. The lunch menu follows closely on the heels of the dinner menu with many overlapping dishes and a few extra, simpler platefuls. Overall, the lunch menu prices are a pound or so cheaper than the evening prices quoted.

The Salt House

The Salt House was once an elegant Victorian street corner pub. But now pretty much all of the place, both inside and out, is painted jet black and it looks like a three-storey stealth bomber has landed in St John's Wood. Granted there's the odd splash of silver or sullen purple, but the decor resembles nothing so much as the old Black Magic chocolate box. Goths may like the black tablecloths, the black napkins, and the black decking under the black outdoor space heaters, but it doesn't really chime in with the food. The Salt House is now owned by the people who run The Salusbury (pg.281), and on taking it over they shut it down for a complete refurb, reopening in the summer of 2003 with a new menu. The food is Italian.

£10 to £50

Address 63 Abbey Rd, NW8
☏ 020 7328 6626
Station St John's Wood
Open Daily 12.30–3.30pm &
7–10.30pm
Accepts All major credit cards
except Diners

Starters range from artichoke and broad bean soup (£5), to an asparagus risotto (£8/11) by way of Mozzarella and Parmesan fritters with chilli jam (£7). The latter are rather like fishcakes made without fish – light inside and crisp outside with an agreeable musty belt of Parmesan. All pasta is home-made and broad noodles made with basil are served with little clams (£7). Or pappardelle may be teamed with rabbit and porcini (£9/12). Then there are seven pukka main courses ranging from eggs Benedict with prosciutto (£7.50), to cartoccio of turbot with spinach and candied citrus peel (£18). If the latter sounds a bit like an Italian restaurant dish, then that is because it is. Order the Salt House sausage sandwich with roast tomatoes and Colman's (£7.50), and what you get is a kind of superstar Brit bruschetta. Take a thick slice of toasted bread, spread it with caramelized fried onions, add a good meaty sausage, sliced, decorate with roast plum tomatoes, then balance another thick slice of toast on top and serve with English mustard. Puds (all £5) range from poached pear with saffron to strawberries with warm zabaglione. The wine list is lengthy, eclectic and not viciously expensive. Service is slick but unfussy.

Fortunately, all the waitresses look good in black; otherwise this place would only be suitable for an undertakers' convention.

Singapore Garden

SINGAPOREAN

(🍴) Singapore Garden is a busy restaurant – don't even think of turning up without a reservation – and performs a cunning dual function. Half the cavernous dining room is filled with well-heeled, often elderly, family groups from Swiss Cottage and St John's Wood, treating the restaurant as their local Chinese and consuming crispy duck in pancakes, moneybag chicken and butterfly prawns. The other customers, drawn from London's Singaporean and Malaysian communities, are tucking into the squid blachan and the Teochew braised pig's trotters. So there are cocktails with parasols and there is Tiger beer. But it's always busy, and the food is interesting and good.

£15 to £35
Address 83a Fairfax Rd, NW6
☎ 020 7328 5314
Station Swiss Cottage/ Finchley Road
Open Daily noon–2.45pm & 6–10.45pm
Accepts All major credit cards
⊛ www.singaporegarden.com

Start with a chiew yim soft shell crab (£7), which is lightly fried with garlic and chillies rather than annihilated in the deep fryer, like the fresh crab fried in the shell (£15), which does offer exceptional crispy bits. If you're feeling adventurous, follow with a real Singapore special – the Teochew braised pig's trotter (£10), which brings half a pig's worth of trotters slow-cooked in a luxurious, black, heart-stoppingly rich gravy. Or try the claypot prawns and scallops (£12), which delivers good, large, crunchy prawns and a fair portion of scallops, stewed with lemongrass and fresh ginger on glass noodles. Very good indeed. From the Malaysian list you might pick a daging curry (£6.75) – coconutty, and not especially hot. Or the squid blachan (£9) – rich with the strange über-savoury taste of prawn paste. Or a simple dish like archar (£4), which is a plate of crunchy pickled vegetables sprinkled with ground peanuts. One option is the mee goreng (£5.50), because this noodle dish is a meal in itself.

At the bottom of the menu you'll find the "healthy alternative" known as Steamboat (£31.50 per person, minimum of two people). This is a kind of party game. Eager participants drop tasty pieces of fresh meat and seafood into a cauldron of broth, which bubbles away at the table, then experience agonies of frustration when they find that they haven't the dexterity to fish them out with chopsticks.

Stoke Newington

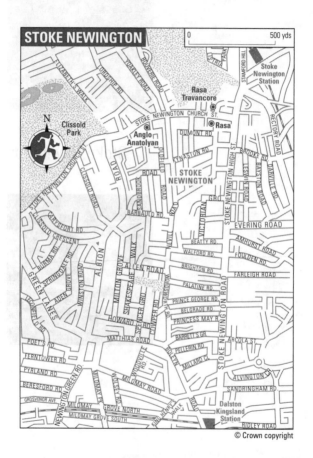

Anglo Anatolyan

The food is sound at the Anglo Anatolyan, the bills are small, and the tables so crowded together that you get to meet all the other diners. But the most intriguing feature of the restaurant is the large and impressive royal crest engraved in the glass of the front door. Under it an inscription reads, "By Appointment to Her Majesty Queen Elizabeth II, Motor Car Manufacturers". Why? Do the Windsors slip up to Stoke Newington when they feel a new Daimler coming on? Predictably, asking the waiters for provenance doesn't help much: they look at you seriously and confide that they "got the door secondhand".

£8 to £20
Address 123 Stoke Newington Church St, N16
℡ 020 7923 4349
Station BR Stoke Newington
Open Mon–Fri 5pm–midnight, Sat & Sun 1pm–midnight
Accepts Mastercard and Visa

Royal warrants aside, the food at the Anglo Anatolyan is usually pretty decent. The bread in particular is amazing: large, round, flat loaves about two inches deep, cut into chunks, soft in the middle and crisp on the outside; it is baked at home by a local Turkish woman and a far cry from the flat, hard, mass-produced pitta pockets of the supermarkets. To accompany it, start with ispanak tarator (£3.15), which is spinach in yoghurt with garlic, and a tremendous, coarse tarama (£2.95). And sigara borek (£3.45) – crisp filo pastry filled with cheese and served hot. And arnavut cigeri (£4.15) – cubes of fried lamb's liver. Dine mob-handed so that you can try more starters. The main courses are more easily summarized: sixteen ways with lamb, one with quails, two with chicken, one with prawn, and two vegetarian dishes. Kaburga tarak (£6.75) is crisp, tasty lamb spare ribs; iskender kebab (£7.75) is fresh doner on a bed of cubed bread, topped with yoghurt and tomato sauce; kasarli beyti (£7.75) is minced lamb made into a patty with cheese and grilled. They are all pretty good.

Like all the Turkish restaurants in this end of town, this is a very laissez-faire kind of place and standards can vary from visit to visit, but when you've eventually had your fill you'll be presented with a hand-written bill, at the bottom of which is printed, "Another cheap night out." This, for once, is simply the truth.

Stoke Newington

Rasa

Rasa has built up a formidable reputation for outstanding South Indian vegetarian cooking. In fact, when diners stop arguing as to whether Rasa is the best Indian vegetarian restaurant in London, they usually go on to discuss whether it is the best vegetarian restaurant full stop. As well as great food, the staff are friendly and helpful, and the atmosphere is uplifting. Inside, everything is pink (napkins, tablecloths, walls), gold ornaments dangle from the ceiling, and a colourful statue of Krishna playing the flute greets you at the entrance. Rasa's proprietor and the majority of the kitchen staff come from Cochin in South India. As you'd expect, booking is essential.

£12 to £30

Address 55 Stoke Newington Church St, N16
☎ 020 7249 0344
Station BR Stoke Newington
Open Mon–Fri 6–11pm, Sat & Sun noon–2.30pm & 6–11pm
Accepts All major credit cards
🌐 www.rasarestaurants.com

This is one occasion when the set meal – or "feast" (£15.50) – may be the best, as well as the easiest, option. The staff take charge and select what seems like an endless succession of dishes for you. But, however you approach a Rasa meal, everything is a taste sensation. Even the pappadoms are a surprise: try the selection served with six home-made chutneys (£3). If you're going your own way, there are lots of starters to choose from. Mysore bonda (£2.75) is delicious, shaped like a meatball but made of potato spiced with ginger, coriander and mustard seeds; or there is kathrikka (£2.75), slices of aubergine served with fresh tomato chutney. The main dishes are good too. Cheera parippu curry (£3.75) is made with fresh spinach and toor dal with a touch of garlic; moru kachiathu (£3.90) combines mangoes and green bananas with chilli and ginger. Or go for a dosa – paper-thin crisp pancakes; masala dosa (£5) is packed with potatoes and comes with lentil sauce and coconut chutney. Puddings sound hefty but arrive in mercifully small portions; the pal payasam (£2.50) is a rice pudding made with cashew nuts and raisins. A fine end to a meal.

The word rasa has many meanings in Sanskrit: "flavour", "desire", "beauty", "elegance". It can also mean "affection" – something that the whole of northeast London feels for this wonderful restaurant.

Rasa Travancore

Rasa Travancore is painted glow-in-the-dark Rasa pink, just like the original Rasa, which faces it across the roadway. It shows a certain amount of chutzpah on the part of any restaurateur to open a new branch opposite head office, but Das Sreedharan has never been shy. Rasa Travancore moves the spotlight onto a particular facet of Ker-

£15 to £35

Address 56 Stoke Newington
Church St, N16
☎ 020 7249 1340
Station BR Stoke Newington
Open Daily 6–11pm
Accepts All major credit cards
🌐 www.rasarestaurants.com

INDIAN

alan cuisine: Syrian Christian cooking, and a very welcome move it is too. All the South Indian flavour notes are there – coconut, curry leaves, ginger, chillies, mustard seeds, tamarind – but as well as veggie specialities, Syrian Christian dishes feature fish, seafood, mutton, chicken and duck.

The menu is a long one and great pains have been taken to explain every dish, although the language can get a bit flowery. Apparently the king prawns in konjufry (£4.95) have been marinated in "refreshing spices" – whatever. But the prawns are very good – plump and with a rich flavour. Or there's Kerala fish fry (£3.95), a large steak of firm-fleshed kingfish dusted with spice and pan-fried. Very delicious. Travancore kozhukkatta (£3.75) is a sort of ninth cousin to those large, doughy Chinese dumplings – steamed rice outside with spiced minced lamb inside. The main course dishes are fascinating and richly flavoured. Kozhy olthu curry (£5.25) – billed as "a famous recipe from Sebastian's mum"! – is a rich, dryish, oniony chicken curry. Lamb stew (£5.95) is a simple and charming lamb curry. Duck fry (£6.95) is dry-fried chunks of duck with curry leaves and onion. Kappayyum meenum vevichathu (£7.95) is a triumph – a soupy fish curry, delicately flavoured and served with floury chunks of boiled tapioca root dusted with coconut. Very moreish. The veg curries are also good: try the Travancore kayi curry (£3.90), "chef Narayanan's signature dish", which is a splendidly richly sauced, coconutty mixed vegetable dish.

Excellent accompaniments are the tamarind rice (£2.50), which has an amazing depth of flavour, and the flaky, buttery Malabar paratha (£2).

Wembley

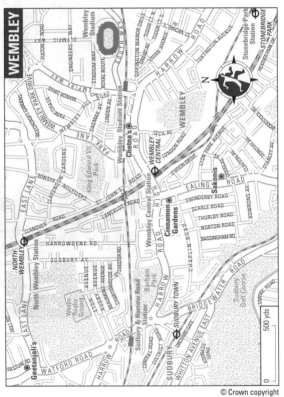

© Crown copyright

Chetna's

Chetna's is a remarkable Indian restaurant – busy enough to need a queuing system. You register your interest at the counter and are given a cloakroom ticket, and when your table is ready your number is called. The restaurant has smart wooden tables and chairs, ceiling fans and some seriously ornate brass chandeliers, but despite these trappings it is still awesomely cheap. The food is very good indeed and the menu is a bit of a surprise, opening with a section headed "seaside savouries" – an odd claim in a vegetarian establishment – and moving through to Chetna's Pizza Corner, confirming once again that when Asians go out to dinner they often want a change from the usual fare. The concept of a large "special vegetable hot pizza" (£5.50) cooked by an Indian chef and made with pure vegetarian cheese, onions and special Chetna sauce – green pepper, corn and hot green chillies – has undeniable charm.

£4 to £10

Address 420 High Rd, Wembley
℡ 020 8900 1466
Station Wembley Central
Open Tues–Fri noon–3pm &
6–10.30pm, Sat & Sun 1–10.30pm
Accepts Mastercard, Switch or Visa
🖰 www.chetnassweets.co.uk

INDIAN/VEGETARIAN

Start with a truly amazing mouthful: Chetna's masala golgapa (£2.60). These are small, crisp golgapas filled with potatoes, onions, moong, chana, green chutney and sweet and sour chutney, and topped with sev. You load them into your mouth and, as you chew, different tastes and textures take over. It's an astonishing sensation. Order more portions than you think you'll need. Also try the kachori (£2.40) – a crisp coat encases a well-spiced ball of green peas. Or there's alu tikki (£2.60) – spicy mash with chickpeas deep-fried. Or there's a dry potato curry (£2.80) – simple and good. The most visually striking dish must be the paper dosa (£4), a giant chewy cone of nutty-tasting pancake with a vegetable sambhar and coconut chutney for dipping.

The award for most comprehensive dish must go to the Delhi Darbar thali (£7.80), which is served with one sweet, one farsan, three vegetables, chutney, vegetable biryani, dhal, raita, papadum and paratha. There's a minimum charge of £3.50 per person at Chetna's – presumably to stop a large family sharing one Delhi Darbar thali for dinner.

Cinnamon Gardens

Cinnamon Gardens is a bright and modern restaurant at the Wembley end of Ealing Road. The dining room is all minty green and apricot with a tiled floor and some ostentatiously modern chairs, which thankfully prove comfortable. The walls are also home to a series of murals that seem to be "naive" versions of the classic sun and sand

£8 to £30

Address 42–44 Ealing Road, Wembley
☎ 020 8902 0660
Station Wembley Central
Open Daily noon–midnight
Accepts Cash or cheque only

"Muriel" that adorned Vera Duckworth's *Coronation Street* living room in the 1980s. This is a Sri Lankan restaurant, and things proceed at a Sri Lankan pace. Don't worry: simply relax and assess the relative merits of Lion lager and Lion stout; soon you will be in just the right mood. Teetotallers may try the Portello, a lurid-purple soft drink with an almost radioactive glow.

Starters include most of the Sri Lankan favourites. There are mutton rolls (two for £1.50), crab claws (£2.75) and the ubiquitous chicken 65 (£4.45), which allegedly must be made with a 65-day-old chicken. There is also a section on the menu devoted to "fried specials", any of which make a great starter when teamed with some bread – try fried mutton (£3.95) or fried squid (£4.40). Another section features devilled dishes, ranging all the way from a devilled potato (£3) to devilled king prawn (£6.25). There is a whole host of hoppers, or rice pancakes, including milk (£2.25 for two), egg (£2.50 for two) and jaggery (£2.50 for two) – the latter rich with unrefined sugar. The Cinnamon special biryani (£5.95) is stunning: dark and richly flavoured, it comes with a bit of everything, including a lamb chop and a hard-boiled egg! From the curries, the chilli chicken (£3.95) is good and hot. Or perhaps crab curry (£4.45), or squid curry (£4.75), appeal? It is also worth noting that the rotis (£1) are very good here, light and flaky, as are the sambols – the seeni sambol (£1.25) is a relatively mild, sweet onion jam, while the katta sambol (£1.75) is an incredibly wild chilli concoction. The service is friendly if a little dozy.

Hidden among the Cinnamon specials is an intriguing dish, "rubbit fried (when available)". Does Bugs know about this?

Geetanjali's

There are a good many Indian restaurants in Wembley, and it would be easy to write off Geetanjali's as just one more of the same. On the face of it, for sure, the menu is pretty straightforward, with a good many old, tired dishes lined up in their usual serried ranks – chicken tikka masala, rogan josh and so on and so forth. But Geetanjali's has a secret weapon, a dish that brings customers from far and wide. Word on the street is that this place serves the best tandoori lamb chops in North London. And when you've tasted them, you'll agree.

£12 to £26

Address 16 Court Parade,
Watford Rd
☏ 020 8904 5353
Station Wembley Central
Open Daily noon–3pm &
6–11.30pm
Accepts All major credit cards
🌐 www.geetanjali-restaurant.com

This chop lover's haven has a large, roomy dining room, and the service is attentive, if a little resigned when you pitch up and order a raft of beers and a few portions of chops – or, as the menu would have it, lamb chopp (£4.20). Of course, the chops are good. Very good. Thick-cut, exceedingly tender and very nicely spiced. Accompany them with a luccha paratha (£2.50), warm and flaky and presented in the shape of a flower with a knob of butter melting into its heart. The alternative is the intriguingly named bullet nan (£2.50), which promises to be hot and spicy, and delivers in good measure. You have been warned. Even if you're not a complete chopaholic, you can also do well here. Go for starters such as the good chicken tikka haryali (£5.90) – chicken breast marinated in green herbs like coriander and mint before being cooked in the tandoor. Rashmi kebab (£3.90) is also good, made from minced chicken and spices. Main courses include mathi gosht (£6.90), which is chicken with fenugreek; lamb bhuna (£6.50); and lamb badam pasanda (£6.90). And should this emphasis on meat leave you craving some of the green stuff, there's sag aloo (£4.20) or karahi corn masala (£4.50).

This is not the cheapest Indian restaurant in Wembley, but it does have a certain style, even extending to the sophisticated peppermint fondant mints that accompany your bill. And it goes without saying that it's worth travelling for the best tandoori chops in North London.

Wembley

INDIAN/VEGETARIAN

Sakoni's

Sakoni's is a topnotch vegetarian food factory. Crowded with Asian families, it is overseen by waiters and staff in baseball caps, and there's even a holding pen where you can check out the latest videos and sounds while waiting your turn. From a decor point of view, the dining area is somewhat clinical: a huge square yardage of white tiling, but the Indian vegetarian food here is terrific. It's old hat to many of the Asian customers

£4 to £10

Address 127–129 Ealing Rd, Alperton
☎ 020 8903 1058
Station Alperton
Open Mon–Thurs & Sun 11am–11pm, Fri & Sat 11am–midnight
Accepts Mastercard, Switch, or Visa
Branches see p.490

who dive straight into what is, for them, the most exciting section of the Sakoni's menu – the Chinese dishes. These tend to be old favourites like chow mein (£5.95) and haka noodles (£4.25), cooked with Indian spicing. Unless curiosity overwhelms you, stick to the splendid South Indian dishes. New to Sakoni's in 2002 – three buffets: breakfast 8am to 11am; lunch noon till 3pm; dinner 7.30pm to 11pm.

Sakoni's is renowned for its dosas. Effectively these are pancakes, so crisp that they are almost chewy, and delightfully nutty. They come with two small bowls of sauce and a filling of rich, fried potato spiced with curry leaves. Choose from plain dosa (£3.50), masala dosa (£4.50), and chutney dosa (£4.60) – which has spices and chilli swirled into the dosa batter. Try the farari cutlets (£3.50); not cutlets at all, in fact, but very nice, well-flavoured dollops of sweet potato mash, deep-fried so that they have a crisp exterior. In fact, all the deep-fried items are perfectly cooked – very dry, with a very crisp shell, but still cooked through. A difficult feat to achieve. Also worth trying are the bhel puri (£3.30), the pani puri (£2.50) and the sev puri (£3.30) – amazingly crisp little taste bombs. Pop them in whole and the flavour explodes in your mouth.

Some say that the juices at Sakoni's are the best in London, and while that may be hyperbole they certainly are very good indeed. Try madaf (£2.50), made from fresh coconut; melon juice (£2.25), which is only available in season; or the orange and carrot mix (£2.50), which is subtitled "health drink".

Further North

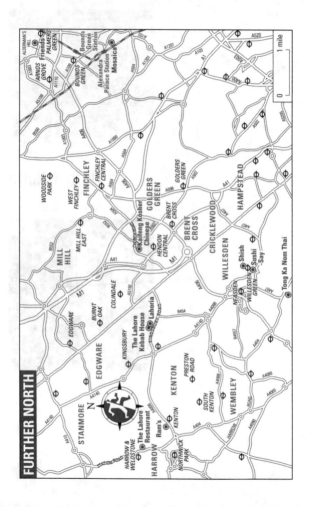

Friends

🍴 It is hard to think of a more unlikely place to find a chic, stylish and aspirational Indian restaurant than Palmers Green, N13. Here there are lots of detached houses, wide streets and smart cars, all is calm and perhaps a tad smug. As you drive along Aldermans Hill you come across a small parade of shops, and occupying a double frontage

£18 to £40

Address 38 Aldermans Hill, N13
☎ 020 8882 5002
Station BR Palmers Green
Open Tues–Fri 6–11pm, Sat & Sun
noon–2.30pm & 6–11pm
Accepts Mastercard and Visa
🌐 www.friends-restaurant.com

is Friends Indian Restaurant. It is a bright place with modern if slightly sparse decor. There's a good deal of bright minty-greeny-blue paint, an apricot-coloured dado and comfortable cane and bamboo chairs. The chef has a very deft touch – spicing is well balanced and flavours are rich and beguiling.

Starters like chicken tikka kali mirch (£3.95) are delicious; it's a juicy chicken tikka with a pungent dusting of black pepper. Or there's a terrific interpretation of "crab pepper fry" (£4.95) – the white crab meat combined with the richer brown meat and classic Southern Indian spices such as curry leaves, fennel seeds and black pepper, with a squeeze of fresh lemon juice to balance the richness. Listed under mains, but an excellent choice as a starter, is adrak ke panji (£7.95) – a pair of thick-cut, meltingly tender lamb chops, they taste vaguely gingery and go well with a roti. Other main-course options include some good Southern Indian dishes like dhania nariyal ka murg (£6.50), which is a chicken curry with plenty of coconut, coriander, curry leaves and fennel. And there's lal mirch ka salan (£7.25), which is a lamb curry made with cinnamon, cardamom and cloves as well as an enticing belt of chilli. Look out for the lacchi paratha (£1.95), which is as buttery and flaky as you could wish for. Amongst the veggie options, chole amchuri (£3.95) is a very simple and very good dish of chickpeas with sour mango powder.

This is accomplished cooking. Service is adept and not over-pushy, and the dining room is comfortable. This is the kind of modern, middle-ranking Indian restaurant we would all like as our local.

Kaifeng Kosher Chinese

The Kaifeng Kosher Chinese restaurant is a one-off. This opulent Chinese restaurant – it was redecorated in 2002 – claims to be, and doubtless is, the only kosher Oriental establishment in Britain. According to the family tree on the wall, the most important family of Kaifeng's former Jewish community is named Chao Lunang-Ching. The inscription adds, rather enigmatically, that "Ezekiel is probably Chao Lunang-Ching Gwlyn Gym". So now you know. The long, narrow dining room is filled with affluent locals, happy to pay smart North London prices that continue to march upwards and have more in common with the West End than the suburbs. But you will get friendly and excellent service that almost justifies the fifteen percent surcharge, and fresh, well-cooked (if a trifle under-seasoned) dishes. If you're Orthodox Jewish, Kaifeng must make a welcome change; if you're not, then seeing how favourite dishes like sweet and sour pork, prawns kung po and so forth turn out kosher-style is a lot of fun.

£25 to £55
Address 51 Church Rd, NW4
☏ 020 8203 7888
Station Hendon Central
Open Mon–Thurs & Sun 12.30–2.30pm & 6–11pm (also Sat from 1hr after sunset to 11pm, Sept–April only)
Accepts All major credit cards
⊛ www.kaifeng.co.uk

Start with the spare ribs (£7.95), which are absolutely delicious, made from lamb instead of pork and arguably even better for it. Hunan chicken with lettuce wrap (£13.50) is also fresh and good, while the usual prawn and sesame-seed toast becomes sesame chicken (£7.95). Of the main courses, the sweet and sour lamb (£14) is slightly less successful – the good, sharp sauce still makes no impression on fairly tough chunks of lamb. But there are some interesting and unfamiliar dishes like beef and straw mushrooms (£14.50), smoked shredded chicken (£13.50), and eggplant in garlic sauce (£6.95). Shellfish dishes, meanwhile, turn into fish, usually sole, which is served in a variety of familiar styles, including steamed with ginger and spring onion (£18.50), and drunken (£18.50) – which means sliced and served in kosher rice wine.

Given its unique status, the Kaifeng is a pretty popular place, and even early in the week it tends to fill quickly. So take the precaution of booking if you're travelling out here specially.

The Lahore Kebab House

This grill house was once linked to the famous Lahore Kebab House in East London. Then, in 1994, Mr Hameed bought the NW9 business, and with it the right to use the name "Lahore Kebab House of East London" anywhere within a five-mile radius of Kingsbury. Although completely independent of the

£6 to £12

Address 248 Kingsbury Rd, NW9
☎ 020 8905 0930
Station Kingsbury
Open Daily 1pm–midnight
Accepts Cash or cheque only

Umberstone Street establishment (see p.173), this unfussy restaurant remains faithful to the spirit of the original. Kebabs here are cheap, freshly cooked and spicy, while the karahi dishes are also worth delving into. This Lahore has the advantage of a drinks licence, so you can now purchase Tusker and Kingfisher beers without having to pop out to one of the neighbouring off-licences.

There's not much point in coming to the Lahore unless you're after some kind of kebab. If you just want a starter bite, there's seekh kebab (75p each). Or, for more serious eating, there's a list of kebabs all with five pieces per skewer: mutton tikka (£2.20); chicken tikka (£3); jeera chicken (£4.20); chicken wings (£4.20); lamb chops (£5). Everyone is very helpful here, and they are happy to make you up a platter – with three pieces of each kebab, for example – and charge pro rata. Unusually, for such a stronghold of the carnivore, there's also a long list of vegetarian dishes, all served in the karahi. Include a couple with your order, perhaps karrai dhal (£3.50), or karrai sag aloo (£3.50), which is particularly rich and tasty. Back with the meats, karrai gosht (£4.70) is a rich lamb curry, while the Chef's Special (£6.50), a hand-chopped keema made with both chicken and lamb, is a revelation. It's very tasty, with recognizable, finely chopped meat – a far cry from the anonymous mince that forms the backbone of keema dishes in so many curry houses. It is thoroughly recommended, as are the breads – tandoori nan (90p) and tandoori roti (60p) – which are fresh and good.

The Lahore's weekend specials all appeal: karrai nehari (£7) brings slow-cooked lamb shanks; karrai bhindi (£4.50) is okra; and karrai karela (£4.50) is made from bitter melons.

The Lahore Restaurant

(icon) Are bring-your-own restos the next big thing? If so, with a BYO drinks policy and open kitchen The Lahore Restaurant is well on its way towards being a ground-breaking sort of place. But that's where the trendiness stops. This homely and unpretentious Pakistani eatery serves grilled meats and karahi dishes. The service is friendly, the food fresh, and the prices are extremely reasonable. The only drawback is discovering that the off-licence next door shuts at nine o'clock on weekday evenings. The room is plain, and a couple of ceiling fans struggle to disperse the fierce heat coming off the grills. When it is just a bit smoky it's not so bad, but sometimes the smoke comes with a chilli pungency that will reduce you to tears.

£6 to £16

Address 45 Station Rd, Harrow, Middlesex
℡ 020 8424 8422
Station Harrow & Wealdstone/ Harrow-on-the-Hill
Open Daily 11.30am–11.30pm
Accepts Cash or cheque only

To start order a couple of rotis (60p) and some grilled meats. Chicken tikka (£3) is sound, a good portion; tandoori chicken wings (six for £4) are great – well marinated, perfectly cooked and spicy. Eat your heart out, Colonel. Tandoori lamb chops (six for £5) are outstanding – thick-cut, heavy with spice, and juicy. Seek kebabs (two for £1.25) have a welcome belt of fresh chilli and green herbs. It would be quite feasible to make a decent meal of starters and bread, but the curries are very good, too, with simple dishes full of flavour like methi chicken (£4.50). When asked the question "Hot, medium, or mild?" it's worth noting that "hot" is not painfully so, and "medium" seems a bit tame. The star turn is the karahi karela gosht (£4.50); the tender, slow-cooked lamb has a rich sauce balanced by the addictive taste of bitter melon. The breads are very good indeed. For an interesting contrast, order a tawa paratha (£1.50) and an onion kulcha (£1.80). The paratha is wholemeal, thick, filling and fried until the outside is flaky-crisp. The onion kulcha is doughy but stuffed with a rich onion mix that includes fresh coriander.

There are no frills at The Lahore Restaurant, and it can be a tad smoky, but the food is very honest, very good and very cheap, and that is a formula that will ensure success anywhere.

Lahoria

This Kingsbury stalwart used to be shabby. Then it was refurbished in pink. Then green. Now pink again, but who cares? Even taking into account the refurbs, it's certain that nobody comes here for the ambience. There's plenty of competition, with half a dozen other Indian restaurants clustered on this stretch of road. No matter – this small place is still busy, particularly at the weekend. What makes the Lahoria stand out, what has kept it going from strength to strength, is the sheer quality of the food, which combines two admirable attributes – simplicity and goodness.

£12 to £25

Address 274 Kingsbury Rd, NW9
☏ 020 8206 1129
Station Kingsbury
Open Tues–Thurs 6–11.30pm, Fri & Sat 5.30pm–midnight, Sun 3pm–midnight
Accepts Mastercard and Visa

So, the food: it's fresh, not painfully hot (unless you want it to be) and well balanced. There are a lot of East African Asian specialities, and dishes come by either the plate or the karai. Start with a plate of jeera aloo (£4.95) – tasty, rich, soft, fried potatoes with cumin, a sort of Indian pommes Lyonnaises. Or have a plate of masala fish (£4.95) – two fat fillets of tilapia cooked in a fresh green masala. You must try the chilli chicken (£6.25), which is nine chicken wings in a dark-green, almost black sludge that is rich with ginger, chillies, coriander and just a hint of tamarind sourness – triumphant but not so hot it hurts. Then there are the tandoori chops (£4.95), which are very good indeed. Also look out for the mari chicken (£6.25), which is chicken marinated in cracked black pepper. For a main course it is hard to give high enough praise to the karai spring lamb (£6.25), served on the bone. It is deliciously rich. Or try a simple classic like karai masala lamb methi (£6.25). The karai red kidney beans (£4.50) and karai bangan ka bartha (£5.25), based on aubergines and onions, are also good bets.

On Friday, Saturday and Sunday, Lahoria offers two notable specials: karai boozi ki goat (on the bone, £6.25) and karai undhiu (£5.50), which is a dish of mixed vegetables. They also have a magnificent chiller full of bottled beers, including Becks, Holsten, Carlsberg, Budweiser and – best of all – Tusker from Kenya.

Mosaica

Up in the high pastures of Wood Green there is a large and hideous concrete "Shopping City" whose main claim to fame seems to be "secure parking". Around the corner is a straggle of large, run-down buildings called The Chocolate Factory that has been colonized by artists, potters, designers and anyone arty needing cheap, no-frills space. You'll find Mosaica hidden at the heart of Building C, and it is an amazing place – spacious, stylish and comfortable. There is a long bar made up of cinder blocks, topped with a twenty-foot sheet of glass. There's a terrace outside in the light well, which will be amazing should we ever get good weather. There's a huge open kitchen. And there are mismatched but comfortable straight-backed chairs. The atmosphere is dead right – stylish but informal, neighbourhood but sharp. The food is a complete surprise. It's terrific.

> **£8 to £40**
>
> **Address** Building C, The Chocolate Factory, Clarendon Rd, off Coburg Rd, N22
> ☎ 020 8889 2400
> **Station** BR Wood Green /Alexandra Palace
> **Open** Tues–Fri noon–2.30pm & 7–10pm, Sat 7–10pm, Sun noon–3pm
> **Accepts** All major credit cards

The two chef-proprietors, John Mountain and David Orlowski, have done time in various West End establishments, but here in N22 they are cooking with real passion. Genuine, unpretentious plating, well-handled fresh ingredients and accurate cooking: this is the kind of stuff that looks simple until you try to do it. The menu at Mosaica is short and changes daily – at lunch the blackboard includes a cheap pasta dish for starving artists. In the evening, starters range from a well-made creamed mushroom and truffle soup (£5.95), to foie gras with toast and pickles (£8.75). Mains range from salmon fillet with purple broccoli and charlottes (£13.95), to rare rib-eye steak with garlic mash and fine beans (£14.95) – the rib-eye sliced and meltingly tender, the mash rich and not over-gluey. Then there may be an epic dish like veal T-bone with braised fennel, olives and tomato (£15.25). The wine list is short and the service more enthusiastic than polished. But the food is great and the prices forgiving.

Puds are notable. How about a perfect chocolate and amaretti biscuit mousse (£5.50); tiramisù (£6); or the enigmatically described "maybe, just maybe crème brûlée" (£6)?

Ram's

£6 to £18

Address 203 Kenton Rd, Harrow, Middlesex
℡ 020 8907 2022
Station Kenton
Open Tues–Sun noon–3pm & 6–10pm
Accepts Mastercard and Visa

INDIAN/VEGETARIAN

Anyone in downtown Mumbai will tell you that India's best vegetarian food comes from the state of Gujarat. And one of the leading contenders for the best of Gujarati food is the city of Surat. Much as European gourmets rate Castelnaudry for cassoulet, in India people go to Surat for the undhiu! Since the end of 2001, Londoners have had their very own Surti restaurant – Ram's. The staff rush around, eager and friendly; their pride in both the menu and their home town of Surat is obvious and endearing. The menu is a long one with plenty of Surti specials, and the food is very good.

Gujarati snacks make great starters. Petis (£2.60) are small balls of peas and onions coated in potato and deep-fried. Kachori (£2.60) are the same kind of thing but with mung daal inside a pastry coat. Patras (£2.60) are made by rolling vegetable leaves with a "glue" of chickpea flour batter; then the roll is sliced across, and each slice becomes a delicate and savoury pinwheel. Stuffed banana bhaji (£2.60) is a sweet and savoury combo. The rata ni puri (£3.50) is a Surti special – slices of purple potato in a savoury batter. Sev khamni (£3.50) is a sludge of well-spiced chickpeas with coconut, served topped with a layer of crisp sev. Flavours are clear and distinct, and some dishes have a welcome chilli heat. Mains do not disappoint. The famous undhiu (£5) (which is billed as a weekend special) is a complex dish of vegetables "stuffed" with a Surti spice paste. It combines aubergines with three kinds of potatoes (purple, sweet and white), as well as bananas and peas. The peas pilau (£1.95) is simple and good. The methi parathas (two for £1.50) are dry and tasty. The puris (£1.20) are fresh, hot and as self-indulgent as only fried bread can be. Drink the Surti lemon soda (£1.50) or the good salt lassi (£1.25), which has a lurking chilli sting.

When the elegantly rolled paan arrives alongside your bill, simply remove the clove holding the leaf shut, pop the whole thing into your mouth, and chew slowly.

Shish

🍴 Shish is pretty slick. A large, curved-glass pavement frontage displays a sinuous bar counter that snakes around the dining room, leaving grills, fridges and chefs' stations in the centre. Diners simply take a stool at the counter, for all the world like being at a modernist sushi bar. All is modern, just as current resto-design fashion dictates, with rough concrete here, polished concrete there, stainless steel everywhere ... Towards the rear are a couple of further kitchens: one primarily for baking fresh flatbreads, and the other for frying, preparation and so forth. This place owes a debt to Israeli roadside eateries, with its falafel and shish kebabs, but the "concept" (all fast-food missions have to have a suitable "concept") is much more inclusive. As proclaimed at the top of the menu, the inspiration for Shish is the food of the Silk Road.

Starters are divided into lots of cold mezze and a shorter list of hot mezze. The tabbouleh (£1.95) needs a bit more coriander and parsley. The cucumber wasabi (£1.95) is pleasant pickled cucumber. The red and green falafel (£2.25) are well made – the red variety is engagingly spicy. The hot bread is as delicious as only good hot bread can be. Kebabs are served in two different ways: either plated with rice, couscous or French fries; or in a wrap. The shish kebabs are really rather good. Mediterranean lamb (£6.95) comes up very tender; apricot and ginger (£5.75) teams chicken with good tangy apricot flavour; the chicken kofta (£4.95) is flavoured with onions, garlic and cumin. The portions all seem decent-sized and there are fish and vegetarian options. Die-hard kebabbers can even insist on a satisfactorily fierce squelch of chilli sauce. This food benefits from being freshly cooked and eaten hot from the grill. It's relatively cheap, too. What's more, Shish is licensed, so there's a cold beer (£1.50) or a glass of wine (£2.50) to turn a quick feed into an enjoyable meal.

In 2002 the private room upstairs was transformed into Shish Above: slightly smarter and pricier menu, slightly more upscale dishes.

£10 to £25

Address 2–6 Station Parade, NW2
☎ 020 8208 9290
Station Willesden Green
Open Mon–Fri 11.30am–midnight, Sat 10am–midnight, Sun 10am–11pm
Accepts All major credit cards except Diners, no cheques

Sushi-Say

Yuko Shimizu and her husband Katsuharu run this small but excellent Japanese restaurant and sushi bar. It has a very personal feel, with just ten seats at the bar and twenty in the restaurant, plus a private booth for five or six. *Shimizu* means pure water, and the cooking is pure delight. It's a tribute to how sophisticated Londoners' palates have become that a restaurant like this

£15 to £40
Address 33b Walm Lane, NW2
☏ 020 8459 2971
Station Willesden Green
Open Tues–Fri 6.30–10.30pm, Sat 1–3.30pm & 6–11pm, Sun 1–3.30pm & 6-10pm
Accepts All major credit cards except Diners

can do well so far out of town. The menu offers a full classical Japanese selection, making it a difficult choice between limiting yourself to sushi or going for the cooked dishes. Perhaps adapting the European style, and having sushi or sashimi as a starter and then main courses with rice, brings you the best of both worlds, and will give you scope to enjoy this small establishment.

Sitting at the sushi bar allows you to watch Katsuharu at work. With a sumo-like stature and the widest grin this side of Cheshire, his fingers magic nigiri sushi of exquisite proportions onto your plate. In the lower price brackets you'll find omelette, mackerel, squid and octopus (£2.40). At the top end there's sea urchin, fatty tuna and yellowtail (£3.40). In between there is a wide enough range to delight even the experts. Nigiri toku (£15.90) brings you eleven pieces of nigiri and seaweed-rolled sushi, and it's a bargain: heavy on the fish and light on the rice. Cooked dishes do not disappoint. Ebi tempura (£10.60) brings you crispy battered king prawns, the batter so light it's almost effervescent, and menchi katsu (£6.50) delivers a deep-fried oval shaped from minced beef and salad. There are set dinners for all tastes, priced from £18.50 to £28.50, and mixed sashimi for £16.50. It's worth trying the home-made puddings, such as goma (sesame) ice cream (£1.90 a scoop). There's also a selection of special sakes, which are served chilled, and even a half-frozen sake (Akita Onigoroshi) at £6. Less a slush puppy than a slush mastiff.

The menu is in English and everyone is very helpful, so dining at Sushi-Say gives you a good chance to develop your knowledge of Japanese food by trying something new.

Tong Ka Nom Thai

At its best, Thai cuisine means intense and distinct flavours – a concept which nearly all of the hundreds of pubs selling Thai grub seem to have mislaid. However the good news is that fresh, cheap and authentic Thai food is alive and well and living on the Harlesden end of the Harrow Road. Tong Ka Nom Thai is a small and garish Thai restaurant

£8 to £15

Address 833 Harrow Rd, NW10
℡ 020 8964 5373
Station Kensal Green
Open Mon–Fri noon–3pm &
6–10pm, Sat 6–10pm
Accepts Cash or cheque only

with a wonderful view of the railway tracks. It is implausibly cheap. The food is very good, the service friendly, and this is a "Bring Your Own" place (although there is a wholly reasonable request on the menu that you buy any soft drinks on the premises).

All the starters are priced at £4. For that, you get six well-spiced tod mun – delightfully chewy Thai fishcakes; or eight popia tod – well-made mini vegetarian spring rolls with a dark, mushroomy filling; or six goong hompha, which are prawns in filo – very nice but not as exciting as the other starters. But the star turn is gai bai toey – six morsels of chicken that are marinated, wrapped in pandan leaf and then fried; they are seriously delicious. The curries, all at £4, are splendid. Gaeng kheaw wan is a well-made green curry which comes with a choice of main ingredients. Other options are a red curry, a yellow curry and a "jungle curry". The house speciality is called "boneless fish fillet" (£4.50), and you would be wise to order it. It's a large hunk of tilapia, and comes in a mesmerizing, light, elegant sauce with plenty of holy basil. The sauces here are good – not thickened to a sludge with cornflour, but rich on their own account. You'll need some rice (£1.20) and you should have a noodle dish – perhaps the pad phrik (£4), which is well balanced. The kitchens here are cramped, with room for only a couple of chefs, as you can see for yourself as you walk past the stoves to the toilet.

At Tong Ka Nom Thai they serve delicious and authentic Thai food. It is truly remarkable that they can do so at what are almost Thai prices.

South

Battersea

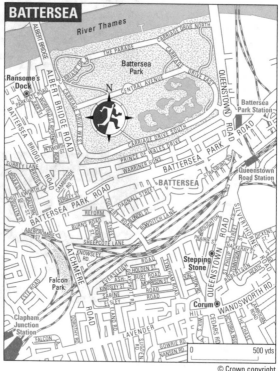
© Crown copyright

Corum

Corum is a perfect example of a gastrobar. The bar part is a runaway success – locals have been known to "book" a particular sofa ahead of time, it can become so crowded. Towards the rear the bar opens out into quite a large restaurant which looks as if it is a page torn from the design manual of modern London restaurants. Blond wood floor, tick. Plain walls with modern art, tick. Subtle lighting, tick. Honey-coloured leather chairs, chocolate leather banquettes, tick. It looks great. Like a thousand other places, but great.

£15 to £30

Address 30–32 Queenstown Rd, SW8
℡ 020 7720 5445
Station Clapham Common/BR Queenstown Road
Open Mon–Fri noon–3pm & 5pm–1am, Sat & Sun noon–1am
Accepts All major credit cards except Diners
ⓦ www.corumrestaurants.com

The menu at Corum is an essay in gastrobar philosophy, and has learned the lesson of old-style brasserie menus – soups, salads, eggs and pasta, seafood, roasts and grills, sides. So you may find a crab risotto with roasted peppers (£6.50/9.75), a Caesar salad (£4.95), eggs Benedict with hash browns (£5/10), Mexican chicken salad (£6.95/11.50), and pan-fried scallops (£7.45/13.95). Nothing alarming there. The surprise is in the very high standard of cooking. The scallops are perfectly cooked and markedly fresh, and they come in a decent portion with an avocado pancetta and spinach salad. This dish works very well. The Caesar salad is very good, classical even to the point of omitting the anchovies now in vogue, with a great lemony dressing. The eggs Benedict is comforting and made with kassler, or smoked pork loin. Other dishes tread the line between classic and over-familiar: there are pork and leek sausages (£12.95), marinated lamb rump with rainbow chard and baby carrots (£13.90), fillet steak (£16.95), veal "Milanese" with Savoy cabbage (£13.50) roast cod (£13.95), salmon fishcake (£11.50), and the Corum burger (£9). These dishes are grand when well made, and at Corum the chef knows his job. The fishcake is large, light and almost fluffy, and it seems hard to criticize a lack of ambition when it is patently obvious that these dishes are very popular indeed.

Puds (all £5.50) are somewhat predictable, with enough sticky toffee, chocolate and the like for the sweetest of teeth.

Ransome's Dock

Ransome's Dock is the kind of restaurant you would like to have at the bottom of your street. It is formal enough for those little celebrations or occasions with friends, and informal enough to pop into for a single dish at the bar. The food is good, seasonal and made with carefully sourced ingredients. Dishes are well cooked, satisfying and

£22 to £65

Address 35–37 Parkgate Rd, SW11
℡ 020 7223 1611
Station BR Battersea Park
Open Mon–Fri noon–11pm, Sat noon–midnight, Sun noon–3.30pm
Accepts All major credit cards
ⓦ www.ransomesdock.co.uk

unfussy, the wine list is encyclopedic, and service is friendly and efficient. All in all, Martin Lam and his team have got it just right. Everything stems from the raw ingredients: the bread may be from Poilâne; the potted shrimps from Morecambe Bay; they dicker with the Montgomerys over prime Cheddar cheeses. The menu changes monthly, but the philosophy behind it does not. There's an extensive brunch menu at the weekend.

Before rampaging off through the main menu, make a pit stop at the daily specials; if nothing tempts you, turn to the seven or eight starters. If it's on, make a beeline for the grilled Norfolk smoked eel, trevisse and ratte potatoes with horseradish sauce (£8.75). It's very rich, very good and very large. Or there may be Perroche goat's cheese crostini with grilled pears and winter leaves (£6.50). Or Morecambe Bay potted shrimps with wholemeal toast (£7.50). Main courses are well balanced – Dutch calf's liver (£15.50) may come with bubble and squeak, braised shallots and pancetta red wine sauce. Or perhaps Trelough duck breast with a pardina lentil and vegetable stew (£17.50) tempts? Or boiled ham hock with steamed leek suet pudding (£11)? Or there may be a "shorthorn" sirloin steak (£22) with foie gras butter and big chips – not just any old steak, but one from a well-hung, Shorthorn steer. Puddings run from the complicated – a hot prune and Armagnac soufflé with Armagnac custard (£7) – to the simple – Greek yoghurt with honey and toasted pistachio nuts (£5).

The wine list makes awesome reading. Long, complex, arcane – full of producers and regions you have never heard of – with fair prices. Advice is both freely available and helpful.

Stepping Stone

(icon) Although outwardly insignificant among the trendy shops in this recently fashionable part of Battersea, Stepping Stone has engendered a fierce loyalty in its clientele. As you enter, there's little to distract the eye. The restaurant is refreshingly unadorned, so there's no question – you're here to eat. Thankfully, the chef likes food and knows how to cook, and the host wants his guests to enjoy themselves. A better for-

£22 to £50

Address 123 Queenstown Rd, SW8
☎ 020 7622 0555
Station Clapham Common/
BR Queenstown Road
Open Mon noon–2.30pm &
7–10.30pm, Tues–Fri noon–
2.30pm & 7–11pm, Sat 7–11pm
Accepts All major credit cards
⊕ www.thesteppingstone.co.uk

mula for running a successful and ultimately satisfying restaurant has yet to be devised. Stepping Stone has taken the admirable decision to oppose the two-sittings-per-table-per-night trend, which means it is essential to book, especially at weekends.

The menu changes every service, so the kitchen is truly market-led. Though reasonably fashionable, the cooking stays well within the kitchen's capabilities. There will be a few simple-sounding dishes, such as goat's cheese and red onion tart (£5.50), and white bean and rosemary soup (£4.50) – good examples of their type – but the menu ranges further for the more adventurous. A veal sweetbreads salad comes with artichokes and roast shallots (£5.50); or maybe honey-roast quail, celeriac rémoulade and lentils (£6.50). Then there are some dual-purpose dishes like Serrano ham and black pudding eggs Benedict (£6/9). Main courses may include dependable options such as rib-eye steak (£14.75), jazzed up by the addition of haggis tortellini and spinach; or swordfish, new potatoes and courgettes, smoked paprika dressing (£13.75). You can expect dishes to be generous, cooked with care and served with a friendly smile. Puddings – treacle tart and clotted cream (£5.25), or apple and rosemary tart with apple ice cream (£4.75)) – are hearty rather than works of art. Commendably, most of the well-planned and mainly European wine list lies under the £25 a bottle threshold.

The Stepping Stone menu footnotes are droller than most – "your meal is a Richard, Frank, Magic, Abigail and Michael *joint* production", "vibrating phones are more pleasing for fellow diners" – so should you lend them yours?

Stepping Stone

Brixton and Herne Hill

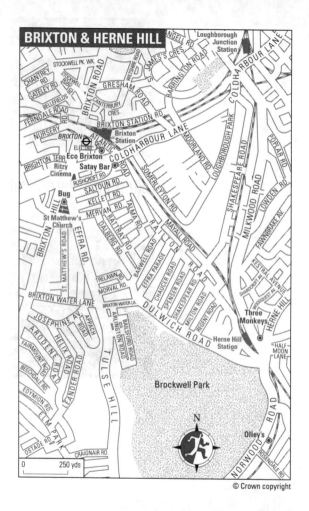

BRIXTON & HERNE HILL

© Crown copyright

0   250 yds

Bug

Bug lurks in the crypt of a converted church. Hardened Presbyterians may feel a little peculiar eating, drinking and making merry in such circumstances, but the less puritanical may even enjoy the thought that it's a short step to the Bug Bar, the trendy club-bar in the neighbouring crypt, and scarcely any further to the nightclub upstairs. The restaurant's subterranean location makes it naturally atmospheric; the large space which is divided into low vaults feels remarkably intimate. The atmosphere in the main area is anything but cryptlike, and the service verges on jolly, plus there's a slick and trendy private dining room called the Cocoon Room.

£15 to £40

Address The Crypt, St Matthews Church, Brixton Hill, SW2
Station Brixton
Open Mon–Thurs 5–11pm, Fri &Sat 5–11.30pm Sun 1–10pm
Accepts MasterCard, Switch, Visa
ⓦ www.bugbrixton.co.uk

Traditionally, the menu has always been mostly vegetarian here, with a fish dish or two to vary the pace, but for a couple of years now a few hesitant meat dishes have been added to the mix. Starters vary from caramelized pear and rocket salad with blue cheese dressing (£3.50); to aubergine masala, onion bhaji, and mint yoghurt dressing (£4.95). There are also a couple of dual-purpose dishes that could be starters or mains – smoked haddock and baby spinach risotto (£4.15/7.50); and seared tuna, guacamole, tomato and cucumber relish (£4.50/8.20). On the main course list, the nut Wellington has survived all the menu revises – nut Wellington en-croûte, braised red cabbage, onion gravy (£7.50); also on offer, pan-fried swordfish steak, sag aloo, red onion and chilli jam (£9.95); free-range chicken breast, pilau rice, satay dressing (£10.50); and spiced lamb meatballs, red pepper mash, mint gravy (£8.50). Puds are simple but good, leading with a warm chocolate tart with orange sorbet (£4.50), and finishing at moody ice creams and sorbets (£2.20/3.60).

The newish, slightly more carnivorous, approach comes into its own at Sunday lunch. Choose from nut roast, organic chicken breast or organic rib-eye steak and enjoy all the trimmings: Yorkshire pud, fondant potato, green beans, rosemary-roasted pumpkin and carrot, and grain mustard onions - £11.95.

Eco Brixton

If you're in Brixton around noon, Eco is a must for your lunch break. Make your way to Brixton Market – London's first market with electric light – and don't be put off by the smell from the fishmonger's shop opposite. Once inside Eco, the whiff soon gives way to more appetizing wafts of cooked cheese and coffee from your neighbour's table. Peruse the menu while you queue among the trailing shoppers – be prepared to share your table – then sit down to one of

PIZZA

£8 to £20

Address 4 Market Row, Brixton Market, Electric Row, SW9
☏ 020 7738 3021
Station Brixton
Open Mon, Tues & Thurs–Sat 8am–5pm
Accepts All major credit cards except AmEx
Branches see p.488
🌐 www.ecorestaurant.com

the best pizzas in South London. Formerly Pizzeria Franco, now Eco Brixton, this place has the same menu as its sister, Eco on Clapham High Street, but the Brixton branch closes at 5pm. It's small and popular, so things can get hectic. Still, the service is friendly, the pizzas crisp and the salads mountainous. Plus there is an identically priced takeaway menu.

All the famous pizzas are here, including a pleasingly pungent Napoletana (£5.90) with the sacred trio of anchovies, olives and capers, and quattro stagioni (£6.90), packed full of goodies. But why not try something less familiar, such as aubergine and sun-dried tomato (£6.50)? Or enjoy la dolce vita (£6.70), where rocket, mushrooms and Dolcelatte all vie for attention? Or even the amore (£6.70), with its French beans, artichoke, pepper and aubergine? Or one of the calzone (£6.90 or £7.20)? It's a difficult choice. For a lighter meal – lighter only because of the absence of carbohydrate – try a salad. Tricolore (£6.20) is made with baby Mozzarella, beef tomato, avocado and olives. Side orders like the melted cheese bread (£3.25) and mushroom bread (£3.75) are highly recommended. For sandwiches, Eco also impresses. Focaccia is stuffed with delights like Parma ham and rocket (£6.25) or Mozzarella and avocado (£5.80).

You could also go for starters, but at lunch they seem a little surplus to requirements. There are eight options, ranging from avocado vinaigrette (£3.90) to Parma ham and rocket salad (£5.25). Puddings are even scarcer – pecan pie (£3.40) or tiramisù (£3.90). Stick with pizza.

Olley's

Olley's is a famous fish and chip shop. It is partly famous because it has won various awards, and partly because of proprietor Harry Niazi's tireless publicity offensive. Olley's takes up two shopfronts just across the road from Brockwell Park: one shop is the take-away and the other is the sit-down restaurant. The restaurant decor revolves around unfinished brickwork and patchy terracotta plaster, reminding you of the Mexican ruin so ably defended by the Magnificent Seven. Even for an eccentric restaurant in SE24, Olley's looks very odd.

£8 to £35

Address 67–69 Norwood Rd, SE24
℡ 020 8671 8259
Station BR Herne Hill
Open Mon & Sun 5–10.30pm,
Tues–Sat noon–10.30pm
Accepts All major credit cards
except Diners
ⓦ www.olleys.info

Start with the avocado with prawn (£3.85) – ripe avo, pink prawns, pinker sauce; or clench your teeth at the kitsch of "Neptune's Punchbowl, a planktonic delight" and try the creamy, home-made fish soup (£3.50), which is surprisingly good – smooth and well seasoned. On to more serious matters: the chips are good here. Niazi believes in pre-blanching, and when done well this technique guarantees chips that are fluffy inside and crisp outside. The mushy peas (£1.50) are commendable and so are the wallies (45p) – which translates as gherkins, for non-Londoners. The fish is a triumph: fresh, white and flaky inside, crisp and golden outside – obviously the fryer knows his craft. Each served with chips, the leader board reads as follows: cod (£8.25); plaice (£8.75); haddock (£8.95); salmon (£9.55); monkfish (£9.95); swordfish (£9.95); halibut (£11.50); and hake (£9.95). Then there is the seafood platter: three prawns, three scampi, three haddies, three plaice goujons, three calamari and chips (£10.75). If you have the temerity to ask for a fish and *large* chips, the plateful that arrives is so large that the staff must be taking the proverbial.

The only puzzle (apart from the Mexican decor and the menu whimsy) is why anyone should come out to a really good fish-and-chip restaurant and choose the "Wild mushrooms in brandy sauce – folded layers of puff pastry filled with fresh mushrooms, courgettes and brown rice, topped with brandy sauce" (£5.90), a dish sadly bereft of either fish or chips.

Satay Bar

The Satay Bar, part of the regeneration of the heart of Brixton, is tucked away behind the Ritzy cinema. First impression of this lively restaurant and bar is one of fun, pure and simple; the term "laid-back" could have been invented for it. The interior is dark and warm, and the nonstop party atmosphere is bolstered by the thumping beat of the background music. If you are old and grizzly it will certainly be too loud for you.

£16 to £32
Address 490 Coldharbour Lane, SW9
☎ 020 7326 5001
Station Brixton
Open Mon–Fri noon–3pm & 6–11.30pm, Sat & Sun noon–midnight.
Accepts All major credit cards
ⓦ www.sataybar.co.uk

If not, settle in, relax and take a look at the art. If you happen to like one of the many paintings adorning the walls, buy it – they are for sale.

Dishes are Indonesian with the chilli factor toned down (for the most part) to accommodate European taste buds. The menu is a testing one – at least when it comes to pronouncing the names of the dishes – but the food is well cooked, service is friendly and efficient, and the prices are reasonable. Your waiter will smile benignly at your attempt to say udang goreng tepung (£6.45) – a starter of lightly battered, deep-fried king prawns served with a sweet chilli sauce. Obvious choices, such as the chicken or prawn satay (£5.95), are rated by some as the best in London. Otherwise try the chicken wings with garlic and green chilli (£5.75) – no less appealing. The hottest dishes are to be found among the curries. The medium kari ikan (£6.95), a red snapper-based, Javanese fish curry, packs a punch even though styled "medium", while the rendang ayam (£5.95), a spicy chicken dish, is only cooled by the addition of a coconut sauce. For something lighter, the mee goreng (£5.25) is a satisfying dish of spicy egg noodles fried with lamb prawns and vegetables; or there's gado-gado (£4.95), a side dish of bean curd and vegetables with spicy peanut sauce, which is almost a meal in itself.

If terminal indecision sets in and you find yourself pinned by the menu like a rabbit in the headlights, try the rijstafel (£13.95 per person, minimum order for two), a combination of six specially selected dishes. This also has a vegetarian option.

Three Monkeys

In the West End and the City, cool restaurateurs are forever buying up old banks, ripping the insides out, slapping on a coat of ultra-chic frosted glass and reopening as the latest thing in slick designer restaurants. It's just a bit of a shock to see such an establishment – complete with a gangplank bridge over the basement bar – in sleepy old Herne Hill. And if that doesn't rock your imagination back on its heels, let's just add that Three Monkeys is an Indian restaurant, albeit an unusual one. The well-written menu steers firmly away from clichéd Indian food.

£25 to £50

Address 136–140 Herne Hill, SE24
℡ 020 7738 5500
Station BR Herne Hill
Open Daily 7–11pm
Accepts All major credit cards
Ⓦ www.3monkeysrestaurant.com

Starters range from shammi kebab (£5.50) – minced lamb rissoles the size and shape of a hockey puck – to something billed as a house special, tandoori aloo joshela (£4.95), which is made from small potatoes marinated in yoghurt and spices before being rolled in melon seeds and cooked in the tandoor. As is the vogue, there is an open kitchen, and the grills and bread are all visibly well made. The main courses run from simple dishes like lamb rogan josh (£9.95) to dishes like chicken tikka makhani (£9.50), which many curryologists assert is the parent of chicken tikka masala. Look out for a range of good fish dishes, and do not be put off by the fact that most of the curries have names unfamiliar to British curry houses; they are authentic, for all that. Try the mean colombo (£10.75), cod that has been given the fiery Chettiyar treatment. Prices are always steepest when you see the words "large" and "prawn". Prawns masala (£12.25) is a laconic title for prawns simmered in a sauce made with vinegar and a spicy Goan masala. Also in the good-but-expensive category is bhindi Jaipuri (£4.95), a dish of okra cut very fine and deep-fried, served with a seasoning of sour dried mango powder.

Three Monkeys flies the flag for culture in Herne Hill. There may be live jazz on Sunday evenings, there are occasional wine-tasting dinners (plus a wine shop), and the restaurant is also pressed into service as an art gallery.

Clapham & Wandsworth

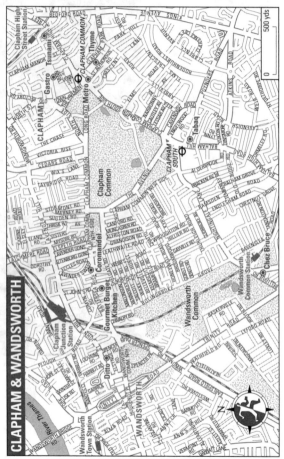

CLAPHAM & WANDSWORTH

Clapham High Street Station

Gastro ● Tsunami

Thyme ● CLAPHAM COMMON

Clapham Common Metro

CLAPHAM MANOR

BEDFORD ROAD

KINGS AVENUE

PARK HILL

THE CHASE

VICTORIA RISE

CEDARS ROAD

WIX'S LANE

LAYBRIDGE ROAD

Clapham Common

CLAPHAM SOUTH

Tabaq

BALHAM HILL

ALDERBROOK

Coromandel

Gourmet Burger Kitchen

Clapham Junction Station

Ditto ●

Wandsworth Town Station

WANDSWORTH RD

River Thames

WANDSWORTH BRIDGE

Wandsworth Common

Wandsworth Common Station

Chez Bruce ●

WANDSWORTH

PLOUGH

500 yds

0

© Crown copyright

Chez Bruce

Bruce Poole's comfortable little restaurant has weathered the storm attendant on gaining a Michelin star with admirable aplomb. All the major pitfalls have been avoided. The regulars may have been nervous, expecting radical change – ameuse whatevers; architecturally tall dishes; prissy service – the downside of star chasing. Good news: Chez Bruce is still delivering honest, unfussy, earthy, richly flavoured food. It is old-fashioned food which avoids the latest gastro-trend and often features the likes of pig's trotters, and rabbit, and mackerel. It is also a real bargain. The star has made one difference, however: the wine list has been extended and refined and is now winning prizes of its own. Prix fixe three-course menus offer lunch for £21.50 (Sun £25), and dinner for £27.50.

£27 to £60

Address 2 Bellevue Rd, SW17
℡ 020 8672 0114
Station BR Wandsworth Common
Open Mon–Thurs noon–2pm &
7–10.30pm, Fri noon–2pm &
6.30–10.30pm, Sat 12.30–2.30pm
& 6.30–10.30pm, Sun noon–3pm &
7–10.30pm
Accepts All major credit cards

FRENCH

The menu changes from season to season and day to day. Generally, the lunch menu is a shortened version of the dinner menu. The kind of starters you can expect are cream of asparagus soup, foie gras and chicken liver parfait with toasted brioche, and terrine of smoked and cured fish with beetroot and horseradish. Or there might be a classic lurking – perhaps vitello tonnato. Main course dishes are deeply satisfying. You could well find rump of lamb with galette Sarladaise, ratatouille and aioli, or roast cod with olive oil mashed potatoes, or roast belly of pork with crackling, lentils, girolles and salsa verde, or roast pigeon with fondant potato, mushroom duxelle and Madeira sauce. This is one of those places where everything on the menu tempts. It's also one of the last strongholds of offal (perhaps the reason why this restaurant is the favourite haunt of so many off-duty chefs?). Look out for sweetbreads, or perhaps calf's liver served with spinach and Ricotta ravioli, sage beurre noisette and Madeira jus.

The sweets here are well-executed classics: proper crème brûlée; clafoutis of plums with clotted cream; tarte Tatin aux poires. No wonder Chez Bruce is booked every evening well in advance. Go for lunch instead – it'll make your day.

Coromandel

INDIAN

The Coromandel Coast (bottom of India, on the right) has lost out in the publicity war with the Malabar Coast (bottom of India, on the left). London has a good many Keralan restaurants (Malabar) and a good many Goan restaurants (Malabar-ish), but Tamil Nadu (Coromandel) isn't so readily front-of-mind.

£17 to £50

Address 2 Battersea Rise, SW11
☎ 020 7738 0038
Station BR Wandsworth Town
Open Daily 11am–3pm & 6.30–11pm
Accepts All major credit cards

This restaurant hedges its bets quite successfully, proclaiming itself "The Southern Indian" restaurant and offering a menu that runs all the way from South Indian vegetarian dishes – dosas and so forth – to Keralan dishes, chilli-rich Chettinad dishes from Tamil Nadu, and Sri Lankan specialities. Spread over two floors, the dining room is brightly painted, modern and busy. Prices are at about the same level as most of the other restaurants hereabouts, which ends up being somewhat higher than you'd expect in a run-of-the-mill curry house. Which is fair enough, as Coromandel is not run-of-the-mill.

On the menu you will find that some of the dishes vary from day to day. There will always be a rasam (£3.45), but some days this will be a spicy lentil concoction; sometimes a pepper soup; and sometimes a tomato rasam. It's one way to keep the kitchen from getting bored. There's also a "surprise" selection of kebabs (£4.95), and Sri Lankan favourites like devilled chicken (£3.95), and mutton rolls (£3.45) – dry curried lamb rolled in bread. Main course stars include a Keralan chicken curry with coconut (£5.95), or there may be a special like Mysore venison (£9.95). From the seafood section try the fish curry (£6.95) or, if available, monkfish Mangalore style (£9.95). The vegetable dishes are good – cadju curry (£6.95) is made with cashews and is rather surprising, if only because the nuts have been cooked until quite soft. Coromandel's breads are also worth investigating, as is their lemon rice (£2.50).

The service is solicitous here, but the staff are clearly concerned lest the food prove too hot for you. So remember to insist that the agreeably fierce South Indian spicing of some dishes is not detuned unless you want it to be.

Ditto

Ditto is split down the middle: half is bar, half is restaurant. You are in Wandsworth, on the borders of Clapham, and this is a neighbourhood restaurant with a local clientele – hold those two images in your mind and you'll have a very clear idea of what this place is like. The bar is busy and loud, the restaurant is busy and loud. Don't even consider popping in at peak time without a booking. Most nights, at just after eight, a trampling herd of affluent nearly forty-somethings leave their au pairs watching over the infants and arrive for nosebag. The service is adroit, the menu is mainly French or Modern British and the food is good but not great. Thankfully the pricing keeps in perfect step with all of the above and delivers pretty good value.

£10 to £40

Address 55–57 East Hill, SW18
☎ 020 8877 0110
Station BR Wandsworth Town
Open Mon– Wed noon–3pm &
7–11pm Thurs & Fri noon–3pm &
7–12.30am, Sat 10.30am–4.30pm
& 7–11.30pm, Sun noon–4pm; bar
food Sun 6–10pm
Accepts All major credit cards
🌐 www.doditto.co.uk

MODERN BRITISH

The menu changes weekly and you can approach it two different ways. There's a set menu offering two courses for £15.50 and three courses for £19.50. There's a choice of three, three and three, and they are not "second-best" dishes. Starters might include a warm game terrine with beetroot vinaigrette, while mains range from duck and cherry sausages to seared fillet of smoked haddock with spring onion brandade. There is also an à la carte. From the starters, a smoked haddock fishcake with capers, tomato dressing (£5.50) is large and spherical; there may be a warm goat's cheese crottin with olives and sun-dried tomatoes (£6.25). Mains range from pan-fried fillet of sea bream, buttered baby gem and sorrel nage (£13.50); to twice-cooked shank of lamb and basil mash (£12.50); pan-fried rib-eye of Scotch beef with wild mushrooms and foie gras butter (£16.50); and lasagne of Swiss chard and asparagus with melted cherry tomatoes (£11.95). Thankfully, the wine list won't make you dive for your wallet – it stretches across continents and from £11.50 to £30 a bottle.

The Sunday menu is an appealing one that starts at eggs Benedict (£4.95) and moves through fishcakes (£5.50) and Cumberland sausage (£7.50) to Sunday roast with vegetables (£9.50). Take the family.

Gastro

Gastro was one of the pathfinders in the steady march to trendiness here in Cla'am, and it has changed accordingly. Where once all was favouritism for regulars, supported by a no-bookings policy, now you may need a reservation to get in. The big table you have to share with other diners is still

£18 to £32

Address 67 Venn St, SW4
℡ 020 7627 0222
Station Clapham Common
Open Daily 8am–midnight
Accepts Cash or cheque only

there and the food is still unabashed about its Frenchness, but there are competing eateries up and down Venn Street, and Gastro is no longer streets ahead.

The staff are French and the menu lists all the Gallic favourites, which tend to be inexpensive and generously portioned. Think yourself back to your last French holiday and enjoy. Under hors d'oeuvres you'll find a pukka soupe de poisson (£4.95) with the classic trimmings. Ordering seafood is straightforward: oysters are sold in sixes (£8.85); mussels arrive à la marinière (£7.40); and crabe mayonnaise (£9.95) is exactly that – a whole crab and mayonnaise. No arguments there! Ordering an assiette Nordique (£7.95) brings a plate of smoked salmon, and smoked monk-fish. The mains will also cosset any Francophile tendencies you may have: daube de chevreuil et sa purée de marrons (£16.50) – venison fillet in red wine sauce; andouillette frites sauce moutarde (£9.40) – that deadly French sausage made from pigs' chitterlings, very much an acquired taste; or an authentically straightforward entrecôte grillé, sauce Béarnaise, frites (£13.50). And there is always boudin noir pommes purées (£10.45) – black pudding, apples and mash – which is as good and as simple as it sounds. Fish dishes are well represented: try bar roti farci au thym et romarin (£14.95). Or half a lobster (£18.95)? For puds think patisserie, and good patisserie at that. House wine is served by the glass, carafe and bottle. The red is better than the white, but not by much. If funds are sufficient, delve further into the short list, or do the sensible thing and order a bottle of top-class French cider (£6.25).

On the menu it stipulates that "at Gastro the chefs will never cook meat more than medium". You have been warned!

Gourmet Burger Kitchen

£14 to £22

Address 44 Northcote Rd, SW11
☎ 020 7228 3309
Station BR Clapham Junction
Open Mon–Fri noon–11pm, Sat
11am–11pm, Sun 11am–10pm
Accepts All major credit cards
except Diners and AmEx
Branches see p.489
⊕ www.gbkinfo.co.uk

BURGERS

On the face of it, the words "gourmet burger kitchen" do not make easy bedfellows. "Gourmet" contradicts "burger", and "kitchen" has an unnervingly homely ring to it. But taken as a whole phrase you can see the intention. "There are burgers here", the proprietors seem to want us to know, "but not those thin, mass-produced ones. Our burgers have flair and originality, but they are not high falutin' burgers; everything is hand-made and good." Anyway, GBK will do for now. The room is cramped and dominated by a large counter behind which there seem to be serried ranks of waitresses and chefs. Everything is pretty casual – you go up to the bar, order and pay, and then your meal is brought to the table.

The menu starts at the "classic – 100 per cent Aberdeen Angus Scotch beef, salad and relish" (£4.95). It also offers the blue cheese burger (£6.60), which adds the tang of Stilton to the main event; the chilli burger (£5.90); the avocado and bacon burger (£6.90); the Jamaican (£6.80) – with mangoes and ginger sauce; the pesterella (£6.90) – with fresh pesto and mozzarella; lamb (£6.90); venison (£6.95); chicken, bacon and avocado (£6.95); or chorizo (£6.95). There is even a "burger" made from Portabella mushroom (£6.30); or the falafel (£5.90), for any bemused vegetarian who strays into this unashamedly carnivorous place. The fries are good and the side salad is excellent, with good fresh leaves and a perky dressing. The Gourmet Burger Kitchen has a good feel to it, and the food is top-quality. Despite the dread word "gourmet", prices are not out of reach.

Consider the Kiwiburger (£6.70). This is made of Aberdeen Angus beef with beetroot, egg, pineapple, cheese, salad and relish. (What, no spatchcocked kiwi? No roundels of kiwi fruit?) This burger is six inches tall, and to take a bite out of it would require the gape of an anaconda. Simply sawing it in half scatters complex garnishes across the plate. But any dish so magnificently eclectic has to be tried. Bizarrely, it tastes pretty good.

Clapham & Wandsworth

Metro

🍴 As you emerge from the southern exit of Clapham Common tube station, Metro is facing you – which is presumably how the place came by its name. Since 2001 when it was taken over by Fran Macmillan (a refugee from the West End where she was front of house in various smart establishments), Metro has settled down to become a steady neighbourhood favourite and some of the

£16 to £40

Address 9 Clapham Common South
Side, SW4
☎ 020 7627 0632
Station Clapham Common
Open Mon & Tues 6–11pm,
Wed–Sun noon–11pm
Accepts All major credit cards
except AmEx and Diners

more extreme and fusiony combination dishes have been tamed. At lunch there are half a dozen dishes on offer with dual pricing so that they may be ordered as starters or mains. In the evening the range is extended and there are some more complex additions.

The food is interesting but mercifully wholehearted. Start with something simple – there is usually a seasonal soup on offer (£4.50); or something modern, such as sesame and pistachio chicken balls (£4.95). Or perhaps crab, Ricotta and spring onion filo parcel with salsa verde (£5). Or – with a nod to the fusion favourites – Cajun crusted salmon fingers on mixed leaf with lime mayonnaise (£5.25). Or medallion of lamb with peanut butter sauce and deep-fried spring onion (£4.95). There are still enough brave combinations of taste and texture for the adventurous diner, but mains are a tad more reined-in: traditional steak and kidney pudding with oysters (£12); baked cod fillet with spinach and Parmesan dumplings and lemon oil (£11.95); goose breast stuffed with foie gras served on sweet potatoes (£13). Puds are sound, if predictable: chocolate and stem ginger pudding with ice cream (£4.25); passion fruit crème brûlée (£4.25); lemon tart with raspberry coulis (£4.25). The service is slick and friendly.

Metro has a very pretty secret garden with a profusion of candles, small terracotta braziers for chilly moments and the reviving green of plants. This is the perfect formula for relaxed dining and is heavily booked by those in the know. And it is uncommonly thoughtful for any establishment to provide blankets for the dogs of Sunday brunchers lingering over the newspapers.

Tabaq

The owners of Tabaq used to drive up from the suburbs to work in a smart West End restaurant, and on the way they would travel along Balham Hill and past Clapham Common. They had set their sights on having a restaurant of their own, smarter than the usual curry house, somewhere they would serve traditional Pakistani specialities. So when

£14 to £25

Address 47 Balham Hill, SW12
℡ 020 8673 7820
Station Clapham South
Open Mon–Sat noon–2.45pm &
6pm–midnight
Accepts All major credit cards
🌐 www.tabaq.co.uk

signs went up outside 47 Balham Hill they took the plunge. They named their restaurant after the tabaq – a large serving dish – and set about dishing up authentic Lahori fare. Over a decade later they have a shelf full of awards and a restaurant full of loyal customers to show for it.

The menu comes with a multitude of sections: starters, grills, seafood, chicken curries, specialities, rice, breads and natural vegetables. To start, go straight for the tandoor and grill section, which features some of the best dishes on the menu, and most commendably carries the boast "we do not add colour to our food". Seekh kabab Lahori (£6.25) is made from well-seasoned minced lamb, and shish kabab lamb (£6.25) is delicious. Or try the masala machli Lahori (£6.25) – fish in a light and spicy batter. As an accompaniment, order raita (£1.95) – yoghurt with cucumber, herbs and spices, and maybe a naan-e-Punjabi (£2.50) of heavy, butter-rich bread from the tandoor, with kachomer (£1.95), a kind of coarse-cut Asian salsa. At this stage of your meal you may well be tempted to choose simply from the salan, or chicken curries. There's murgh taway ka makhani (£8.50) – this sauce is thought to be a buttery ancestor of chicken tikka masala – or murgh palak (£7.25), chicken and spinach. Maybe you'd like to try one of the dishes that won the Tabaq chef one of his many awards? Zaikadaar haandi gosht (£8.50) is a rich dish of lamb marinated in yoghurt and cooked in a traditional haandi, or cooking pot. And there are good biryanis, too.

Desserts include one item you do not immediately associate with Pakistani cuisine – baked Alaska (£12), which serves two and must be ordered in advance.

Clapham & Wandsworth

Thyme

(🍴) When Thyme opened towards the end of 2001, no one really guessed how very good it was going to be, but by 2003 it had even picked up an award or two, and was clearly somewhere to watch. In its new incarnation the restaurant is a good deal more user-friendly than before, chairs are more comfortable

£25 to £80

Address 14 Clapham Park Rd, SW4
☎ 020 7627 2468
Station Clapham Common
Open Tues–Sat 6.30–10.30pm,
Accepts All major credit cards
except Diners

and the decor less challenging. The food is ambitious and good, the prices are fair, the service is friendly ... This is an engaging little restaurant where the kitchen tries hard and succeeds more often than it fails.

The idea is that you approach dinner as a multi-course affair. The menu is written to support this strategy, with three dishes at £6, then three at £7, three at £8, three at £9 and three at £10 – you get the idea. There are also two dishes for sharing by two people at £25 and £30. Portions are good, and some of the dishes masquerading as starters are easily large enough to be sold as mains. Velouté of butternut squash with tortellini of salt cod (£6); pressed terrine of foie gras and confit cod, reduction of Banyuls (£7); and crisp fillet of brill, braised beef and carrots, buttered greens (£9) makes an economical and interesting three-course dinner at £22. Dishes are innovative and the standard of cooking is accomplished. warm salad of quail, tarte fine of wild mushrooms, parfait of foie gras (£8); mousseline of oysters, seared scallop, vinaigrette of cockles, smoked bacon (£8); roast pigeon from Bresse, pithivier of Savoy cabbage, sauté of foie gras (£10). The dishes for sharing are magnificent – pot-roast rump of lamb, celeriac Dauphinoise, roast vegetables (£25 for two) or perhaps etuvée of turbot, braised baby leeks, soft herb emulsion (£30)? Puds (all £5) include a white chocolate and yoghurt soup, and chestnut "Tiramisù" pears with clementine ice. Cheeses come from La Fromagerie and add a £5 supplement.

The wine list is unaggressively priced, and there are two epic tasting menus available every day – four courses with four glasses of wine £50, and five with five for £70.

Tsunami

Tsunami opened towards the latter part of 2001, and within weeks the proprietors could have filled a scrapbook with glowing reviews. The good news is that, while the restaurant is now bedded down successfully, standards seem to be holding up well. The dining room is surprisingly large, and elegant in a minimalist, Japanesey sort of way. All the staff are outstandingly helpful and friendly, and the kitchen bustles away in full view through a long serving hatch. The restaurant is at the end of Clapham High Street that is nearest to Brixton, and it is very much an area in transition. Scruffy shops have given way to trendy bars and these are just starting to be supplanted by ambitious restaurants, of which Tsunami is the perfect example.

> **£14 to £40**
>
> **Address** Unit 3, 1–7 Voltaire Rd,
> SW4
> ☎ 020 7978 1610
> **Station** Clapham North
> **Open** Mon–Fri 6–11pm, Sat
> 6–11.30pm
> **Accepts** All major credit cards
> except AmEx and Diners

The food is very good, the presentation on the plate is quite outstanding, and the bill is not over-the-top. For once all those pretty-as-a-picture arrangements seem to stem from a genuine love of the beautiful. Order a few starters to share. The butternut ebi with creamy spicy sauce (£4.95) is very good – plump prawns in crispy overcoats. Or there's sunkiss sashimi – seared with hot olive oil and dressed with ponzu: salmon (£5.50), scallop (£5.95). Or the kawari age (£4.95) which is tempura made with black cod. Best of all is the tuna tataki (£6.95), which is a sashimi made with seared tuna and dressed with a sharp ponzu dressing. Each slice is raw in the middle and firm around the edge – very delicious indeed. The sushi here look good. The tempura is light and there are lots of interesting vegetable tempura (two pieces £1 to £2.80). From the main dishes, an old favourite, hira unagi - grilled marinated eel (£9.95) – comes with rice and miso soup, and "prime Scottish fillet beef" (£11.95) comes with balsamic teriyaki soy. Or perhaps a innovative dish like pan-fried foie gras in den-miso (£14) appeals?

If you do feel adventurous, look under "oysters" and you'll find the oyster shooter (£5.50) – sake, oyster, ponzu, momji daikon, quail egg yolk and spring onion – Japanese Clapham's answer to the prairie oyster.

Greenwich & Blackheath

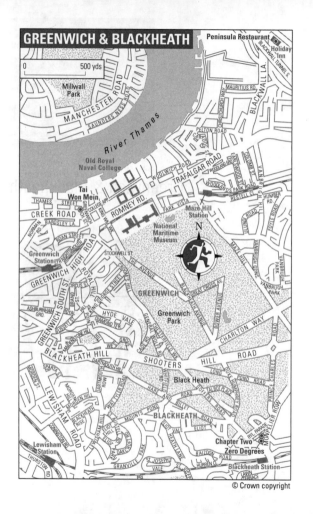

GREENWICH & BLACKHEATH

Peninsula Restaurant

Holiday Inn

0 — 500 yds

Millwall Park

MANCHESTER ROAD

SAUNDERS NESS ROAD

River Thames

MAURITIUS RD.

BLACKWALL

BLACKWALL TUNNELS

PELTON ROAD

Old Royal Naval College

WOOLWICH ROAD

TRAFALGAR ROAD

Tai Won Mein

THAMES STREET

CREEK ROAD

ROMNEY RD.

PARK VISTA

Maze Hill Station

N

Greenwich Station

STOCKWELL ST

National Maritime Museum

THE AVENUE

GREENWICH HIGH ROAD

GREENWICH SOUTH STREET

ROYAL HILL

HYDE VALE

GREENWICH

GREAT CROSS AV

Greenwich Park

BOWER AVENUE

CHARLTON WAY

BLACKHEATH HILL

DARTMOUTH HILL

SHOOTERS HILL ROAD

LEWISHAM ROAD

Black Heath

BLACKHEATH

Lewisham Station

THURSTON RD.

GRANVILLE

ST. JOSEPH'S VALE

Chapter Two
Zero Degrees

Blackheath Station

© Crown copyright

Chapter Two

(🍴) Occupying a bright, sunny position (weather permitting) in a small smart parade of shops just off the heath, Chapter Two seems to promise good things from the outside. Its clean, half-clear, half-frosted glass frontage allows you to glimpse the well-dressed diners enjoying themselves within. And when you enter you'll find yourself in a sleek, modern space, with light wood and metal complemented by richly coloured walls, all coming together to set off crisp linen and sparkling glassware. The whole place has a professionally run air, exuding comfort and confidence.

£16 to £45

Address 43–45 Montpelier Vale, Blackheath, SE3
☎ 020 8333 2666
Station BR Blackheath
Open Mon–Thurs noon–2.30pm & 6–10.30pm, Fri & Sat noon–2.30pm & 6–11pm, Sun noon–3.30pm & 7–9.30pm
Accepts All major credit cards
🌐 www.chaptersrestaurant.co.uk

FRENCH

This feeling of competence also embraces the menu. Dinner is a set price affair: £16.50 for two courses; £19.50 for three, from Sunday to Thursday, going up to £22.50 on Friday and Saturday evenings. There's nothing particularly unusual or showy on offer, but there's plenty of choice among the reasonably classic, well-thought-out dishes, and they use decent ingredients to good advantage. Among the first courses you may find caramelized parsnip velouté with parsnip crisp and truffle oil; or a wild mushroom and Parmesan risotto; or pan-fried scallops, mild curry and Sauternes cream with an orange salad (which attracts a £3.50 supplement). Main courses range from the likes of roast cod with spinach and shellfish chowder; or assiette of Cambridge pork, apple Tatin and sage jus. Portions are generous and presentation is top-class. The puds are mainly tried-and-tested favourites: warm chocolate fondant; warm blueberry madeleine with strawberry ripple ice cream and a florentine biscuit; baked almond cheesecake; home-made ice cream.

Chapter Two is a decent local restaurant, special enough for annual occasions but not so expensive as to prohibit more regular visits. Service is professional rather than pally, and someone has given the wine list some thought – there's a wide range of wines from around the world, available at ungreedy prices, including a fair choice by the glass. If you've a nose for a bargain, visit for lunch, when the menu is much the same as the evening but prices fall to £14.50 for two courses and £16.50 for three (Sunday lunch, £13/16).

Peninsula

(icon) The Peninsula restaurant is in a strange location. Sited on a promontory (defined by trunk roads on two sides and with a major roundabout at its peak), you'll find the Peninsula occupying the ground floor of the Holiday Inn Express hard by the Millennium Dome. The dining room is large and functional, with space for a couple of hundred diners and even on a weekday the dim sum

£8 to £35
Address The Holiday Inn, Bugsby's Way SE10
☏ 020 8858 2028
Station North Greenwich
Open Mon-Fri noon–11.30pm, Sat 11am–11.30pm, Sun 11am–11pm (dim sum daily until 5pm)
Accepts All major credit cards

trade is brisk. There are large family tables complete with highchairs and thoughtful Chinese tots chewing chunks of squid. You can buy a Chinese newspaper or drink a Chinese beer, there's an imposing bar with the obligatory vase filled with an oversize display of bright tropical flowers. The main menu features all the usual favourite dishes, but it is the dim sum that makes this place stand out.

There are two dim sum menus: a small book-like one on the table, and a list of specials on posters around the rooms – treasure egg puff pastry; or deep-fried yam sandwiched with prawns (both £2.80). From the main menu the cheung fun are sound (even if the flobby white casing is a little robust): you can choose from pork, vegetarian, beef (£2.60) and king prawn (£3.20). Other good choices are the mini spring rolls (£1.90); the paper-wrapped prawns (£2.60); the char sui buns (£1.90); the glutinous rice in lotus leaf (£3.20) comes as one large parcel but is suitably rich, sticky and self-indulgent; the chives dumplings (£1.90) – thin enough to see the green shards through the pastry. The cooking is very sound here, and the prices represent very good value indeed, something you would guess at as soon as you see how exceedingly busy this restaurant is. But the real wonder of the Peninsula is more where it is than what it is. An unexpected find.

Towards the end of the dim sum menu there is a special selection – sliced cuttlefish in ginger sauce (£4.50) is a terrific dish. Duck tongue in garlic sauce (£4.50) is interesting; it is just a pity that the tongue is not the tastiest or the largest part of the duck.

CHINESE/NOODLES

Tai Won Mein

(🍴) And it's a welcome back to this guide for unpretentious noodle house Tai Won Mein, an establishment sorely tried by the Dome shenanigans when it was shut down for over a year to facilitate pavement widening! Tai Won Mein's simple signs urge you to "eat fast food" – and the stark interior with its long, low benches reinforces the message. But, while quality is often sacrificed for speed of service, that is certainly not the case here. Good-quality food, together with extraordinarily reasonable prices, mean that this place is always busy. At the weekend, when the nearby markets are in full swing, you must expect to wait for a seat. This will give you a chance to get to know your prospective table-neighbour while you queue.

£5 to £12

Address 39 Greenwich Church St, SE10
☎ 020 8858 1668
Station BR Cutty Sark Gardens
Open Daily 11.30am–11.30pm
Accepts Cash only

Table decoration is sparse and your placemat doubles as the menu. Starters include spring rolls (£3.10) and fried spare ribs (£3.10). Make sure you ask for the chilli sauce. Main courses are divided into rice, noodles and ho fun (which are a kind of ribbon-like noodle, flatter and softer than the usual); the noodle section is then subdivided into fried noodles and soup noodles. The house special soup noodle (£3.80) is served in an enormous bowl, a steaming vat of egg, prawn, beef, squid, crab meat, mussels, fresh greens and, finally, noodles. Less colourful, but certainly no less satisfying, is pork with noodles in soup (£3.20). The fried noodle dishes are equally imposing – huge plates piled high with such delights as mixed seafood (£3.80). Then there's ho fun with king prawn in soup with vegetables (£3.80), and fried ho fun with roast pork and duck (£3.80). Rice dishes – chicken with curry sauce (£3.20) or ribs with black bean sauce (£3.20) – are equally popular. Sadly, Tai Won Mein is a pudding-free zone.

You can wash down the main courses with Sapporo (£2.90), a crisp Japanese beer. For the health-conscious, how about the mixed fruit juice (£1.60) – a blend of apple, orange and carrot? Sounds odd, tastes great. In the two-year forced absence from this guide Tai Won Mein's prices have only risen by 15p! Hurrah.

ITALIAN/PIZZA

Zerodegrees

0° – as the logotype, napkins, menus and so forth would have it – is a lively fun factory in the heart of sedate and respectable Blackheath. The proprietors have taken the idea of the microbrewery, a formula that has been honed to perfection in the West End, and put together a lively venue. It's a grand-looking space, all aluminium cladding and stainless-steel brewing equipment, with a large bar which dominates and a small area for seating and eating by the open kitchen.

£8 to £20

Address 29–31 Montpelier Vale, Blackheath SE3
℡ 020 8852 5619
Station BR Blackheath
Open Daily noon–11.30pm
Accepts All major credit cards except Diners
Ⓦ www.zerodegrees
-microbrewery.co.uk

The menu is an obvious one. Other beer places do wood-fired pizzas – so does Zerodegrees. Other beer places do special sausages – so does Zerodegrees. Other beer places do mussels ... you've guessed it: so does Zerodegrees. It's an engagingly simple idea and, given that this is a loud, happy place full of people keen to get blatted by some pretty decent beers, the food admirably fulfils its role as a solid counterweight. If you want starters, it's best to keep it simple: garlic bread (£2.50); dough balls (£2.20); a trio of crostini (£4.50); marinated artichokes (£4.25). There are a handful of pasta dishes, all at £8.95. Moody sausages come with mash (£6.95), mussels come in a kilo pot with frites and mayo (£10.95) and there are eighteen different pizzas all tasting suitably smoky and ranging from traditional cheese to the most popular choice, which is Peking duck (with roasted duck breast, crispy tortilla chips, spring onions and hoi sin sauce) by way of American hot and all the usual suspects (£5.50 to £7.95).

Five different beers are brewed on the premises: a Pilsner; a good, hoppy-tasting pale ale; a black lager; a wheat ale; and a "special" which changes regularly to stop you getting bored. The pricing is simple: halves (£1.15); pints (£2.30); four-pint jugs (£8.25); and, at happy hour, which is in force from 4pm to 7pm Monday to Friday, all pints are £1.50. Beer and loud music – everything you need to get happy, and then a pepperoni pizza to follow. It may not be original, and it's certainly not for the middle-aged, but it works.

Kennington & Vauxhall

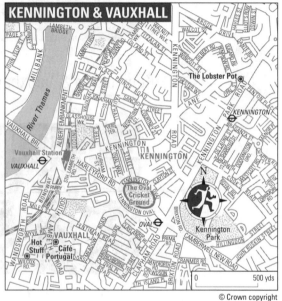

KENNINGTON & VAUXHALL

PAGE ST
MILLBANK
LAMBETH
BRIDGE
JOHN ISLIP ST
WALNUT TREE WLK
FITZALAN'S
WALCOT ST
BROOK
DRIVE
CARDIGAN
GASWELL'S RD
ALBERT RD
KENNINGTON
BLACK PRINCE ROAD
SANCROFT
STREET
The Lobster Pot
KENNINGTON
PARK ROAD
KENNINGTON
River Thames
ALBERT EMBANKMENT
CLASSHOUSE WK
GODING ST
JONATHAN STREET
TYTER TER
KENNINGTON
LANE
KENNINGTON
OVAL WAY
KENNINGTON
ROAD
KENNINGTON
Vauxhall Station
VAUXHALL
STH LAMBETH
HARLEYFORD RD
DURHAM ST
CLAYTON ST
KENNINGTON ROAD
CLAYTON ST
BROAD WAY
PARRY ST
MILES ST
SOUTH
The Oval
Cricket
Ground
KENNINGTON OVAL
OVAL
BRIXTON ROAD
N
Kennington
Park
WANDSWORTH ROAD
WYVIL RD
LANSBY RD
VAUXHALL
FENTIMAN ROAD
CLAYLANDS
CAMBERWELL NEW ROAD
JOHN RUSKIN STREET
HILLINGDON
Hot
Stuff
Café
Portugal
CLAPHAM ROAD
DORSET
MEADOW ROAD
HANDFORTH RD
SWDSON
PRIMA RD
ST ISLAND RD
CRANMER RD
WILCOX RD

0   500 yds

© Crown copyright

Café Portugal

When setting up a bar, café or restaurant, the first item on any proud new Portuguese owner's shopping list must be the telly. All the televisions in South Lambeth Road seem to be turned up loud, and the one in the bar of Café Portugal is no exception (thankfully, the one in the restaurant half of the operation is not always switched on). Portuguese restaurateurs have all mastered the trick of integrating their establishments with the community and Café Portugal is a laid-back, easy-paced kind of eatery with distinctly dodgy mud-orange decor. The food is workmanlike and appears authentically Portuguese, as do some of the television programmes.

£11 to £27

Address Victoria House, South Lambeth Rd, SW8
℡ 020 7587 1962
Station Vauxhall
Open Mon–Sat 8am–11pm, Sun 10am–10.30pm
Accepts All major credit cards except Diners

PORTUGUESE

There is now a rather twee menu which comes complete with a small photo of the dish in question – rather like those models in the windows of Japanese restaurants. To start with you can opt for calamares fritos (£3.70), and sopa do día (£2.20), the soup of the day. Or more interesting dishes like ameijoas a Café Portugal (£3.80), which are clams and must be a step up on that trusty old Portuguese special, avocado with prawns (£3.30). The menu goes on to display a dozen fishy options: lobster, sea bass, Dover sole, three monkfish dishes and three ways with salt cod. Of the latter, the most adventurous sounding, bacalhau à Gomes de Sá (£9), turns out to be a stunning and gloriously simple dish of salt cod cooked in the oven with potatoes, onions and chunks of hard-boiled egg. For the meat-eater there's carne de porco à Alentejana (£9), another all-in-one, home-cooked kind of meal in which small chunks of pork are served with some clams, chorizo and chopped pickled vegetables, then small cubes of crisp-fried potato are scattered over the top. The resulting dish is a grand blend of tastes and textures. At Café Portugal, puddings are largely pastries and you are doomed if you don't like eggy confections.

The wine list here is a Portuguese affair, and reasonably priced, so look out for interesting little numbers from the Dão and the Douro. Café Portugal caters to its knowledgeable, mainly Portuguese, clientele.

Kennington & Vauxhall

Hot Stuff

🍴 This tiny restaurant, run by the Dawood family in south Lambeth, is something of an institution. It has only a few seats and offers simple and startlingly cheap food to an enthusiastic local following. The food is just what you would expect to get at home – assuming you were part of Nairobi's Asian community. Trade is good and has been the catalyst for a refurb – now all is soft blues and orange with an array of different-coloured chairs.

£10 to £20

Address 19 Wilcox Rd, SW8
☏ 020 7720 1480
Station Vauxhall/Stockwell
Open Mon–Fri noon–10pm, Sat 4–10pm
Accepts All major credit cards
🌐 www.eathotstuff.com

The starters are sound rather than glorious, so it's best to dive straight into the curries. There are a dozen chicken curries and a similar number of lamb dishes, all priced at between £3.25 and £5.35. It is hard to find any fault with a curry that costs just £3.25! The most expensive option is in the fish section – king prawn biryani, which costs £7.50; not much more than you would pay for a curried potato in the West End. The portions aren't monster-sized, and the spicing isn't subtle, but the welcome is genuine and the bill is tiny. Arrive before 9.30pm and you can sample the delights of the stuffed paratha (£1.50) – light and crispy with potato in the middle, they taste seriously delicious. Chickpea curry (£2.60), daal soup (£2.50) and mixed vegetable curry (£2.25) all hit the spot with vegetarians. For meat-eaters, the chicken Madras (£3.40) is hot and workmanlike, while the chicken bhuna (£3.50) is rich and very good. However, the jewel in the crown of the Hot Stuff menu is masala fish (£4.25), which is only available from Wednesdays to Saturdays; thick chunks of tilapia are marinated for 24 hours in salt and lemon juice before being cooked in a rich sauce with coriander, cumin and ginger.

Hot Stuff closes prudently before the local pubs turn out, and part of the fun here is to watch latecomers – say, a party of three arriving at 9.50pm and seeking food. Promising to eat very simply and very quickly may do the trick, as this restaurant is driven by the principles of hospitality and puts many more pretentious establishments to shame. Bring your own alcohol, as no corkage is charged.

The Lobster Pot

You have to feel for Nathalie Régent. What must it be like to be married to – and working alongside – a man whose love of the bizarre verges on the obsessional? Britain is famed for breeding dangerously potty chefs, but The Lobster Pot's chef-patron, Hervé Régent, originally from Vannes in Brittany, is well ahead of the field. Walk down Kennington Lane towards the restaurant and it's even money as to whether you are struck first by the life-size painted plywood cutout of Hervé dressed in oilskins, or the speakers relaying a soundtrack of seagulls and melancholy Breton foghorns.

£10 to £35

Address 3 Kennington Lane, SE11
℡ 020 7582 5556
Station Kennington
Open Tues–Sat noon–2.30pm &
7–11pm
Accepts All major credit cards
🖰 www.lobsterpotrestaurant.co.uk

VERY FRENCH/FISH

These clues all point towards fish, and doubtless Hervé will appear to greet you in nautical garb, moustache bristling, and guide you towards his best catches of the day. The fish here is pricey but it is fresh and well chosen. Starters range from well-made, very thick, traditional fish soup (£6.50) to a really proper plateau de fruits de mer (small £11.50, large £22.50). The main course specials sometimes feature strange fish that Hervé has discovered on his early-morning wanderings at Billingsgate. There are good spicy dishes too, such as filet de thon à la Créole (£14.50), which is tuna with a perky tomato sauce, and monkfish with Cajun spices and white butter sauce (£15.50). Simpler, and as good in its way, is la sélection de la mer à l'ail (£14.50), which is a range of fishy bits – some monkfish tail, an oyster, a bit of sole, tiny squid, and so on – all grilled and slathered in garlic butter. The accompanying bread is notable, a soft, doughy pain rustique, and for once le plateau de fromage à la Française (£6) doesn't disappoint.

The Lobster Pot's weekday set lunch (£10 for two courses, £13.50 for three) makes lots of sense. It could get you moules gratinées à l'ail followed by filet de merlan sauce créole and crêpe sauce à la mangue. One of the most popular options in the eight-course Menu Surprise (£39.50 per person) – three fish dishes, then meat and so on – the chef's choice, and wholly dependent on what's good at the market.

Putney

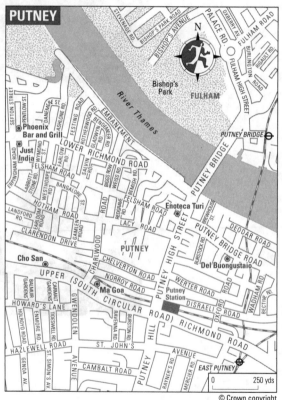

PUTNEY

N

Bishop's
Park

FULHAM

River Thames

PUTNEY BRIDGE

EMBANKMENT

SEFTON STREET

PENTLOW ST

DANEMERE ST

DANEHURST RD

ASHLONE RD

FESTING ROAD

ROTHERWOOD RD

BENDEMEER RD

GLADWYN RD

STEVENAGE RD

BISHOP'S PARK ROAD

BISHOP'S AVENUE

OSBERTON RD

PALACE RD

FULHAM ROAD

BURLINGTON

BIGAULT RD

FULHAM HIGH STREET

Phoenix
Bar and Grill

Just
India

LOWER RICHMOND ROAD

WYMND ST

FELSHAM ROAD

FARLOW ROAD

SALVIN

BIGGS ROW

WEISS RD

BEMISH RD

EFFINGHAM ROAD

ABBOTT'S RD

STONE RD

WESTHORPE RD

BANGALORE ST

FELSHAM ROAD

Enoteca Turi

PUTNEY BRIDGE ROAD

BURSTOCK ST

BREWHOUSE ST

DEODAR ROAD

HOTHAM ROAD

LANDFORD RD

EARLSTHORPE RD

GAMLEN RD

REDGRAVE RD

LACY ROAD

CHARLWOOD

ROAD

CLARENDON DRIVE

PUTNEY

PUTNEY HIGH STREET

Cho San

UPPER (SOUTH

CHELVERTON ROAD

CIRCULAR

NORROY ROAD

Ma Goa

ROAD)

Putney
Station

WERTER ROAD

Del Buongustaio

BALMUIR
GARDENS

CARMALT
GARDENS

GWENDOLEN

BURSTOCK RD

RAVENNA RD

DISRAELI RD

RICHMOND ROAD

OXFORD ROAD

WADHAM RD

RECTIVE RD

HOWARD'S LANE

HOLROYD ROAD

ENMORE RD

TIDESWELL RD

AVENUE

PUTNEY HILL

ST. JOHN'S

AVENUE

RAYNER'S RD

MERCIER RD

EAST PUTNEY

HAZLEWELL ROAD

GENOA AV

ST SIMON'S AV

CAMBALT ROAD

0   250 yds

© Crown copyright

Cho-San

(🍴) Too many Japanese restaurants use extremely high prices and ultra-swish West End premises to keep themselves to themselves. As a European adventurer basking in the impeccably polite and attentive service, it's hard not to feel a little anxious. What should you order? How do you eat it? Will it taste nice? How much does it cost? If you have ever been assailed by

£8 to £35

Address 292 Upper Richmond Rd, SW15
☏ 020 8788 9626
Station BR Putney
Open Tues–Fri 6.30–10.30pm, Sat & Sun noon–2.30pm & 6.30–10.30pm
Accepts All major credit cards

JAPANESE

these worries you should pop along to Cho-San in Putney. This small, unpretentious, family-run restaurant opened in 1998 and has built up a steady trade. As well as a host of knowledgeable Japanese drawn by the good fresh food and sensible prices, there are interested Londoners tucking into sushi with gusto. On one occasion these devotees included a 12-year-old girl, who, judging by her uniform, had dropped in for dinner on the way home from school.

The menu is a book. And one worth reading. This is your chance to try all those dishes you have never had, without wounding your pocket. The sushi is good. The sashimi is good. And a giant boat of assorted sushi and sashimi, with miso soup and dessert, costs £19.90. But why not try some more obscure sushi? The prices of the fancy ones range from £2.50 to £5.90 for two pieces. Or, if you prefer your fish cooked, choose the perfect tempura cuttlefish (£7.90) – a stunning achievement, its batter light enough to levitate. And then there are always the kushiage dishes, where something is put onto a skewer, gets an egg and bread-crumb jacket and is treated to a turn around the deep-fryer. Ordering tori kushiage (£5.60) gets you two skewers, each of which holds two large lumps of chicken and a chunk of sweet onion. Delicious. Or opt for tempura king prawn (£9.90). Then there are the meat dishes, the fish dishes, the rice dishes, the soba noodles, the udon noodles ... and the hot sakes, cold sakes and beers. You could eat your way to a good understanding of Japanese food here. Ask the charming, helpful staff and get stuck in.

Newcomers should take the easy option: a profusion of seven-course set meals costing between £17.90 and £19.90.

Del Buongustaio

🍴 On the first day of each month it's all change at Del Buongustaio as they unleash a new menu on the appreciative residents of Putney. The menu here features well-cooked, authentic food with a sprinkling of less familiar dishes from Cinderella regions like Puglia and Piedmont, as well as some painstakingly researched gems that once graced tables in Renaissance Italy. The dining room is light, airy and pleasantly informal. The

£16 to £45

Address 283 Putney Bridge Rd,
SW15
☎ 020 8780 9361
Station East Putney
Open Mon–Sat noon–3pm &
6.30–11pm, Sun noon–3.30pm
Accepts All major credit cards
except Diners
🌐 www.theitalianrestaurant.net

cooking is good too, with authentic dishes and friendly service. Take time to study the wine list, which is particularly strong on classy bottles from less familiar provinces.

Who knows what the next menu will bring? But you can hazard a guess that there will be interesting pasta dishes, such as a splendid spaghetti aragosta con pomodori fresci (£7.95/12.85) – spaghetti with lobster and fresh tomatoes. Or perhaps tortelli di fagiano con fonduta di Taleggio (£6.30) – pheasant ravioli with a Taleggio cheese fondue: rich or what? The piatto pizzicarello (£7.80), described with disarming modesty as a "plate of savouries", is a regular starter option. And in season there may be the torta rinascimentale di fave, ricotta e prosciutto (£6.50), an amazing multi-layered cake of broad beans, prosciutto, Ricotta and Fontina cheese that comes with a rocket and egg sauce. Main course dishes may include lamb, sea bass, veal, pork, chicken, guinea fowl, cod or perhaps a Swiss chard and Ricotta pudding. Or tonno e verdure con salsa al basilico e limone (£14.50) – grilled tuna with Mediterranean vegetables with basil and lemon. Look out for the rustic dal campo side dishes, particularly verdure al vapore (£2.95), which is mixed seasonal greens. The multi-choice set lunch deal brings three courses for £12.95.

It's worth saving space for a dessert if only for the eight splendid pudding wines, served by the glass, including Vin Santo (£3.80), the befuddlingly alcoholic Aleatico di Puglia (£3.80) and a 1995 Recioto della Valpolicella (£4.50). There is also a huge selection of merciless grappas...

Enoteca Turi

If you like your Italian food a little more adventurous than the usual, then it is worth making the journey to Putney and Giuseppe Turi's pretty little restaurant. Every dish is based on fresh ingredients and, like some other notable venues, Enoteca offers a very genuine and personal version of Italian regional

£15 to £65

Address 28 Putney High St, SW15
☎ 020 8785 4449
Station Putney Bridge
Open Mon–Sat 12.30–2.30pm &
7–11pm
Accepts All major credit cards

ITALIAN

cooking. Turi himself hails from Apulia, and many dishes are based on recipes from this area. Enoteca takes its name from the Italian term for a smart wine shop, so it's hardly surprising that wines are feature prominently in the scheme of things. There's a monumental list of more than 90 specialist Italian wines and a separate by-the-glass menu offering 11 Italian regional wines – an excellent way to educate the palate.

As for the food, at lunch there is a shortened version of the dinner menu and dishes are a couple of pounds cheaper. In the evening you'd do well to start with salad of artichoke, pear, walnuts and Pecorino (£7.50); or perhaps a plate of antipasto pugliese (£7.50) – marinated, grilled vegetables served with a fava puree. Pasta choices may ravioli di castagne e ricotta (£8.50 at lunch, £10.50 at dinner); pappardelle con ragù d'anatra (£8.50 at lunch and £11.50 for dinner). Main courses may include stinco d'agnello con puree di patate e cipolline – lamb shank with spring onion and potato puree (£14.50); or petto d'anatra (£15.50) – duck breast served with lentils and baked fresh Ricotta. There is always a fresh fish of the day and a dish of the day. Desserts will test your mettle – go for the torta di cioccolata con nocciole (£5.50), a blockbusting chocolate and hazelnut cake, or perhaps the particularly good, authentic tiramisù (£5).

Though there are many good restaurants in this area, Enoteca has a loyal following and, except for Monday and Tuesday nights, it is essential to book. If you're more of a wine bluff than a wine buff you'll be grateful for the discreet numbers printed beside each dish on the menu – they represent the recommended wines, all of which are available by the glass.

Just India

Just India is a thoroughly modern Indian restaurant. The decor is modern, the food is modern (and features authentic regional dishes), and brunch is served on Sundays. Both dishes and the prices are more sophisticated than in most high street curry houses as befits the knowledgeable diners of the Lower Richmond Road! The chef has set up

£18 to £40

Address 193 Lower Richmond Rd, SW15
℡ 020 8785 6004
Station BR Putney
Open Tues–Sat 6.30–11pm, Sun noon–2.30pm & 6.30–11pm.
Accepts All major credit cards

here after learning his craft at Veeraswamy (see p.358), one of London's more exalted Indian restaurants. The room is long, comfortable and gives a general impression of calm – something that is carried through to the service.

The menu is an interesting read; it is always a delight to find a few unfamiliar dishes. Starters may include a salad made with lotus leaves and aubergine (£3), a complex creation of rolled lotus leaves bound together with gram flour, steamed, and then fried before being presented on the aubergine. Prawn balchao (£4) teams large prawns with a healthy belt of South Indian spice. Malai murg tikka (£3) is the gentle yoghurty chicken tikka. A methi seekh kebab (£3) is simply presented and strong with fenugreek. Main courses are in a similar original vein. A Karwari fish curry (£8) is a good dish, rich with an unusual spicing of trifala (a west coast touch). Or there's a Keralan chicken curry (£7) – hot, with mustard seeds, red chillies, ginger and curry leaves plus a dash of coconut milk. The lamb rogan josh (£7) is delicious, although the description is a tad over-elaborate "lamb cooked in the traditional 'awad' way with a unique flavour of rogan (tinged flavoured and spiced oil) and josh (strong punch of knuckle juice and marrow)". Side dishes are good, there is a great vegetable dumpling and yoghurt curry called kadi pakora (£3). Also avial (£3) – veg with coconut, yoghurt and mustard seeds – there's a strong South Indian streak here.

Indian restaurants often have trouble filling the tables at lunchtime, so Just India is only open in the evening. The exception being Sunday, when brunch is big – a lazy and gentle Indian brunch running through the afternoon. What a good idea.

Ma Goa

Despite the stylish ochre interior, complete with fans and blond wooden floor, despite the café-style chairs and tables, and the computer system to handle bills and orders, the overwhelming impression you are left with when you visit Ma Goa is of eating in somebody's home. This place is as far as you can possibly get from the chuck-it-in-a-frying-pan-and-heat-it-through school of curry cookery. The food is deceptively simple, slow-cooked and awesomely tasty. And it is authentically Goan into the bargain.

£14 to £30

Address 244 Upper Richmond Rd, SW15
☏ 020 8780 1767
Station BR Putney/East Putney
Open Tues–Sat 6.30–11pm, Sun 12.30–3pm & 6–10pm
Accepts All major credit cards
ⓦ www.magoa.co.uk

The menu is fairly compact: half a dozen starters are followed by a dozen mains, while a blackboard adds a couple of dishes of the day. Shrimp balchao (£4) is a starter made from shrimps cooked in pickling spices and curry leaves. Sorpotel (£4/7) is made from lamb's liver, kidney and pork in a sauce rich with roast spices, lime and coriander. The Ma Goa's sausage (£4) is rich, too, with palm vinegar, cinnamon and green chillies. Main courses are amazing. The spices are properly cooked out by slow cooking, which makes lifting the lids of the heavy clay serving pots a voyage of discovery. Porco vindaloo (£8.65), sharp with palm vinegar, is enriched with lumps of pork complete with rind. Gallina kodi (£7.95) is a gentle guinea fowl curry made with rosewater. Ma's fish caldin (£8.75) is kind of fish stew with large chunks of fish in a coconut-based sauce. Or there's kata masala (£7.65), a chicken dish served on the bone (hooray) and heavy with cinnamon, black pepper, ginger and lime. Vegetarians are equally well served. Bund gobi (£3.50/6.50) is stir-fried, shredded cabbage with carrots, ginger and cumin, while beringella (£3.50/6.50) is an aubergine dish made with pickling spices. The rice here is excellent.

On the specials board you might be lucky enough to find lamb kodi (£8), described as "lamb with cloves, garlic and chilli". On the electronic message winging its way to the kitchen, this is altered to "Bella's lamb" – dishes here really are made from family recipes.

Phoenix Bar and Grill

🍴 This restaurant is a member of London's leading family of neighbourhood restaurants, and is related to Sonny's (see p.398). Anyone fancying their chances in what is a cut-throat marketplace would do well to study these establishments. They are all just trendy enough, the service is just slick enough and the cooking is marginally better than

£16 to £50

Address 162–164 Lower Richmond Rd, SW15
☎ 020 8780 3131
Station BR Putney
Open Mon–Sat 12.30–2.30pm & 7–11pm, Sun 12.30–3pm & 7–10pm
Accepts All major credit cards

you would expect, with competitive pricing. Grub-wise, the Phoenix has a secret weapon: Franco Taruschio (of Walnut Tree fame) didn't much enjoy retirement and he consults at Phoenix to keep himself busy. There's a large, white-painted room inside and a large, white-painted courtyard out front where you can eat alfresco.

Signor Taruschio's ever-changing menus draw on his heritage (the Marche in Italy) and that of his family (Thai influences), and the menu here includes some of the famous dishes that made the Walnut Tree a place of foodie pilgrimage. Chief among them is the epic eighteenth-century truffled lasagne, or vinicsgrassi maceratesi (£14.50). This is ambrosial stuff, and you can also order it as a starter (£8.95). Other starters may include a warm Thai salad of scallops and prawns (£7.50); home-cured bresaola with artichokes, rocket and Parmesan (£6.75); and goujonettes of lemon sole with Thai dipping sauce (£5.50). Mains range from courgette risotto with Pecorino (£10.50); to pan-fried pigeon breast with braised red cabbage, caraway and juniper sauce (£12.50); or mixed grilled fish with grilled Mediterranean vegetables (£15). Puds range from dark chocolate fondant with ginger ice cream (£5.50); to spume Amaretto (£5.95); and apple fritters (£5.25).

The set lunch and "early bird" dinner (order by 7.45pm and go home by 8.45pm) are grand value at £13.50 for two courses and £16.50 for three. Try Jerusalem artichoke soup, then venison sausages with castelluccio lentils, culminating in lemon and lime semi-freddo. This would be good value even without the imprimatur of Franco Taruschio, and it's worthy of the attentions of any early bird.

Tooting

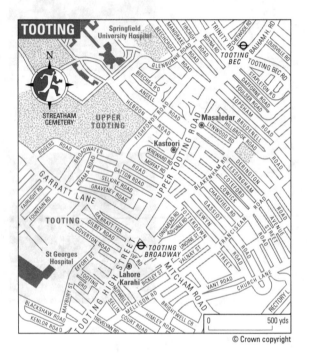

© Crown copyright

Kastoori

(🍴) Anyone who is genuinely puzzled that people can cope on – and indeed enjoy – a diet of vegetables alone should try eating at Kastoori. Located in a rather unpromising-looking bit of town, Kastoori is a Gujarati "Pure Vegetarian Restaurant". The food they serve is leavened with East African influences, and so delicious that you could invite even the most hardened carnivore and be pretty

£12 to £20

Address 188 Upper Tooting Rd, SW17
☎ 020 8767 7027
Station Tooting Broadway
Open Mon & Tues 6–10.30pm,
Wed–Sun 12.30–2.30pm &
6–10.30pm
Accepts Mastercard and Visa

INDIAN/VEGETARIAN

sure that they would be as entranced as everybody else. The large and cavernous restaurant is run by the admirably helpful Thanki family – do be sure to ask their advice, and act on it. Kastoori's most recent face-lift has changed the decor from pink to blue and yellow, but thankfully the quality of the food has stayed the same.

First onto the waiter's pad (and indeed first into the mouth, as they go soggy and collapse if made to wait) must be dahi puri (£3.25) – tiny crispy flying saucers filled with a sweet-and-sour yoghurty sauce, and potatoes, onions, chickpeas and so forth. You pop them in whole; the marriage of taste and texture is a revelation. Samosas (three for £1.95) are excellent, the onion bhajis (five for £2.75) are also a revelation – bite-sized and delicious, a far cry from the ball-of-knitting served in most high-street curry emporia. Then make sure that someone orders the vegetable curry of the day (£4.85), and others the outstanding cauliflower with cream curry (£4.95) and special tomato curry (£4.95) – a hot and spicy classic hailing from Katia Wahd. Leave room for the chilli banana (£5.25), bananas stuffed with mild chillies – an East African recipe – and mop everything up with generous helpings of puris and chapatis (both at £1.40 for two).

The smart move is to ask what's in season, as the menu is littered with oddities that come and go. For example, there's a "beans curry" subtitled "Chef's Choice" (£4.95). Another interesting and esoteric dish is drumstick curry (£5.25). Drumsticks are thin, green Asian vegetables about eighteen inches long and twice as thick as a pencil. You chew the flesh from the stalk. This is a place where it pays to experiment.

Lahore Karahi

£9 to £22

Address 1 Tooting High St, SW17
☏ 020 8767 2477
Station Tooting Broadway
Open Daily noon–midnight
Accepts Cash or cheque only

(¶) Though the bright neon spilling onto the pavement beckons you from Tooting High Street, spiritually speaking, the Lahore Karahi is in the curry gulch of Upper Tooting Road. It's a busy place, and behind a counter equipped with numerous bains-marie stand rows of cooks, distinguishable by their natty Lahore Karahi baseball caps, turning out a daily twelve-hour marathon of dishes. Prices are low, food is chilli-hot and service is speedy. Don't be intimidated: simply seat yourself, don't worry if you have to share a table, and start ordering. Regulars bring their own drinks or stick to the exotic fruit juices – mango, guava or passion – all at just £1.

Unusually for what is, at bottom, an unreconstructed grill house, there is a wide range of vegetarian dishes "prepared under strict precautions". Karahi karela (£2.95) is a curry of bitter gourds; karahi saag paneer (£3.50) teams spinach and cheese; and karahi methi aloo (£2.95) brings potatoes flavoured with fenugreek. Meat-eaters can plunge in joyfully – the chicken tikka (£2.25), seekh kabab (£1.20 for two) and tandoori chicken (£1.75) are all good and all spicy-hot, the only fault being a good deal of artificial red colouring. There are also a dozen chicken curries and a dozen lamb curries (from £4.25 to £4.50), along with a dozen specialities (from £4.25 to £8 for king prawn karahi). Those with a strong constitution can try the dishes of the day, like nihari (£5.50), which is lamb shank on the bone in an incendiary broth, or paya (£4.95), which is sheep's feet cooked until gluey. Breads are good here: try the methi naan (£1.50) or the tandoori roti (60p).

The Lahore Karahi comes into its own as a takeaway, and there's usually a queue at the counter as people collect their considerable banquets – not just chicken tikka in a naan, or portions of curry, but large and elaborate biryanis as well – meat (£3.75), chicken (£3.75), prawn (£5.95) or vegetable (£2.95). For wholesome, fast-ish food, the cooking and the prices here are hard to beat.

Masaledar

What can you say about a place that has two huge standard lamps, each made from an upturned, highly ornate Victorian drainpipe, topped with a large karahi? When it comes to interior design, Masaledar provides plenty of surprises, and a feeling of spaciousness. This establishment is run by East African Asian Muslims, so no alcohol is allowed on the premises, but that doesn't deter a loyal clientele, who are packing the place out. Along with several other restaurants in Upper Tooting Road, Masaledar has had to expand, and has added another 25 covers. The food is fresh, well spiced and cheap – there are vegetable curries at £3.25 and meat curries for under £5 – and, to cap it all, you eat it in an elegant designer dining room.

£8 to £20

Address 121 Upper Tooting Rd, SW17
℡ 020 8767 7676
Station Tooting Bec/Tooting Broadway
Open Daily noon–midnight
Accepts Mastercard and Visa

INDIAN

As starters, the samosas are sound – two meat (£1.95) or two vegetable (£1.95). Or try the chicken wings from the tandoor (five pieces £2.50), or the very tasty lamb chops (four pieces £3.75). You might move on to a tasty, rich chicken or lamb biryani (£4.50). Or perhaps try a classic dish like methi gosht (£4.75) – this is strongly flavoured and delicious, guaranteed to leave you with fenugreek seeping from your pores for days to come. Then there's the rich and satisfying lamb Masaledar (£4.95), which is disarmingly described as "our house dish cooked to tantalize your taste buds". The breads, however, are terrific, especially the wonderful thin rotis (70p). Look out for the various deals that range from "All day lunch platter £2.95" to "birthdays, parties, conferences ... private parties of up to 120".

Sometimes the brisk takeaway trade and the fact that all dishes are made to order conspire to make service a bit slow. And despite, or because of, the absence of alcohol, you can have an interesting evening's drinking. Mango shake (£1.95) is rich, very fruity and not too sweet; order one before your meal, however, and greed will ensure that you have finished it by the time your food comes. Both the sweet and salty lassi (£1.50) are very refreshing, as is the "fresh passion juice" (£2.50).

Tower Bridge & Bermondsey

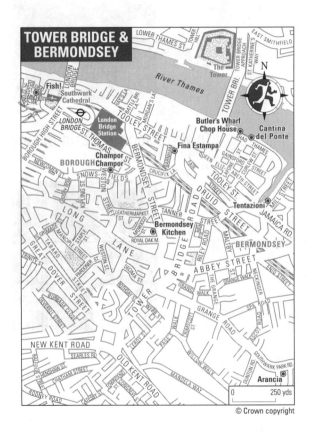

TOWER BRIDGE & BERMONDSEY

LOWER THAMES ST

TOWER HILL ST

EAST Smithfield

The Tower

TOWER BRIDGE APPROACH

ST KATHERINE'S WAY

TOWER BRI.

River Thames

N

LONDON BRIDGE

Fish!

Southwark Cathedral

CATHEDRAL STREET

CLINK STREET

BATTLE BRI. LA

MORGAN'S LA

LONDON BRIDGE STREET

LONDON BRIDGE

London Bridge Station

ST. THOMAS ST

TOOLEY STREET

Butler's Wharf Chop House

Cantina del Ponte

SHAD THAMES

Fina Estampa

BERMONDSEY STREET

QUEEN

GAINSFORD ST

ELIS LACINE ST

ABETH ST

THAMES STREET

MILL STREET

Champor Champor

BOROUGH

SNOWS

NEW MEN

BOROUGH HIGH STREET

NEWCOMEN

REDCROSS WAY

KIPLING ST

SNOWSFIELDS

WESTON STREET

CRUCIFIX LA

TALE

DRUID STREET

TOOLEY ST

Tentazioni

JAMAICA RD

LONG LANE

LEATHERMARKET ST

TANNER ST

Bermondsey Kitchen

MORocco ST

Royal Oak M.

BRIDGE ROAD

RILEY ROAD

MALTBY

BERMONDSEY

GREAT DOVER STREET

TRINITY ST

TABARD ST

MANCIPLE STREET

STAPLE ST

WESTON ST

PARDONER ST

DECIMA ST

ABBEY STREET

THE GRANGE

GRANGE WALK

NECKINGER

ENID STREET

TOWER BRIDGE ROAD

BURBAGE ROAD

BARTELL CLOSE

ROTHSAY ST

GRANGE WALK

SEA ROAD

GRANGE ROAD

SOUTHWARK PARK RD

NEW KENT ROAD

SEARLES RD

BAZELEY

SHENSHAW ST

CHATHAM STREET

RODNEY ROAD

CATESBY ST

OLD KENT ROAD

LEROY ST

PAGE'S WALK

CRIMSCOTT ST.

TOWNSEND

CONCORDE ST

WILLOW WALK

MANDELA WAY

DUNTON RD

Arancia

| 0 | | 250 yds |

© Crown copyright

Arancia

Gentrification has spread through this part of town; this is yet another area where house prices have climbed beyond reason. Arancia has to live with these changing times. Ten years ago this patch was all pie and mash and car chases. Now sensible and authentic Italian food is quite acceptable – and the proprietors of Arancia are to be congratu-

£10 to £20

Address 52 Southwark Park Rd, SE16
☎ 020 7394 1751
Station BR South Bermondsey
Open Mon & Tues 7–11pm,
Wed–Sun 12.30–2.30pm & 7–11pm
Accepts Mastercard and Visa

ITALIAN

lated on keeping the food cheap enough to attract the long-term residents, while at the same time good enough to ensnare newcomers. Success on all fronts. This is an old-fashioned, regularly changing, seasonally inspired menu. It also a sign of nervous times in restaurant land that if anything prices here may have fallen a little – making Arancia a bargain whether you are bourgeois or Bermondsey.

Starters might include zuppa di ceci pancetta (£3), a chickpea soup served with bruschetta. Or you might find insalata di baccalà (£4), a salad of salt cod, squid and roast peppers (£4). Or bruschetta cipolla e Taleggio (£4), a winning combination of caramelized shallots and gooey cheese. There's usually a pasta dish, perhaps gnocchi alla romana (£4) served plainly with butter and Parmesan. For main course there may trota al forno (£9) – baked trout spiked with Strega and served with a fennel and orange salad. You can also bank on dishes like fegato aceto di modena (£9) – pan-fried calf's liver finished with a splash of balsamic vinegar and served with mashed potato. Vegetarians are catered for, too: tortine di zucca (£9) – a tart made with pumpkin and pine nuts and served with a marinated mushroom salad. The puddings are adventurous: perhaps a rather good chocolate semifreddo (£3.30); or pear and almond tart (£3.50).

The pursuit of bargain prices is also the theme of the all-Italian wine list. They are certainly inexpensive wines, and they are all drinkable, but if you're after something really splendid you'll be out of luck. The proprietors of Arancia also run an outside catering business. With food as simple and as good as this, it should be worth investigating.

Tower Bridge & Bermondsey

Bermondsey Kitchen

When all the old pubs in a neighbourhood have been converted into gastropubs, the next logical development is to start building gastropubs, from scratch. The Bermondsey Kitchen may well be at the forefront of this trend. A pub has been created. But it is a pub where the bar space is junior partner to a large dining area; where the range of draught beer is severely curtailed; and

£15 to £30

Address 194 Bermondsey St, SE1
℡ 020 7407 5719
Station London Bridge
Open Mon–Sat 12.30–3pm &
6.30–10pm, Sun 11.30am–4pm
(brunch)
Accepts All major credit cards
except AmEx

where the dominant element is the large open kitchen. The mainspring of this place is one of a growing band of Eagle alumni to fly the nest, and as you would expect, with such provenance the basics are in place. An ever-changing menu is commendably short: four starters, four mains, three puds. This formula has certainly hit the spot and the Kitchen is packed - even midweek you would be wise to book.

The presentation of the dishes here is gratifyingly straightforward; there is a welcome absence of towers and complication. Among the starters black pudding comes on a thick slice of fried bread with a fried egg on top (£4), good to eat but you cannot help feeling grateful that you're close to Guy's Hospital in case the cholesterol gets you. Sea bass escabeche is a healthier option and comes with a good baby spinach and red pepper salad (£5). Beetroot, carrot and salsify fritters (£4) come with aioli and are very light and crisp – more like tempura than fritters. Main courses split fish, veggie and two meat. The meat-based dishes are well balanced: a long skewer of char-grilled lamb kebabs (£10) with pickles, flatbread and carrot and harissa salad is accurately cooked; and a "Scarborough" beef stew comes with mash and red cabbage (£11): a good stew. The fish dishes are also unfussy – grilled salmon with purple sprouting (£12) – and so are puds – chocolate pudding with crème fraîche (£4). The Bermondsey Kitchen may be modern-looking but it sticks to a true gastropub ethos, and genuine gastropub prices.

One of the side dishes intrigues: "celeriac and porcini gratin" (£2.50), a rich and delicious mess of potato and celeriac slices glued together with vaguely cheesy crusty bits.

Butlers Wharf Chop House

Butlers Wharf Chop House – another Conran creation – really deserves everyone's support. For this is a restaurant that makes a genuine attempt to showcase the best of British produce. There's superb British meat, splendid fish, and simply epic British and Irish cheeses. What's more, the Chop House wisely caters for all, whether you want a simple dish at the bar, a well-priced set lunch or an extravagant dinner. The dining room is spacious and bright, and the view of Tower Bridge a delight, especially from a terrace table on a warm summer's evening.

£15 to £40

Address 36e Shad Thames, SE1
☎ 020 7403 3403
Station Tower Hill/London Bridge
Open Restaurant Mon–Fri & Sun noon–3pm & 6–11pm, Sat 6–11pm; bar Mon–Sat noon–3pm & 6–11pm, Sun noon–3pm
Accepts All major credit cards
🌐 www.conran.com

BRITISH

Lunch in the restaurant is priced at £19.75 for two courses and £23.75 for three. The menu changes regularly but tends to feature starters such as pheasant and pigeon ballottine; or Loch Fyne smoked salmon; or a clam and mussel salad with cucumber, tomato and dill. Mains will include dishes like fish and chips, and slow-roast belly pork with prunes, as well as the house speciality of spit roasts and grills. They do a flawless roast rib of beef with Yorkshire pudding and gravy, and excellent braised oxtail with mashed potato. After that you just might be able to find room for a pud like rhubarb crumble tart with vanilla ice cream, even if the sticky toffee pudding is a dish too far. Dinner follows the same principles but is priced à la carte. Thus, there may be starters like hot-smoked eel served with horseradish and bacon (£7.50), half a lobster mayonnaise (£16.50). Mains may include steak, kidney and oyster pudding (£13.50); charcoal-grilled lamb chops with fried potatoes and green sauce (£16.50); or grilled lemon sole (£16.50). There's also steak and chips, priced by size – from £16.50 for an 8oz sirloin to £25 for a 12oz fillet. Or poached chicken and potato pie (£14.50). Butlers Wharf is also one of the few places in London where you can have a savoury to end the meal – Welsh rarebit (£3.50).

The bar menu is appealing: two courses for £8, three for £10. You might choose crab soup, roast lamb and lemon tart – a pretty good tenner's worth.

ITALIAN

Cantina del Ponte

Jostling for attention with the Pont de la Tour, its more renowned and considerably pricier Conran neighbour, the Cantina del Ponte does not try to keep up, but instead offers a different package. Here you are greeted with the best earthy Italian fare, presented in smart Conran style. The floors are warm terracotta, the food is strong on flavour and colour, the service is refined, and the

£10 to £35

Address Butlers Wharf, Shad Thames, SE1
☎ 020 7403 5403
Station Tower Hill/London Bridge
Open Mon–Sat noon–3pm & 6–11pm, Sun noon–3pm & 6–10pm
Accepts All major credit cards
🌐 www.conran.com

views are superior London dockside. Book ahead and bag a table by the window or, better still, brave the elements in summer and sit under the canopy watching the boats go by. Inside is OK but less memorable, and the low ceilings are a bit claustrophobic if you're seated at the back.

The seasonal menu is a meander through all things good, Italian-style, with a tempting array of first courses, and mains that include pizza, pasta and risotto, not to mention side orders, puddings and cheeses. Simple, classic combos like Mozzarella with grilled polenta and salsa rossa (£5.75) always appeal. Or grilled squid with chilli and rocket (£5.95). Veggie dishes like pumpkin and Ricotta tortellini with butter and sage (£9.95) are good, or how about a classic like risotto con funghi (£9.95)? Pizzas are equally filling, and feature all the old favourites, like quattro stagioni (£7.20), Margherita (£4.95) and Napoli (£6). Main courses range from fillet of sea bass with Jerusalem artichoke mash and lemon olive oil (£13.95); breast of guinea fowl with Umbrian lentils, zampone and salsa verde (£12.95); to calf's liver with cipollini onions and polenta (£12.95); and lamb shank with rosemary potatoes and porcini (£13,95). Puds veer from tiramisù (£4.95), through torta di cioccolata and noci (£4.50), to panna cotta with rhubarb (£5.25).

As well as competitive set menus (lunch and pre-theatre), priced at £10 for two courses and £12.50 for three, Cantina does a mean line in takeaway pizzas – always presuming that you live near enough to fetch it yourself, or perhaps that you like a serious snack when you get home after dinner out.

Champor Champor

You are unlikely to stumble into Champor Champor by accident. Nearby Bermondsey Street has its share of eateries and galleries, but in Weston Street Champor Champor is all alone, surrounded by concrete, which makes the brightly painted, genuinely eccentric little restaurant all the more remarkable. The two proprietors describe the food as "creative Malay-Asian" and the chef – Adu Amran Hassan - not only handles the presentation of the dishes but also the interior design. He makes a good job of both. The food is tough to categorize, but the presentation is sophisticated and stylish and all the flavours are agreeably upfront.

£24 to £50

Address 62 Weston St, SE1
☏ 020 7403 4600
Station London Bridge
Open Mon–Sat 6.30–10.30pm
(lunch by appointment)
Accepts All major credit cards
🌐 www.champor-champor.com

The menu changes with the seasons and offers two courses for £19.90 and three for £24.90. To start, there may be grilled calamari served with calamansi-cured scallop, Khmer prahok and smoked fish dip; or Nonya yam and celery cake, coconut vinaigrette, preserved mustard leaf chutney. Do not be disheartened by the unfamiliarity of these dishes; ingredients are carefully matched and flavours work well. Or there may be buffalo phat phet salad: this is terrifically good. With this dish you are presented with a stone mortar and in it is a hot (both in terms of temperature and bird's-eye chillies) stir-fry of buffalo meat, garlic and holy basil leaves. Take a brave leap and order in hope rather than in knowledge – a strategy made possible by helpful and attentive service. Main courses arrive on trays – tiger prawn curry tempoyak brings a rough-hewn bowl of fine noodles, a bowl with a salad of tiny red chard leaves and sesame seeds, and a splendid curry with several large and meaty prawn tails. Ordering the Malay wedding duck red curry gets you a bowl of nutty, sweet brown rice, a leaf salad, and an excellent, rich, spicy duck curry. Even the desserts are suitably exotic – "tropical fruit arrack trifle, roti chanai biscotti" touches several bases.

The wine list is also refined but priced fairly, and there is a range of moody Asian beers – Mongolian Baddog (£2.90) anyone? Or perhaps Hite (£2.90) from South Korea – pleasantly light, but malty?

Fina Estampa

PERUVIAN

While London is awash with ethnic eateries, Fina Estampa's proud boast is that it is the capital's only Peruvian restaurant. Gastronomy may not be the first thing that springs to mind when one thinks of Peru, but the husband-and-wife team running the place certainly tries hard to enlighten the customers, and bring a little downtown Lima to London

£15 to £30

Address 150 Tooley St, SE1
℗ 020 7403 1342
Station London Bridge
Open Mon–Fri noon–2.30pm &
6.30–10.30pm, Sat 6.30–10.30pm
Accepts All major credit cards
ⓦ www.finaestampa.co.uk

Bridge. With its fresh cream-, gold- and coffee-coloured interior, Fina Estampa has a warm and bright ambience, and the attentive, friendly staff add greatly to the upbeat feel of the music.

The menu is traditional Peruvian, which means there's a great emphasis placed upon seafood. This is reflected in the starters, with such offerings as chupe de camarones (£6.95), a succulent shrimp-based soup; cebiche (£5.95), a dish of marinated white fish served with sweet potatoes; and jalea (£9.50), a vast plate of fried seafood. Ask for the salsa criolla – its hot oiliness is a perfect accompaniment. There is also causa rellena (£5.50), described as a "potato surprise" and it is exactly that: layers of cold mashed potato, avocado and tuna fish served with salsa – the surprise being how something so straightforward can taste so good. Main courses – the fragrant chicken seco (£10.95), chicken cooked in a coriander sauce; or the superb lomo saltado (£12.95), tender strips of rump steak stir-fried with red onions and tomatoes – are worthy ambassadors for this simple yet distinctive cuisine. Perhaps most distinctive of all is the carapulcra (£10.95), a spicy dish made of dried potatoes, pork, chicken and cassava – top choice for anyone seeking a new culinary adventure.

One particularly fine, and decidedly Peruvian, speciality is the unfortunately named Pisco sour (£3.50). Pisco is a white grape spirit and the Peruvian national drink, not dissimilar in taste and effect to tequila. Here they mix Pisco with lemon, lime and cinnamon, then sweeten it with honey, add egg white, and whip it into a frothy white cocktail, which is really rather good.

Fish!

You feel like a fish at Fish! The restaurant's huge windows and glass ceiling contribute to a tank-like feeling. They also contribute to high noise levels and a general party ambience. The restaurant is large and there's a courtyard for alfresco eating, plus bar seating for armchair chefs who like to watch the real ones at work. The turbulence of the restaurant industry has left its mark on the Fish! chain, which is now a good few links shorter than when in its pomp. The menu is a little shorter, which is probably an improvement.

£22 to £50

Address Cathedral St, SE1
☏ 020 7407 3803
Station London Bridge
Open Mon–Sat 11.30am–11pm,
Sun noon–10pm
Accepts All major credit cards
Branches see p.489
⊕ www.fishdiner.co.uk

FISH

The good intentions of the place, however, are still apparent. The Marine Stewardship Council logo is splattered about and the restaurant is a "GM free zone". From the printed list of fishy contenders – down to 15 from 22 – a number will be available depending on what the market has come up with. You select your favourite; from those available, choose whether you want it steamed or grilled; and then choose salsa, Hollandaise, herb butter, garlic butter, lemon mayonnaise to go with it. Create your own combo. Prices range from £11.95 for plaice to £14.95 for sea bass, or £16.50 for John Dory. Portions are large and the fish is as good and fresh as you'd expect. The traditional menu also offers starters like prawn cocktail (£5.95), while main dishes include fishcake (£9.50); tuna burger with chips (£10.95); seafood linguine (£9.95); or fish and chips with mushy peas (£10.95). And, for poor lost carnivores who have rather missed the point, there is even a grilled free-range chicken breast (£11.50). If you like a traditional approach to fish, Fish! won't disappoint. Puddings include stalwarts like chocolate fondant (£4.95), and bread-and-butter pudding (£4.95), the latter rich with double cream, and apple crumble with custard (£4.50). The house white, a Sauvignon (£12.95), is light, crisp and fairly priced.

Fish!'s enlightened approach adds interest to eating, whilst not being too preachy. There's also a Fish! shop next door for wet fish and sauces, and a touch-screen recipe machine.

ITALIAN

Tentazioni

🍴 This small, busy and rather good Italian restaurant has crept up behind Sir Terence Conran's Thameside flotilla of eateries and is giving them a terrific run for their money. The food is simple, high-quality peasant Italian, with strong, rich flavours. The pasta dishes are good here, as are the stews, and the wine list is interesting. As well as a splendid three-course Regional Menu (£26) that changes on a monthly basis, there is a Menu Degustazione, which gets you five courses for £36. The set lunch has been discontinued but there is "lunch club" for regulars that offers an attractive 30 percent discount.

£10 to £20

Address 2 Mill St, SE1
ⓣ 020 7237 1100
Station Bermondsey/Tower Hill
Open Tues–Fri noon–2.30pm & 7–10.45pm, Mon & Sat 7–10.45pm
Accepts All major credit cards
ⓦ www.tentazioni.co.uk

All the starters can be turned into main courses, and the menu changes to reflect the seasons and the markets. You may find choices such as ravioli di zucca con burro e salvia (£9/13) – pumpkin ravioli; or gnocchetti di semolina e zenzero, salsa di gamberi e pomodorini arrostiti (£8/12) – gnocchetti with ginger and prawns; or a simple-sounding dish like zuppa di funghi porcini con gâteau di farro (£8) – a soup of ceps and cracked wheat. Main courses offer hammer blows of flavour. Frito misto di pesce con carciofi e salsa all'agro dolce (£18) – mixed fried fish with sweet and sour sauce; while merluzzo arrostito con finocchi gratinati all'aglio e vermut (£15) is roast cod with garlic and vermouth. Or how about a dish like filetto di maiale e polenta saltata al ginepro con sugo di melanzane e salvia (£16) – pork fillet with juniper-sautéed polenta? Or maybe salmone dorato con semi di sesamo, tortino di riso e salsa alla camomilla (£15) – salmon with a sesame seed crust, served with a rice cake and camomile sauce appeals? For pudding it is hard to better the sformatino di ricotta con salsa al caffè (£7), a delicious Ricotta pudding with coffee sauce, although the "chocolate ecstasy" (£7) has many fans.

The "Degustazione" provides a very tempting option. How does this sound: spicy baby squid salad; then the pumpkin ravioli mentioned above; then the mixed fried fish; and the pork fillet; chocolate ecstasy? A pretty rewarding way to part with £36.

Wimbledon & Southfields

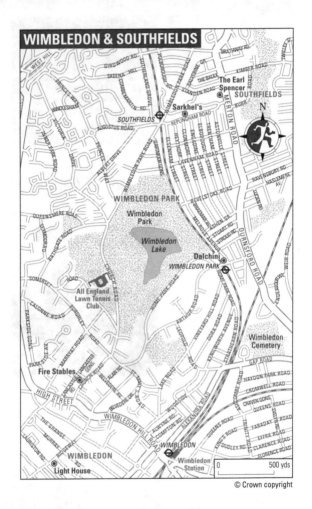
© Crown copyright

Dalchini

Dalchini is an Indian word for cassia (a spice rather like cinnamon), it stems from the words dal, meaning bark, and chini, meaning China. Which makes it jolly appropriate for this small and friendly family restaurant, as Dalchini serves the kind of Chinese food that has emigrated to Bombay. This is Chinese with a pronounced Indian accent – lots of spice and a good deal of chilli. The restaurant is run by Udit Sarkhel's

INDIAN/CHINESE

(see p.383) wife Veronica, who is Hakka Chinese and comes from a long line of Chinese restaurateurs based in Bombay. In 2003 the Sarkhels convinced the planning authorities to allow them to convert the ground-floor shop and deli into a restaurant dining room, and Dalchini was able to move up out of the basement into more agreeable surroundings.

A good strategy is to toy with a few starters and then turn to the specials list for the classic Indo-Chinese dishes. Start with the chicken lollipops (£3.95); or the pepper garlic fish (£3.95) – cod that has been given an Indo-Chinese twist. Or perhaps the red pumpkin fritters (£3.75) appeal? The corn cream (£3.75) is that rarity – a vegetarian dish that really shines. Whether you are keen on Indian or Chinese food, the Dalchini main courses are great fun. There is chilli chicken (£6.25), a big seller in Bombay, sweet and chilli-hot; or "American chicken chop suey" (£7) – the story goes that chop suey was a dish first devised by Chinese coolies working on the American railroads. Or stewed lamb and tofu with yellow bean sauce (£6.25) – slow-cooked with chilli and a few water chestnuts. Or the house signature dish, which is ginger chicken (£6.25). Or show off with the standing pomfret (£9.95), a cunningly deboned fried pomfret that is presented upright as if swimming. As an accompaniment to all this, vegetable Hakka noodles (£4.25) fit the bill.

You also deserve to try one very different dish: goat meat curry (£6.25), a simple Calcutta-style curry with potato. Or for pudding, how about honey noodles with ice cream (£4.25)? These are egg noodles as you've never seen them before!

The Earl Spencer

The Earl Spencer is a cracking new gastropub. This rambling, high-ceilinged boozer reopened in mid-January 2003 and now the denizens of SW18 are beginning to realize just how lucky they are. The Earl is sibling to the long-established Havelock in Brook Green (see p.467), and the lessons learned over the years in W14 have been put to good advantage here in Southfields. The room is plain, large and bare. The bar serves

£10 to £30

Address 260 Merton Rd, Southfields, SW18
℡ 020 8870 9244
Station Southfields
Open Mon–Sat 12.30–2.30pm & 7–10pm Sun noon–3pm & 7–9.30pm
Accepts Mastercard & Visa

decent beer. Portions are large. Prices are very reasonable. Service is friendly, and the wine list offers sound value. The menu is an ever-changing one, things run out, dishes are seasonal. The standard of cooking is very high.

"Mulligatawny soup, coriander and raita" (£4) is a real blast from the past, but a welcome one for all oldies who remember the hot sweet taste of the Heinz tinned version. At the Earl, this soup is thick with lentils and fresh coriander leaves, and comes with an island of yoghurty onion raita. Very good indeed. The most pricey starter turns out to be stunning value: for £6.50 you get a plate of sound Caesar salad with two large, perfectly cooked scallops, each wrapped in crisp bacon. There's no pretentious presentation, no towering mounds of rocket, no artfully balanced scallops. You get good, fresh, well-cooked food. A pork chorizo and chicken liver terrine (£5) has strayed from the menu at the Havelock; it is just as good south of the river. If anything the main courses are even more satisfying; pan-fried veal kidneys (£9) come in a bowl on spring greens, lentils and with a wild mushroom cream. The kidneys are perfectly cooked, flavours and textures complement one another. A salt beef stovie (£8.50) – which is a kind of Scottish potato-cake-cum-hash, sits on green beans, is topped with a fried egg and comes with a moat of decent mustard sauce. Puds are sound, not fancy.

You could have a whole roast pigeon with red cabbage and mash; or a fillet of sea bream, with new potatoes and Jerusalem artichokes; and still not break the £9.50-a-dish barrier. This is how gastropub food should be.

The Fire Stables

By gastropub standards The Fire Stables (which opened as long ago as 2001) is now something of a veteran. And it is a veteran that has won its share of awards. Even in busy Wimbledon the bar does good trade, and the spacious restaurant also prospers. The chairs are comfortable and the tables big enough, the high ceiling and large windows give a spacious feel, the floor is made of painted floorboards – in short everything is "gastropub-normal".

£12 to £40

Address 27–29 Church Rd, SW19
℡ 020 8946 3197
Station Wimbledon
Open Mon–Fri noon–3pm &
6–10.30pm, Sat noon–4pm &
6–10.30pm, Sun 11am–4.30pm &
6–10pm
Accepts All major credit cards

MODERN BRITISH/GASTROPUB

The menu changes daily and the food is well presented and reasonably priced. Starters range from Jerusalem artichoke soup w truffle oil (£4.50) to a foie gras and chicken liver parfait w red onion marmalade (£5.75). You may already have spotted the typographical idiosyncrasy, which wears pretty thin pretty quickly. They don't write "with" at the Fire Stables, what they put is w. So you get char-grilled squid w chilli jam (£6.50) – this could get irritating by the time you get to cheese w Bath Olivers (£5). A starter of Portobello mushrooms w gremolata and mozzarella on bruschetta (£6) is much more successful – good mushies, very tasty. Or perhaps boudin noir w caramelized apple and mustard sauce (£5.50)? Main courses include slow-roast pork belly w Puy lentils and red cabbage (£9.50); roast cod w Parma ham, spinach and mustard sauce (£14); spaghettini w tiger prawns, chilli, garlic and parsley (£11); breast of duck w fondant potato tian aubergine and semi-dried tomato (£13.50); roast skate w butter bean cassoulet and mustard sauce (£13.25) and saddle of venison w Dauphinoise potato and braised red cabbage (£14.50). A fennel, fine herb and goat's cheese risotto (£10.50) is pressed into service for vegetarians (no w for them!). Puds (all £5) are desirable if predictable numbers, such as bread-and-butter pudding; sticky toffee pudding w vanilla ice cream; pear and almond tart w crème fraîche; and baked cheesecake w raspberry coulis.

On Sunday at brunchtime the lunch menu is extended by two or three eggy-type dishes. Brunch is the new lunch out in Wimbledon.

MODERN EUROPEAN

Light House

Light House is a strange restaurant to find marooned in leafy suburbia – you would think that its modern, very eclectic menu and clean style would be more at home in a city centre than in a smart, quiet, respectable neighbourhood. Nevertheless it continues to do well. The restaurant has gone through several changes of chef and yet still manages to keep the feel of the menu much the same. First impressions always count, and a light, bright interior – cream walls and blond wood – plus genuinely friendly staff make both arriving and eating at Light House a pleasure.

£20 to £50

Address 75–77 The Ridgway, SW19
℗ 020 8944 6338
Station Wimbledon
Open Mon–Sat noon–2.30pm & 6–10.30pm, Sun noon–2.30pm
Accepts All major credit cards except Diners

At first glance, the menu is set out conventionally enough in the Italian style: antipasti, primi, secondi, contorni and dolci. But that's as far as the Italian formality goes – the influences on the kitchen here are truly global. Starters may range from Cornish crab and Arbroath smokie potato cake with tuna carpaccio, ginger and yuzu dressing (£7); to carrot and coriander soup with crème fraîche (£5); or char-grilled Tomino in vine leaves with roast butternut squash, Marcona almond and melon salad (£6); or roast aromatic duck with steamed pancakes, Thai salad and sour plum and sesame dipping sauce (£6.50). It would be very easy to get this sort of cooking wrong, but in fact Light House makes a fair job of it. Among the "secondi", dishes like roast Trelough duck breast with celeriac, balsamic roast onions and cranberry compote (£14) jostle with combinations like almond-crusted cod with wok-fried courgettes and mustard dressing (£14.50). Perhaps the cooking is a little overcomplicated, but it's well executed and intriguing. Puddings have a retro note but can still surprise – steamed sultana and pine nut pudding with grappa and espresso custard (£5.20); or Bailey's and fudge semifreddo with butterscotch (£5.20).

Someone had a lot of fun choosing the wine list – a selection of about twenty each of whites and reds, which crosses as many frontiers as possible. If you want a bargain, go for lunch – the "set lunch" (Tuesday to Saturday) is a steal at £12.50 for two courses.

Sarkhel's

Before opening his own place in SW18, Udit Sarkhel was heading the kitchens of the famous Bombay Brasserie in the West End, where he had all the latest kit and a large brigade of chefs. Moving to Sarkhel's in Southfields must have been like resigning as conductor of an orchestra and setting up a one-man band, but it is certainly a huge asset to South London. And South London has certainly responded – the dining room seems to be enlarged at least once a year. Today Sarkhel's is a large, elegant restaurant, serving well-spiced food with a number of adventurous dishes scattered through the menu – the hot, fresh Chettinad dishes are particularly fine. Moreover, it's a pleasant, friendly, family-run place offering good cooking at prices, which, though not cheap, certainly represents good value (particularly the bargain set lunch at £9.95 or the Express at £5 – neither available on Sunday). Booking is recommended.

£11 to £35

Address 199 Replingham Rd, Southfields, SW18
☎ 020 8870 1483
Station Southfields
Open Tues–Thurs noon–2.30pm & 6–10.30pm, Fri & Sat noon–2.30pm & 6–11pm, Sun noon–2.30pm & 6–10.30pm
Accepts All major credit cards except Diners
ⓦ www.sarkhels.com

Start by asking Udit or his wife if there are any "specials" on. These are dishes which change according to what is available at the markets. You might be offered a starter of Tareli macchi (£4.25) – fish cooked in a spicy batter, a famous Bombay Parsee dish. Or vagatore bangde (£5.95), which is a mackerel boned out and stuffed with shrimp balchao, and it's pleasantly chilli-hot. The khass seekh kebab (£4.25) is as good as you'll find anywhere. For main course dishes, check the specials again – it might be something wonderful like a kolmi nu Patia (£8.75), a spicy Parsee prawn dish. On the main menu, try the chicken reszala (£7.25), a rich dish that is the speciality of Calcutta Muslims; or perhaps the jardaloo ma gosht (£7.25), a sweet and sour lamb dish made with apricots. All are delicious, without even a hint of surface oil slick. Be sure to add some vegetable dishes. Perhaps the baigan patiala (£5.95), which is a dish of cubed aubergine and cashew nuts stewed with a touch of ginger and chilli.

There are also frequent regional festivals – ask if you're puzzled by strange dishes, as you'll get good advice and fabulous food.

Further South

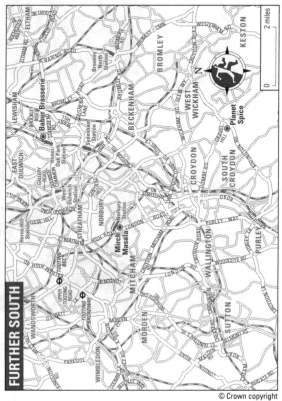

FURTHER SOUTH

© Crown copyright

Babur Brasserie

🍴 The Babur Brasserie is a stylish and friendly restaurant serving elaborate and interesting dishes which bear no resemblance to ordinary curry house fare – an unexpected find in SE23. The food is both subtle and elegantly presented and, while it does cost a touch more than most suburban Indian restaurants, you are still paying a great deal

£10 to £25
Address 119 Brockley Rise, SE23
☏ 020 8291 2400
Station BR Honor Oak Park
Open Daily noon–2.30pm & 6–11.30pm
Accepts All major credit cards
🌐 www.babur-brasserie.com

less than you would in a French or Italian place of similar quality. There is a buffet lunch on Sunday (£8.95) at which children eat free if they are less than seven years old.

How nice to be faced with a list of appetizers and see so few familiar dishes, like fish kola (£3.95) – bite-size bits of white fish battered and deep-fried; salmon samosas (£4.25); malai murgh tikka (£3.95), a grown-up chicken tikka with cashew nut marinade; or alloo choff (£3.25), potato croquettes with spice and a cashew crust. Main courses are just as good. Try chicken Chettinad (£7.50) – a South Indian dish that is traditionally served hot with chillies; or "Classic Madras monk-fish" (£9.95) – setting aside the availability of monkfish in downtown Madras, this is a good, hot fish curry finished with fresh curry leaves, mustard, coconut and tomato sauce. Beef xacutti (£8.25) is a complex curry made with an awesomely long list of spices including fenugreek and star anise. Then there are a dozen fresh vegetable dishes – vegetarians will applaud the thali option (£12.50) of picking three from the list with tarka sagdal, raita, rice and a naan bread. On the subject of bread, try the lacha paratha (£2.25), a flaky paratha made with ghee. The dessert menu is more extensive and more elaborate than usual, too, running the gamut from rasmalai with mango (£3.50), to kulfi (£3.75), that dense and tasty Indian ice cream.

Hing, or asafoetida, is a spice that has not only a distinctive flavour but also what translates into a rude name. In oonbhariu (£4.95) – a dish from the vegetables section – it is blended with lovage and cumin to accompany bananas, sweet potato, baby aubergines and shallots. Particularly delicious, and not stinky at all.

Mirch Masala

You'll find Mirch Masala just up London Road from Norbury station. It may not look much from the outside, but it deserves a place on any list of London's top Indian restaurants – something South London's Asian community appears to have cottoned on to. As befits such a culinary temple, the chefs take centre stage. The kitchen is in full view and you can watch the whole cooking process, which culminates, as likely as not, in a chef bringing the food to table. They are certainly prone to wandering out while you are enjoying the last of your starters to ask if you're ready for your main course. What's more, at the end of the meal they are also happy to pack up anything you don't finish so that you can take it home. Take advantage, and over-order! This is a very friendly and unpretentious place serving spectacular food at low prices, which makes for very contented diners indeed.

£6 to £16

Address 1416 London Rd, SW16
☎ 020 8679 1828
Station BR Norbury
Open Daily noon–midnight
Accepts All major credit cards except AmEx and Diners
🌐 www.mirchmasalarestaurant .co.uk

Start with a stick each of chicken tikka (£2.50) and lamb tikka (£2.50), crusted with pepper and spices on the outside, juicy with marinade on the inside. Very good indeed. Or try the butter chicken wings (£3), cooked in a light, ungreasy sauce laden with flavour from fresh spices and herbs. Then move on to the karahi dishes, which are presented in a kind of thick aluminium hubcap. The vegetable karahis are exceptional, so go for the butter beans and methi (£3.50) – an inspired and delicious combination of flavours – or karahi valpapdi baigan (£4), which is aubergines cooked with small rich beans. Among the best meat dishes are the deigi lamb chops (£4.50), and the deigi saag gosht (£5) – spinach, lamb and a rich sauce. Even something simple like karahi ginger chicken (£5) proves how good and fresh-tasting Indian food can be. Rice (£1.50) comes in a glass butter dish complete with lid. Breads include a good naan (70p) and an indulgent peshwari naan (£2) for anyone dead set on pushing the boat out.

A meal at Mirch Masala will be a memorable one. As they say on the menu, "Food extraordinaire. You wish it – we cook it."

Planet Spice

Planet Spice is a fish out of water. Even the presence of the latest transport innovation, the much-vaunted tramway, cannot prepare you for the surprise you get when you arrive here. The restaurant (a sister establishment to the Babur Brasserie, see p.387 and you'll find that dishes migrate from one restaurant to the other) is located at the junction of two major roads and in premises that have been used for everything from a Greek restaurant to a dance school. Today the building houses an exceptional Indian restaurant. If Planet Spice were in the West End, it would be the critics' favourite.

£15 to £32

Address 88 Selsdon Park Rd, Addington, South Croydon
℡ 020 8651 3300
Station Croydon Tramway
Open Mon–Sat noon–2.30pm & 6.30–11.30pm, Sun 12.30–3.30pm & 6–11.30pm
Accepts All major credit cards
🌐 www.planet-spice.com

The chefs have had to make certain compromises. The takeaway side of things is still dominated by old-style dishes – korma, Madras, chicken tikka masala – and any sit-down customers perplexed by the main menu can opt for these. The main menu, however, is agreeably sophisticated and really is the one you should work from. Start with the Mysore chilli chicken (£3.95), chilli-hot chicken nuggets; or spicy crab and smoked salmon balls (£4.95), another deep-fried dish; or prawn and mint samosas (£4.25); or tandoori scallops (£5.95). Or an old favourite like ragda pattice (£3.75) – Mumbai street food, a kind of über potato cake. Main courses are distinguished by accurate and well-balanced spicing and unusually careful cooking. Try the swordfish balchao (£9.95), a hot and sour Goan sauce. Team it with the lime and cashew nut rice (£2.25). Or there's kori gassi (£7.50) – a Mangalorean chicken dish. Otherwise, try a dish like satkora tarkari (£8.50), which is a Bengali dish made with the small, sour plums called shatkora. Or there's the tawa sea bass (£11.95), which is a marinated sea bass pan-fried and served with upma (a kind of Indian couscous) and raw mango. If all this sounds a bit exotic, then there is always the Nilgiri chicken (£7.75), which is a gentle chicken dish made with coriander and mint.

These are ambitious dishes, handled well. It is undoubtedly due to the able chefs in the kitchen. Not what you'd expect of a curry house in Addington.

West

Barnes & Sheen

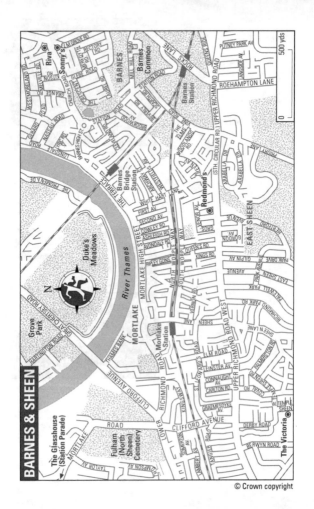

The Glasshouse

(🍴) In 2003 The Glasshouse held the well-deserved star it first picked up in Michelin's 2002 guide. Chef Anthony Boyd honed his craft at the Michelin-bedecked Square (see p.86) and Chez Bruce (see p.331), and at The Glasshouse he has made a good job of combining the rich flavours of Chez Bruce with the sophistication of The Square. What's more, the restaurant is on

£16 to £50

Address 14 Station Parade, Kew Gardens, Surrey
℡ 020 8940 6777
Station Kew Gardens
Open Mon–Sat noon–2.30pm & 7–10.30pm, Sun 12.30–3pm
Accepts All major credit cards except Diners

FRENCH

the doorstep of Kew Gardens underground station, which makes it easy for anyone who can get onto the District Line. The interior has a clean-cut, modern feel to it and the chairs are worthy of lavish praise – they are blissfully comfortable, an aspect of dining which is all too often over-looked. The food is good. Very good.

The main menu is a simple, one which changes daily and usually gives you the choice of nine starters, eight mains and eight puds. From this menu three courses cost £30, but there is a limited set lunch menu (two choices each course), which costs just £12.50 for two courses and £17.50 for three. All of these options are snatch-their-hand-off bargains. The imaginative and straightforward cooking owes much to French cuisine. Starters range from a warm salad of wood pigeon with deep-fried truffled egg; through crisp mackerel with watercress, capers, Charlotte potatoes and grain mustard; to scallop and shrimp tortellini, crab bisque, tomato and chives. Main courses vary from a classic beef Wellington with all the trimmings (including a small supplement to the bill), to roast sea bass with aubergine caviar, braised baby fennel, capers and aioli. The slow-roast pork belly with apple, sage and choucroute tarte fine will appeal to serious eaters. Puddings have a deft touch and include old favourites like hot chocolate fondant and steamed golden syrup sponge pudding. The wine list is short and thoughtfully drawn up, with one or two unusual selections.

Service at The Glasshouse is masterful, and will leave you feeling thoroughly cosseted. However, it's just as well to note their warning – "Please order taxis at least 25 minutes before they are required" – as you are in the wilds of Kew.

Redmond's

MODERN BRITISH

When Redmond and Pippa Hayward opened this small neighbourhood restaurant towards the end of the 1990s, it was head and shoulders above anything else the locale had to offer. A few years down the line and "Barnes & Sheen" may not quite be a match for Soho, but there are a good many very decent places to eat. Redmond's is one of the best, propelled by a telling combo of very good cooking and reasonable prices. They tweak the menu on a daily basis, so it reflects the best of what the season and the markets have to offer. The dinner menu is not particularly short – about six or seven starters and mains – and proves astonishing value at £28.50 for three courses. There is also a competitive lunch menu: £16.50 for two courses and £19.50 for three. What's even more astonishing is that the list is not splattered with supplements or cover charges. And the food here really is very good indeed: well seasoned, precisely cooked, immaculately presented.

£18 to £45

Address 170 Upper Richmond Rd West, SW14
☎ 020 8878 1922
Station BR Mortlake
Open Mon–Fri noon–2pm & 7–10.30pm, Sat 7–10.30pm, Sun noon–2.30pm
Accepts Delta, Mastercard, Switch or Visa

If the terrine of ham hock, foie gras and baby capers is available when you visit, pounce. Redmond's charcuterie is accomplished: it will be multi-layered, multi-textured and superlative-inducing in every way. There may also be roast home-salted cod with Puy lentils and shallot cream; or perhaps a ballottine of quail and foie gras mousse, mushroom and green bean salad, sherry jus. Main courses combine dominant flavours with elegant presentation – roast fillet of smoked haddock and seared scallops with cauliflower puree and curry oil; pea, mint and red onion risotto with shaved Parmesan and asparagus; char-grilled rib-eye steak with Dijon cream, pommes Anna and Savoy cabbage. Or for classicists – roast boned saddle of lamb, gratin dauphinois, Madeira jus. The puddings are wonderful, too: poached spiced pears with Marsala ice cream and dark chocolate sauce; banana parfait with mandarin sorbet.

The short wine list is littered with interesting bottles at accessible prices. There are halves, magnums, pudding wines and just plain bargains.

Riva

(🍴) Andrea Riva has always been something of a darling of the media, and his sophisticated little restaurant exerts a powerful pull, strong enough to convince even the snootiest of fashionable folk to make the dangerous journey into the unknown territory on the south bank of the Thames. When they get there they find a rather conservative-looking restaurant, with a narrow dining room decorated in a sombre blend of dull greens and faded parchment, and chairs which have clearly seen service in church. As far as the cuisine goes, Riva provides the genuine article, so most customers are either delighted or disappointed, depending on how well they know their Italian food. The menu changes regularly with the seasons.

£25 to £45

Address 169 Church Rd, SW13
ⓣ 020 8748 0434
Station BR Barnes Bridge
Open Mon–Fri noon–2.30pm & 7–11pm, Sat 7–11.30pm, Sun noon–2.30pm & 7–9.30pm
Accepts All major credit cards except Diners

ITALIAN

Starters are good but not cheap. The frittelle (£9.50) is a tempura-like dish of deep-fried Mediterranean prawn, salt cod cakes, calamari, sage and basil, with a balsamic dip. If it is on the menu, you must try bocconcini di bufala – buffalo mozzarella with baby spinach, cherry tomatoes and chiodini mushrooms (£7), vibrant and deliciously oily. The brodetto "Mare Nostrum", a chunky, saffron-flavoured fish soup (£7), is also superb, a delicate alternative to its robust French cousin. Serious Italian food fans, however, will find it hard to resist the sapori Mediterranei (£21 for two), which gets you grilled scallop and langoustines; baccalà mantecato and polenta; eel and lentils; mussels in tomato pesto; and grilled oysters. Among the main courses, rombo al rucola (£18.50) is a splendid combination of tastes and textures – a fillet of brill with a rocket sauce and mashed potato. Fegato and polenta unta (£14.75) – calf's liver served with garlic polenta and wild mushrooms – delivers a finely balanced blend of flavours.

If there's anybody out there who still thinks that pizza and pasta are the Italians' staple diet, Riva's uncompromising regional menu proves otherwise. The house wines are all priced at a very accessible £12.50. Of the whites, the pale-coloured Tocai is crisp, light and refreshing.

Sonny's

If the scientists are to be believed, we must evolve or die, and if they're looking for corroborating evidence they'll find it at Sonny's. This "neighbourhood stalwart" has grown into something more polished. Barnes-ites have been supporting Sonny's since Modern British cuisine was just a twinkle in a telly chef's eye. The interior is modern but gratifyingly unthreatening and there is a busy, casual feel about the place. Sonny's shop next door sells a good many of those little delicacies that you would otherwise have journey to the West End to procure. In the spring of 2003 Sonny's acquired a new head chef - Helena Puolakka formerly head chef of La Tante Claire, until that resto left the Berkeley Hotel in late 2002. Knightsbridge's loss is Barnes's gain!

£18 to £38
Address 94 Church Rd, SW13
☎ 020 8748 0393
Station BR Barnes Bridge
Open Mon–Sat 12.30–2.30pm & 7.30–11pm, Sun 12.30–3pm
Accepts All major credit cards

The menu changes on a regular basis to reflect the seasons, so you might find starters like velouté of Jerusalem artichoke, hazelnut bread crisp (£4.50), or a terrine of chicken and leek with tarragon jelly (£6.25), or even, on a more whimsical note, ballottine of foie gras with glazed grapes, and Poilâne toast (£8). Main courses may take a classic combination like pan-fried calf's liver with Alsace bacon, then add Brussels sprouts and a red onion and lime compote (£12). There tend to be some attractive fish dishes, too: grilled halibut with crunchy onion tart, sweet potato cream (£14.50), say, or poached monkfish tail on a ragout of haricot blanc and chorizo (£14). Or there is the grandstand option (£33, for two people) a roast Challans duck, shitake and sweetcorn relish and a foie gras sauce. The service is welcoming and the wine list provides some sound bottles at sound prices.

Puddings are comfortable: sorbets, jellies, raspberry brûlée, served with biscotti (£5.25). If Barnes is your neighbourhood, you will be glad of the set dinner option: two courses for £16, three for £19.50.

The Victoria

It would be nice to live in West Temple Sheen. The name has a good ring to it. The houses are palatial and pricey, both Sheen Common and Richmond Park are close at hand, and then there's The Victoria, a truly outstanding gastropub. The Victoria made the transition from pub to gastropub in late 2000. Since then it has had a conservatory, squashy sofas and painted floorboards – very smart. And they have

£12 to £30

Address 10 West Temple Sheen,
SW14
℡ 020 8876 4238
Station BR Mortlake
Open Mon–Fri noon–2.30pm &
7–10pm, Sat noon–3pm & 7–10pm,
Sun noon–3pm & 7–9pm
Accepts All major credit cards
ⓦ www.thevictoria.net

MODERN BRITISH/GASTROPUB

even added seven bedrooms (which are described as simple but stylish), so now it should probably be called a hotel. Just when you thought that you had mastered the distinction between restaurants and gastropubs ... The Victoria hangs onto gastropub status by virtue of its accessible prices. What you're getting is restaurant cooking, a restaurant wine list and restaurant service, and you're getting it on the cheap.

The menu changes daily – or even more frequently than that, should items run out – and features half a dozen starters and the same number of mains and puds. Starters may offer garbure (£4.95), serious soup; or a classic like quiche Lorraine (£4.95); or potted trout with pickled cucumber salad (£6.95). There is also the Victoria tapas plate (£8.95) – very popular. Mains are steady dishes well executed. Wild mushroom risotto with pissenlit and truffle oil (£10.95); slow-roast belly pork with fennel, tomatoes and crispy polenta (£11.95); grilled sea bass with couscous salad and pomegranate relish (£15.95); coq au vin (£12.95). These are all examples of those special, simple-sounding dishes that are hard to get right. Desserts are top stuff. It's a pleasure to watch punters savouring buttermilk pudding with poached Yorkshire rhubarb (£4.95), or taunting chocoholics with warm chocolate pudding with crème fraîche and white chocolate (£5.95).

The Victoria changes the menu on Saturday, when it becomes altogether brunchier, with simpler dishes and a number that overlap, serving as either starters or mains – think eggs Benedict (£6.95), or lamb and mint sausages with onion gravy (£5.95/7.95).

Chelsea

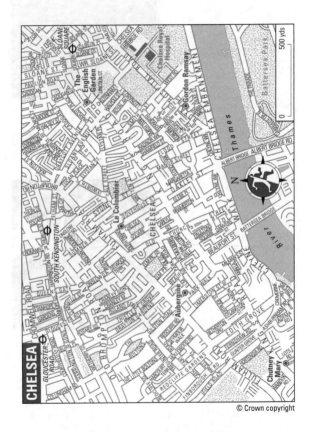

CHELSEA

© Crown copyright

Aubergine

It's hard to imagine it, but a decade or so ago this neck of the woods was a bleak-ish place to eat out. Aubergine changed all that, and it merits the accolade "old-established". Now it is both familiar enough, and light and airy enough, for even the most discerning of ladies who lunch. The best of everything in season and a talented kitchen make

£35 to £100

Address 11 Park Walk, SW10
℡ 020 7352 3449
Station South Kensington/
Earl's Court
Open Mon–Fri noon–2.30pm &
7–11pm, Sat 7–11pm
Accepts All major credit cards

FRENCH

for a busy place, so booking is a must. The arrival of a new front of house from Le Gavroche coincided with a rejigging of the set lunch offer that is now amongst the most competitive in town. Amuses-gueules, three courses, coffee, petits fours, half a bottle of water and half a bottle of wine costs just £32. This is an outrageous bargain.

A lunch that comprises mousse of foie gras, fricassee of chanterelles, followed by lobster tortellini, lobster butter sauce, and then banana soufflé, banana ice cream, with all the bells and whistles of a high-flying restaurant and half a bottle of Pouilly-Fuissé, doesn't read, look or taste like £32 worth. Even at full throttle the main dinner menu offers three courses for £50, which is not so very fierce for cooking of this calibre (although supplements hang on the coat-tails of lobster, turbot, cheeses and the like). Starters may include boudin of pigeon with confit turnips, and morel jus; or an assiette of foie gras – mousse, ballottine and sauté; or pan-fried scallops with pea puree, smoked bacon jus. Main courses include dishes such as fillet of John Dory with a casserole of peas, onions and bacon; assiette of corn-fed duck; roast veal sweetbread studded with truffle, caramelized onion puree; These are well-conceived and well-executed dishes, beautifully presented. Desserts are equally accomplished – assiette of orange; prune and Armagnac ice cream; poached pear with a vanilla parfait. The service is accomplished and unobtrusive. The Menu Gourmand at £70 will spin the experience out by presenting seven pixie portions.

The only cautionary note relates to the wine list, where the prices bolt swiftly out of reach for all but the most special of special occasions.

Chelsea

Chutney Mary

In the spring of 2002 Chutney Mary shut down for a thorough refurbishment and the locals held their breath, worried that the restaurant they had grown fond of since the mid-1990s would be changed out of all recognition. Good news! A sensitive design job has meant that, while everything looks new and chic, it is still as comfortable as ever. The lighting designer (seduced from his day job as a theatrical lighting expert) has done a particularly fine job and it is hard to tell that the moonlight – which plays over the tree in the conservatory as night falls – is not the real thing. This is not a cheap restaurant but it is a good one. The men in the kitchen know their job and turn out refined Indian food. Food so good that in 2003 Chutney Mary won Indian Restaurant of the Year at the London Restaurant Awards.

£30 to £90

Address 535 King's Rd, SW10
℡ 020 7351 3113
Station Fulham Broadway
Open Mon–Fri 6.30–11.30pm, Sat noon–3pm & 6.30–11.30pm, Sun noon–3pm & 6.30–10.30pm
Accepts All major credit cards
🌐 www.chutneymary.com

Start with the crab cake (£9.50) – spankingly fresh crab, loosely bound and top-and-tailed with a potato rosti. Delicious. Or there's the tokri chaat (£6), which is an edible basket filled with various street-food treats and topped with yoghurt and chutney. Or the crab claws with black pepper and garlic (£9.50) – huge tender claws swimming in a sea of garlic butter. Vegetarians will enjoy the platter of mixed tikki (£6.50) – different crisp-coated patties served with excellent chutneys. Mains are equally impressive. Mangalore prawns (£16) are giant prawns, chilli-hot and tamarind-tangy. Nalli gosht (£14) is a splendid lamb curry, served on the bone, with intense flavours. Or there's duck with apricots (£16.50) – pink duck breast and a Parsee masala. From the side dishes, the sarson ka saag (£4.50) – mustard leaves cooked with lotus root – stands out; as does the butter beans methi malai (£3.50). Breads are good here – lacchi paratha (£2.75).

The dessert menu (all at £5.50) is also inspired. There is a strawberry brûlée with garam masala; a dark chocolate fondant served with orange-blossom lassi; and small eclairs stuffed with Srikhand (a sweetened cottage cheese/yoghurt) and served with chocolate sauce.

Le Colombier

Viewed from the pavement outside on Dovehouse Street, you can see that Le Colombier was once a classic, English, street-corner pub. But now it's a pub that has a small, glassed-in area in front, covered with tables and chairs. How very Parisian, you might think, and you would be right. This is a French place. It is run by Monsieur Garnier, who has spent most of his career in the slicker

£15 to £30
Address 145 Dovehouse St, Chelsea Square, SW3
☎ 020 7351 1155
Station South Kensington
Open Mon–Sat noon–3pm & 6.30–11pm, Sun noon–3.30pm & 6.30–10.30pm
Accepts All major credit cards

reaches of London's restaurant business. With his own place he has reverted to type and everything is very, very French.

The menu is French, the cooking is French, the service is French and the decor is French. When the bill comes, you tend to be surprised – first that it is no larger, and second, that they ask for pounds not euros. The cooking is about as good as you would have found in a smart Routiers in rural France during the 1970s – before such places became hard to find. Starters include such bistro classics as oeufs pochés meurette (£5.80), soupe de poissons (£5.30), and feuilleté d'escargots à la crème d'ail (£6.80). And there are oysters, goat's cheese salad, duck liver terrine, and tomato and basil salad. Listed under "les poissons" there is filet de loup de mer rôti au thym (£16.90); and coquilles St Jacques aux champignons sauvages (£14.80), which is scallops with wild mushrooms. Under "les viandes" there is steak tartare, pommes frites (£14.80); filet de boeuf au poivre (£16.80); and magret de canard aux olives (£14.50). Under "les grillades" are the steaks and chops. Puddings include crêpes Suzette (£4.90) and omelette Norvégienne pour deux (£12), which is also described as "baked Alaska" – something of a geographical conundrum.

Service is as French as the menu itself, but Le Colombier is not some trendy retro caricature. None of the atmosphere is posed. If this seems like a provincial French eatery, it's because that's what it is. The fact that it is located in Chelsea makes the set menu for lunch and early dinners (two courses for £13; on Sunday £15) very good value indeed.

Chelsea

The English Garden

(🍴) This Chelsea stalwart is part of Searcy Corrigan Restaurants and after an initial period when it found itself somewhat out on a limb in far away Chelsea, latterly it has acquired its own persona. There's a maple-wood bar, lashings of soft, creamy and biscuity tones, and a judicious use of grey British slate, the service is slick and this is a relaxed

£22 to £50
Address 10 Lincoln St, SW3
☎ 020 7584 7272
Station Sloane Square
Open Mon 6–11pm, Tues–Sat
noon–3pm & 6–11pm, Sun
noon–3pm & 6.30–10.30pm
Accepts All major credit cards

and comfortable place to eat. The menu still owes a good deal to the principles and ambitions of head office, and the well-conceived Modern British food relies on good combinations of strong flavours, and carefully matched textures, with the whole being underpinned by a welcome reliance on seasonality.

The menu changes twice a day, and the pricing is simple: lunch is £19.50 for two courses and £23 for three; dinner is £25 for two and £29 for three. Less than £20 for potted smoked mackerel with beetroot, shallot and dill, followed by confit duck leg, braised cabbage, rosemary jus, and then chocolate pot with kumquat marmalade and white chocolate ice cream? This is good value. Or perhaps ballottine of salmon with a citrus salad, followed by crisp pork belly, celeriac and caramelized quince, and finishing with farmhouse cheeses? In the evening these dishes would be bolstered by one or two more serious numbers. Starters might include braised crubeen, black pudding and apple puree, or a warm salad of chickpeas with an escabeche of red mullet. Mains might be dishes such as stuffed "Kentish Ranger" chicken, creamed cauliflower and harissa; roast cod with Jerusalem artichoke puree; baked skate wing, capers, brown shrimps and dill; and seared scallops with apple and fennel, pancetta and horseradish. Puds are indulgent: try ginger madeleines with poached pear and vanilla cream; or a panna cotta with poached Yorkshire rhubarb.

Elsewhere in the Garden are two elegant private rooms that can be joined together, creating space for parties of 10, 20 or 30. There is an irresistible temptation to say that everything in the garden is rosy.

Gordon Ramsay

Gordon Ramsay is on a roll. His new-ish resto within Claridges (see p.81) continues to delight the critics, and he has added the dining room at the Connaught, and the Grill Room at the Savoy to his increasingly large sphere of influence. At Chelsea, his restaurant continues to be packed. Thankfully, the prices are not as high as you might fear. There are two fixed-price à la carte

£35 to £140

Address 68–69 Royal Hospital Rd, SW3
℡ 020 7352 4441
Station Sloane Square
Open Mon–Fri noon–2pm & 6.45–11pm
Accepts All major credit cards
⊛ www.gordonramsay.com

FRENCH

menus at both lunch and dinner (£65 for three courses, £80 for seven), and a steal of a set lunch (£35 for three courses). Even if you add £5 for a glass of good house wine, this offers the more accessible face of truly great cooking – as long as you can get a booking.

The menu here is constantly evolving and changing. On the main menus, look out for a ravioli of lobster and langoustine poached in a lobster bisque and served with a lemongrass and chervil velouté; or a carpaccio of pigeon from Bresse with shavings of confit foie gras, baby artichokes and a Parmesan salad – this is a stunning dish of unusual delicacy; or caramelized slices of pig's foot with veal sweetbreads and a celeriac rémoulade and a salad of green beans – as robust and delicious as you could wish for. And those are just starters! Mains intrigue: fillet of turbot poached in red wine with radicchio and celeriac risotto; cannon of Cornish lamb with confit shoulder (cooked for eight hours) with salsify, caramelized onions, buttered spinach and rosemary jus; and saddle of Scottish venison with creamed cabbage, beetroot fondant and sautéed wild mushrooms. Even the desserts fascinate – hot chocolate fondant with milk mousse and ice cream; or if there are two of you opt for the assiette de l'Aubergine – pud lover's heaven. To order successfully here, just pick a dish or even an ingredient you like and see how it arrives; you won't be disappointed. This restaurant is a class act through and through.

You will have to book at Gordon Ramsay, but, sensibly enough, reservations are taken only a month in advance, avoiding a potentially huge backlog. Book now, and count the days.

Ealing & Acton

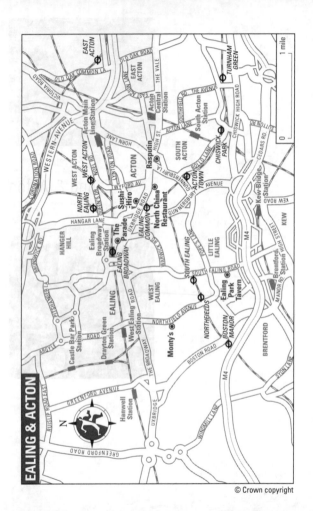

EALING & ACTON

© Crown copyright

Ealing Park Tavern

In 2001, when it was transformed from a lager and football hovel into a tidy pub and eatery, this establishment reverted to its original name – the Ealing Park Tavern. The new owners were the people behind another fine gastropub, St John's (see p.262), so it is no surprise that they have made a decent fist of it. It is a handsome place and, like its North London sibling, is founded on the simple premise that hospitality is important. The

£12 to £40

Address 222 South Ealing Rd, W5
℡ 020 8758 1879
Station South Ealing
Open Mon 6–10.30pm, Tues–Fri noon–3pm & 6–10.30pm, Sat noon–4pm & 6–10.30pm, Sun noon–4pm & 6–9pm
Accepts All major credit cards except Diners

bar has two or three decent real ales and a blackboard featuring decent bar snacks like proper pork pies. The wine list is short but gives a fair choice around the £15-a-bottle mark, topping out at £35. The dining room has a tall counter separating it from an open kitchen and the menu is chalked up on a blackboard. What makes the Park Tavern so popular is the food.

The menu is short one – seven or eight starters and half a dozen mains – but it is thoughtfully written, changes daily and there is something for everybody. Starters may include a carrot and orange soup (£4.25); steamed mussels in beer, chorizo and red onion (£5); or seared marinated salmon with horseradish cream (£5); or a venison and duck liver terrine (£5), which is very good eating. Main courses are well presented, substantial and seem pretty good value. There may be a haunch of venison, braised red cabbage, cassis jus (£11.75); or a char-grilled sirloin, root vegetable cake, Béarnaise sauce (£12.50); or pork fillet wrapped in bacon and sage, wholegrain Hollandaise (£11). Fish dishes tend to be a good option: how does a fish stew made with hake, sea bass, bream, mussels and langoustines (£11.50) sound? Puds are comforting and comfortable – crème brûlée, rice pudding, chocolate mousse.

At lunchtime they cut the menu down a bit and add in some simpler dishes like shepherd's pie, stews and casseroles, each dish ends up costing £2 or £3 less than in the evening. The food is good at the Ealing Park Tavern, prices are reasonable, the atmosphere is informal and the service is friendly. We could all do with a local like this one.

Monty's

(🍴) Once upon a time, the now-defunct Ealing Tandoori held West London curry lovers in thrall – it was the undisputed first choice. Then, in the late 1970s, the three main chefs left to open their own place, which they called Monty's, on South Ealing Road. As business boomed, two of the chefs moved on to set up independently. But as all three co-owned the name "Monty's", they all use it, and that is why there are now

£12 to £24

Address 54 Northfield Ave, Ealing, W13
ⓣ 020 8567 6281
Station Northfields
Open Daily noon–2.30pm & 6–11.30pm
Accepts All major credit cards
Branches see p.489
ⓦ www.montys.uk.com

three different Monty's, all fiercely independent but each with the same name and logo. Unlike many small Indian restaurants, these are "chef-led", which is a key factor in making Monty's in Northfield Avenue an almost perfect neighbourhood curry house. You won't find banks of flowers or majestic staircases, the tables are too close together and you may be crowded by people waiting for a takeaway. But the cooking is classy, the portions are good and prices are fair. This is a restaurant that has a fine grasp of what its customers want.

A complimentary plate of salady crudités arrives with any chutneys and poppadoms ordered, but starters are the exception rather than the rule here – perhaps because of the well-sized main course portions. Trad tandoori dishes are good, like the tandoori chicken (£4.75 for two pieces). Or there is hasina (£6.50), lamb marinated in yoghurt and served as a sizzler. The boss here remembers introducing the iron-plate sizzlers at the Ealing Tandoori years ago and claims that his were the first in Britain. Breads are delicious – pick between nan (£1.75) and Peshwari nan (£2.50). But the kitchen really gets to shine with simple curry dishes like methi gosht (£7.25) – tender lamb (and plenty of it) in a delicious sauce rich with fenugreek; and chicken jalfriji (£7.25), which is all that the dish should be. Vegetable dishes also shine – both brinjal bhaji (£3.80) and sag paneer (£3.80) are delicious.

Monty's is one of very few local curry houses to serve perfectly cooked, genuine basmati rice. So the plain boiled rice (£2.10) – nutty, almost smoky, with grains perfectly separate – is worth tasting on its own.

North China Restaurant

The special Peking duck, which always used to require 24 hours' advance notice, is now so popular that the restaurant cooks a few ducks every day regardless. So you don't always have to pre-order. But then you do, because it is so popular that they cannot guarantee that you'll get one unless you order it. The North China has a 24-carat local reputation, it is the kind of place people refer to as "being as good as Chinatown", which in this case is spot-on, and the star turn on the menu doesn't disappoint.

£14 to £25

Address 305 Uxbridge Rd, Ealing Common, W3
℡ 020 8992 9183
Station Ealing Common
Open Mon–Thurs & Sun noon–2.30pm & 6–11.30pm, Fri & Sat noon–2.30pm & 6pm–midnight
Accepts All major credit cards
⊛ www.northchina.co.uk

CHINESE

Unlike most other – upstart, deep-fried – crispy ducks, the crispy Peking duck here comes as three separate courses. Firstly there is the skin and breast meat, served with pancakes, shreds of cucumber and spring onion, and hoisin sauce. Then there is a fresh stir-fry of the duck meat with beansprouts, and finally the meal ends with a giant tureen of rich duck soup with lumps of the carcass to pick at. It is awesome. And the price, £42, is very reasonable, working out at just over £3 per person per course. If you're dull and just want the duck with pancakes, the price drops to £32. So what goes well with duck? At the North China the familiar dishes are well cooked and well presented. You might start with barbecued pork spare ribs (£4.80), or the lettuce wraps (£3.30 per person, minimum two people), which turns out to be our old friend "mince wrapped in lettuce leaves" made with prawn and chicken. For a supplementary main course, prawns in chilli sauce (£7.25), although not very chilli, is teamed with fresh water chestnuts and tastes very good. Singapore fried noodles (£4.20) is powered by curry powder rather than fresh chilli, but fills a gap.

The genuinely friendly service at the North China stems from the fact that it is a family restaurant. If the genuine Peking duck does not appeal, perhaps you should consider the North China's other high-ticket item. When lobsters are good at market they go onto the menu at a seasonal price of about £22.50 per lobster.

RUSSIAN

Rasputin

You'll find the "Rasputin Russian Restaurant and Wine Bar" up at the Ealing end of Acton High Street. This restaurant used to be a dark cave-like sort of room, but after a refurb it is now, in the words of the proprietors, "modern". It's still a jolly place, and the

£14 to £30
Address 265 High St, Acton, W3
☎ 020 8993 5802
Station Acton Town
Open Daily 6–11.30pm
Accepts Mastercard and Visa

Russian specialities are homely and delicious, with an authentic emphasis on game in season. All this must be noted before you have made any inroads into the 20 different vodkas, which come both as single shots and – take care here – "by the carafe".

With the menu comes a plate of cucumber, cabbage, green tomatoes and peppers, all markedly salty and with a good vinegary tang. For a starter, try pierogi – rich little dumplings that come stuffed with a choice of potato and cheese, meat, or sauerkraut and mushrooms; they are all priced at £3.95 a portion. The blinis – small buckwheat pancakes – are also good; try them with smoked trout (£5.50) or, if you enjoy the special thrill of finding a bargain, with Sevruga caviar (£24.95). The Moscovite fish platter (£8.95) is also delicious. At Rasputin they are constantly tinkering with the menu and there usually seem to be several versions extant at once. Hold out for the golubtsy (£9.95), which is permanently under threat of banishment from the menu and is now called "cabbage parcels" – this is a simple but satisfying dish of cabbage leaves stuffed with meat and rice. Very wholesome and very good. Or there's a chicken Kiev made with tarragon butter (£9.90). Fish fans may want to try the salmon fillets in dill sauce (£10.95). Desserts are rather staid – crème brûlée (£3.50) or pancakes filled with a choice of chocolate, walnuts or fruit preserve (£3.50). Also interesting is the Russian tea served in a glass and holder. It is made with tea, lemon and a splash of vodka (£2.50), with a small bowl of honey alongside for sweetening.

If you are of fearless disposition (or possibly if you are a Russian exile), then the formidable game mixed grill is for you: wild boar chop, venison steak, pigeon breast, pheasant sausage and so forth, all for £14.95.

Sushi-Hiro

Sushi-Hiro is a very self-effacing sort of restaurant. The sign outside says "Sushi-Hiro, Japanese Gourmet Foods", and if it were not for the constant stream of Japanese people calling for sushi boxes to go, the blanked-out windows would make it look a bit like one of those very discreet "specialist" shops. When you push open the door you find

£15 to £40

Address 1 Station Parade, Uxbridge Rd, W5
℗ 020 8896 3175
Station Ealing Common
Open Tues–Sun 11am–1.30pm & 4.30–9pm
Accepts Cash only

JAPANESE

that half the room is given over to a waiting area for takeaway customers, there is a sushi counter with stools and a handful of tables and that's about it. The ceiling is high, the lighting bright, and all is spotlessly clean. It can be bit intimidating, but take heart: all the experts agree that Sushi-Hiro serves some of the best sushi in London.

The menu offers sushi in various guises. You are given a miniature clipboard with a small form to fill in your order and that's when it all gets tricky, as there are 50 or so boxes to tick. The best strategy is to start with the chef's selection of superior nigiri (£12), which brings 10 pieces of sushi – tuna, salmon, herring roe, turbot, bass, red clam, scallop, salmon roe, red bream and sweet shrimp. Try them all and then repeat the ones you like the most. The sushi here is very good: the rice is soft and almost warm, the balance between the amount of rice and amount of topping is just about perfect, and the fish is squeakily fresh and very delicious. When you've taken the sting out of your appetite with the chef's choice, consider trying a piece of eel (£1.80) – very rich; mackerel (90p) – a revelation, light and not oily at all; pickled plum roll (£2.20 for four) – made with rice, pickled plum and shiso leaves, an addictive flavour; or salmon roe (£1.50) - salty and sticky. Then round things off with a small bowl of rather splendid miso soup (£1), which comes with a couple of little clams lurking in the depths. These are all sophisticated flavours and textures.

This establishment works to Japanese rules, so beware of the opening times, which are "early" by European standards, and the cash-only rule, which means they do not even take cheques.

Earl's Court

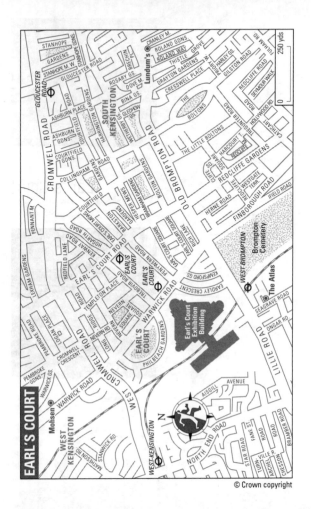

EARL'S COURT

© Crown copyright

The Atlas

(icon) Once upon a time, pubs were for boozing. You got sarnies maybe, and pickled onions if you were lucky. But fortunately The Atlas is part of the great gastropub revolution. This was the first gastropub set up by brothers Richard and George Manners and it works well; so well in fact that by 2003 they had added three more. George is IC the cheffing side: he trained at gastropub

£15 to £30

Address 16 Seagrave Rd, Fulham, SW6
☎ 020 7385 9129
Station West Brompton
Open Mon–Sat 12.30–3pm & 7–10.30pm, Sun 12.30–3pm & 7–10pm
Accepts Mastercard, Switch or Visa

headquarters – The Eagle in Farringdon (see p.191). The flavours come mainly from Italy with the occasional North African and Spanish diversion, but there are no concessions. The menu is chalked on the board at lunch and becomes a tad more formal in the evening; both depend on what's in supply and what has inspired the kitchen.

Starters may include a Tunisian chicken and chickpea soup with honey and cinnamon (£3.50); slow-roast tomato and Feta salad – capers, basil and rocket – bruschetta (£6.50); or a risotto all'Isolana – a Venetian risotto with pork, tomatoes and oregano (£6.50). Main courses range from grilled Italian sausages, spiced black beans with cumin and coriander, tomato and chilli jam (£8); roast tenderloin of pork with rosemary and pancetta, celeriac and chestnut gratin (£11); to grilled blue-fin tuna steak with peperonata (£11.50). Or there's Moroccan pheasant and apricot tagine – ginger, saffron and toasted almonds, couscous salad (£10.50). Or grilled rib-eye steak with roast field mushroom and cavalo nero with cream (£12). The dessert selection is short and to the point, with dishes such as baked quince with maple syrup, cinnamon and cream (£4), or Donald's chocolate and almond cake with ice cream (£4).

The wine selection is also chalked up, and there are some unusual offerings served by the glass, which makes The Atlas a good venue for wine lovers in search of a bit of impromptu tasting. Everyone else will be pleased to have found an eatery where you can get a decent pint. The Atlas is busy, noisy, friendly and young, and the food is good into the bargain. You're likely to end up sharing a table, so get there early.

Earl's Court

Lundum's

(🍴) This is a genuine family restaurant – four Lundums work in the business. This site on the Old Brompton Road is home to London's premier Danish restaurant. The Lundums would be the first to admit that there is not a lot of competition; in fact this may well be London's only Danish restaurant, which gives them something of a head start. There's nothing particularly Danish about the room, which is pleasantly light and airy with huge mirrors and a skylight: much the same as in previous incarnations. But the staff proudly produce interesting (and delicious) dill-flavoured aquavit, which they import specially. They also import the Danish sausages and all manner of other delicacies. The food is elegantly presented, competently handled and ... Danish. At lunchtime it's trad Danish; in the evening, modern Danish. You cannot help but be swept along by the tidal wave of commitment and charm.

£25 to £65

Address 119 Old Brompton Rd, SW7
℡ 020 7373 7774
Station Gloucester Road/South Kensington
Open Mon–Sat noon–11pm, Sun noon–4pm (brunch)
Accepts All major credit cards

At dinner (£17.25 for two courses, £21.50 for three) the menu, which changes seasonally, reads like a lot of other menus – smoked salmon gravadlax, roast lamb, pan-fried cod. Best, then, to visit at lunch (£12.50 for two courses, £15.50 for three), when there are more Danish dishes on offer. Go à la carte across the shoal of herrings (£4.50/6.25) – simply marinated, or spicy, or lightly curried, or sour with dill. As well as classic open sandwiches (£3.75–£7.75) you can also choose a smorrebrod m/lunt (£6.25 to £7.50) of fiskefrikadeller (fish meatballs) or frikadeller (meat meatballs). There are also platters: the Danish (£15.25) contains herrings, meatballs, plaice and salad; or there's an all-fish platter (£16.25). Or try the Medisterpolse (£9.75) – Danish sausage with red cabbage. Desserts are indulgent and the aquavit deadly.

"Gammel Ole – Danish Old cheese (18 months) served on rye bread and lard with onions, aspic and rum dripping" (£4.75). At first glance this dish, on the lunch menu, doesn't read well. But persevere, because it is really good, with flavoursome strong cheese and a seductive combination of tastes.

Mohsen

🍴 Just suppose that you are visiting Homebase on the Warwick Road. As the traffic thunders past, spare a thought for the people who still live here. For, indeed, across the road you will see signs of habitation – two pubs, one a Young's house, the other selling Fuller's beer, and between them Mohsen, a

£8 to £25

Address 152 Warwick Rd, W14
☎ 020 7602 9888
Station Earl's Court
Open Daily noon–midnight
Accepts Cash or cheque only

IRANIAN

small, busy Persian restaurant. This shouldn't come as a complete surprise, as you are not so very far from the nest of Iranian shops on Kensington High Street, but for somewhere so hidden Mohsen tends to be gratifyingly busy. There is nothing better than a loyal core of knowledgeable Middle Eastern customers to keep up standards in a Middle Eastern restaurant.

In the window is the oven, where the bread man works to keep everyone supplied with fresh-from-the-oven sheets of bread. This bread is terrific – wholemeal, large and flat, but not too flat, with a perforated surface and a sprinkling of sesame seeds that gives a nutty crunch. The waiters conspire to see that it arrives in a steady stream and never has a chance to get cold. The starters list is largely made up of things to go with the bread. You must have sabzi (£3), which is one of the most delicious and health-oriented starters in the world. It is a basket containing a bunch of fresh green herbs – tarragon, flat parsley and mint – plus a chunk of Feta. Eat it with your bread. Or there's maast o mouseer (£2.50), which is a dish of yoghurt and shallots. Or chicken livers cooked with mushrooms (£3). Homous (£2.50) is good. The main courses tend to revolve around grilled meat – joojeh kabab (£9.40), for example, is a poussin, jointed, marinated, grilled and served on rice. Then there is chello kabab-e-barg (£11), which is outstanding – a tender fillet of lamb flattened and grilled. It is traditionally accompanied by an egg yolk.

Look out for the dish of the day. On Wednesday it is kharesh badenjan (£7), a stew of lamb and aubergines. And always be sure to finish with a pot of aromatic Iranian tea (£3), served in tiny, elegant, gilded glasses.

Fulham

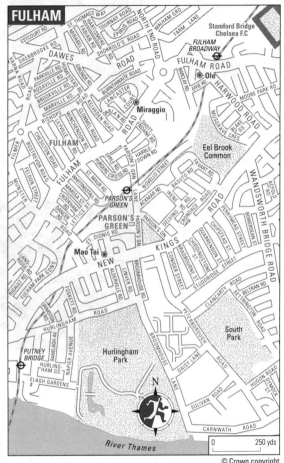

Mao Tai

(icon) Mao Tai is much more Chelsea than Chinatown, both in appearance and in the kind of food it serves. It's a pretty restaurant, cleverly lit, well decorated and with brisk, efficient service. The menu has recently undergone reappraisal and the ground has shifted away from the fiery Sichuan influences to something more suave. The clientele is just what you would expect from an area that is the very apple of any estate agent's eye. Such surroundings – and, to be fair, such food – do not come cheap. Still, you'll leave well fed and well looked after, as both the cooking and service are slick and chic.

£15 to £55

Address 58 New Kings Rd, SW6
(T) 020 7731 2520
Station Parsons Green
Open Mon–Fri noon–3pm &
6.15–11.30pm, Sat 12.30–3pm &
6.15–11.30pm, Sun 12.30–3pm &
6.15–11pm
Accepts All major credit cards
Branches see p.489
(W) www.maotai.co.uk

CHINESE

Start with steamed scallops (£7.85 for two). These are usually a pretty good indication of things to come, and at Mao Tai they are well cooked – just firm without having become rubbery. Salt and pepper prawns (£7.85) are very fresh but somewhat disconcertingly fried in their shells, so the lovely crispy bits end up on the side of the plate. Dumplings feature as in pork and ginger; prawn, chive and chilli; mushroom and spinach; and pea shoot and prawn (all cost £6.40 for six). Also good in the starters section are the salt and pepper Chesapeake Bay soft-shell crabs (£7 each). From the fish section choose Tianjin turbot steamed on the bone (£15.50) – these are serious restaurant dishes at serious prices – or perhaps sirloin strips with lemongrass and cracked black pepper (£12) appeals? The claim is that all dishes are made with free-range Angus beef. Onwards to sautéed chicken with orange blossom honey and pineapple (£8.50). Or rabbit with lemongrass and garlic (£8.50) – there is a modernist influence blowing through the kitchen here, perhaps in response to the opening of a second Mao Tai at the ever-trendier Brompton Cross. In the vegetable section there's broccoli in oyster sauce (£5.85), and seasonal pea shoots (£8.50).

In the face of all these rather exalted prices the Mao Tai feast (£24.70 per person for a minimum of two) and the set lunch (£12.50 per person) strike a welcome chord.

Miraggio

Bright café-style gingham table-cloths and a simple rustic air belie the quality behind this family-run establishment. Your first sign of this is the appetizing display of antipasti in the window. There are mouth-watering wafer-thin strips of char-grilled courgette and aubergine, nutty little boiled potatoes with virgin olive oil and roughly chopped flat-leaf parsley, strips of grilled peppers, small and large mushrooms and an aubergine and tomato bake with tiny melted Mozzarella cheeses. It's enough to stop even the most jaded foodie in their tracks.

£15 to £40

Address 510 Fulham Rd, SW6
℗ 020 7384 3142
Station Fulham Broadway
Open Tues–Thurs 12.30–3pm &
7.30–11pm, Fri 12.30–4pm &
7.30–11pm, Sat 12.30–4pm &
7.30–10.30pm, Sun 12.30–4pm
Accepts All major credit cards
except Diners

For starters, choose the antipasti della casa (£8.50) and you'll get the window dishes. Otherwise, try scamorza al prosciutto (£7), grilled smoked Mozzarella topped with ham, or melanzana alla Parmigiano (£6.50), baked aubergine rich with cheese. Pastas include the usual suspects, with some less familiar dishes like bucatini all'matriciana (£7.50), which is bucatini with bacon and tomatoes, or linguine zucchini e scampi (£9). There are plenty of meat and fish choices, too, including spigola all griglia (£14), grilled sea bass; calamari fritti (£13.50), a dish of perfectly cooked deep-fried squid; grigliata mista di pesce (£18) – the classic mixed fried fish; abbacchio scottadito (£10), simple grilled lamb; and filetto spinaci e patate (£15), a carefully cooked fillet steak with spinach and potatoes. If you're not already having spinach with your main course, try a side order of spinaci burro e Parmigiano (£4). Popeye would faint with pleasure. Puddings include what is claimed to be the best tiramisù in the area (£5), and zoccolette (£4.50), a home-made profiterole with a Nutella filling. The kitchen is open to the dining room, so you can see your food being cooked, which makes for great entertainment.

Also remarkable is that Miraggio is currently a bring-your-own-bottle establishment (£2 corkage per bottle), so your choice of wine is very wide indeed. This is a delightfully straightforward place, and a grand place to enjoy good home-style Italian cooking in Fulham.

Olé

(🍴) You can't miss Olé. It's bright and modern with blond wood everywhere, and right opposite Fulham Broadway tube. Olé is a combination bar and restaurant. The bar is open for drinks if you're not hungry and there's the restaurant at the back if you are. This is the sort of place where you may start by going for a drink, and end up eating and being pleasantly surprised by the food.

£15 to £40

Address Broadway Chambers,
Fulham Broadway, SW6
℡ 020 7610 2010
Station Fulham Broadway
Open Mon–Sat noon–3pm &
5–11pm, Sun 6–11pm
Accepts All major credit cards
ⓦ www.olerestaurants.com

The menu, which changes monthly, is modern Spanish and geared to tapas-style sharing. Larger main courses are confined to the daily specials board, and the reasonably priced wine list, which changes every three months, is exclusively Spanish.

The menu is divided into Frias (cold dishes), Calientes (hot dishes) and Ensaladas (salads). For the conventional there are favourites like jamón Serrano (£5.75), boquerones (£3.90), patatas bravas (£3.20), chorizo al vino blanco (£4.50) and gambas al ajillo (£4.95). The gambas are sweet and hot, with garlic, chilli and olive oil. For the more adventurous there are dishes like calabacín relleno de jamón y queso con almendros y crema de queso (£3.95). This translates as "layers of courgette stuffed with ham and cheese, topped with cream of almonds and cheese sauce". It is delicious, and incredibly rich. Tortillas abound here. Instead of just tortilla española (£4.10), there are four more: with pimentos (£4.50), with chorizo (£4.50), with tuna (£4.50) and with a spinach cream filling (£4.20). All are freshly made. Meat-eaters can enjoy tapas like solomillo de cerdo con verduras al vapor, a la esencia de mostaza (£4.80) – fillet of pork with steamed vegetables and mustard essence; carne de buey a la plancha con verduras y salsa de tomate y datiles (£4.50) – beef fillet with vegetables and date sauce; or pollo a la plancha con surtido de pimientos y crema de ajo (£4.50) – grilled chicken with peppers and cream of garlic. For the sweet of tooth there are eight puddings (all under £4).

Olé also features two notable Spanish beers: Estrella Galicia (£2.65), from northern Spain, and Damm (£2.70), from Barcelona.

Hammersmith & Chiswick

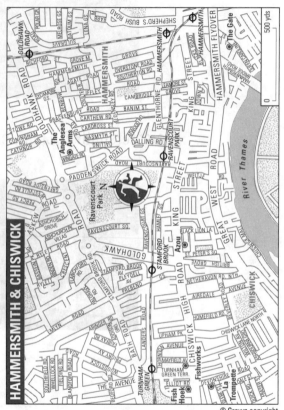

HAMMERSMITH & CHISWICK

© Crown copyright

The Anglesea Arms

Do not make the mistake of thinking that this establishment is merely a pub. The Anglesea serves very good food indeed, and as well as being one of the very first notable gastropub it is still one of the shining lights. The menu changes at least twice a day, dishes are crossed out as they run out, but when you've achieved "favoured local" status,

£11 to £27

Address 35 Wingate Rd, W6
℡ 020 8749 1291
Station Ravenscourt Park
Open Mon–Sat 12.30–2.45pm & 7.30–10.45pm, Sun 1–3.30pm & 7.30–10pm
Accepts Mastercard and Visa

MODERN BRITISH/GASTROPUB

you can ask for something simple that's not even on the board. Pitch up early, claim a seat, and not only will you dine well but you'll leave feeling good about the bill.

Who knows what will be chalked up on the blackboard when you visit? The menu is both eclectic and attractive, and prices have an upper limit of about £6 for starters and £11 for mains. You might end up choosing between Cornish mackerel rillette, beetroot, horseradish and chives (£4.95); and pigeon, quail and foie gras terrine, with brioche and onion marmalade (£5.95). Or between an open tart of aubergine, courgette, Feta and mint served with tzatziki (£4.75); and something simple like six Irish oysters, shallot relish and Guinness bread (£6.95). Main courses could be pot-roast stuffed saddle of lamb, white beans, curly kale and rosemary gravy (£10.25), or honest, market-fresh fish dishes like roast fillet of cod, new potatoes, clams, fennel, slow-cooked tomato and dill butter (£9.95); or seared gilt-head bream, savoury polenta, peperonata, black olives and basil oil (£10.25). To round things off, a British cheese in perfect condition, perhaps Cornish Yarg served with chutney, leaves and water biscuits (£4.75), or more puddingy-type puds like cherry clafoutis, crème fraîche ice cream (£4.50). This cooking is about as far from the kind of grub you'll be offered in a thousand chain pubs as you can get.

As befits food such as this, there's a wine list to match. A dozen wines are on offer by the glass, and the choice is thoughtful. Not very many restaurants, and very few pubs, offer a range of pudding wines by the bottle, half-bottle and glass – a far cry from the builders' overalls and pints of Guinness that once ruled the roost here.

Azou

Azou opened at the very end of 1999, so by London restaurant standards it can now claim to be old-established! It is a small, comfortable, informal North African restaurant where you can enter into the spirit and end up sitting on the floor on a cushion. This is a family business and the Benarab family go out of their way to make you welcome: service is attentive. The kitchen knows its business, and the classics – tagines, couscous, grills – are presented with some panache.

£10 to £30

Address 35 King Street, W6
☎ 020 8563 7266
Station Stamford Brook/ Ravenscourt Park
Open Mon–Fri noon–2.30pm & 6–11pm, Sat & Sun 6–11pm
Accepts All major credit cards

The menu is split into various sections. First there is a list of kemia, by way of starters. These are the North African equivalent of tapas and include all the favourites, from dips like hummus (£3.50) and baba ganoush (£3.95) to bourek (£4) – those little pastries filled with cheese or mince – and "briks" from Tunisia (£4.50), which are deep-fried filo parcels of potato, tuna and egg. Or there are foules mesdames (£4), a hot salad of broad beans. One classic that should not be missed is the mechouia (£4.50), which is a salad of grilled tomato and pepper. The main courses are arbitrarily divided up. Under "couscous", vegetarian (£8.50) teams vegetables and chickpeas; "fish" (£12) fish, shellfish and prawns, or there's "royale" (£14.50), which brings lamb shank, chicken breast and Merguez sausage. Under "Tagines" there's the tagine fish (el hoot) (£12.50); Casablanca (£9.95) is made with lamb shank, artichoke hearts and peas. Or the tagine el ain (£9.95), lamb shank with prunes, apricots and almonds. From the "Azou Specialities", the tagine romanne (£8.95) appeals – chicken in sweet and tangy pomegranate sauce with almonds, raisins and caramelized onions. These dishes are well made and fairly priced. There's a sound Moroccan wine for a reasonable £13.50 a bottle and an interesting beer from Casablanca (£2.90).

The ultimate dish at Azou is only available if ordered in advance. "Mechoul" is laconically described as a whole lamb, marinated, spiced and roasted. It is served with starters as a buffet for up to twelve people – a snip at £280.

Fish Hoek

£16 to £45

Address 6–8 Elliot Road, W4
℡ 020 8742 0766
Station Turnham Green
Open Tues–Sat noon–2.30pm &
6.30–11pm, Sun noon–3pm &
6–10.30pm
Accepts All major credit cards
except AmEx and Diners

At the end of 2001, Pete Gottgens opened this restaurant dedicated to South African fish. By 2003 it had proved so successful that he was able to close down his other nearby establishment and concentrate full time on fish. Which would not be surprising were it not that he has chosen to do so in leafy Chiswick, which is some way from the abundant waters of the Cape. But due to the efficiency of the air-freight industry, fish can be landed and iced in South Africa and then pitch up in W4 in about the same time as they would take to get from Aberdeen. The restaurant is a light and airy place with those glassed-in super-bay window areas that Parisians are so fond of jutting out onto the pavement.

The menu changes daily and features an impressive array of South African fish – 25 or so choices, and most of them can be had as half or full portions. Try out three half-portions and live a bit! Grilled Cape swordfish loin, garlic and honey-roast pumpkin, fresh chilli, garlic and chives (£7.50 to £15); Natal sardines, grilled with rock salt with mixed salad leaves and peri peri mayonnaise (£7.25 to £14.50); pan-seared Eastern Cape squid, lime and orange segments (£7.75/15.50); line caught Aghuilas musselcracker, new potatoes, spring onions (£9.25/18). The names and provenance are as exotic as the fish themselves. Some non-South African fishes stray onto the list – there may be Cuban mahi mahi (£7.25/14.75), line-caught Cornish sea bass fillet with sautéed potatoes (£15) – but the stuff from SA is well worth trying, as are the monster prawns from Mozambique called tiger giants (£16/29.50). Fish Hoek is a pleasant and informal restaurant where they take a good deal of trouble over simple fish cookery.

The walls are lined with Hemingway-esque black-and-white photos of big-game fishing. These are from the Gottgens' family albums and, if you look at the shot to the right of the door to the toilets, you can see the proprietor of Fish Hoek – he's the small boy trotting along beside his father and that enormous fish.

Fishworks

🍴 There's something spooky about this part of Chiswick; as well as a splendid array of food shops they now have two fish restaurants (see Fish Hoek p.433). One neighbourhood fish restaurant would be impressive, but to have a choice is remarkable. Fishworks opened in the spring of 2003 and is the London end of a chainlet that links branches in Bath, Bristol and Christchurch. The vibe is right at Fishworks. The front of the restaurant is a wet-fish shop that stays open until 10.30pm to make those dinner parties a tad easier and, hurrah, the fish looks and smells fresh. Inside is a pretty, modern dining room with a gardeny bit at the rear. Service is friendly and attentive, the wine list is interesting and not too rapacious; all in all a very satisfying place.

> ### £15 to £60
>
> **Address** 6 Turnham Green Terrace, W4
> ☏ 020 8994 0086
> **Station** Turnham Green
> **Open** Tues–Sat noon–2.30pm & 6–10.30pm
> **Accepts** All major credit cards except Diners
> ⊛ www.fishworks.co.uk

There's a longish menu and a very long list of specials on a blackboard. From the starters, crisp-fried goujons of sole (£7.50) are fresh, crisp and fried. Very nice. If the blackboard lists braised crab with wine and parsley (£8.50), pounce. This is terrifically good, a large crab in manageable hunks arrives at table in a copper pan with lots of buttery juice. Hours of fun. Or how about Cornish razor clams with garlic glaze (£10)? Or steamed River Fowey mussels with wine and parsley (£5.50/9)? Or grilled marlin (£13)? Or a "chunk of halibut with Hollandaise sauce" (£16.50) – very good indeed? There is a serious fruits de mer (£45 for two). And there are "whole fish – for the table": a wild sea bass for two (£18 per person); a Newlyn brill for five (£16 per person); or a turbot to feed four (£16 per person). Vegetables are simple and good, a dish of buttered spinach leaves (£1.75) is outstanding. The bread is good. This is a comfortable place where the fish are both skilfully chosen and skilfully cooked.

The wine list is eclectic and there are some interesting bottles at accessible prices. Start with half a bottle of cold Manzanilla San Leon (£12.50), and look out for the unusual Pazo Ribeiro (£16.75) – from Galicia: dry, white and zingy.

The Gate

The extraordinary thing about The Gate, which is tucked away behind the Hammersmith Apollo, is that you hardly notice that it's a vegetarian restaurant. This is enjoyable dining without the meat. It's not wholefood, it's not even healthy; indeed, it's as rich, colourful, calorific and naughty as anywhere in town. The clientele is a quiet and appreciative bunch of locals and pilgrims – it's unlikely that anyone could just stumble across this hidden-away, former artists' studio, which Adrian and Michael Daniel have leased from the nearby church since 1990. The airy decor and the high ceiling give it a serene, lofty feel, which may be The Gate's only nod to veggie solemnities. Basically this place is about good food and has been so successful that there is now a Gate 2 in Belsize Park (see p.245).

£16 to £35

Address 51 Queen Caroline St, W6
℡ 020 8748 6932
Station Hammersmith
Open Mon–Fri noon–2.45pm & 6–10.45pm, Sat 6–11pm
Accepts All major credit cards
Branches see p.489
ⓦ www.gateveg.co.uk

VEGETARIAN

The short menu changes monthly, but starters are always great. There's usually a tart, like the butternut squash and Gruyère tart (£5.75), which elsewhere, with its sophisticated salad, would be served as a main course. Also excellent are the couscous and Feta cheese fritters (£5.75), which have a pistachio crust and are served with a red and green coulis. Portions are invariably hearty, so it's a good idea to share starters in order to pace yourself and sample all the courses. The mains are generally well executed. Tortilla (£10.50) is a corn tortilla with two fillings – butternut with lime and beetroot and goat's cheese with turtle bean and chipotle chilli salsa. Or there's a red Thai curry (£9.50), made with a long list of vegetables. Puddings are splendid: there may be a tarte Tatin (£5.50); rhubarb and plum crumble (£5). Those without a sweet tooth should go for the cheese platter (£5) – it comes with oat biscuits and bread.

The drinks list is extensive, with all manner of freshly squeezed juices (£2.25), herbal teas (£1.50 to £3) and coffees (£1.35 to £1.75), while the wine list tops out at £24 (except for champagne) and has something for everyone – vegan, vegetarian, organic-only and carnivore alike.

La Trompette

FRENCH

(YI) La Trompette opened in 2001, and in the blink of an eye the restaurant had settled in, won the hearts and minds of Chiswickians and accumulated a lengthy waiting list for tables. This state of affairs wasn't a great surprise as Trompette is a thoroughbred from the same stable as Chez Bruce (see p.331), The Glasshouse (see p.395) and The

£25 to £65

Address 5–7 Devonshire Rd, W4
☏ 020 8747 1836
Station Turnham Green
Open Mon–Sat noon–2.30pm &
6.30–10.30pm, Sun 12.30–3pm &
7–10pm
Accepts All major credit cards

Square (see p.86). It's a pleasant dining room with a good deal of light oak and chocolate leather on show. The food is very good, the wine list is comprehensive, the pricing is restrained and the service is on the ball.

The prix fixe arrangements are straightforward: lunch is £19.50 for two courses, and £21 for three (rising to £25 on Sunday); dinner is £30 for three courses. The head chef is Ollie Couillard, who served time at both Chez Bruce and The Square. He is a very good cook. Dishes tend to have French roots and to be dependent on fresh, seasonal produce. The menu changes on a day-to-day basis. Presentation is simple but elegant. Starters may include such delights as grilled brochettes of duck hearts with chips cooked in duck fat and a ravigotte sauce; or seared scallops with pork belly, Jerusalem artichoke puree and lentil vinaigrette (which attracts a £5 supplement); or cream of garlic soup; or terrine de campagne – charcuterie is a strong point of the kitchen here. Mains are rich and satisfying. In the appropriate season you might be offered roast loin of veal with snails, ceps bordelais and truffled creamed potatoes; or a ragout of sea bream, oysters and mussels with champagne, crème fraîche and chives; or duck magret with foie gras sausage, caramelized apples and port sauce. Or two people may consider forking out the extra £10 supplement and having the côte de boeuf with chips and Béarnaise sauce. This is a very good restaurant indeed.

Puds range from classics such as an assiette citron; chocolate profiteroles; or gâteau Basque with rhubarb and orange compote; to superb savoury finales like baked Vacherin with garlic thyme, white wine and crusty loaf. Enjoy!

Notting Hill

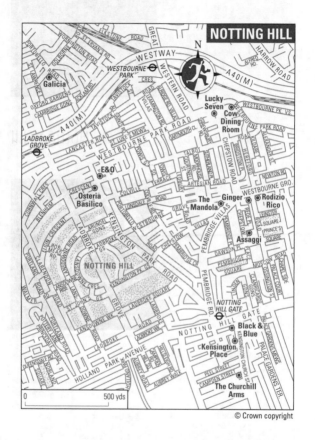

NOTTING HILL

© Crown copyright

0   500 yds

Assaggi

Assaggi is a small, ochre-painted room above The Chepstow pub. It's generally full at lunch and booked well in advance in the evenings. The prices are unforgiving and, on the face of it, paying so much for such straightforward dishes could raise the hackles of any sensible diner. But the reason Assaggi is such a gem, and also the

£32 to £70

Address 39 Chepstow Place, W2
℗ 020 7792 5501
Station Notting Hill Gate
Open Mon–Fri 12.30–2.30pm &
7.30–11pm, Sat 1–2.30pm &
7.30–11pm
Accepts All major credit cards

reason it is always full, is that selfsame straightforwardness. The menu may appear simple but it is littered with authentic and luxury ingredients, and the cooking is very accomplished indeed. Prepare yourself for a meal to be remembered.

You'll find a dozen starters – with the option to have the pastas as main courses – and half a dozen main courses. Start with pasta, maybe tagliolini con ragù di pesce (£8.95/10.95), a dish of perfectly cooked pasta with a fishy sauce. Or a plate of sensational bufala Mozzarella (£8.25). Or grilled vegetables with olive oil and herbs (£8.75). Or bresaola punta d'Anca (£8.25). Or there may be a dish like capesante con salsa alla zafferano (£10.95) – a simple plate of perfectly cooked, splendidly fresh scallops. Main courses are even more pared down: calf's liver (£15.95); a plainly grilled veal chop with rosemary (£18.95); branzino alla griglia (£19.95) – grilled sea bass. Those with serious intent can try the whole leg of milk-fed baby lamb – a dish for two people and with a wait of 45 minutes (£48). Particularly memorable. But even a humble side salad of tomato, rucola e basilico (£4.75) is everything you would wish for. Puddings change daily and cost £5.95. Look out for panna cotta – a perfect texture – and the beautifully simple dish made from ultra-fresh buffalo Ricotta served with "cooked" honey. To accompany, the short wine list features splendid and unfamiliar Italian regional specialities.

Assaggi is known for its bread. This is the famous Sardinian carta di musica – very thin, very crisp and very delicious. It's like a kind of Italian poppadom, only better. The name came about because, when well made, the papery texture is reminiscent of the sheets of vellum on which music was first written.

STEAK

Black & Blue

🍴 Say the words "steak house" to a Londoner and they immediately conjure up a very 1960s image – lots of tartan and red plush, with hapless tourists reaffirming their worst misgivings about British food. The time is right for a decent chain of steak houses. And Black & Blue may just be the first of a new breed. For a start, this establishment, which is part of gradually lengthening chain, has the very best provenance for

£12 to £40

Address 215–217 Kensington Church St, W8
☎ 020 7727 0004
Station Notting Hill Gate
Open Mon–Thurs & Sun noon–11pm, Fri & Sat noon–11.30pm
Accepts Mastercard and Visa
Branches see p.487

its meat. All the steak here comes from Donald Russell of Inverurie – the company which is king of the Aberdeen Angus beef trade.

Black & Blue certainly looks like a smart modern restaurant. There are banquettes, a good deal of wood panelling, a stylish bar and some rather nice vintage Bovril posters – a restaurant designer has been hard at work here. Starters are predictable. There's a prawn cocktail (£5) – half a dozen large prawns in pink stuff. Or you could have butterfly prawns with a sweet chilli dip (£5). Or there's that American abomination, a whole deep-fried onion (£5). Thereafter there are burgers (which are pretty good), an "all day breakfast", salads, baguettes, two chicken dishes, prawns and tuna – ignore them all in favour of the steaks. The steaks are good. Aberdeen Angus is well-flavoured meat and, commendably enough, when you say rare you get rare. Each steak comes with a very decent mixed salad of watercress, flat parsley and rocket – steer clear of the proffered dressings – and tolerable fries. There are five steaks offered: sirloin, rib-eye, fillet, T-bone and a côte de boeuf for sharing. Pricing is straightforward: sirloin 6oz/£12, 10oz/£16; rib-eye 10oz/£15; fillet 6oz/£16, 8oz/£19; T-bone 14oz/£19; côte de boeuf 21oz/£24. There's a small choice of simple desserts: chocolate mousse and lemon tart (both £5) are served with clotted cream.

The wine list is not long but is agreeably ungrasping and peaks at a bottle of premier cru Rully at £25, while there are simple reds on offer around the £12 mark, which is pleasant reading on any restaurant wine list.

The Churchill Arms

(🍴) In the ever-expanding field of pub restaurants, the Churchill is something of an old stager. It was possibly one of the first in London to offer Thai food. Do you wonder why we see so few pubs selling Indian food, incidentally? Or Chinese food? Could it be because of the grand profit margins on Thai cuisine? Well, whatever the motivation behind it,

£7 to £20

Address 119 Kensington Church St, W8
℗ 020 7792 1246
Station Notting Hill Gate
Open Mon–Sat noon–9.30pm, Sun noon–4pm
Accepts Mastercard and Visa

the Churchill has nurtured its clientele (who are largely students and bargain hunters) over the years by the simple expedient of serving some of the tastiest and most reasonably priced Thai food in London. The main dining area is in a back room featuring acres of green foliage, but don't despair if you find it full (it fills up very quickly) – meals are served throughout the pub. Service is friendly but, as the food is cooked to order, be prepared to wait – it's worth it. If you really can't wait, precooked dishes such as chicken with chillies (along with that other well-known Thai delicacy, Stilton ploughman's) are also available.

Dishes are unpronounceable, and have thoughtfully been numbered to assist everybody. The pad gai med ma muang hin-maparn (no.15 – £5.50) is a deliciously spicy dish of chicken, cashew nuts and chilli served with a generous helping of fluffy boiled rice.. The khao rad na ga prao (no.5 – £5.50), is described as very hot. Not an understatement. This prawn dish with fresh chillies and Thai basil is guaranteed to bring sweat to the brow of even the most ardent chilliholic. For something milder, try the pad neau nahm man hoi (no.17 – £5.50), beef with oyster sauce and mushrooms; or the khao rad na (no.3 – £5.25), a rice dish topped with prawns, vegetables and gravy. Both are good. Puddings are limited in choice and ambition, but for something sweet to temper the heat, try apple pie (£2.50) – a strange accompaniment to Thai food, but surprisingly welcome.

One of the refreshing things about the Churchill is you get restaurant-standard food with drinks at pub prices, and they even do takeaways in traditional foil trays.

Cow Dining Room

(🍴) The Cow is something of a conundrum. On the one hand it is a genuine pub – a proper pub, with beer and locals – and on the other, owner Tom Couran has managed to make it something of a meeting place for Notting Hill's smarter residents. Downstairs all is fierce drinking and cigarette smoke, while upstairs you'll find an oasis of calm and, at its centre, a small dining room. It is a good place to eat. The atmosphere is informal but the food is accomplished.

£20 to £55

Address 89 Westbourne Park Rd, W2
☎ 020 7221 5400
Station Westbourne Park
Open Mon–Fri 7–11pm, Sat 12.30–2.30pm & 7–11pm, Sun 12.30–3.30pm & 7.30–10.30pm
Accepts All major credit cards except Diners

The chef here is James Rix, who formerly served time in Alastair Little's Frith Street establishment. The menu changes on a daily basis and delivers fresh, unfussy, seasonal food, and if anything dishes are slightly cheaper than they were in the last edition of this guide – quite an unusual occurrence, but one that we should encourage!

Starters put together tried and tested combinations of prime ingredients such as wild garlic and white bean soup (£5.25); baked buffalo Mozzarella, roasted tomato and red pepper sauce (£7); breast of wood pigeon with lentils and salsa verde (£6.50); or Galician-style braised octopus with potatoes and paprika (£8). Main courses cover most of the bases, from aubergine and Ricotta ravioli with sage butter sauce (£15.50); through whole roast lemon sole with parsley and garlic butter (£13); to whole roast squab pigeon with sauté of morels, peas and pancetta (£17). The menu finishes triumphantly with slow-roast belly of "Old Spot" pork with black pudding and Pommery mustard sauce (£16.75). Puddings are a suitable mix of the comfortable and the desirable: crème brûlée (£4.75); chocolate mousse cake with a blood orange salad (£4.75); poached champagne rhubarb with custard (£4.50). Or you could go for cheese, which comes with the imprimatur that signifies well-chosen and well-kept cheeses – "Neal's Yard" cheeses with oatcakes (£6.25).

The menu encourages diners to commence proceedings with a glass of champagne orange cocktail (£6.50) or kir royale (£6.50). But the staff will happily fetch you some of the excellent De Koninck beer from downstairs if these more exotic fizzies don't tempt.

E&O

E&O (it stands for Eastern & Oriental) is geared to non-traditional eating. You're encouraged to abandon the starter and main course convention, and order a mix of small and large dishes to share. Cooking is based on Japanese with added eponymous influences. The venue itself is modern Japanese in feel and is relaxed at the same time as being stylish. Forks, knives, spoons and chopsticks sit in stone pots on the table, and cloth napkins are piled high. It's no-rules eating and your fingers are as useful as anything else. Staff are knowledgeable and take trouble to explain if you're unfamiliar with dishes or the spirit of the place. But even more than the taste, it is the presentation of the food that makes it exceptional.

£25 to £50

Address 14 Blenheim Crescent, W11
℡ 020 7229 5454
Station Notting Hill Gate/Ladbroke Grove
Open Mon–Sat noon–11pm, Sun 1–10.30pm
Accepts All major credit cards
Ⓦ www.eando.nu

ASIAN ECLECTIC

The menu divides into soups, dim sum, salads, tempura, curries, futo maki rolls/sashimi, barbecue/roasts, specials, sides and desserts. Edamame, soy and mirin (£3.00) is a dish of soybeans in the pod to pop and suck out. Fun and delicious. Among the dumplings chicken and snow pea (£5), and mushroom and chestnut, green tea dumplings (£6) stand out; chilli-salt squid (£5.50) is well-seasoned crispy squid served in a Japanese newspaper cone; baby pork spare ribs (£5.50) come with a sauce good enough to eat with a spoon. Oyster tempura (£2 each) is ambitious and delicious. In the barbecue/roasts section, black cod with sweet miso (£19.50) is as good as this fish gets. Under curries you'll find green five vegetable curry (£9) and mussaman lamb shank (£12.50). When you get to the puds you must choose from ices (£5); chocolate pudding (£6.50), which comes with a 20-minute wait; banana parfait with tempura banana and milk chocolate ice (£6.50); and a shockingly transcultural ginger tiramisù (£6.50). Wines are well chosen and reasonably priced, and there's a selection of six teas (£2.50) served in large Chinese pots.

E&O is deservedly popular, and it has two sittings for dinner. It is both essential to book and difficult to get a table. An option is the separate bar, which has a dim sum menu.

Galicia

As you walk up the Portobello Road it would be only too easy to amble straight past Galicia. It has that strange Continental quality of looking shut even when it's open. Only make it through the forbidding entrance, however, and Galicia opens out into a bar (which is in all probability crowded), which in turn opens into a small, 40-seat restaurant (which is in all probability full). The tapas at the bar are straightforward and good, so it is no surprise that quite a lot of customers get no further than here. One regular once confided that some of the best Spanish dishes he had ever sampled were given to him as tapas in the bar while he was waiting for a seat, and that when he finally got the elusive table he had eaten so much that he was forced to surrender it to someone in greater need. So, first secure your table ...

£14 to £35
Address 89 Westbourne Park Rd, W2
☎ 020 7221 5400
Station Westbourne Park
Open Mon–Fri 7–11pm, Sat 12.30–2.30pm & 7–11pm, Sun 12.30–3.30pm & 7.30–10.30pm
Accepts All major credit cards except Diners

...then cut a swath through the starters. Jamón (£4.50) is a large plate of sweet, air-dried ham; gambas a la plancha (£6.25) are giant prawns plainly grilled; and pulpo a la Gallega (£5.50) is a revelation – slices of octopus grilled until bafflingly tender and powdered with smoky pimentón. Galicia does straightforward grilled fish and meat very well indeed. Look for the chuleto de cordera a la plancha (£8.40), which are perfect lamb chops, or lomo de cerdo (£7.75), which are very thin slices of pork fillet in a sauce with pimentón. Or there's the suitably stolid Spanish omelette, tortilla (£5.25). And you should have some chips, which are very good here. The wine list is short but also full of opportunities for exploration – you may find yourself the proud possessor of a Vega Grand Riserva for just £18.90. Or then again, that bin may have run out.

Galicia is a pleasant place without pretension. The waiters are all old-school – quiet and efficient to the point of near-grumpiness. The overall feel is of a certain stilted formality. The clientele is an agreeable mix of Notting Hill-ites and homesick Iberians, both of which groups stand between you and that table reservation, so book early.

Ginger

(🍴) Given that nearly every curry house on nearly every high street in the land is owned and manned by Bangladeshi businessmen, you might think that Ginger, which serves traditional Bangladeshi food, would be pretty run-of-the-mill. Until you eat there, that is. This is a restaurant that offers genuine Bangladeshi home

£18 to £45

Address 115 Westbourne Grove, W2
ⓣ 020 7908 1990
Station Notting Hill Gate/
Bayswater
Open Daily 6–11pm
Accepts All major credit cards
ⓦ www.gingerrestaurant.co.uk

cooking. Not the sweet and tomatoey dishes worked up to suit the British palate, but the real deal. Expect lots of fish dishes, and delicious light stews (known as jhols). Plus attentive service, a thoughtful wine list, and some slick cocktails. But, most important of all, the men in the kitchen really know their stuff. Genuine Bangladeshi cooking has long deserved a decent showcase, and at Ginger it has finally got one.

There are some stunning dishes. Start with the bekti macher kebab (£4.50) – a firm white fish, given the tandoor treatment. From the other end of the spectrum, try the shingara (£2.95) – imagine a solid vegetable samosa that has been made with shortcrust pastry, like a deep-fried pasty. The katti kebab (£3.95) is also good – roast lamb in a kind of wrap. The difficult choices continue among the main courses. Surma macher biryani (£8.95) is epic – a fish biryani! Bangladeshis are besotted with fish – try the macher kobiraji (£8.50), which is an aromatic fish curry from West Bengal. Carry on to the raj ash kalia (£13.50), which is a Bengali stir-fry of duck; or the moni puri prawns (£13.50), a dish named after one of the tribespeople of Bangladesh. There are a good many prawn dishes on the menu – try the ajwani chingr jhol (£10.95), which presents king prawns in a thin sauce that is both hot and sour. Lau dal (£3.95) is a revelation: moong lentils cooked with white pumpkin and garlic. The parathas (£1.95) are very good – flaky and suitably self-indulgent.

Puddings are sweet. And when you are talking sweet in "Bengali" terms you are well off the normal scale. If you think you're up to it, just attempt the mishti doi (£3.50), which is a lurid, set yoghurt. Toothkind it is not.

Kensington Place

(Y) The first thing to know about Kensington Place is that it is noisy. The dining room is large, echoing, glass-fronted and just plain noisy. It's the racket of hordes of people having a good time. Rather than background music, there's the busy hum of confidences, shrieks of merriment, and the clamour of parties. The service is crisp, the food is good and the prices are fair. The menu changes

£18 to £60

Address 201–207 Kensington Church St, W8
☎ 020 7727 3184
Station Notting Hill Gate
Open Mon–Sat noon–3.30pm & 6.30–11.45pm, Sun noon–3.30pm & 6.30–10.15pm
Accepts All major credit cards

from session to session to reflect whatever the market has to offer, and there is a set lunch that offers a limited choice of three good courses for £16 during the week and £18.50 on Sunday. By way of example: you might have razor clams with parsley and garlic, followed by fricassee of wild rabbit with prunes and bacon, and then a chocolate and coffee Japonais with cocoa sorbet. This is fine value for money.

Rowley Leigh's food is eclectic in the best possible way. The kitchen starts with the laudable premise that there is nothing better than what is in season, and goes on to combine Mediterranean inspirations with classic French and English dishes. Thus you may find, in due season, starters like fish soup with croutons and rouille (£6.50), escarole salad with pears and Roquefort (£6), pumpkin and sage risotto (£6.50), or omelette fines herbes (£5.50). These are sophisticated dishes, and well-chosen combinations of flavours. Main courses might be cod with champ and prawn sauce (£15.50), noisettes of venison, "agro dolce" (£17.50), ballottine of guinea fowl with leek and apricot stuffing (£14.50), or steamed Dover sole with cucumber shrimps and dill (£19).

The dessert section of the menu offers what may be one of London's finest lemon tarts (£6) and some well-made ice creams (£5). There are also traditional favourites with a twist: bread-and-butter pudding made with panettone (£6.50), or hot bitter chocolate mousse (£6.50). And for hardened pudding addicts there is the ultimate challenge – the grand selection (£12.50). Indulge yourself (or share) and take a glass of Tokaji Aszu 5 Puttonyos (£5.50) alongside.

Lucky Seven

Following the success of the Cow (see p.442), Tom Conran has shifted his attention a few hundred yards up the road to a site which was previously a shabby and agreeably seedy little Portuguese café-restaurant-drinking den. Now it is the considerably glossier Lucky Seven, an American diner freshly trans-

£8 to £24
Address 127 Westbourne Park Rd, W2
☎ 020 7727 6771
Station Westbourne Park
Open Mon–Sat 7am–11pm, Sun 7am–10.30pm
Accepts Cash or cheque only

planted to Notting Hill. The kitchen runs across the back behind a high counter and the tiny dining area accommodates 36 people in two sets of booths. There are engraved mirrors. A Pepsi clock. Sally didn't meet Harry here, but doubtless she will soon.

The menu is on a peg-board over the kitchen and it opens with breakfast dishes: two eggs any style (£3.75); with sausage (£4.25); with bacon (£4.25); with Portobello mushrooms (£4.25) – wending its way through omelettes (£3.95) and eggs Benedict (£5.95) to buttermilk pancakes (£3.75). Then there's a section of "soups, stews, salads, sides" before it moves towards "sandwiches and fries". In the evening there's a blue-plate special dish (£6.50 to £8), which ranges from club sandwich to gammon and eggs. The range of chips (all £2.25) is formidable. You can have fries, fat chips, or home fries – the fat chips are best, well crisped and chunky. The fries are a little on the dry side (perhaps a tad too thin?), and the home fries are made from peel-left-on segments of fried potato that are so large as to seem claggy. The burgers are well made, although on the small side for serious trenchers – but, as they start at just £4.25 for the "Classic hamburger", perhaps that is best resolved by ordering two Classics. In the stews section you will come across such delights as New England clam chowder, chicken noodle soup, and a Cuban black bean chilli (all £2.50 a cup, £4.75 a bowl).

Lucky Seven is a small, agreeably informal place serving sound enough food at sound enough prices. It is full of vaguely trendy customers who seem to approve wholeheartedly of both grub and prices. And the fat chips are very good, needing no more than a hint of Mr Heinz's red elixir to attain perfection.

The Mandola

(YI) The food at The Mandola is described as "urban Sudanese", and as that means forgoing some of the more traditional Sudanese delicacies – strips of raw liver marinated in lime juice, chilli and peanut butter springs to mind – it seems like a good bet. This would be a small, seriously informal, neighbourhood restaurant but for the fact that it attracts people from all over town. They have not only taken over the shop next door, but have also had to institute a two sittings-a-night policy. Despite such minor irritations there's much to praise. The staff are so laid-back as to make worriers self-destruct on the spot. The restaurant is unlicensed, so everything from fine wine to exotic beer is available (corkage £2) – if you choose to bring it with you.

£12 to £22

Address 139–141 Westbourne Grove, W11
☎ 020 7229 4734
Station Notting Hill Gate
Open Mon 6–11pm, Tues–Sun noon–11pm
Accepts All major credit cards
🌐 www.mandolacafe.co.uk

To start there is a combo of dips and salads, rather prosaically listed as "mixed salad bar" for two (£10.50). There are a few Middle Eastern favourites here, given a twist, and all of them are strongly and interestingly flavoured. Salata tomatim bel gibna (£3.50) is made from tomatoes, Feta and parsley; salata tahina (£3.25) is a good tangy tahini; salata aswad (£4.20) is a less oily version of the Turkish aubergine dish iman bayeldi; salata daqua (£3.50) is white cabbage in peanut sauce; and tamiya (£4.75) is Sudanese falafel. All are accompanied by hot pitta bread. As for main courses, samak magli (£10.50) shows just how good simple things can be – fillets of tilapia are served crisp and spicy on the outside, fresh on the inside, with a squeeze of lime juice. Chicken halla (£9.50) is cooked in a rich, well-reduced tomato sauce that would be equally at home in a smart Italian eatery. Lovers of the exotic can finish with the Sudanese spiced coffee, scented with cardamom, cinnamon, cloves and ginger – you get your own flask and coffee set, enough for nine tiny cupfuls, for £4.

It is lucky that the bowl for the crushed green chilli with lime, onions and garlic (£1.75) is stainless steel, as the contents must be one of the hottest things in the known universe.

Osteria Basilico

Long before Kensington Park Road became the borough's hottest spot for outdoor dining, there was always a restaurant on this corner. When Duveen closed, the restaurant cat stayed on to have the next establishment named in its honour – Monsieur Thompson. Then, in its turn, Monsieur T became Pizza by Numbers. Finally, in 1992 came Osteria, which has flourished ever since. Daytime star-gazing is enlivened by arguments between parking wardens, clampers and their victims, while the traffic comes to a standstill for the unloading of lorries and for a constant stream of mini-cabs dropping off at the street's numerous restaurants. At dusk you get more of the same, with the streetlights struggling to make the heart of Portobello look like the Via Veneto.

£12 to £45
Address 29 Kensington Park Rd, W11
☎ 020 7727 9372
Station Ladbroke Grove/ Notting Hill Gate
Open Mon–Fri 12.30–3pm & 6.30–11pm, Sat 12.30–4pm & 6.30–11pm, Sun 12.30–3.30pm & 6.30–10.30pm
Accepts All major credit cards except Diners

Inside, pizza and pasta are speedily delivered with typical chirpy Italian panache to cramped, scrubbed tables. Go easy on the baskets of warm pizza bread, as the antipasti (£6) – various grilled and preserved titbits arranged on the antique dresser – are a tempting self-service affair. Of the other starters, frittura di calamari e gamberoni (£6.80) and carpaccio di manzo con pesto, rucola e parmigiano (£7.50) are both delicious. Specials change daily and have no particular regional influence – perhaps a classic like fettuccine con tartufo bianco, parmigiano e salsa al rosmarino (£13.50). Among the permanent fixtures, spigola alla griglia con olio aromatizzato (£14.50) is a simply grilled sea bass; while costolette d'agnello con pomodori freschi e melanzane (£12) is char-grilled lamb cutlets with fresh tomato and aubergine. Pizzas vary in size depending on who is in the kitchen – perhaps staff with shorter arms throw the dough higher, resulting in a wider, thinner base – but all are on the largish size. Pizza Diavolo (£7.50) comes with mozzarella and a good, spicy pepperoni sausage.

There's a house Chianti at £9.50, but it's much better to opt for the Montepulciano d'Abruzzo (£15.50), a pretty decent wine at a pretty decent price.

Rodizio Rico

BRAZILIAN

If you're a lover of smoky grilled meat, Rodizio Rico will come as a godsend. In southern Brazil this restaurant would be pretty run-of-the-mill stuff, but in W11 churrascarias are the exception rather than the rule. Rodizio can be a puzzling experience for first-timers. There's no menu and no prices – but no problem. *Rodizio* means "rotating", and refers to the carvers who wander about the room with huge skewers of freshly

£20 to £35

Address 111 Westbourne Grove, W2
☎ 020 7792 4035
Station Notting Hill Gate/
Bayswater
Open Mon–Fri 6.30pm–midnight,
Sat 12.30–4.30pm &
6.30pm–midnight, Sun 1–11pm
Accepts All major credit cards
except Diners

grilled meat from which they lop off chunks on demand – rather like the trolleys of roast beef at Simpson's in the Strand. You start by ordering and then help yourself from the salad bar and hot buffet. As the carvers circulate, they dispense bonhomie as they cut you chunks, slivers and slices from whichever skewer they are holding. You eat as much as you like of whatever you like, and then pay the absurdly reasonable price of £17.90 a head.

When you're up helping yourself to the basics, look out for the tiny rolls, no bigger than a button mushroom, called pão de queijo – a rich cheese bread from the south of Brazil. Also bobo, a delicious kind of bubble and squeak made from cassava and spring greens. Return to your seat and await the carvers – they come in random order, but they keep on coming. There's lamb, and ham, and pork, and spare ribs, and chicken, and silverside beef (called lagarto after a similarly shaped iguana!). Then for offal aficionados there are grilled chicken hearts. But the star of the show is picanha – the heart of the rump, skewered and grilled in huge chunks. Taste it and the arguments over the relative merits of rump and fillet are over forever – the "rumpers" would win by a landslide. Brazilians seem to revere the crispy bits, but if you want your meat rare you only have to ask.

South Americans rate the impossibly sweet soft drink Antarctica Guarrana (£2) very highly. "Just like the guarana powder you can get in the chemist's shop," they insist. If the lure of alternative rainforest stimulants doesn't appeal, house wines start at a reasonable £11.50 a bottle. And, as you would expect of a Brazilian establishment, the coffee is very good indeed.

Richmond & Twickenham

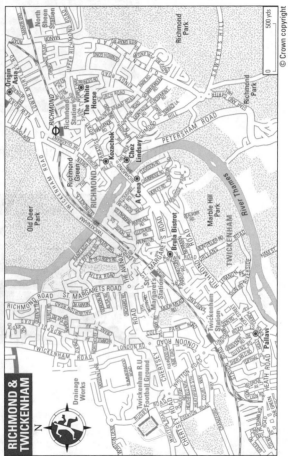

A Cena

If you stumble over Richmond Bridge towards Twickenham, A Cena is the first restaurant on the left. It is a relative newcomer and from day one has seemed an ambitious sort of place. This place is more Knightsbridge than Richmond, but seems to have survived those always-difficult first couple of years in some style. There is a bar area to the front that aims to tempt streetwise locals with modish cocktails; there are large displays of lemons; all is trendy, all is modern. The menu changes to suit the seasons and the markets, and the food is good – simple in the best kind of way, with clever combinations of flavour and texture. These are straightforward Italian dishes and all the better for that. The only caveat is that portions are on the small side, especially when viewed in conjunction with their price tags.

£20 to £50

Address 418 Richmond Rd, Twickenham, Middlesex
☎ 020 8288 0108
Station Richmond/BR St Margarets
Open Tues–Sat noon–2.30pm & 7–10.30pm, Sun noon–2.30pm
Accepts All major credit cards except AmEx

FRENCH

Dishes are admirably seasonal – start with the wild fennel soup (£5.50), or pan-fried sweetbreads with Marsala and artichokes (£8). Simple dishes like mozzarella di bufala with baked radicchio (£7.50) always appeal. The pasta of the day and the risotto are well made; dishes like a risotto Valpolicella (£6.50/11.50) vie with pea and mint ravioli with a spicy lamb sausage sugo (£7). Main courses read and eat well: grilled sea bass with braised cavolo nero, fennel seeds and capers (£15.50); veal cutlet Milanese with Swiss chard (£15.50); polenta fritters with tomato, spinach and Parmigiano (£12.75); or black pepper chicken with smashed artichokes (£15). The puds are good – the home-made espresso ice cream (£5) is truly awesome, and the chocolate tartufo (£5) is seriously rich, and so it should be.

Some pundit somewhere once defined the differences between French and Italian food by saying that while French cuisine uses skill and artifice to hide the shortcomings of poor ingredients, in an Italian kitchen the aim is to do as little as possible and allow truly wonderful ingredients to speak for themselves. Whoever it was hit the nail on the head. A Cena may just convince you it is true.

Richmond & Twickenham

Brula Bistrot

In 1999, two friends who worked in smart central London restaurants decided that the time had come to open their own place. They chose St Margarets as a locale and, as they were called Bruce Duckett and Lawrence Hartley, they called their restaurant Brula. It had a tiny, yellow-painted dining room and an equally modest kitchen. It was very much a family affair. Within 18 months Brula had become so successful that they had to move across Crown Road into larger premises. Now the Brula Bistrot (the name was enlarged, in keeping with the new premises) is no longer a cramped affair. There are large windows with a profusion of rather elegant stained glass. Thankfully, the food and philosophy have endured – well-cooked French bistro food, limited choice, low, low prices.

£11 to £25

Address 43 Crown Rd, St Margarets, Surrey
℡ 020 8892 0602
Station BR St Margarets
Open Mon–Fri 12.30–2pm & 7–10.30pm, Sat 12.30–2pm & 7–10.30pm
Accepts Delta, Electron, Solo or Switch

You have to admire anyone who has the good sense not to mess with something that works really well. Lunch at Brula Bistrot will cost you £9 for one or two courses and £11 for three. Extra veg (should you want any) costs a further £2.50; an espresso to finish is £1.50. The menu changes on a weekly basis, so you might face a choice of celeriac rémoulade, soft egg and chives; duck rillette with onion marmalade; or rustic fish soup with rouille. Then on to beef meatballs with thyme dumplings; fish of the day with soy and ginger dressing; or spinach and mushroom tart. Finally, your pick of the puds. All very French, and all rather nostalgic, evoking that dimly remembered rural France when you could pitch up at any bistro de gare and be sure of a good, cheap, satisfying meal. In the evenings they go à la carte (starters between £4.50 and £7.50; mains £11 to £13.50; puds £4) and add an extra dish to make four choices for each course – perhaps escargots de Bourgogne to start with, and venison steak with creamed endives and a red wine sauce to add gravitas to the main courses.

The Frenchness even extends to the list of suggested apéritifs at the top of the evening menu: kir (£3.50), Pilsener (£3), or kir royale (£7.50). And, should you spurn these blandishments, the wine list is short and agreeably priced – a Chablis Premier Cru Fourchaume was sighted at £25.

Chez Lindsay

At first glance, Chez Lindsay looks rather like Chicago in the 1920s – all around you people are drinking alcohol out of large earthenware teacups. The cups are in fact traditional Breton drinking vessels known as bolées, the drink is cider, and Chez Lindsay lists a trio of them, ranging from Breton brut traditionnel to Norman cidre bouché. This

£7 to £27

Address 11 Hill Rise, Richmond, Surrey
℡ 020 8948 7473
Station Richmond
Open Mon–Sat 11am–11pm, Sun noon–10pm
Accepts Mastercard and Visa

small, bright restaurant has had a loyal local following for a good many years. Most people are attracted by the galettes and crêpes, though the menu also includes a regularly changing list of hearty Breton dishes – especially fish. It's a place for Francophiles: both the kitchen and the front of house seem to be staffed entirely by Gauls, which in this instance means good service and tasty food.

Start with palourdes farcies (£5.95), where nine small clams are given the "snail butter" treatment – lots of garlic. Or the moules à la St Malo (£5.75), which are cooked with shallots, cream and thyme. Then you must decide between the galettes or more formal main courses. The galettes are huge buckwheat pancakes, large and lacy, thin but satisfying. They come with an array of fillings: egg, cheese and ham (£6.25); scallops and leeks (£8.75); Roquefort cheese, celery and walnuts (£6.50); and "Chez Lindsay" (£6.50) – cheese, ham and spinach. The other half of the menu features a good steak frites (£12.75) and lots of fish and shellfish. The "gratin de Camembert, vivanneau et crevettes" (£11.75) is an interesting dish – a gratin containing red snapper, prawns and Camembert. Or the bar grillé (£15.75) – a whole grilled sea bass with salad and new potatoes. Or even choucroute de mer (£13.25). Ask the amiable staff about off-menu goodies, which, depending on the market and the season, might be anything from exotic fish to roast grouse.

At lunch, the menu de midi delivers two courses – a salad and a galette – for just £5.99, and there is always a three-course prix fixe at £14.99. Real pud enthusiasts will save themselves for the chocolate and banana crêpe (£4.50).

Kozachok

Tourists will know Richmond as that funny little town on the Thames that cannot quite make up its mind whether it is in London or not. What is less immediately obvious is that it is also a good place to go and eat Ukrainian food. This is a significantly eccentric restaurant. Everything within is painted – bowls, decorative cruets, even the walls, have naive cartoon murals. And bunches of twigs have been used to decorate the ceiling. You will feel as if you have strayed onto a set during the filming of *Smiley's People*. Service is more akin to treacle than quicksilver, and the food is limited in choice and stolid in demeanour. "Why bother?" you will probably be asking. You should eat at Kozachok because you will enjoy yourself. The service is genuinely welcoming, the food is un-fussed-about-with and the vodka (along with the excellent Obolon Ukrainian beer) will leave you giggling irresponsibly.

£18 to £40
Address 10 Red Lion St, Richmond, Surrey
☎ 020 8948 2366
Station Richmond
Open Tues–Thurs 6.30–11pm, Fri & Sat 6.30–11.15pm, Sun 6.30–10pm
Accepts All major credit cards except Diners

There are half a dozen starters. Far and away the best is the blini. This is a large and fluffy creation, about 1in deep and 3in across, crisp outside, and very delicious – probably "best ever" when topped with aubergine ikra (£4.95), smoked salmon (£5.50), salmon caviar (£7.50), or – best of all – marinated herring (£5.75). Drunken salmon is also good (£6.95) – home-salted, vodka-cured salmon. Or there is ruletka (£4.75), which is sliced aubergine rolled around cheese. Mains include a Ukrainian speciality called varenki (£8.75), which is like grandparent ravioli filled with potato and cheese. From Siberia there are pelmeni (£8.75) – thick dumplings stuffed with mince and served with sour cream; not for the faint-hearted. Or there's shashlik (£8.95), a pork kebab which will seem a bit tame if you're drinking properly. Pud means mind-numbing and artery-clogging pancakes, as light as sandbags.

Vodka comes in a wide variety of guises here. And you will be fine right up to the moment when someone suggests beer chasers and you agree. Kozachok is a charming place, run by genuine people who have a real grasp of hospitality.

Origin Asia

🍴 The section of Kew Road that runs up to Richmond has always been something of a restaurant gulch. So it was no surprise when, in March 2002, Origin Asia opened its doors. This is an aggressively modern, markedly stylish, somewhat over-the-top Indian restaurant – all of which would count heavily against it if the food were not very good indeed. The large restaurant is divided into four sections, the most attractive of which is

£18 to £38

Address 100 Kew Rd, Richmond, Surrey
☎ 020 8948 0509
Station Richmond
Open Mon–Sat noon–2.30pm & 5.30–11pm, Sun noon–2.30pm & 5.30–10.30pm
Accepts Mastercard and Visa
🌐 www.originasia.co.uk

INDIAN

the one at the back with a grand view of the open kitchen. In the front section the "goldfish-bowl" feeling is just about mitigated by a rather splendid Indian glass chandelier; the middle sections are agreeable; but the back is the place to be.

Starters like chaman-ki-chat (£3.25) are most intriguing; this is made from fresh sharp fruits – apple, strawberry, kiwi fruit – cubed and made into a salad with chunks of boiled potato, cubes of salty home-made paneer (Indian cheese) and a tangy, spicy dressing. An original dish that works well. Or how about something from the tandoor? Go for adrak-ke-panje (£10.50) – five top-class tandoori lamb chops, with well-seasoned, tender meat. Like the surroundings, some of the dishes are a little over-the-top. Methi-ke-scallops (£12.50) is one of them – the scallops are perfectly cooked, soft and sweet, and the methi sauce is a belter, strongly flavoured and well balanced. But together? Try the gosht saagwala (£8.50) instead. This is an epic dish – a simple spinach and lamb curry, but the fresh spinach is still green and perky, the lamb is tender, and the sauce rich. A well-flavoured, traditional combination. Or chicken haramasala (£6.95) – an interesting green chilli paste. There are also plenty of vegetarian dishes that tempt – the Punjabi-di-dal (£5.95) is a good, buttery-rich dal. The breads are outstanding: lacchedar Kerala paratha (£2.25) is flaky and delicious, and there are rotis (£1.75). The simple jeera rice (£2.95) is also wholly successful.

There are a few tables outside, which will have a powerful appeal if and when there is weather clement enough to use them.

INDIAN

Pallavi

(icon) This is a small outpost of an extensive Indian restaurant empire. Pallavi is one of the simplest and the cheapest, and started its days as a large takeaway counter with just a few seats, then moved over the road from the original site to these smart new premises. The cooking has travelled well, and still deserves the ultimate compliment – it is genuinely home-style, with unpretentious

£10 to £23

Address 1st Floor, 3 Cross Deep
Court, Heath Rd, Twickenham,
Middlesex
℡ 020 8892 2345
Station BR Twickenham
Open Daily noon–3pm & 6–11pm
Accepts All major credit cards
⊛ www.mcdosa.com

dishes and unpretentious prices. True to its South Indian roots, there is an impressive list of vegetarian specialities, but the menu features just enough meat and fish dishes to woo any kind of diner.

Start with that South Indian veggie favourite, the Malabar masala dosa (£3.50). This huge, crisp pancake is made with a mixture of ground rice and lentil flour, and is a perfect match for the savoury potato mixture and chutney. There's also a meat masala dosa (£4.95), described on the menu as a "non-vegetarian pancake delicacy" – full marks for accuracy there. Or try the delightfully named iddly (£3.50), a steamed rice cake made with black gram, which is eaten as a breakfast dish in India. Whatever you open with, have some cashew nut pakoda (£2.95), a kind of savoury peanut brittle made with cashew nuts, which is wholly delicious. The main dishes are simple and tasty, and are served without fuss. For unrepentant carnivores, chicken Malabar (£3.95), keema methi (£3.95) or kozhi varutha curry (£3.95) all hit the spot. But there are also some interesting fish dishes, including the fish moilee (£5.95). Veggies are good too: try parippu curry (£2.15) – split lentils with cumin, turmeric, garlic, chillies and onions; or cabbage thoran (£2.50) – sliced cabbage with carrots, green chillies and curry leaves. The pilau rice, lemon rice and coconut rice (all £2.20) are tasty, and parathas are even better – try a green chilli or a sweet coconut paratha (both £2.50).

In this posh new incarnation, Pallavi is fully licensed, so you are no longer obliged to bring your own carryout. Thankfully, the lassi (£1) is still just as good.

The White Horse

All over town, pubs are being torn away from the traditional breweries and transformed into ever trendier gastropubs, but in this instance Fuller's brewery were somewhat ahead of the game. Several years ago they gave a free hand to the management at one of their pubs in Richmond and encouraged them to modernize their approach to the food they offered. A number of chefs have

£12 to £30

Address Worple Way, Richmond, Surrey
☎ 020 8940 2418
Station Richmond
Open Mon–Sat noon–3pm & 6.30–10pm, Sun noon–4pm & 6.30–9pm
Accepts All major credit cards except Diners

MODERN BRITISH/GASTROPUB

come and gone, but the White Horse is still something of a jewel in Fuller's crown – particularly if you want to eat out. The pub is still a pub, dark decor but with good, large tables that are well spread out – no sitting in your neighbour's pocket here. The food and pricing are also spot-on, as is confirmed by a steady trade.

The menu is a short one, and all the better for it. Half a dozen starters and five main courses change twice a day to accommodate whatever is best from the market. There might be parma ham and rocket salad with Parmesan shavings (£5.50). Or a broccoli and goat's cheese soup with croutons (£3.75); char-grilled tuna steak with green olives, French beans and tomato (£6); or Stilton and roast vegetable melt on toasted olive bread (£5). Main courses are also simple, like pan-fried cod fillet (£10.50), which comes with caper butter and new potatoes); or the linguine with pesto cream, rocket and grilled asparagus (£7.50). Or roast pork with crackling and apple sauce, roast potatoes and winter vegetables (£10.50). The wide-ranging wine list tops out while still reasonably priced. What's more, there is the intelligent option of a 250ml glassful of any one of seven different wines (£4). Puds are seasonal, so you might be tempted by bread-and-butter pudding with crème anglaise (£4.50), or banana tarte Tatin with vanilla ice cream (£4.50). And if they don't get you, then the dark chocolate pot (£4.50) probably will.

The lunch menu is a more reserved version of the evening offering, but one that features some interesting sandwiches, How does minute steak with roast wild mushrooms (£6) sound? Or smoked salmon, cucumber and capers (£5.50)?

The White Horse

Shepherd's Bush & Olympia

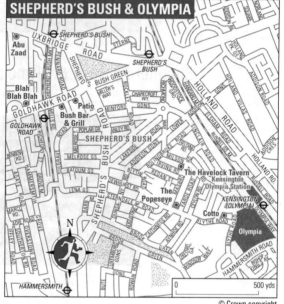

SHEPHERD'S BUSH & OLYMPIA

Abu Zaad

Blah Blah Blah

UXBRIDGE ROAD

SHEPHERD'S BUSH

SHEPHERD'S BUSH

SHEPHERD'S BUSH GREEN

MILLER'S WAY

CHARECROFT WY.

MINFORD GDNS.

GOLDHAWK ROAD

Patio
Bush Bar
& Grill

GOLDHAWK ROAD

BENBOW RD.

SHEPHERD'S BUSH ROAD

SHEPHERD'S BUSH

POPLAR GR.

ANLEY RD.

MELROSE GS.

BATOUM GS.

LAKESIDE RD.

LENA GS.

DEWHURST RD.

STERNDALE RD.

BLYTHE RD.

REDAN S.

IRVING RD.

MELINA

The Havelock Tavern
Kensington
Olympia Station

The
Popeseye

Cotto

BLYTHE ROAD

KENSINGTON
(OLYMPIA)

Olympia

HOLLAND ROAD

HOLLAND VILLAS ROAD

ADDISON ROAD

RUSSELL RD.

FESTING RD.

HAMMERSMITH ROAD

N

BROOK GREEN

BUTE GDNS.

ROWAN RD.

HAMMERSMITH

0   500 yds

© Crown copyright

Abu Zaad

To reach the dining room here you must first wend your way through lots of tables full of happy people, some grazing by the pastries (£4.30 per lb), some gossiping in front of the counter filled with the numerous meze, some at the coffee-making area. Then turn left at the open kitchen, where there's a char-

£12 to £20

Address 29 Uxbridge Rd, W12
℡ 020 8749 5107
Station Shepherd's Bush
Open Daily 11am–11pm
Accepts All major credit cards except AmEx

coal grill, stews ready for reheating, and a full-sized bread oven. Abu Zaad is a busy place and a friendly one – the food is good and awesomely cheap. Finally you go up a few steps to a raised area, where the rich green walls look as if they are decorated with metal panels. Very Damascene.

This may be the cheapest place in London to experiment with meze, as (whether hot or cold) most cost about £2. Here £2 will buy you a large portion of makanic – meaty, chipolata-sized sausages; baba ganouj – delicious aubergine mush; or foul medames – boiled fava beans with chickpeas, tomato and lemon juice; or hummus. A stunning haystack of tabbouleh is more expensive at £2.50, but comes with spankingly fresh chopped parsley and mint. Ordering a dish called falafi (£1.50) brings four crisp and nutty falafel. You must try the fattoush (£2), a fresh, well-dressed salad with croutons of deep-fried flatbread. In fact, all meze you order will arrive with a basket of delicious fresh flatbread. The food is described on the menu as "Damascene Cuisine" but most of these dishes are claimed by every Middle Eastern chef. Drink a glass of carrot and apple juice (£1.50) and feel healthy. The menu goes on to list dozens of main courses, from rich casseroles to charcoal grills, and they are all priced at about £4.90. There's a good case for not bothering with a main course here; simply order seven or eight meze between two.

On the menu at Abu Zaad there is a two-stage cartoon of a man with a donkey cart making collections and deliveries; the caption runs as follows: "Mr Abu Zaad used to collect meals from traders' wives and deliver them to traders in the souk." Things are different in the Uxbridge Road, but it's easy to imagine that the food is just as good.

VEGETARIAN

Blah Blah Blah

(🍴) Following an unkind comment in an earlier edition of this guide (something along the lines of "looks a bit like a funeral parlour"), Blah repainted the outside and now faces the world in deep maroon with gold lettering. Inside the status is still quo. The floors, tables and chairs are wooden, there are blinds rather than curtains, and the only decorations of note are driftwood and old iron lamps. Add wallpaper music and the echoing noise levels become formidable. It is alleged that this is the restaurant where Paul McCartney asked for the music to be turned down.

£16 to £25
Address 78 Goldhawk Rd, W12
☏ 020 8746 1337
Station Goldhawk Road
Open Mon–Sat 12.30–2.30pm & 7–11pm
Accepts Cash or cheque only

The menu casts its net not widely and you can expect dishes with all manner of influences. Among the starters there may be cream of asparagus soup (£3.95); an avocado, citrus and Mexican salad (£4.95) – the Mexican interest being represented by tortilla chips; a Greek salad (£4.50); and an aubergine, chickpea and spinach puri (£4.95) – pepped up with a pathia sauce and a brinjal pickle. Dodging over to Italy, there's a tortino made with sweet potatoes (£4.95) – roast sweet potatoes and leeks in the Italian answer to a soufflé. Main courses are similarly eclectic. Saffron fazzoletti (£9.50) is handkerchief pasta layered with Mozzarella and Jerusalem artichokes. And there may be a Indonesian laksa (£9.95) – noodles with tofu spring rolls in spicy coconut broth; or a simple roast fennel tart (£9.95) – puff pastry, the fennel cooked with cream and white wine. Or roast pumpkin tyropizza (£9.50), with Feta and filo adding the Greek elements to this dish. Puds (all £4.95) are rewarding: chocolate and pear tart with ice cream; white chocolate muffin; or banana and toffee profiteroles with butterscotch sauce to keep the local dentists prosperous.

Blah Blah Blah offers well-prepared food that just happens to be vegetarian, rather than the kind of heavy, wholemeal and meaningful fare you would expect from a more in-your-face vegetarian restaurant. It is unlicensed, so bring your own. There is a very reasonable corkage charge of £1.25 per person.

Bush Bar & Grill

The Bush end of the Goldhawk Road was once the preserve of curry houses, cafés, the street market and a pie-and-mash shop. In 2001 they were joined by the Bush Bar, full of renegade stylistas who had migrated west from Notting Hill. You could see this place as a successful bridgehead for the sophisticated, complete with serried ranks of bottles, smart raised booths and smartly dressed punters. The large dining area is busy and the whole place has an agreeable buzz to it.

£12 to £45

Address 45a Goldhawk Rd, W12
☎ 020 8746 2111
Station Goldhawk Road
Open Mon–Sat noon–3pm &
6.30–11.30pm, Sun noon–4pm &
6.30-10.30pm
Accepts Mastercard and Visa
ⓦ www.bushbar.co.uk

MODERN BRITISH

The Bush Bar & Grill captures the informal, pacey bustle of a classic brasserie rather well. Service is brisk and with attitude, and the food comes flying out over the pass from an open kitchen that runs the length of the room. The menu changes on a monthly basis and in 2003 they adopted a policy of sourcing as much British produce as possible, and favouring organic producers. Starters may include butter bean and morel soup, truffle oil (£5.25); pressed quail terrine, soused grapes and rocket (£5.75); and fresh Cornish crab cake, sweet chilli dressing (£7.75). Salads range from avocado, tomato and pousse (£5.50/8.50) to a squid and crispy pork salad (£7/11.50). From the grill there's sea bass fillet, grilled baby courgettes, rocket and chilli salsa (£13.75); and Aberdeen Angus rib-eye steak and chips (£15.50) – all the beef here is from Donald Russell of Inverurie. Puddings are a tad predictable: bread-and-butter pudding (£4); tarte Tatin (£4.50); crème brûlée (£4). This restaurant has the measure of its customers, serves admirably unfussy food, and has prices that are grounded in reality. The wine list at the Bush Bar & Grill is also extremely encouraging. In such a chic establishment, a reliable house wine (Armit's French Red or White) priced at £11 deserves a warm welcome, and even a top bottle like Château Leoville Barton 1997 has an agreeably ungrasping price tag of £52.

There's a good-value set menu that runs at lunch and pre-theatre (6.30pm to 7.30pm): £12.50 for two courses and £15.50 for three. That should tempt them away from the nearby BBC canteen.

MODERN BRITISH

Cotto

(icon) From the outside, Cotto, which stands on a corner site in a residential neighbourhood behind Olympia, is nothing special. Acres of plate-glass frontage reveal a sprinkling of tables around a large central bar area. Once you have taken in the clean white walls, the dark ribbed carpet and the collection of primary-coloured abstract paintings on

£15 to £50

Address 44 Blythe Rd, W14
℡ 020 7602 9333
Station Kensington (Olympia)
Open Mon–Fri noon–2.30pm &
7–10.30pm, Sat 7–10.30pm
Accepts All major credit cards

the walls, there is precious little decoration … and therefore minimal distraction from the real purpose of this restaurant, which is to provide good grub for discerning local residents.

The balance of the menu will strike a chord with foodies. Though the restaurant has an Italian name (*cotto* means "cooked"), its menu draws from both English and French traditions. It seems that the cooking is firmly rooted in the best of all approaches: treating ingredients with respect and striving to get the most out of each of them. The menu – which changes regularly to follow the seasons – is not long, but there's plenty of variety, and the deal is a simple one: two courses for £15.50 and three for £18. The six starters might include a celeriac soup; a house terrine; or salt cod and pancetta flan with parsley sauce. Main courses usually include a proper vegetarian choice, such as a wild mushroom risotto, as well as a couple of fish options, like baked sea bream with cuttlefish and bouillabaisse sauce; or seared scallops with lentils and garlic mash (one of the few selections that attracts a supplement, of £4.50). Meat dishes may include braised belly pork with leeks and truffles; and poached breast and roast leg of chicken. Puddings, such as pecan and cranberry tart, or chocolate and griottines terrine, will please any sugar addict.

Eating at Cotto is a satisfying experience, and the food is served with good manners and grace. You should be aware, though, that the bill can escalate, especially if you give the wine list full play. But a visit for lunch is much more affordable: two courses are offered at £12, and three at £15. The dishes may not be as complex, but the same philosophy applies as at dinner.

The Havelock Tavern

The Havelock is one of those pubs marooned within a sea of houses; in this instance it's the sea of houses just behind Olympia. It's a real pub, with a solid range of beers as well as an extensive wine list. What is most attractive, though, is the attitude that lies behind the menu, which is chalked up daily on the blackboard. As the chef half of the pro-

£8 to £25

Address 57 Masbro Rd, W14
℡ 020 7603 5374
Station Shepherd's Bush
Open Mon–Sat 12.30–2.30pm &
7–10pm, Sun 12.30–3pm &
7–9.30pm
Accepts Cash or cheque only

prietorial partnership says, "We're in the business of feeding people." And that's just what they do, serving up seasonal, unfussy food – the kind of fresh, interesting, wholesome stuff you wish that you could get around to cooking for yourself. The bar seats 75 and during the summer there's a terrific garden complete with vines and a pergola. Service involves stepping up to the bar and ordering what you want, so there's no service charge to bump up what are very reasonable prices indeed.

The menu is different every session, with more "one-hit" dishes served at lunch, when most customers are pressed for time. Starters might be deep-fried monkfish, Vietnamese dipping sauce and lime (£6); spiced red lentil and coriander soup (£4); chorizo, chickpea, snail and tomato stew with crostini (£5.50); or deep-fried buffalo Mozzarella fritters, with roast tomatoes, baby spinach, black olive dressing (£6). Main courses range from pot au feu of salt beef, spring greens, new potatoes, carrots and apple crème fraîche (£8.50); to roast fillet of cod, mashed potato, spinach, bacon and red wine sauce (£10.50). Or a classic like slow-cooked Chinese belly pork, with noodles and bok choi (£9.50). Puddings are equally reliable – try the warm rice pudding with prunes and Armagnac (£4), or the toasted banana bread, butterscotch sauce and vanilla ice cream (£4).

A great deal of effort goes into selecting slightly unusual wines for the blackboard wine list. Many of them are offered at bargain prices, but the biggest seller is still a glass of the house red. Popular rumour has it that the Havelock is one of Simon Hopkinson's favourite eateries. No wonder.

Patio

(🍴) The ebullient Eva Michalik (a former opera singer) and her husband Kaz have been running this Shepherd's Bush institution for more than a decade, and it's not hard to see why the show is still on the road. At Patio you get good, solid Polish food in a friendly, comfortable atmosphere, and for a relatively small amount of money. And this little restaurant is a people-pleaser – you

£13 to £26

Address 5 Goldhawk Rd, W12
℡ 020 8743 5194
Station Goldhawk Road/
Shepherd's Bush
Open Mon–Fri noon–3pm &
6pm–midnight, Sat & Sun
6pm–midnight
Accepts All major credit cards

can just as easily come here for an intimate tête-à-tête as for a raucous birthday dinner. The food is always reliable and sometimes it's really excellent. There are two floors; downstairs feels a little cosier and more secluded.

The set menu (available at lunch and dinner) is Patio's trump card. For £12.90 you get a starter, main course, dessert, petits fours … and a vodka. The menu changes daily – ask Eva to tell you what's new and you could get something that's not yet listed. Starters may include plump and tasty blinis with smoked salmon; wild mushroom soup; Polish ham; and herrings with soured cream. Everything is fresh and carefully prepared. For mains, there's a good selection of meat, fish and chicken dishes – the scallops in dill sauce, when available, are outstanding. Or you might try a Polish speciality such as golabki (cabbage stuffed with rice and meat), which is also available as a vegetarian dish; or chicken Walewska (chicken breast in fresh red pepper sauce); or sausages à la Zamoyski (grilled with sautéed mushrooms and onions). Main dishes come with a hearty selection of vegetables such as roast potatoes, broccoli and red cabbage. Be prepared, too, for high-octane puds, such as the Polish pancakes with cheese, vanilla and rum – the fumes alone are enough to send you reeling. Also good is the hot apple charlotka with cream. For those after more variety, including a scattering of non-Polish dishes, the à la carte offers further choice, and for not a great deal more money.

Patio is a good night out. The piano crammed in near the entrance is often put to use by a regular customer, and there are frequent sightings of a roving Gypsy quartet.

The Popeseye

Just suppose you fancy a steak. A good steak, and perhaps a glass (or bottle) of red wine to go with it. You're interested enough to want the best, probably Aberdeen Angus, and you want it cooked simply. The Popeseye is for you. This quirky restaurant is named after the Scottish word for rump steak, and every week the proprietor buys his meat not from Smithfield or a catering butcher, but from the small butcher his family uses in the north of Scotland. The meat is Aberdeen Angus and the restaurant is a member of the Aberdeen Angus Society. The dining room is small, things tend to be chaotic, and the atmosphere is occasionally pretty smoky. As to the food, there is no choice: just various kinds of steak and good chips, with home-made puddings to follow. Oh, and the menu starts with the wine list. You choose your drink, and only when that's settled do you choose your steak – specifying, of course, the cut and the size (and they come very big here), and how you want it cooked.

£18 to £80

Address 108 Blythe Rd, W14
☎ 020 7610 4578
Station Hammersmith
Open Mon–Sat 7–10.30pm
Accepts Cash or cheque only
Branches see p.489

STEAK

There are those times when, for nearly everyone, only a large piece of meat will do. You may have curry days, fish days or pasta days, but for red meat days the Popeseye really hits the spot. Now – about these steaks. Popeseye comes in 6oz, 8oz, 12oz, 20oz and 30oz (at £9.45, £12.45, £16.95, £21.95 and £32), as does sirloin (£12.45, £15.45, £19.95, £25.45 and £38), and fillet (£13.95, £18.45, £22.95, £31.45 and £45.50). All prices include excellent chips, and a side salad is an extra £3.45. Puddings are priced at £4.75 and come from the home-made school of patisserie – such delights as apple crumble, sticky toffee pudding and lemon tart.

The wine list is an ever-changing reflection of what can be picked up at the sales and represents good value. There are fine clarets and Burgundies, plus the best of the Rhône, Australia, Argentina, Chile and Spain – and there are also two white wines on offer for people who have lost the plot. Ask advice. People have been seen here happily drinking Château La Lagune 1986 for £75 a bottle, which – despite being a tidy sum –is also a bargain.

Southall

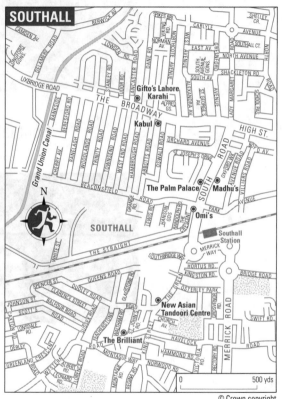

SOUTHALL

The Brilliant

The Brilliant is a Southall institution. For more than twenty years the Anand family business has been a nonstop success and it is now a bustling 250-seater. For 25 years before that, the family's first restaurant, also called The Brilliant, was the toast of Kenya. The food at The Brilliant is East African-Asian, and very good indeed. There are changes afoot here in that you can see that the Anand family is pulling back slightly.

£15 to £30

Address 72–76 Western Rd,
Southall, Middlesex
☏ 020 8574 1928
Station BR Southall
Open Tues–Fri noon–2.30pm &
6pm–midnight, Sat & Sun
6–11.30pm;
Accepts All major credit cards
ⓦ www.brilliantrestaurant.com

There are some new chefs in the kitchen and, starting in 2003, the restaurant no longer closed for August – presumably the Anands no longer feel that they have to do it all themselves. It is also to be expected that as The Brilliant starts hiring chefs from outside, so the menu will go more mainstream. Let's hope that the legendary high standards prevail.

To start with, you must try the butter chicken (£8 half, £16 full). A half-portion will do for two people as a starter. This dish is an enigma: somehow it manages to taste butterier than butter itself – really delicious. There's also jeera chicken (£8/16), rich with cumin and black pepper. And chilli chicken (£9/18), which is hot, but not quite as hot as it used to be! If you're in a party, move on to the special menu section – these come in two portion sizes, suggested for three people and five people. Methi chicken (£17.50/32.50), masaladar lamb (£17.50/32) and palak chicken (£17.50/32) are all winners. Alternatively, choose from among the single-portion curries, which include masala talapia (£9), a fish curry of unimaginable richness with good firm chunks of boneless fish. Well-cooked basmati rice costs £3.50 and, as well as good rotis (£1), the breads list hides a secret weapon, the kulchay (£1). This is fried, white-dough bread, for all the world like a very flat doughnut. Hot from the kitchen they are amazing – it's best to order a succession so that they don't go cold.

Ask to try the pickles – carrot, sharp mango and hot lime. They are splendid. And the Kenyan beer Tusker (£2.50), with its label rather engagingly designed like a banknote.

Gifto's Lahore Karahi

🍴 In Southall they know a good thing when they taste it. Gifto's Lahore Karahi specializes in freshly grilled, well-spiced meats and exceptionally good breads, backed up by a few curries and one or two Lahori dishes. It is a sign of the towering success that there have been regular renovations, refurbs and expansion but the emphasis is still on a no-frills operation. A row of grinning

£9 to £17

Address 162–164 The Broadway, Southall, Middlesex
☎ 020 8813 8669
Station BR Southall
Open Mon–Thurs noon–11.30pm, Fri–Sun noon–midnight
Accepts All major credit cards
ⓦ www.gifto.com

chefs seem to juggle with the three-foot skewers as meat goes into the tandoor caked in a secret marinade and comes out perfectly cooked and delicious. Despite having 100 seats downstairs and the same again upstairs, there is a still a queue outside at the weekend.

Whatever else you order, you need some bread. Peshwari nan (£1.80) is a triumph, hot from the oven, flavoured with garlic and fresh herbs, and liberally slathered with ghee and sesame seeds. It's hard to imagine it bettered. To accompany it, you might start with an order of chicken tikka (£3.80), which is juicy and strongly spiced. Or go straight for a portion of five lamb chops (£5.50), encrusted in tandoori paste and grilled until crisp. Or try pomfret fish (£8.90) from the tandoor, a worthwhile extravagance. Curries include sag gosht (£6.20), which is chunks of lamb in a dark-green, velvety spinach base; Nihari lamb (£6.20), cooked slowly on the bone in a rich gravy; and, more unusually, batera – quail – curry (£6.20). The menu describes paya (£6.20) as "lamb trotters in thick gravy" – a gravy created by three hours' cooking in a pot with ginger, onions and garlic. For specialists only, perhaps. Very delicious, and supposed to "purify the blood", is the karela gosht (£6.20), a telling combination of bitter melon and lamb. The side dishes will tempt all-comers, especially the tarka dhal (£4.20), which is rich and buttery.

You can specify your seasonings for all the Lahore's dishes – mild, medium or hot. Hot is very hot and will have you calling for a large mango shake (£2). All drinks at the Lahore are soft, though you can bring your own beer or wine (no corkage is charged).

Kabul

(🍴) Find the Himalaya Shopping Centre and wend your way past the silk merchants and the shops selling exotic CDs. Head up the escalator and to the left you'll find the Kabul, which has taken over the space allocated to an entire shop. It's a spacious restaurant with comfortable chairs, dark-blue tablecloths and a series of banquettes running

£5 to £15

Address 1st Floor, Himalaya Shopping Centre, Southall, Middlesex
☏ 020 8571 6878
Station BR Southall
Open Daily noon–midnight
Accepts Mastercard and Visa

along the wall. At one end of the room there's an open kitchen where the chefs work quietly and without fuss. The menu splits into two sections: Afghan food and Indian food. Curiosity should compel you to try some Afghan dishes, but the cooking seems to be of a high standard whatever you order. Portions are very large and prices very competitive.

Start with dumplings – ordering the Afghan starter called mantu gosht (£5.99) brings a dinner plate covered in large savoury dumplings filled with spiced lamb. Ashak are also dumplings and come in meat and non-meat versions – the vegetarian ones (£4.99) are amazingly good, light dumplings with dough so thin that you can see the green leaves of the filling through the skins. Also notable is the showr-na-kath (£1.99), a bowl full of chickpeas in a thin, green, herby, chilli-warmed liquid. You eat them with a spoon, or more sensibly with some of the excellent Afghan nan bread (£1.20). For mains, the quabuli murgh (£5.99) is a large plate of delicious rice pillau made with plenty of sultanas and garnished with shreds of carrot; on top of it is a tender chicken drumstick, and it comes with a bowl of curry with a large minced lamb cake hidden in its depths. Another winner is the karahi tukham (£2.50), which is a small karahi full of light, buttery, rich and spicy scrambled eggs. Stray onto the Indian side and you will not be disappointed: karela gosht (£5.40) is well seasoned and the striking taste of the bitter melon acts as a perfect foil for the richness of the other dishes on the table. The food is good here, and large portions make it very good value as well.

On your way out, stop and shop – there's an intriguing poster on the stairs singing the praises of tooth jewellery.

Southall

Madhu's

(🍴) Madhu's reopened in spring 2003 after a prolonged refurbishment following a serious fire. Before it shut down Madhu's was at the smart end of the Southall scale, but upon its re-opening Madhu's is even smarter still. The decor is chic; there's a new logo (a red M with a flourish); and the staff (of which there seem to be a great many) are all dressed in black. As you walk in you cross a glass panel in the floor which appears to have a river running under it – water feature heaven. You'll find smart white asymmetric china; serried ranks of highly polished cutlery and Louis Roederer Crystal on the wine list at £350 a bottle. Take heart: the cooking has not lost its way.

£25 to £50
Address 39 South Rd, Southall, Middlesex
☎ 020 8574 1897
Station BR Southall
Open Mon & Wed–Fri 12.30–3pm & 6–11.30pm, Sat & Sun 6–11.30pm
Accepts All major credit cards

The food here is predominantly East African-Asian, and is well spiced with good, full-on flavours – thank goodness nothing has been toned down. Starters are pricey but portions are good – try the famous butter chicken (£8): very tender, very delicious but sadly still dyed a lurid orange. Or there are the lamb chops (four for £8) – well spiced and juicy. Anyone homesick for Africa will relish the mogo jeera (£3), cassava pan-fried with cumin. Main courses also come in large portions. Masala fish (£8) is a hunk of tilapia in a rich tomatoey sauce. The simple dishes are also well made – sag gosht (£8) is a good choice, lamb cooked with fresh spinach and agreeably spicy. The vegetable section also hides some treasures: a dish of bhune karele (£6) is particularly fine – a bitter gourd is stuffed and then oven-roasted – a vibrant dish. Breads are good, particularly the bhatura (£1.50), which is a fluffy cross between chapati and doughnut. If you can avoid the allure of the Crystal, you'll find Tusker and Whitecap beers at £3 a bottle. Make sure that they are cold.

Among the appetizers you'll find nyamah choma (£7), which has a strange provenance for a dish served in Southall as it derives from a Masai original (Madhu's East African heritage showing through). Nyamah choma is made from lamb spare ribs marinated in chilli and lemon juice and then cooked in the tandoor. Chewy, spicy, tangy, and very good indeed.

The New Asian Tandoori Centre

On the menu at the New Asian Tandoori Centre it states, "Famous and suitable venue for business and social gathering", and so it is. Despite having two names – this establishment is also called the Roxy Restaurant – the NATC is a large, light and airy place. It is made up from three shopfronts and splits into three rooms: on the right there's a

£8 to £18

Address 114 The Green, Southall, Middlesex
℡ 020 8574 2597
Station BR Southall
Open Mon–Thurs 8am–11pm, Fri–Sun 8am–midnight.
Accepts No credit cards

INDIAN

seriously busy takeaway operation, in the middle a no-frills canteen and on the left a smarter dining room complete with a bar and ornamental stonework. This is one time when you can stick to the "middle path" with confidence. Service is friendly and, except for the tandoori dishes, the food arrives briskly.

The menu offers the kind of strongly flavoured food you would expect in a Punjabi cafe. Start with good jeera chicken (£6), rich with cumin; or there are simple savoury kebabs – chicken (£1) and lamb (90p). Or vegetable pakora (£1.30). The boneless fish tikka (£3.50) is stunning – large, firm-fleshed chunks of fish, well spiced and not at all dried out. With the rather good breads in support – chapatis (60p); bhaturas (60p), naans (80p) – a few starters and grilled meats could easily make a meal. But it would be a pity to miss out on the main course dishes. The menu is split into two halves: vegetarian and non-vegetarian. There is a good bhindi dish (£3.50), fine soggy aubergines; Bombay aloo (£3); a curry made with karela (£3.50) – bitter melon; chana dal (£3), a delicious rich yellow chickpea sludge. Meat-eaters will enjoy the butter chicken (£6); the bhuna chicken (£5.50); the economically named lamb curry (£5.50); and the bhuna lamb that is only served on Saturday and Sunday (£5.50). Also worth trying are the simple dishes like chicken korma or lamb korma (both £6). As well as beers, lassis and soft drinks, the menu rather charmingly offers a "peg" of Black Label for £2.50.

When asked if the eponymous Roxy, whose name features on the plate-glass windows, would put in an appearance, the waiter replied, "He is always here." Food for thought?

Omi's

Omi's is a small, no-frills eatery with a kitchen that seems at least as spacious as the dining area. The explanation for this lies down the street, where you'll find one of Southall's larger banqueting and wedding halls. Omi's is a thriving outside-catering operation and has never been purely a restaurant: until some years ago, the food shared a counter with a van-rental business; and a couple of years ago Omi's fulfilled a long-held dream and expanded into the next-door property, doubling their capacity to eighty seats. But you'll still find tasty, Punjabi/Kenyan-Asian dishes, lots of rich flavours and great value. The idea of opening for a bit longer each day and even on Sunday is often discussed – best ring and check.

£5 to £12
Address 1 Beaconsfield Rd, Southall, Middlesex
☎ 020 8571 4831
Station BR Southall
Open Mon–Thurs 11am–9pm, Fri & Sat 11am–9.30pm
Accepts All major credit cards

The food is cooked by a formidable line-up of chefs in the back, doubtless knocking up dishes for diners with one hand while masterminding the next Indian wedding for eight hundred with the other. There's a constant stream of people picking up their takeaways. The starters are behind the counter: chicken tikka (£3) is good and spicy, while aloo tikki (50p) is a large, savoury potato cake, delightfully crisp on the outside. Or try the masala fish (£2.75), a large slab of cod thickly encrusted with spices. Go on to sample a couple of the specials. Aloo methi (£3.50) – potatoes cooked with fenugreek – is very moreish indeed. All the curries are commendably oil-free and thrive on the cook-and-reheat system in operation here. They are best eaten with breads – parathas (70p), rotis (40p) and the mega-indulgent, puffy fried bhaturas (50p) are all fresh and good.

If you feel a sudden tightening of your fist, you'll warm to the multi-course set meal on offer here – it costs a miserly £4.50, either vegetarian or non-vegetarian. This is very sound, very cheap food served with a minimum of fuss. You shouldn't expect frills but you will bask in the warmth of real hospitality. West End emporia, please note this kind of atmosphere and these prices!

Palm Palace

The Palm Palace may be short on palms, and it is not palatial by any manner of means, but the food is great. This is the only Sri Lankan restaurant among the restaurant turmoil that is Southall, and the menu features a great many delicious and interesting dishes. As is so often the case with Sri Lankan food, the "drier" dishes are particularly

£9 to £18

Address 80 South Rd, Southall, Middlesex
℡ 020 8574 9209
Station BR Southall
Open Daily noon–3pm & 6–11.30pm
Accepts All major credit cards

appealing, and there is a good deal of uncompromising chilli heat. The dining room is clean and comfortable in a sparse sort of way, and service is friendly and attentive.

Starters are very good here. Try the mutton rolls (£1.50) – long pancake rolls filled with meat and potatoes. Or there's the fish cutlets (£1.50), which are in fact spherical fishcakes very much in the same style as those you find in smart West End eateries, but better spiced and a tenth of the price. Move on to a "devilled" dish: mutton (£4.50), chicken (£4.50) or, best of all, squid (£4.95). With a dark tangy-sweet sauce with chilli bite, these dishes combine spices with richness very well. There was a time when every curry house in the land featured Ceylon chicken, but here you'll find a short list of real "Ceylon" curries including mutton (£3.95) – they're good, if straightforward. Try the chicken 65 (£4.50), whose name is said to refer to the age of the chicken in days; any younger and it would fall apart during cooking, any older and it would be tough. The hoppers (Sri Lankan pancakes) are good fun – string hopper (£2.50); egg hopper (£1.25); milk hopper (£1). Try a simple vegetable dish as well – sag aloo (£2.50) brings fresh spinach and thoughtfully seasoned, well-cooked potato.

Beer lovers must order a big bottle of Lion Stout (£3.50), which is dark, dangerous and delicious. As well as being eight percent alcohol, it brings with it a ringing endorsement from Michael Jackson, the "beer hunter" himself. Look at the back label and you will find not only his portrait, but also a short eulogy – "chocolatey, mocha, liqueur-like", and so forth. This beer is surprisingly good with spicy food.

Palm Palace

Further West

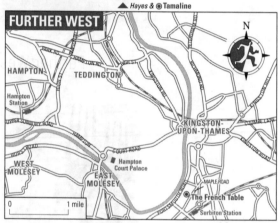

▲ Hayes & ◉ Tamaline

FURTHER WEST

HAMPTON

TEDDINGTON

Hampton Station

KINGSTON-UPON-THAMES

UPPER SUNBURY ROAD

COURT ROAD

WEST MOLESEY

Hampton Court Palace

EAST MOLESEY

MAPLE ROAD

◉ The French Table

Surbiton Station

0 — 1 mile

© Crown copyright

The French Table

(🍴) The French Table serves well-cooked, modern French/Mediterranean food. The restaurant is owned by Eric and Sarah Guignard; he cooks and she runs the front of house. Things have gone from strength to strength for this small, elegant, modern restaurant and it seems to have bedded in well. The menu is an interesting one because, despite a good many modern influences,

£15 to £45

Address 85 Maple Rd, Surbiton, Surrey
☎ 020 8399 2365
Station BR Surbiton
Open Tues 7–10.30pm, Wed–Fri noon–2.30pm & 7–10.30pm, Sat 7–10.30pm, Sun noon–2.30pm
Accepts Mastercard and Visa

MODERN EUROPEAN

Guignard's food is rooted in the French classics – as befits a cook who has served time in various Michelin-starred establishments.

Flavours are upfront and the seasoning spot-on. There is a deft handling of different textures and presentation is commendably unfussy. Things change regularly, but starters may include dishes like deep-fried scallops with an asparagus and lime leaf risotto (£6.80); or terrine of marinated salmon, potato and dill (£5.50). The kitchen's classical approach shows in starters like the duo of foie gras (£8.90) – a ballottine with trad "quatre épices" and a tranche pan-fried with warm Mozzarella. Main course dishes are robust and delicious: calf's liver with crushed sweet potato, crispy wild mushroom ravioli, black peppercorn sauce (£13.80); brandade of cod with julienne of roast red peppers and fresh herbs (£13.50); or there may be poached halibut with tomato risotto, chicory tartlet and beetroot jus (£14.20). Simple dishes are also well handled – try millefeuille of sweet potato and artichokes with pistou (£10.50). Puds are good – pear tart; profiteroles; coconut mousse – all £4.95. The wine list here is largely French and gently priced, the service is friendly and everybody seems to be trying very hard indeed – as befits an "owner-driver" establishment.

The set lunch is a bargain at £12.50 for two courses and £15.50 for three (Sunday lunch £16.50 for three courses). Gratinée of pumpkin with Parma ham and Parmesan; followed by medallion of veal with celeriac, wild mushrooms and Madeira sauce; and then strawberry tart with white chocolate mousse for just £15.50 would make a grand lunch anywhere, but in Surbiton it is downright miraculous.

Tamaline

Since it opened in the late 1980s, this scruffy little restaurant in Hayes (along the Uxbridge Road, just west of the Southall strip) has had a well-deserved reputation for Sri Lankan seafood dishes. The only confusing factor is the name – for most of its life this place was called Thamoulinee, and that is still what it says on the menu

£8 to £20
Address 128 Uxbridge Rd, Hayes, Middlesex ☎ 020 8813 6170 Station BR Southall Open Daily 6pm–midnight Accepts Cash or cheque only

covers. Whatever it may be called, this is a friendly, informal place, and even had a slight refurbishment in 2003. Food is made with care (which can mean slowly) presented without frills, and is very delicious. Relax and take your time – there is always the television banging out Tamil TV to keep you amused.

Start with the mutton rolls (two for £1.50), which are short, crisp and chewy spring rolls with a hearty mutton filling. Bonda (four for £2) are also good – savoury spheres of fried mash. Fried crab claws (four for £2.25) is an interesting dish of minced crab formed into lumps and fried crisply – like a vastly improved crabstick. The devilled squid (£4.50) is truly wonderful – tiny squidlets stuffed and cooked until meltingly tender. Very rich. The sambols are well done – these are a sort of condiment like chutney which you use to add flavour to rice or bread. Try the coconut sambol with Maldive fish (£2) – the rich, sweet coconut contrasts well with the salty, savoury fish. The flat, flaky, buttery breads are sensational; the plain gotthamba roti (£1.10) is only eclipsed by the egg roti (£2), which has an egg cooked between the layers. The food is good and spicy here (although dishes can be made as mild as you wish), the bill is a gentle one, and you get two names for the price of one.

One of the most famous Sri Lankan specialities is the hopper. These are dish-shaped, crispish, bready sorts of things which can be made plain, with milk, or with an egg. If you yearn to try them, do not visit Tamaline on Friday, Saturday or Sunday as the lady who does the hoppers doesn't like to come out at the weekend, and so they are off the menu. You have to admire such an explanation.

index

index

index of restaurants with branches

Alounak

44 Westbourne Grove, W2
℡020 7229 0416
Bayswater

10 Russell Gdns, W14
℡020 7603 1130
Shepherd's Bush/
Olympia (when open)

L'Artista

917 Finchley Rd, NW11
℡020 8731 7501
Golders Green

61 The Parade, High St,
Watford
01923 210055
Watford High St

17 Central Circus, NW4
℡020 8202 7303
Hendon Central

120 Station Rd,
Edgware, Mddx
℡020 8951 5533
Edgware

Bank

Aldwych
1 Kingsway, WC2
℡020 7379 9797
Holborn

Westminster
45 Buckingham Gate,
SW1
℡020 7379 9797
St.James's Park

Barcelona Tapas Bar

1a Bell Lane, E1
℡020 7247 7014
Aldgate/Aldgate East

Barcelona II
℡020 7377 5111
15 St Botolph St, EC3
(entrance in Mddx St, E1)
Aldgate East/Liverpool St

Barcelona III
Lordship Lane, Dulwich,
SE22
℡020 8693 5111
E.Dulwich/Forest Hill/
Herne Hill

Barcelona IV
13 Well Ct, off Bow Lane,
EC4
℡020 7329 5111
St Paul's

Belgo

Centraal, 50 Earlham St,
WC2
℡020 7813 2233
Covent Garden

Noord, 72 Chalk Farm Rd,
NW1
℡020 7267 0718
Chalk Farm

Bierodrome

173-174 Upper St, N1
℡020 7226 5835
Highbury & Islington

44-48 Clapham High Rd,
SW4
℡020 720 1118
Clapham Nth/Common

67 Kingsway, Holborn
WC2
℡020 7242 7469
Holborn

Black & Blue

215-217 Ken Church St
W8
℡020 7727 0004
Notting Hill Gate

105 Gloucester `Rd, SW7
℡020 7244 7666
Gloucester Rd

Boisdale

15 Eccleston St SW1
℡020 7730 6922
Victoria

22 New Globe Walk, SE1
℡020 7928 3300
Borough/London Bridge

The Toucan

29 Carlisle St, W1
℡020 7437 4123
Leicester Square

94 Wimpole St, W1
℡020 7499 2440
Oxford Circus

5 Old Jewry, EC2
℡020 7606 8765
Bank/Moorgate

La Trouvaille

12a Newburgh St, W1
℡020 7287 8488
Oxford Circus

353 Upper St, N1
℡020 7704 8323
Angel Islington

Wagamama

(also Kingston, Manchester, Nottingham, Dublin)

4 Streatham St, WC1
℡020 7323 9223
Tottenham Ct Rd

10a Lexington St, W1
℡020 7292 0990
Piccadilly Circus

101a Wigmore St,W1
℡020 74090111
Bond St/Marble Arch

11 Jamestown Rd, NW1
℡020 7428 0800
Camden Town

26 Kensington High St, W8
℡020 7376 1717
High St Kensington

Harvey Nichols SW1
℡020 7201 6000
Knightsbridge

1a Tavistock St, WC2
℡020 7836 3330
Covent Garden

14a Irving St, WC2
℡020 7839 2323
Leicester Square

8 Norris St, SW1
℡020 7321 2755
Piccadilly Circus

Unit 1a Citypoint Moor Lane EC2
℡020 7588 2688
Moorgate

109 Fleet St EC4
℡020 7583 7889
St Pauls/Blackfriars

N1 Centre Parkfield St N1
℡020 7266 2664
Angel

By Tower 42, 22 Old Broad St, EC2
℡020 7256 9992
Broad St

YO! Sushi

52 Poland St, W1
℡020 7287 0443
Oxford Circus

Harvey Nichols, 5th Floor SW1
℡020 7201 8641
Knightsbridge

19 Rupert St, W1
℡020 7434 2724
Piccadilly Circus

Selfridges Food Hall, W1
℡020 7318 3944
Marble Arch/Bond St

02 Centre Finchley Rd NW3
℡020 7431 4499
Finchley Road

County Hall, Belvedere Rd SE1
℡020 7928 8871
Waterloo

95 Farringdon Rd EC1
℡020 7841 0790
Farringdon

Whiteley's Bayswater, W2
℡020 7727 9392
Bayswater

myhotel, Bedford Sq WC1
℡020 7636 0076
Tottenham Ct Rd

Paddington Station, W2
℡020 7706 9550
Paddington

N1 Centre Parkfield St N1
℡020 7359 3502
Angel

Zilli Fish

36-40 Brewer St, W1
℡020 7734 8649
Piccadilly Circus

Zilli Café
42-44 Brewer St, W1
℡020 7287 9233
Piccadilly Circus

Signor Zilli
40 Dean St, W1
℡020 7734 3924
& Zilli Bar
℡020 7734 1853
Leicester Square

Zilli Fish Too
8-18 Wild St, WC2
℡020 7240 0011
Covent Garden

index of restaurants by cuisine

Categories below are pretty self-explanatory, though note that "Indian" includes Bangladeshi, Indian and Pakistani restaurants.

Fusion

Carnevale 213
Hoxton & Shoreditch

The Providores 74
Knightsbridge & Belgravia

Gastropubs

The Anglesea Arms 431
Hammersmith & Chiswick

The Atlas 419
Earl's Court

The Barnsbury 268
Islington

**The Cow
Dining Room** 442
Notting Hill

The Drapers Arms 270
Islington

Duke of Cambridge 271
Islington

The Eagle 191
Clerkenwell

Ealing Park Tavern 411
Ealing & Acton

The Earl Spencer 380
Wimbledon & Southfields

The Engineer 231
Camden Town & Primrose
Hill

The Fire Stables 381
Wimbledon & Southfields

The Fox 216
Hoxton & Shoreditch

**The Havelock
Tavern** 467
Shepherd's Bush &
Olympia

The House 272
Islington

St John's 262
Holloway & Highbury

The Salt House 287
St John's Wood & Swiss
Cottage

The Salusbury 281
Maida Vale & Kilburn

The Victoria 399
Barnes & Sheen

The Well 196
Clerkenwell

The White Horse 459
Richmond

Greek

The Real Greek 217
Hoxton & Shoreditch

Souvlaki & Bar 194
Clerkenwell

Hungarian

The Gay Hussar 125
Soho

Indian

See also Sri Lankan.

Babur Brasserie 387
Further South – Forest Hill

Benares 79
Mayfair & Bond Street

Bengal Village 170
Brick Lane & Spitalfields

The Brilliant 473
Southall

Café Naz 171
Brick Lane & Spitalfields

Café Spice Namaste 182
The City

Chetna's 297
Wembley

Chor Bizarre 80
Mayfair & Bond Street

Chowki 123
Soho

Chutney Mary 404
Chelsea

The Cinnamon Club 150
Victoria & Westminster

Modern European

North African

North American/ Burgers

See also Southwest
American

INDEX OF RESTAURANTS BY CUISINE

index of restaurants by name

A–Z note: The Eagle appears under E not T, La Trompette under T, and Al Duca under D. But Café Pacifico is a C, San Daniele an S and Alastair Little an A. Well, you have to have rules.

index